RUSSIAN–MUSLIM CONFRONTATION IN THE CAUCASUS

This book presents two important texts, *The Shining of Daghestani Swords* by al-Qarakhi and a new translation for a contemporary readership of Lev Tolstoi's *Hadji Murat*, illuminating the mountain war between the Muslim peoples of the Caucasus and the imperial Russian army from 1830 to 1859. The editors offer a complete commentary on the various intellectual and religious contexts that shaped the two texts and explain the historical significance of the Russian–Muslim confrontation. It is shown that the mountain war was a clash of two cultures, two religious outlooks and two different worlds. The book provides an important background to the ongoing contest between Russia and indigenous people for control of the Caucasus. The two translations are accompanied by short introductions and by a longer commentary intended for readers who desire a broader introduction to the tragic conflict in the Caucasus whose effects still reverberate in the twenty-first century.

Thomas Sanders is Associate Professor of Russian History at the U.S. Naval Academy. **Ernest Tucker** is Associate Professor of Middle East History at the U.S. Naval Academy. **Gary Hamburg** is Behr Professor of European History, Claremont–McKenna College, U.S., specializing in the cultural and intellectual history of imperial Russia.

SOAS/ROUTLEDGE STUDIES
ON THE MIDDLE EAST
Series Editors
Benjamin C. Fortna, *SOAS, University of London*
Ulrike Freitag, *Freie Universität Berlin, Germany*

This series features the latest disciplinary approaches to Middle Eastern Studies. It covers the Social Sciences and the Humanities in both the pre-modern and modern periods of the region. While primarily interested in publishing single-authored studies, the series is also open to edited volumes on innovative topics, as well as textbooks and reference works.

ISLAMIC NATIONHOOD AND COLONIAL INDONESIA
The Umma below the winds
Michael Francis Laffan

RUSSIAN–MUSLIM CONFRONTATION IN THE CAUCASUS
Alternative visions of the conflict between Imam Shamil and the Russians,
1830–1859
*Edited and Translated by Thomas Sanders, Ernest Tucker
and Gary Hamburg*

RUSSIAN–MUSLIM CONFRONTATION IN THE CAUCASUS

*Alternative visions of the conflict between
Imam Shamil and the Russians, 1830–1859*

*Edited and translated by
Thomas Sanders, Ernest Tucker
and Gary Hamburg*

With an extended commentary
'War of Worlds' by Gary Hamburg

Routledge
Taylor & Francis Group

LONDON AND NEW YORK

First published 2004
by Routledge
2 Park Square, Milton Park, Abingdon, Oxon, OX14 4RN

Simultaneously published in the USA and Canada
by Routledge
270 Madison Ave, New York NY 10016

Routledge is an imprint of the Taylor & Francis Group

Transferred to Digital Printing 2010

© 2004 Thomas Sanders, Ernest Tucker and Gary Hamburg

Typeset in Baskerville by Taylor & Francis Books Ltd

British Library Cataloguing in Publication Data
A catalogue record for this book is available from the British Library

Library of Congress Cataloging in Publication Data
A catalog record for this book has been requested

ISBN10: 0–415–32590–0 (hbk)
ISBN10: 0–415–47879–0 (pbk)

ISBN13: 978–0–415–32590–5 (hbk)
ISBN13: 978–0–415–47879–3 (pbk)

Publisher's Note
The publisher has gone to great lengths to ensure the quality of this reprint
but points out that some imperfections in the original may be apparent.

CONTENTS

Preface   vi
Acknowledgments   viii
Note on transliteration   ix
Chronology   x
Maps   xii

Introduction   1

PART I   7

*The Shining of Daghestani Swords in Certain
Campaigns of Shamil (Selected Passages)*
Muhammad Tahir al-Qarakhi   11
TRANSLATED AND ANNOTATED BY ERNEST TUCKER
AND THOMAS SANDERS

PART II   75

Lev Tolstoi, *Hadji Murat*   77
TRANSLATED AND ANNOTATED BY THOMAS SANDERS
AND GARY HAMBURG

PART III   169

**War of worlds: A commentary on the two texts
in their historical context**   171
GARY HAMBURG

Glossary (compiled by Ernest Tucker)   250
Index   256

PREFACE

But surely he is great and holy because he is a man, a madly and
tormentingly beautiful man; a man of the whole of mankind.

Maxim Gorky on Lev Tolstoi, Reminiscences of
Tolstoi, Chekhov and Andreev

There was one nation which would not give in, would not acquire
the mental habits of submission—and not just individual rebels
among them, but the whole nation to a man. These were the
Chechens ...

Alexander Solzhenitsyn on the
Chechens, The Gulag Archipelago

This work began as a post-Soviet project and ended as more of a post-modernist
one. In the early 1990s, in dismay over the general level of misinformation on
the history of Russian–Chechen relations, we began to search for ways to alert
the educated public to the complexities of that history. An obvious point of
reference for newcomers to the Caucasus region is Lev Tolstoi's posthumously
published novella, *Hadji Murat*, whose title character was a major figure in the
mountain war of the mid-nineteenth century. Unfortunately, English readers
commonly encounter this little gem in the incomplete, unsatisfactory rendition
by Tolstoi's English disciple, Aylmer Maude. The Maude version is rife with
archaic Anglicisms and punctuated by dialogue whose meaning is sometimes as
remote as the peaks of the Caucasus. We decided, therefore, to begin our project
by providing readers with a more accessible translation of *Hadji Murat*.

We also wanted our readers to have access to at least one indigenous account of
the Caucasus's unhappy history. To capture the mountaineers' voices, we chose to
translate Muhammad Tahir al-Qarakhi's *The Shining of Daghestani Swords in Certain
Campaigns of Shamil*. A scribe who enjoyed the confidence of Imam Shamil, the military and religious leader of the anti-Russian forces during the mountain war of
1830–1859, al-Qarakhi was exceptionally well placed to know the principal events
of the war and to convey the mountaineers' singular perspective on those events.
Moreover, since *The Shining of Daghestani Swords* derives from the Middle Eastern
tradition of chronicling and hagiography, our translation gives readers the chance to

examine the formal divergence between mountain techniques of representation and the more familiar European genre of historical fiction.

Thus, our book presents two perspectives on the Caucasus: Tolstoi's enlightened European viewpoint and al-Qarakhi's indigenous interpretation. The commentary at the end of this work analyzes the war of worlds between imperial Russia and the Islamic mountaineers. Because of the currency of the subject matter, the eminence of Tolstoi, and the privileged proximity of al-Qarakhi to Imam Shamil and to the imam's view of the conflict, we think this book is an excellent case study of cultural collision. As such we hope it will be of interest to specialists in Russian and Middle Eastern studies, to teachers of world and European history courses, and to the educated public in the English-speaking world and beyond.

Thomas Sanders, Ernest Tucker and Gary Hamburg

ACKNOWLEDGMENTS

This book is very much a joint effort. Tucker translated al-Qarakhi directly from the Arabic version of the text collated by the Soviet Arabist A. M. Barabanov. Sanders translated Barabanov's Russian variant of al-Qarakhi's text into English too, and those two English translations were utilized to prepare the translation presented here, one that seeks to balance both fidelity and clarity. With the same goal in mind, Hamburg and Sanders collaborated on the translation of Tolstoi from the Russian.

Tucker and Sanders wrote draft essays dealing with the mountain and Russian sides, respectively. Hamburg incorporated that material into his commentary, significantly extending and elaborating upon these preliminary essays. Students at Notre Dame and midshipmen at the Naval Academy have read and reacted to the translations at various points in the process, and their responses have helped refine the translation. As colleagues at the Naval Academy, Tucker and Sanders had the advantage of proximity in consulting on issues relating to the texts. Hamburg, meanwhile, solicited an expert reaction to the portion of the commentary on al-Qarakhi from his friend and colleague, Paul M. Cobb. The Tolstoi section was read critically by Nancy L. Ickler. We wish to thank Ivan Jaksic, Andrzej Walicki, and Elise Kimerling Wirtschafter for reading the entire commentary and furnishing their constructive criticisms, and Jon Parshall for creating the maps.

Sanders and Tucker received summer research support from the Kennan Institute and from the Naval Academy Research Council, whose support they now gratefully acknowledge. Hamburg gratefully acknowledges support from the History Department at Claremont McKenna College, which reacted with warmth and critical discernment to his commentary.

Most importantly, Sanders would like to thank his wife Jolene and children Brooke and Joseph; Tucker, his wife Sarah and children Claire and Carl; and Hamburg, his wife Nancy and children Michael and Rachel. Without their support and devotion, this project could not have happened.

We want our readers to know that executing this project has been an exhilarating challenge that has paid us large intellectual dividends. We wish each reader comparable rewards in coming to terms with that place beyond the Caucasus's towering ridge where, as the Russian poet Mikhail Lermontov once hinted, genuine freedom may perhaps abide.

Thomas Sanders, Ernest Tucker and Gary Hamburg

NOTE ON TRANSLITERATION

In order to preserve the distinctive voices of the two texts, we have retained Arabic versions of names in the al-Qarakhi translation but used the Russian versions of all names in the Tolstoi translation. The glossary gives a list of important name variants. Arabic adjectival versions of place names, such as "al-Qarakhi" for someone from Qarakh, are also indicated in the glossary. In general, the versions of names used in this work are taken from Moshe Gammer, *Muslim Resistance to the Tsar: Shamil and the Conquest of Chechnia and Daghestan* (London: Frank Cass, 1994), although diacritical marks have been omitted. Note the following exceptions to this rule: "Baku" is used instead of "Baqu" and "Hadji Murat" is preferred over "Hajimurad" since the former has become the conventional Western spelling for Tolstoi's work and for its main character.

CHRONOLOGY

1796	Shamil was born in Gimrah, a mountain village in Daghestan.
1829	Ghazi Muhammad rose up against the Russians in Daghestan as the first imam of a Sufi resistance movement.
1832	Ghazi Muhammad died and was replaced as imam by Hamza Bek.
1834	Hamza Bek died and Shamil became the third imam.
1839	Shamil made an unsuccessful stand against the Russians at Akhulgoh.
1840s–1850s	Intermittent military campaigns waged by Shamil and his followers continued against the Russians in Daghestan and Chechnia.
1851	Hadji Murat defected to the Russians, but was killed in 1852 when he tried to go back to the mountains.
1851–1855	Lev Tolstoi served in the Russian army, first in the Caucasus, and later in the defense of Sevastopol during the Crimean War.
1853–1856	Crimean War.
1859	Shamil made a last stand against the Russians on the mountain plateau of Ghunib, but ultimately had to surrender to them there. Shamil was sent to Kaluga, where he lived until 1866 when he moved to Kiev.
1871	Shamil died on the *hajj* pilgrimage and was buried in Medina.

The CAUCASUS

Muzlik

Chechnia

Sukhumi

Vladikavkaz

RUSSIA

Black
Sea

Georgia

Tiflis

Batumi

OTTOMAN

Aleksandropol'

Kars

Erivan

Russia

Austria-
Hungary

Aral
Sea

EMPIRE

Black Sea

Caspian
Sea

Ottoman

Mediterranean
Sea

Iran

Afg.

Empire

India

Beyazit

39°

4,000   13,124
3,000   9,843
2,000   6,562
1,000   3,281
100   328
0   0
Below sea level

National
Boundaries

Rivers

Van

0   25   50   75   100 kilometers

0   25   50   75   100 miles

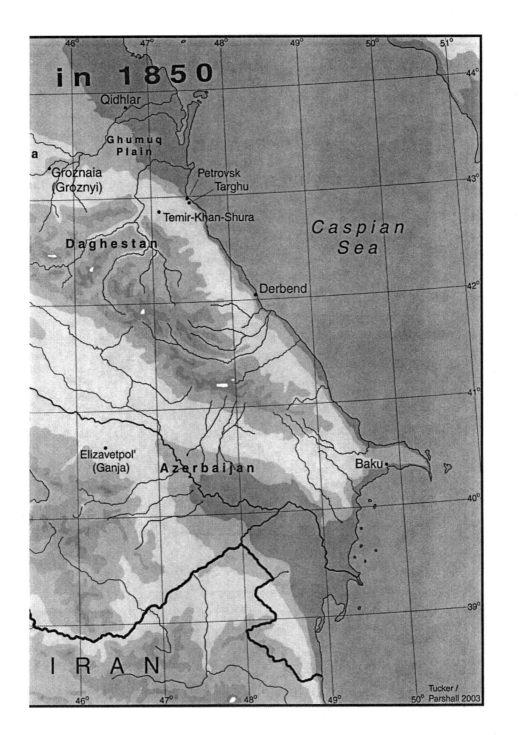

in 1850

Qidhlar

Ghumuq
Plain

a

Groznaia
(Groznyi)

Petrovsk
Targhu

• Temir-Khan-Shura

Daghestan

Caspian
Sea

Derbend

Elizavetpol'
(Ganja)

Azerbaijan

Baku•

IRAN

Tucker /
Parshall 2003

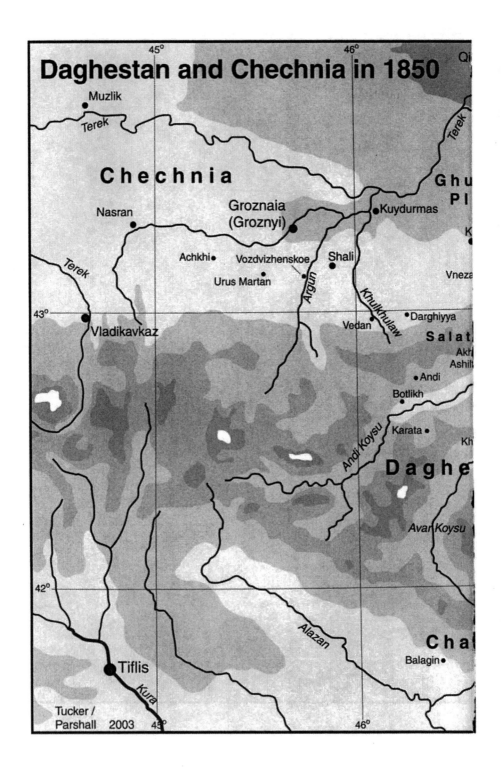

Daghestan and Chechnia in 1850

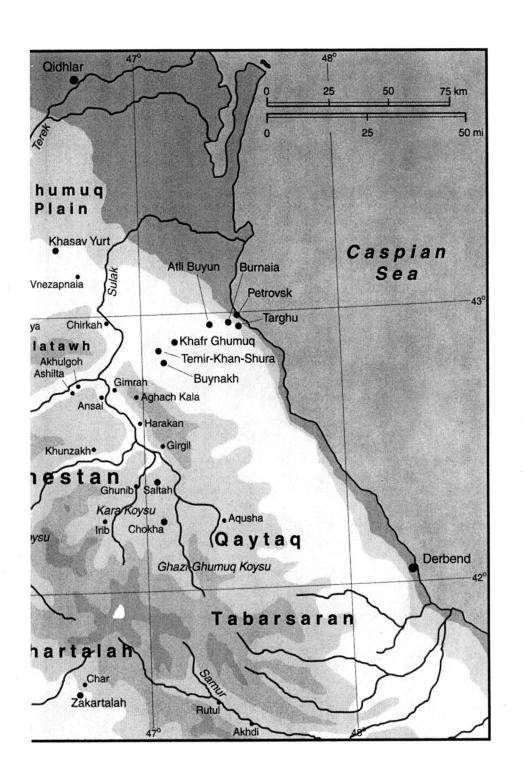

Qidhlar

47°

48°

0   25   50   75 km

0   25   50 mi

Terek

humuq
Plain

Khasav Yurt

*Caspian
Sea*

Vnezapnaia

Atli Buyun   Burnaia

Petrovsk

43°

ya   Chirkah

Targhu

latawh

●Khafr Ghumuq

Akhulgoh
Ashilta

Temir-Khan-Shura

Gimrah

Buynakh

Ansal

●Aghach Kala

●Harakan

Khunzakh●

●Girgil

nestan

Ghunib Saltah

Kara Koysu

●Aqusha

oysu

Irib   Chokha

Qaytaq

Ghazi Ghumuq Koysu

Derbend

42°

Tabarsaran

hartalah

Char

Samur

Zakartalah

Rutul

47°

Akhdi

48°

INTRODUCTION

For the past two centuries the rugged flanks of the Caucasus have been contested ground—the site of religious strife, imperial conquest, wars of national liberation, revolutions, ethnic cleansing, banditry, kidnapping, financial skullduggery, and sheer madness, but equally the locus of profitable cultural interaction, extraordinary intellectual creativity, deeply felt patriotism, family loyalty, heroic persistence, and nobility of soul. The region's outsized contradictions have intoxicated travelers, tantalized journalists, and fascinated scholars, generating a veritable flood of publications about the customs, ethnographic complexities, shifting confessional identities, and peculiar histories of the mountain peoples. In the wake of such prodigious reportage, often expertly done, one may wonder if anything about the Caucasus remains unsaid, if any detail of its social life has been overlooked, if any grievance of its multitudinous peoples has gone unrehearsed. The Caucasus would seem to be one of those rare places where no one is forgot, nothing forgotten.

For an outsider, however, the task of understanding the tangled modern history of the Caucasus remains daunting, if only because the region's most instructive voices have spoken in an assortment of tongues—Russian, Arabic, Turkish, Persian, Georgian, Armenian to name a few—each the product of an ancient culture, each bearing within its semantic web complex assumptions about God and the ideal contours of human society. Where the mute stones speak in recondite languages, even the most sensitive of ears may detect only meaningless sound and endless fury.

The present book is an experiment in listening through cacophony. The investigation has the primary object of attending scrupulously to two powerful representations of the 1830–1859 mountain war between Russia and the indigenous peoples of the North Caucasus. Our first text, written in the stylized Arabic that served as the religious lingua franca in the North Caucasus and in most of the Islamic world, is a historical chronicle of the mountain war recorded largely in the 1850s. Entitled *The Shining of Daghestani Swords in Certain Campaigns of Shamil*, the chronicle is the only comprehensive history of the war from the insurgents' perspective. Its author, Muhammad Tahir al-Qarakhi, composed the text under the direct supervision of the insurgent leader, Imam Shamil. In it we hear,

1

through the medium of a scribe's account, Shamil's voice, but also unmistakable echoes of the Prophet Muhammad himself, of myriad Muslim hagiographers, and of the Sufi brothers who sought to make human society conform to God's design. We have chosen to translate those portions of al-Qarakhi's text that best illustrate the war's religious dimensions, Shamil's character, the clash between Shamil and his rival Hadji Murat, and the war's aftermath. So far as we know, this translation of *The Shining of Daghestani Swords* is the first to appear in English.

The second text is Lev Nikolaevich Tolstoi's fictional history of the mountain war, *Hadji Murat*. The last of Tolstoi's great novels, *Hadji Murat* presents a single episode of the mountain conflict—Hadji Murat's 1851 defection to the Russians and his tragic death in spring 1852—as a microcosm of the entire bloody war. Using techniques he had employed in *War and Peace*, Tolstoi constructs around Hadji Murat elaborately researched portraits of the principal military and political figures on both sides of the belligerency. His ambition is to analyze how absolute power corrupts everyone it touches, from European bureaucrats to "Asiatic" satraps, how it despoils nature, mocks God, and transforms human societies into prisons.

English readers already have access to two translations: the archaic version of Aylmer Maude and the chatty 1977 redaction by Paul Foote. The present translation, by Thomas Sanders and G. M. Hamburg, strives to convey to readers the poetic compression and calculated strangeness of Tolstoi's Russian. It also tries to encode in American English, a language ever more informal and democratic in sensibility, the class-specific rhythms and idioms of Tolstoian discourse. These features are crucial components of *Hadji Murat* that must be communicated if the English translation is somehow to approximate the original story's unsettling power.

By what logic do we combine in our book two texts so radically different, one a formal Arabic chronicle by a virtually unknown Sufi adept, the other a work of historical fiction by a universally recognized master? Beyond a bare coincidence of subject matter, the two texts would seem to have nothing in common. Moreover, as we shall see, there is no evidence that either writer knew the other. Must we then explain our choice by asserting that only by the juxtaposition of these two incongruous texts could we fathom the cultural disparity between subaltern mountaineers and the Russian hegemons? Half-tempted to make such an arbitrary assertion, we nevertheless prescind from it, preferring instead to justify our choice on the following three grounds.

First, in spite of their obvious differences, al-Qarakhi and Tolstoi had a great deal in common. Both were religious—al-Qarakhi being a Muslim scholar working in the Sufi tradition and Tolstoi being a self-styled Christian anarchist who, late in life, became fascinated by Islam's social teachings. Both men took active part in the mountain war: al-Qarakhi fought as an insurgent soldier until physically unable to do so; Tolstoi joined Russian raids and artillery bombardments of Chechen villages in the early 1850s. Both men wrote accounts of the war during actual combat: al-Qarakhi's first redaction of *The Shining of Daghestani*

Swords was composed in the mid-1850s, whereas Tolstoi's earliest writing about the Caucasus war, material he later incorporated into *Hadji Murat*, dated to 1854. Each writer corrected his first account of the war by adding documentary evidence and oral testimony that appeared after the fighting had ended. In each case, the writer selected a literary genre familiar in his own culture: al-Qarakhi chose the historical chronicle and hagiography, Tolstoi selected the novella (*povest'*) form. Yet each writer modified the genre as the material demanded: al-Qarakhi's chronicle gradually evolved from a formalized annalistic first redaction toward a looser, but more analytical narrative; Tolstoi's *Hadji Murat* moved from narrative short story toward polemical history. Thus, each writer stretched a familiar genre in an unfamiliar direction, producing a hybrid form adapted to the curious subject matter of the mountain war. Neither writer lived to see his final report of the Caucasus war into print: al-Qarakhi entrusted the manuscript of *The Shining of Daghestani Swords* to his son Habibullah, while Tolstoi turned the manuscript of *Hadji Murat* over to his literary executor, V. G. Chertkov.

Second, in spite of their formal differences, al-Qarakhi's *Shining of Daghestani Swords* and Tolstoi's *Hadji Murat* mapped in exquisite detail the power constellations operating during the mountain war. From al-Qarakhi we learn how Imam Shamil exercised personal authority from the initial campaign to impose Islamic law in Daghestan to the political showdown with Hadji Murat in 1851, and from thence to the climactic defeat of the insurgency by Russian forces in 1859. We see that the imam's charismatic leadership depended on a remarkable command of the military art, on conspicuous personal bravery, and dogged persistence against heavy odds, but also on the capacity to collaborate with senior Muslim divines and to coexist for long periods with headstrong rivals like Hadji Murat. Meanwhile, Tolstoi's history sketched precisely how senior Russian officials reacted to significant events in the mountain conflict and asserted their will in the warring region. *Hadji Murat* gives us a chilling but accurate guide to Russian field officers' legendary cruelty toward the insurgents, the generals' casual disregard for casualties among their own serf soldiers, and to imperial ministers' cynical palace intrigues over these matters of life and death. Tolstoi's painstaking study of Tsar Nicholas I and of the making of Russian military plans for the Caucasus informs us that bureaucratic authority in an absolute regime necessarily entailed systematic deception, arbitrariness, and irrationality. Under Tolstoi's sharp pen, Nicholas assumed the guise of (self-)deceiving, murderous megalomaniac, for, in Tolstoi's opinion, only such a personality could have presided over Russia's (self-)destructive war effort. *Hadji Murat*'s characterization of Imam Shamil was no less devastating, but we may read it not only as criticism but as Tolstoi's backhanded acknowledgment that, in tough-mindedness, in political resourcefulness and manipulative theatricality, the imam was fully the match of the All-Russian Emperor. Whatever al-Qarakhi's and Tolstoi's subjective judgments of the war leaders, their descriptions of power relations on the two sides are uncannily apposite.

Third, all similarities now aside, two unlike texts may in fact provide an opportunity to mark cultural dissonance, even to plumb the gap between two divergent civilizations. Al-Qarakhi's *Shining of Daghestani Swords* limned a religious movement that aspired to order collective life by maximizing individual self-control, that awarded social prestige to the most nearly selfless individuals, that promised the community's eternal gratitude to individual martyrs. In embracing otherworldly ideals, al-Qarakhi's Daghestani swordsmen did nothing they thought out of the ordinary: they subjected themselves to God's will just as their forebears had done and just as other Muslims will do so long as the world persists. The stronger the Russians' intrusive presence in the Caucasus and the greater the peril to the mountaineers' religious autonomy, the more attached the mountaineers became to their Muslim ways. Indeed, if we listen closely to al-Qarakhi's chronicle, we may hear the historical hammer blows forging a militant Islamic identity.

In *Hadji Murat* Tolstoi observed the mountaineers' peculiar customs, including their religious behaviors. The text represents villagers at prayer, *murids* during their ritual ablutions, Imam Shamil meeting with his spiritual counselors. Yet, as we shall demonstrate below, Tolstoi did not capture the mountaineers' distinctive religious sensibility. On the one hand, he strove to identify in Islam the ethical principles he presumed to be common to all religions. On the other hand, he censured Islamic leaders' resort to political violence, finding in such coercion an immoral, inauthentic, corrupt use of religion comparable to the misguided Russian Orthodox sponsorship of state violence. In both respects, Tolstoi reduced Islam to a this-worldly phenomenon. But Islam (like Christianity and Judaism) is more than a code of ethics or vehicle of power: it is a way to approach an omnipotent God, whose will shapes the universe and governs human destinies. By diminishing religion to its mundanity, by domesticating *al-Mumit*, God the Giver of Death, Tolstoi made it impossible for himself and his future readers to grasp what drove the mountaineers' insurgency.

We believe that, at the source of Islamic civilization, there is a particular religious code, a set of beliefs about God's nature and human beings' necessary relationships to God that, in one way or another, constitutes itself in the fabric of Muslim society and imposes distinctive intellectual parameters on believers. If we do not comprehend that code, we shall not understand the civilization dependent upon it. Tolstoi's failure of religious intuition, we argue, marred *Hadji Murat*, a fictional history that was in so many other respects remarkable for its empathetic embrace of mountain ways. Nor was Tolstoi's lapse of sympathetic insight unique to him: we think it symptomatic of the Russian governing and political elites' inability or unwillingness to understand the indigenous peoples of the Caucasus. In other words, we discern in *Hadji Murat* a pattern of failing to recognize what was most distinctive about Russia's Caucasian Other.

Methodologically, the present book combines traditional tools of philology, textual criticism and comparative intellectual history with certain techniques of post-modernist inquiry. For example, we approach the Caucasus war as a clash between a hegemonic power and subaltern peoples, a collision of alterities, a war of worlds. We see Hadji Murat himself as a liminal figure whose movements between belligerent camps enabled Tolstoi to write about the symmetries of power constellations on both sides of the conflict, while simultaneously exploring the asymmetry of the power actually wielded by the warring groups. We assume that the mountaineers' Islamic identity was, in large part, encoded in privileged religious texts, but we also demonstrate that, in considerable measure, that identity was historically constructed: its "genetic" component was gradually actualized in the mountaineers' defensive responses to Russian incursions into the Caucasus. We do not contend that our methods are the only ones appropriate to studying the Caucasus. Still less do we pretend to make prescriptive theoretical claims on its behalf. We do assert, however, that our methods of analyzing al-Qarakhi's *Shining of Daghestani Swords* and Tolstoi's *Hadji Murat* are appropriate to the material at hand and helpful in carrying out our research enterprise.

This book consists of three parts. The first part contains substantial portions of al-Qarakhi's *Shining of Daghestani Swords* with brief introductory remarks about the text and its author. The second part includes a new translation of *Hadji Murat* preceded by a short introduction. The object of these two parts is to offer readers direct access to both translations without the encumbrance of lengthy prefatory materials. Part III is a long commentary on the two texts. The commentary locates each document in its specific biographical, literary, and historical context, then analyzes each text as a representation of the mountain war. The commentary assumes its readers' acquaintance with *The Shining of Daghestani Swords* and *Hadji Murat*; otherwise, it is written for general readers possessing no prior knowledge of the Caucasus.

Our intention is to put in the reader's hands a book that can be used in various ways, according to that reader's particular interests. Those interested in the Caucasus itself, in Arabic literary culture, in Islam, and the Middle East may want to refer only to the al-Qarakhi chronicle; meanwhile, Russophiles and Tolstoi enthusiasts may choose to move straight to the new translation of *Hadji Murat*. Specialists in the fields listed above will probably find it worth their whiles to study the commentary. In it they will find nothing new on the mountain war from conventional political or military perspectives. However, we think that we have provided new insights into the al-Qarakhi chronicle, into the mountain insurgency as a defensive cultural movement, and into the relationship between Imam Shamil and Hadji Murat. We also believe that our analysis of Tolstoi may lead researchers into some productive new ways of conceptualizing his so-called religious conversion and to new avenues for thinking about his late fiction. Postmodernist historians of culture may see in our arrangement of material suggestive new techniques for representing alterity. By organizing our material in untraditional fashion-first al-Qarakhi, then Tolstoi, then a commentary almost equally divided between the two texts—we try self-consciously but not arbitrarily to de-center our investigation. We attach equal weight to the "unknown" al-Qarakhi and the "master" Tolstoi, equal weight to the indigenous belief systems of the Caucasus and to the Russian (mis)understanding of them. We employ these techniques neither to advance any ideological agenda of our own nor to promote ourselves as experts of any sort. We know well that the Caucasus has been hard on ideologues and self-professed experts. Our only goal is to facilitate in some small measure the understanding of that beautiful region's tragic past.

Part I

INTRODUCTION

The Bariqat al-Suyuf al-Daghistaniyya fi Ba'di al-Ghazawat al-Shamiliyya (The Shining of Daghestani Swords in Certain Campaigns of Shamil), *written not in a language of the Caucasus but in Arabic, reflected the Islamic education of its author: Muhammad Tahir al-Qarakhi (died 1882). Al-Qarakhi, presumably from the area around Qarakh in Daghestan, served as Shamil's scribe and adviser from about 1850 until the death of his own father later that decade.[1] He produced this work to present Shamil's story as an inspiration for Muslims struggling to live a righteous life and build a good society.*

The Shining of Daghestani Swords *joined a long series of Muslim biographies that began with the* Sira *(the main account of Muhammad's life written in the eighth century CE). The earliest depictions of great military campaigns conducted in God's name* (ghazawat) *were the stories of Muhammad's initial confrontations with unbelievers who had attacked him and his followers. This work also bears resemblances to another classic Islamic literary genre: the* manakib *accounts of holy men's virtues and excellences, particularly those about great Sufis. Shamil was a leading figure (although not formally considered a spiritual master) of the Naqshbandi Sufi order, which had spread from Ottoman lands into the Caucasus at the beginning of the nineteenth century and remains strong around the world today, particularly in Turkey and South Asia. More than some other Sufi groups, the Naqshbandis believed that the best way to achieve the ultimate Muslim goal—union with God—was to emphasize strict obedience to Islamic law in all actions. With its greater focus on action than contemplation, Naqshbandi doctrine easily became a rallying force for native Muslim resistance to Russian expansion in the Caucasus, which began to accelerate in the 1820s.*

Shamil was a disciple and distant relative of Ghazi Muhammad, who had been recognized by the Daghestanis as their first imam (Muslim spiritual/political leader) in 1829. When Hamza Bek, the second imam, was killed, Shamil became the third imam in 1834 and remained this community's leader until 1859. In that year, he surrendered to the Russians, but was considered to have remained the imam until his death in 1871 on a pilgrimage to the Islamic holy cities of Mecca and Medina. Shamil was buried in Medina.

It is not surprising that The Shining of Daghestani Swords *portrayed Hadji Murat, Tolstoi's hero, as unreliable, since he fled to the Russians after being sentenced to death by Shamil. An intriguing aspect of the work is how it differs from previous ghazawat accounts by celebrating Shamil's peaceful surrender to the Russians. His surrender was not depicted in this work as a shameful capitulation but as the reasonable response of a wise man to a difficult situation. Shamil was shown retaining his dignity and honor as he experienced the modern wonders of St. Petersburg, hardly the way earlier accounts of Muslim warriors had ended. Shamil was shown, after his death, being brought to Medina to rest among the great Muslim holy men—a happy repose for someone who had struggled so hard to promote justice for those of his faith. The reader must evaluate these selections from* The Shining of Daghestani Swords *to assess whether al-Qarakhi, at the end of his work, was simply resigned to Shamil's defeat by superior modern forces, whether he was consoled by Shamil's success in reaching Medina, or whether Shamil's quest for God in the next world had transcended military defeat in this world. With such uncertainty,* The Shining of Daghestani Swords *conveyed some of the unease felt by the Muslim world as it encountered the juggernaut of Western expansion during the nineteenth and twentieth centuries.*

It took several decades after its composition for The Shining of Daghestani Swords *to be circulated widely. Al-Qarakhi's son Habibullah put it into final form after his father's death. Habibullah almost succeeded in getting it published in Daghestan after the turn of the century but was stopped by Russian imperial censors. At that time, the text was seized by tsarist authorities and did not reappear until 1934, when scholars at the Soviet Academy of Sciences located four versions of it. The entire text and its Russian translation were published by 1946.[2] Versions of al-Qarakhi's work appear to have been circulated earlier in the Islamic world, given its several Ottoman and modern Turkish translations, the most recent of which was published in 1987.[3] The selections included here are all based on the version of the text from the oldest extant manuscript (dating from around 1872) discovered by A. M. Barabanov, a promising young Soviet scholar from the Caucasus who was killed in World War II soon after he had completed his thesis on al-Qarakhi and published a Russian translation of the text in the spring of 1941. His academic mentor, I. Iu. Krachkovskii, edited and published Barabanov's original edition of the Arabic text after the war in 1946. Barabanov's Russian translation of al-Qarakhi was used extensively in the preparation of this edition.*

The work should not be read as a linear history in the modern Western sense. It portrayed Shamil as a leader by recounting particular stories in great depth without always providing information about everything that happened. The Shining of Daghestani Swords *covered Shamil's whole career by focusing on episodes that revealed how Shamil embodied the Naqshbandi Sufi ideal of the leader. Al-Qarakhi showed him as a man mystically in touch with God but also very faithful to the letter of Islamic law. Hence, we urge the general reader not to get lost in the swirl of place and personal names, but rather to focus on what the stories reveal about the mountain peoples' conception of the nature of the struggle and about the nature and source of Shamil's legitimacy as imam.*

The Shining of Daghestani Swords *told a number of dramatic stories about how Shamil demonstrated his right to rule in many episodes through his career. One good example can be found in its description of how he was nearly mortally wounded at a battle in Gimrah, yet survived to continue battling the Russians until he could pause to bury the first imam, Ghazi*

Muhammad. This point of this story was not to focus on the narrative details of exactly what had happened between the Russians and Shamil's forces in Gimrah, but rather to show how Shamil's survival of a mortal wound, his escape to fight another day, and his supervision of the burial of Ghazi Muhammad all revealed him to be a man who embodied the union of mystical and orthodox Islam throughout his career.

For this reason, only a few selections from al-Qarakhi's entire text are presented here. These are accounts of key points in Shamil's career, such as when he became the imam, to illustrate how al-Qarakhi, the devoted follower, portrayed his master, Shamil.

THE SHINING OF DAGHESTANI
SWORDS IN CERTAIN CAMPAIGNS
OF SHAMIL
(SELECTED PASSAGES)[4]

Muhammad Tahir al-Qarakhi
(translated and annotated by Ernest Tucker and Thomas Sanders)

[Muhammad Tahir al-Qarakhi began his work by praising Shamil and his predecessors, Ghazi Muhammad and Hamza, as leaders who guided Muslims in the north Caucasus to obey Islamic holy law (*sharia*) instead of following tribal customary law (*adat*). Shamil's legitimacy was based on how he promoted Islamic practice and belief in the region. Obedience to religious law is immensely important for Muslims because of the belief that God revealed this law in its final form in the Quran. In the particular circumstances of the nineteenth-century Caucasus, military resistance to the Russians was often twinned with religious study, recalling that in Islam, *jihad* (literally "striving in the path of God") encompasses more than just holy war. It includes all efforts to promote and defend Islamic values and beliefs.]

In the name of God, the Merciful, the Compassionate. There is no power and strength save with God, the Exalted, the Great!

Praise God who favors with great rewards those who fight for the faith instead of the shirkers! (O God, may He be Exalted!)[5] Bless our master Muhammad, his family and companions, and grant them salvation.[6] Bless those who follow them in struggle, *jihad*, learning, and teaching. The people of Daghestan in this late age called themselves "Muslims," but no one was summoning them to [obey Islamic] law or to avoid what is forbidden.[7] No, they were subjecting themselves to customary law, and even their [so-called] Islamic judges impelled the people to obey it.[8] They praised authorities [on customary law] for implementing and enforcing it, calling it "justice."

(Praise God!) How vile were their reprehensible actions in their assemblies and associations, especially in collaboration with the Russian infidels. Some even joined them to fight Muslims. Others mixed [their lineages with them, combining their] ancestors, children, brothers, and grandchildren with them day and night. Yet others gave their children to the infidels as hostages, seeking a sop from them. Some set up an idol from among their idols: a lord, in other words, whose conduct pleased the Russians. They chose him to serve the tsar, sought his

11

favor, and considered his laws necessary for organizing the affairs of this world and the next, yet viewed the true faith [Islam] that God had decreed as corruption.[9] Indeed, we incline to God and return to Him!

God blessed them by sending the brave and renowned scholar, the wise and careful man whose [words] should be obeyed, the martyr Ghazi Muhammad (May the most Holy and Praised One sanctify his secret!), to renew the study of *sharia*, to correct the transgressions of Muhammad's sublime religious community, to revive the abandoned signs of Islam that had been utterly forgotten, and to impose the long-neglected rule of the *Quran*.[10] Next, [God] established the brave, intrepid, and intelligent scholar, the hard-charging martyr Hamza of esteemed foreign descent, in his [Ghazi Muhammad's] place and had him continue these efforts (May God make his earth light and heaven his ultimate home!).[11] The able scholar Shamil was then sent: a respected, well-known man with fight in his soul who could endure suffering and injury. [He became] known in the east and the west for the effects of his *jihad* so that the people of Mecca and Medina, the scholars of Balkh and Bukhara, and pious people from [all] parts of the world ... said prayers for [his] victory, success, and prosperity.[12]

People's hearts in St. Petersburg, Moscow, and Siberia became frightened purely through the grace of God. Despite [living in] a poor country of meager subsistence, where most people were heading straight to hell due to their greedy dependence on the infidels for what they owned ... [Shamil and his followers] performed miraculous deeds and [waged] great military campaigns, facing certain destruction at the hands of the great and powerful Russians and ... their apostate helpers. To admonish those who reflect on things carefully, we have recorded some of those events and holy battles as lessons for future generations and models for the perceptive. We called this *The Shining of Daghestani Swords in Certain Campaigns of Shamil*, because [Shamil] witnessed the careers of the first two [leaders], was distinguished in most of [his campaigns], and [endured] the hardships of hostility and separation. It collects all the details in several volumes and will astonish the ears and eyes. (The Lord does what He will. God bless the victorious!)

The beginning of Ghazi Muhammad's leadership

[In 1829, a gathering of notables in the Caucasus acclaimed Ghazi Muhammad as their first imam: the religious and political leader of a Muslim Daghestani anti-Russian resistance movement there. This took shape just as Russia had begun to consolidate its control of the region after defeating Iran in a three-year war. Ghazi Muhammad had been a top disciple of Sayyid Jamal al-Din al-Ghazi-Ghumuqi, a leader (*shaykh*) in the Caucasus of the Naqshbandi Sufi order. While Jamal al-Din emphasized a more passive spiritual focus, Ghazi Muhammad called for active struggle (*jihad*) against the Russians.[13] Although not formally considered a true spiritual leader himself, Ghazi Muhammad led a resistance movement against the Russians in Daghestan from 1829 until he was killed on October 29, 1832. In its account of Ghazi Muhammad's leadership, *The Shining of Daghestani Swords* showed how the beginning of Shamil's career foreshadowed his later achievements.]

In 1242 AH [= 1826 CE],[14] God wanted to renew religion and to have good preferred to bad, as well as to distinguish some [Muslims] in campaigns and some in martyrdom. From a nation blessed by bounty and delighted by much wine, he raised up a man with no tribe to shelter him and no power with which to dominate. He was Ghazi Muhammad al-Gimrawi (May God sanctify his secret!),[15] the heaven-favored scholar who led them. He called on [Muslims] to obey the *sharia*, practice it, and reject customary law.[16] He spoke thunderously on this subject and composed a letter denouncing the people [of Daghestan] as infidels. It was a poem titled "The Splendid Proof of How the Daghestani Authorities Rejected [True Belief]" and here is a part [of it]:

> The chronicles of customary law are collections of poetry by followers of the treacherous one who is stoned [Satan].
> The Lord will decide who is the loser: Muhammad or he who supports vile custom.
> When the followers of Ahmad [Muhammad] grasp the strong cable [Islam], [Those others] will not find even a weak protector,
> In the future, they will know which of these two [groups'] promises will be fulfilled,
> when they witness a day of calamitous visions.
> The Merciful One [God] will banish a people who love him [Satan] from white Kawthar on the day when secrets are revealed [Judgment Day],[17]
> If the one who follows customary law were equal to the one who follows *sharia*,
> Then there would be no difference among us between the pious and the debauched.
> Why [else] were messengers sent, the *sharia* established, and the *Quran* revealed with its rules?
> What kind of repose could there be in a place where the heart is not at ease, and the authority of God not accepted?
> A place where the shining forbearance [of Islam] is repudiated, and where ignoramuses abandoned [by God] rule.
> Its vilest site is considered its Ka'ba, and its sinful are [considered] its just.[18]
> The well-known faith [of Islam] has become unknown.
> Its emir considers corrupt acts good,
> and falls short in forbidding the sins he encounters.
> If Muhammad were alive now,
> his Indian blade would be unsheathed.
> Their spokesman rejects what I have said to him,
> [but] it should not be hard to grasp what is known by intuition.
> O exiles from Islam, you who have gone astray,
> Let there be peace upon the one who [lies] buried in the dust.

The noble Hashimi[19] Prophet whose intercession is accepted,
the esteemed messenger: Muhammad.
Until now, these people have all been spreading distress and hostility,
Their situations and actions guided them
against the commandments of God, His prohibitions, and His guidance.
Because of this people's sins, they became divided.
The unbelievers and their enemies ruled them.
Indeed, I grieve for this people [who had once been] raised up and [offered]
intercession,
Since ruin has fallen on their heads.
If you do not see that obeying your Lord is good,
then go and serve the one who has caused fear and terror [Satan].

After [hearing] this, their tempers cooled and they accepted what he said. Then
he went to the region of Chirkah and called on people there to do the same
thing. After nearly a month [of his preaching] they agreed. He won over group
after group there, both the willing and the unwilling.

A trustworthy source told me that a servant of the great *shamkhal* said to him
that an enraged Ghazi Muhammad once came to the *shamkhal* by himself. In a
harsh voice, he gave him an order: "Establish the *sharia* in your territory!"[20] The
shamkhal's face lost its color. When he went limp and responded, "I will do this! I
will do this!" Ghazi Muhammad left. The *shamkhal* told his servant, "By God, I
almost wet my robe from fear of him." He made as if he were going to fulfill this
promise but did nothing. (Thanks be to God, Lord of the universe!)

Then the blessings of the *shaykhs* of the *tariqat* [the Naqshbandi Sufi order]—
the scholar Muhammad Efendi al-Yaraghi and Jamal al-Din al-Ghazi-Ghumuqi
(May God have mercy on them!)—were spread around.[21] These blessings helped
establish *sharia* like spring rain helps plants grow. Ghazi Muhammad wrote a
message addressed to all regions that was friendly to believers but warned those
who were haughty and rebellious against God:

> In the name of God, the Merciful, the Compassionate. He is the
> Creator.... We are servants of God, all-powerful Victor over all, the
> Creator who resists all who oppose the *sharia* of [God's] preferred ones
> and [those who oppose] the behavior of the righteous. Peace be upon
> those who "hear the word, follow its best meaning,"[22] and adopt Islam
> as their faith.
>
> O wretched ones, know that we have given our souls and lives to exalt
> God's word. We have dedicated ourselves to pleasing God. "If you have a
> trick, then use it."[23] Do not hide your [true] situation from yourself so
> that even you can't see it. When we come out into the open fields in front
> of people, evil will rise in the morning for those who were warned and
> did not obey![24] "If you come back [to the faith], then you will keep your
> wealth. Do not oppress, and you will not be oppressed."[25] When cold

takes off its clothes and heat puts them on, we shall come upon you with an army that you will never be able to match. We will seize you cowering from your villages and you will be brought low. Indeed, we will make you taste the penalty of this life short of the supreme penalty [of death] so that you might turn back [to Islam].[26] We have come out with humility among the believers, but forceful with the infidels, in order to help our repentant and worshiping believer brothers, peace be upon you until the Day of Judgment!

As for those kind brothers, be patient and fear God in the hope that you will flourish and God will remove the evil with which the infidels oppress [you]. God will not improve the situation of the corrupt. Hold steady until we can come to [help] you. Do not obey the command of the corrupt. "Do not lose heart and do not grieve, for you are the most exalted."[27] Peace be upon him who follows right guidance, and abandons the false! We will punish as they deserve all those we meet who do not know the meaning and form of the *fatiha*, the testament of faith, prayer, and the other pillars,[28] as well as [those who follow] infidel sayings, do bad deeds, and commit multitudes of other great sins.[29] (Let there be peace!)

The beginning of Ghazi Muhammad's mobilization

When Ghazi Muhammad saw the gap between those who tried to implement *sharia*, those who worked to extinguish its light in order to exalt [tribal] customs and practices, and others who vacillated between these [two groups], he mobilized an army to move through the villages and countryside in order to guide the obedient, straighten out the crooked, and smite sinful local lords. He entered Qaranay and Irpili, took control of them, disciplined their inhabitants, and sent the judge of Qaranay and its other leaders to the Gimrah jail.

He proceeded into Harakan where they submitted to him. Their religious scholar, the famous Sa'id, then fled to the lowlands that were under Russian control.[30] The wine jugs in his house were poured out and [Ghazi Muhammad] moved on to Ansal.[31] He treated people there kindly and convinced them to accept the *sharia* and surrender to Islam. It is related as a sign of his prestige that he said to them, "You are confident that you will go back to what you used to do: heading to the lowlands to sell apples and wine. A second one [Hamza Bek] will come against you with force, and you will see what a third one [Shamil] will do to you."

He arrived in [the region of] Baqulal. [Ghazi Muhammad] established *sharia* among its inhabitants and [punished] Mekhelta's judge by beating him. The [people of Mekhelta] submitted to [Ghazi Muhammad]. He called on them to wage war on 'Andal. The village of Ghaghal battled him. Men from Mekhelta and others became martyrs there while many from 'Andal were killed too. The ['Andal force] was defeated and transformed into a humble, meek group that obeyed his orders and prohibitions.

15

The first battle of Khunzakh

Since [Khunzakh's] people and its leader had produced great discord and strife, causing much evil, rebellion, and sinful behavior, he attacked them with a substantial force and headed into the territory of their leader Pakhu Bike.[32] It is said that when the army came into it, she stood conspicuously on the roof [of her house], encouraging her men. Ghazi Muhammad brought with him the force from Hindal [there]. He appointed his best student and companion Shamil to command the Baqulal forces. [Shamil] led them in an attack on the town from the direction of the cemetery. Bullets showered them like hail falling from the sky. [Shamil] went into a house and barricaded its door, followed by about thirty of his young followers. Many from Baqulal and other places became martyrs there. The group [from Hindal] that had come with Ghazi Muhammad from the eastern side [of town] ran away, [but] it is said that the men from Baqulal [who were with Shamil attempted to] block these Hindal troops as they were trying to leave.

The villages in the regions of Baqulal and Khunzakh settled down. A Mekhelta man [came to] Khunzakh and reported that this had happened. He told the people barricaded in the house to come out, saying, "You will not be harmed."

Fearing treachery, Shamil waited until dawn and then his group came out. When he returned to Baqulal, people gathered around him and harshly criticized him: "All this strife comes from the bad luck you brought!" They took away his weapons and hat. They were about to kill him when Darvish Nur Muhammad al-Inkhawi, together with his companions and Hadith al-Mililti, son of the [newly] appointed judge [there], saved him. This happened on the night of 1 Ramadan 1245 AH [= February 24, 1830 CE] at the end of winter.

The hypocrites rejoiced at this event. People who remained uncertain about whom to support began to incline towards them. Others showed laziness and neglected [their religious duties]. Ghazi Muhammad and his companions settled down in fields outside the village [of Gimrah], where they built dwellings and a mosque for themselves made out of earth. Shortly after [Ghazi Muhammad] returned from the battle at Khunzakh, there was a severe earthquake (which will be discussed later) and a great plague broke out among the people. They began to seem as if they had just woken up from being unconscious.[33]

Due to Pakhu Bike's treachery, the Russians were able to mount an attack on [Ghazi Muhammad's] forces on the night of 10 Dhu al-Hijja [1246 AH = June 2, 1830 CE] and a battle followed.[34] The men of Gimrah handed two condemned men over to [the Russians] as hostages for a peace agreement. Ghazi Muhammad did not make [any agreement with the Russians, though]. In fact, this battle led him to [push on and] seize Aghach Qala.

Hamza in Chartalah

By the fall of 1246 AH [1830 CE], the second year after the [Russian] fortress [in Chartalah] was built, Hamza received Ghazi [Muhammad]'s permission to lead a large force to nearby Ghuluda, where he was met by the Char people and their allies. When the Russians came out to attack, Hamza and the Char group fought back and killed many of them, driving them back into the fortress. [The Russians] left behind a cannon, so the [Muslims] took it and plundered the [belongings of the Russian] dead. They tried every trick to destroy this cannon, but could not.

When Hamza saw that he could not drive the infidels out of the [Chartalah] fortress, he sought protection [from them] for the Char region. He went into the fort with Shaykh Sha'ban al-Buhnudi. The two were imprisoned there as hostages and [later] sent to Tiflis. They stayed there awhile and were later released under a truce in exchange for two boys to take their place. Hamza remained at home studying until he heard that the boy who had replaced him had died. Then, he went right to Ghazi Muhammad.

The first battle at Aghach Qala

In the spring of the sixth year [of his leadership (1246 AH/1831 CE)], Ghazi Muhammad set out with about 150 men to do battle at Aghach Qala, which is about an hour away from Ghazanish. The *shamkhal* and Ahmad Khan went after them [there] leading [an army of] all the people of the lowlands, but their attack turned into a shameful rout. Most of those lowlands people went over to him [Ghazi Muhammad] and submitted to his authority. The Russians came back and camped near Uritirk. A group that was in their fort came out to attack led by 'Ali Sultan al-Ansali and they were defeated and killed. Two men became martyrs there and Darvish Nur Muhammad al-Inkhawi was wounded.

Then the Russians advanced to Kafr Ghumuq [two days' march from Gimrah], while Ghazi Muhammad went with his army to Atli Buyun, an hour away from the Targhu fortress. Russian troops attacked them from two sides and they fought back on both. The [defenders at Atli Buyun] killed many [Russians] and inflicted a serious defeat on them there. The Russian troops regrouped for another assault but were too afraid to launch an attack. [The Ghazi] swept into the village of Piri Awul where the treasury and belongings of the *shamkhal* and other notables were kept. [Ghazi Muhammad] seized everything there [as booty] and sent it to Aghach Qala.

The battle at Targhu fortress

Next, he moved against the Targhu fortress and launched a headlong attack on it. It is said that [his forces] entered it through the cannon ports in its walls. A man from Gimrah came to Ghazi Muhammad bearing the good news that the fort had been taken. Ghazi Muhammad corrected him, "The fort has not yet been taken, but something is happening there that God desires. Go back there and I will follow [you]." While they were fighting at the fort, fire broke out in the powder magazine near our troops. It blew up and killed nearly twelve hundred of our men, of whom eighty were from Chirkah. The Russians mounted another attack after this incident. Ghazi Muhammad charged at them three times and the brave Nur Muhammad al-Tsubuti killed a soldier with his sword who had intended to bayonet Ghazi Muhammad.

Addendum: Shamil's son Jamal al-Din was born about 20 days after this event. (Praise God!)

The siege of the fortress of Indiri and the campaign of Aghdash Awukh[35]

'Abdullah al-'Ashilti led an army from Salatawh to besiege Indiri and its fort. Ghazi Muhammad joined them. They laid siege to it for about a month and a half. Then Ghazi Muhammad learned that the Russians were moving against them. He allowed his armies to return [to their homes] and most of the troops, who were rabble, did go away. [A force of Russians] who had [just] arrived there then fought a great battle with the soldiers who remained with him. He regrouped and ensconced [his forces] in Chumal, an inaccessible spot between Indiri and Awukh. Groups of Russians gathered and went into Aghdash Awukh, setting it on fire. Two brothers there inflicted terrible casualties on them and were martyred outside the village. It is reported that when their mother found them, she was neither sad nor wept. On the contrary, she was happy about their martyrdom. She was only sad that her other son could not join them because he had been traveling. "Patience is beautiful and we seek help from God!"[36]

The Russians began to pull back as Ghazi Muhammad waged war on them. He killed many and drove them back to Indiri, capturing a fine cannon that he sent to Chirkah. He moved the people of Indiri to settle in place that he had bought for fifty tomans from the treasury and then went back to his house. When the Russians finally arrived at Kafr Ghumuq, Ghazi Muhammad laid siege to the fort of Derbend. He continued to attack it for nearly two weeks as several big battles took place there.

Then Muhammad Efendi al-Yaraghi (May God protect his secret!), the man familiar with God, and his followers met up with Ghazi Muhammad when he was in Tabarsaran.[37] He went back with them, taking them first to Irpili and then to Chirkah.

The conquest of Qidhlar fort

In the fall, Ghazi Muhammad assembled an army, suspecting that the Russians were moving towards Kilbakh. He advanced from the direction of Chechnia towards Qidhlar and conquered it, capturing lots of property and prisoners there. A Circassian said that he had been in Qidhlar when it was captured and that so many flocks of black ravens had flown out then that they blocked the sun. The cries of the ravens swirling above the fortress distracted the Russians and threw them into confusion. After Ghazi Muhammad's force left, the ravens gradually drifted away.

Leading a large force from Qidhlar, the cursed [Russian] commander pursued [him back] to Chirkah. With Muhammad Efendi al-Yaraghi's permission, the [Muslims] there made peace with him and gave him back the [captured] cannon. [Muhammad] Efendi moved to the village of Ihali. The people of Indiri and their comrades returned to their native villages. [Ghazi Muhammad] mobilized an assault on the fort at Buraw.[38] As he approached it, he was knocked off his horse by the blast of wind from a shell fired from an infidel cannon near him and he retreated.

The second incident at Aghach Qala

The Russians and all the people of the lowlands marched against Aghach Qala. Ghazi Muhammad was not there, but Shamil, Hamza, and Sa'id al-Ihali were inside its fort. Shamil had come with his Gimrah comrades to confront the enemy. When the fighting turned serious, all but three of his companions became separated from him. [Helped] by firing [from inside the fort] behind them, [Shamil and his men] routed an enemy force coming from one direction and then retreated back into the fort. Hamza, Shamil, and several of their comrades fought hard. They killed many of the infidels, who had surrounded the fort on all sides but could not get into it. They continued fighting until nightfall when the enemy pulled back. The fort's defenders started stripping the dead [of their belongings] and finally abandoned it.

Ghazi Muhammad's mobilization against Chechnia

When Ghazi Muhammad's neighbors in Chirkah and other villages shifted [their loyalty] to the infidels, he mobilized an army to attack the Chechens in the spring in order to reform them and to wage holy war [*ghaza*] in their area. The man familiar with God, Muhammad Efendi al-Yaraghi, accompanied him on this campaign. He went into Chechen territory and burned several of their villages. Five hundred Russian cavalrymen attacked them in Kuydurmas, but the [Muslims] killed most of them, leaving only three survivors. They plundered them and took their equipment, including two cannons and such things. A large Russian force arrived to attack them the next day. Ghazi Muhammad's army then withdrew and sent the two cannons to the village of Bayan.

A memorable digression about some of Ghazi Muhammad's glorious deeds and acts of distinction: Ghazi Muhammad came back from Chechnia saying, "These armies are coming after me and I will be martyred at the door of my house." He began building a fortification in the narrow parts of the Argun valley by digging trenches and dwellings there. He worked on this until the early fall.

It is related that a Gimrah woman, a cousin to [both] Ghazi Muhammad and Shamil, said that she had once visited Ghazi Muhammad in the Argun region in the company of some other women. When he told them, "I will be leaving you soon," they wept. They asked, "Who will we have [to guide us] after you?" He answered, "Shamil will be good for you." When they pressed him, asking "Who could [possibly] help us like you?" Ghazi Muhammad replied, "His life will be long. I saw two tree trunks in a dream: one was me and the other, Shamil. As the trunks floated down the river, Shamil's rose out. It was a cypress, whose usefulness is said to endure forever."

It is said that once Shamil was coming back from a visit to [Ghazi Muhammad]. Looking towards him, [Ghazi Muhammad] asked, "How would it be for him, if only he knew what will happen to him in the future?"

There once had been with Ghazi Muhammad an immigrant scholar from the lowlands whom Muhammad Efendi respected, loved, and made his close companion. He was called "Hasan Husayn."³⁹ When they retreated from Chechnia, they left him there. A short while later, a man came from Chechnia and reported, "This Hasan Husayn went over to the Russians. When he attacked us alongside their troops, we killed him." Ghazi Muhammad was taken aback and wept, but then said, "Indeed we are from God and we return to Him."⁴⁰ He told Shamil, "If ever I turn away from what we are doing, kill me without delay, so that I may not be described by God's words: 'We grant them respite that they may grow in their iniquity.'"⁴¹ End [of story]. [He said] this for fear of having a bad end like this [man]. (May God grant us a good end!)

A reliable source told me on the authority of the *shamkhal* Abu Muslim's servant that a letter from [a man who lived at] the holy tomb [of Muhammad in Medina] (May God bless its holiness and grant it peace!) was delivered to [the *shamkhal*] that literally read, "I have been seeing in a dream the Prophet [Muhammad] (May God bless him and grant him peace!), standing all alone, but now I see another man with him." I asked him who that man was and he said, "It must be Ghazi Muhammad," since the letter went on to describe the appearance and characteristics [of someone resembling Ghazi Muhammad]. The man then had written, "By God most Great, O Abu Muslim! I am writing you to ask: 'Did Ghazi Muhammad have those characteristics and this description?'"

Abu Muslim summoned a famous scholar, the lame Hajiyaw al-'Uruti. He gave him the letter and asked him whether Ghazi Muhammad was [being described] in it. Hajiyaw replied, "By God, I was a close associate of Ghazi Muhammad for twelve years during his education and he was as described. I could not describe him as [well] as this letter, even though I was his [close] friend."

I also heard that this scholar Hajiyaw al-'Uruti used to say, "Had Ghazi Muhammad and I lived before the time of the Prophet [Muhammad], I would have said that [Ghazi Muhammad] was a prophet."⁴² He also told me that Ghazi Muhammad studied in a particular village when he was young. One old man who lived there had a close association with Muhammad Efendi al-Yaraghi and Ghazi Muhammad. He told us that Muhammad Efendi used to say, "We can say, you and I, that Ghazi Muhammad not only seeks the best in what he pursues, but that he has *kashf* [mystical understanding of everything] except the very throne and chair [of God]."⁴³ (May God protect their secrets and enrich us with their treasures!)

A reliable person informed me on the authority of another reliable source from Gimrah that after the return from the battle in Khunzakh [see below], some people from the town who were in the mosque after the noon prayer were saying things in front of Ghazi Muhammad to rebuke him, such as "This man has fomented great unrest and brought the world down on the people." Ghazi Muhammad, infuriated and exasperated by their words, shouted the name of God at them. Then the mosque began to shake, which scared those people. They said, "Come let us repent [what we have done]!" Ghazi Muhammad quickly stood up, replied, "I have already repented," and went to his house.

That [shaking] was caused by a severe earthquake that struck Daghestan at that time. The scholar Murtaza 'Ali al-Dhuldi al-Qarakhi told me that he and Ghazi Muhammad were once with some men in a house in 'Ashilta. Ghazi Muhammad lay down, having covered himself with his cloak. Suddenly, he rose up and said, "There is no power and strength save with God." They said to him, "What did you see?" He answered, "I saw nothing." They repeated the question and he replied, "It was as if the Russians had been approaching us." Just then, they heard the voice of a rider who came up to Ghazi Muhammad and said, "A *naib* sent me to tell you that the Russians are coming from such-and-such a place." Ghazi Muhammad ordered him, "Tell the *naib* not to be afraid. They are coming for me, not for him." He made ready to depart ['Ashilta] and then left.

One sign of his intense piety was that he wore a patched shirt. Since there was a lot of cloth in his house, his followers asked, "Why don't we cut you a [new] shirt from this linen?" He replied, "This does not belong to me. It is for the common good and the poor."

The *ghaza* in which Ghazi Muhammad became a martyr and Shamil was injured

[After Ghazi Muhammad's forces had retreated from Chechnia,] the Russians were advancing [behind them] but [Ghazi Muhammad and his followers] still had not finished fortifying their positions. Men from 'Uthmanu and Qachar, as well as Chamaw al-Qaytaqi, Jamal al-Chirkawi, and Sa'id al-Harakani joined the Russian side. Ghazi Muhammad went to the Gimrah valley, barricaded its narrow part, and built shelters behind the barricades. During the night before the battle, which occurred on Monday, 3 Jumada II, 1248 AH [= October 29, 1832 CE], Shamil dreamed that his small and large guns would be destroyed [i.e., would not fire] and that the enemy would then climb up on the roof of a house [he was in], break a hole in it, and shoot rifles into it, but he would escape from it.

The Russians [and their allies] attacked them on that day. The battle raged from morning until afternoon. Our army fled as Ghazi Muhammad and Shamil went into a house behind the barrier [they had dug as a defensive fortification] with about thirteen men. Ghazi Muhammad said to Shamil, "you do not live here," as if he did not want him to stay there. There was a lot of gunpowder stored there. The enemy surrounded the house. Some of them climbed on its

21

roof and poked holes in it. The [Muslims] shot from inside the house to return [enemy] fire. Shamil's gun jammed. The men on the roof were sticking their guns through the holes and shooting at those inside, just as Shamil had seen in his dream. Ghazi Muhammad ordered his troops to rush out the door of the house. They and Ghazi Muhammad crowded around it, but no one went out. There was much chanting of the phrases "I ask God's forgiveness" and "There is no god but God."

Ghazi Muhammad took out his sword and charged. His cousin, Muhammad Sultan, charged with him. Shamil [couldn't get to the door, because of the crowd, so he] ordered the others to charge with Ghazi Muhammad, but no one pushed forward. He said, "See if Ghazi Muhammad has been killed." It was reported that he had just fallen. Shamil felt no sadness or grief, but remarked, "The time of 'let us not cry' has come for Ghazi Muhammad. Fair-eyed houris will attend the martyrs before the separation of their souls, and let us hope that they await us in heaven."[44]

Shamil was afraid that [the Russians] would ignite the gunpowder inside the house as they shot through the roof. He ordered those [inside with him] to charge out but they wouldn't. He pulled out his sword, shoved his scabbard inside his belt, rolled up his sleeves, hitched up his robe, and charged through the door. His headgear and turban were knocked off when he hit the top of the doorway. Shamil struck a soldier with his sword who was standing by the door. He fell face down and "cast down his beard" [i.e., died]. He hit another soldier who also fell. A third solider stabbed Shamil in the chest with his rifle bayonet and ran him through. Shamil grabbed the bayonet with one hand and felled the attacker with his own sword. The fallen man's rifle fell away from him.

[The Russians] around him saw this and ran away, but he went after them. Because of the crowd of people, they could not fire their weapons at him. One soldier shot a bullet, but it did not hit Shamil. He stabbed that man many times, but the man shielded himself with his felt cap. They said his name was Khan Mukhul and that he returned from that battle gravely injured. God knows best whether he died from his wounds or not.

Another soldier threw a stone at [Shamil]. It hit his left shoulder blade and broke his collarbone. The pain grew so bad that he could not breathe. He did not fall down, though. It was said that perhaps this was due to the *baraka* [spiritual power] that had nourished his body and primed him for holy battle from the time when they had returned from Chechnia.[45] As he was running around, not worrying about saving himself from their attack, he heard someone rushing behind him shouting, "God, God!" It happened to be the *muezzin* [prayer caller] who had been with them in that house.

[Shamil] ran after him. As they moved away from the crowd, many fired but did not hit them. The [enemy] did not pursue them after that, even though they were all around them on the road to Gimrah. Shamil grew weary from carrying his sword and gave it to the *muezzin*. Somewhat later, after they had gotten away from the enemy, Shamil fell behind a rock to die and the *muezzin* hid himself nearby. [Shamil] told him to get away, but the man refused. At that moment, he realized that the sun had not yet set behind the mountains and remembered that he had not called out the afternoon prayer. Shamil urged him to do it. When he had completed two prostrations, he threw up blood and swooned.

They stayed there until the sun and moon had set. They climbed farther up to reach the top of a mountain and spent a bitterly cold night there. Despite the fact that Shamil had no hat, his chest was full of blood, and his other garments were soaked with it, a continuous hot wind blew from the hole in his chest. It was emanating from his body and it warmed up the two of them. He said, "This wound has been better for me tonight than one hundred coins." When morning came, he rode a horse [that he borrowed nearby] to where his children were staying.

The Russians remained a week in Gimrah and demanded the corpse of the martyred Ghazi Muhammad. Some Gimrah hypocrites who were their allies brought it to them. The famous scholar Sa'id al-Harakani ordered that [the body] not be buried in Gimrah's soil. He said that the [Russians] ought to be told that if they buried him there, the *murids* would visit his grave, gather [often] at it, and stir up discord and sedition. They agreed with him and carried it to Targhu. They dried and preserved it there, where it was kept for a long time and finally buried. During the time when Shamil ruled a state [*dawla*] and his control extended to Targhu, he sent someone there to dig up this grave. They carried [the coffin] back to Gimrah and reburied it. He built a blessed mosque over it. May God protect its secret and may He grant us His blessings! Husayn, son of Ibrahim al-Gimrawi, said that when he was in Derbend, he read an account [stating] that eight thousand Russians had perished at Ghazi Muhammad's hands during a three-year holy war [*ghaza*]. (Thanks be to God, Ruler of the two worlds!)

Then Shamil moved to Ansal with his family. He was unable to sleep for some twenty nights. A doctor came and attached [medicinal] pieces of wax to his body, so he slept for twenty-four hours. He woke up and asked, "Have I performed the noon prayer?" They said "No, you omitted your prayers." He said, "How disgraceful for you [not to have woken me up]!" They replied, "You slept from yesterday morning until this moment." He did not travel [from there] until the end of [the month of] Sha'ban [1248 AH = December, 1832 CE]. He then visited the teacher Muhammad al-Yaraghi in the village of Balagin.

What later happened to Shamil in Gimrah

On the first day of Ramadan [1248 AH = January, 1833 CE], he went to Gimrah. While he was going to the prayer room to perform ablutions before praying, he ran into some women sitting out on the [side of the] road working wool. He passed by them and said, "Do they think *sharia* died together with Ghazi Muhammad?" He thought that they would be gone before he came back but found them as they had been on his return. He [now] saw a decrepit old man with them who had no loincloth and was carrying a thick staff. Shamil took the staff from him and reprimanded him, asking, "Have you been instructed to sit among these women?" He fell down and exposed his private parts. Shamil began to beat the women. They all ran away, except one. She was stubborn and he beat her several times. When she saw that he was not going to leave her [alone], she ran away, screaming, "I am being killed!" Shamil went back to his own house. The son of this woman ran to their [Gimrah] judge to complain about this behavior. The judge was Hasanalmuhammad al-Harikuli. He was someone whose foot Ghazi Muhammad had kissed, saying, "This *sharia* is the religion of our Lord. It is not something exclusively bestowed upon me. Follow it and raise it up. Do not allow ignorant louts to do you evil according to their whims. Do not be lenient about this and do not take advice from them."

The judge's assistant quickly arrested Shamil. He was sentenced to be punished because he had tried to enforce the law without [the judge's] permission. He responded with "hearing and obedience" [to the judge's sentence] and was taken away.[46] The flogger gave him twenty lashes with his whip. During the flogging, he felt something dripping from his chest wound. He touched it with his hand and felt blood. He showed the blood to the flogger and told him, "You've ripped open my wound. You will be held responsible for this." Frightened, the flogger replied, "We thought your wound had healed. Otherwise, why would we have hit you?"

It was Friday and [Shamil] attended the mosque that day. He asked the judge for permission to speak. Shamil asserted that it was all right for [any] man to enforce [Islamic] law without the ruler's permission. He said that the judgment against him was wrong, because what he did [was just, since] the faith of God does not die when those who maintain it die.

He said, "In fact, those who are better than Ghazi Muhammad have died. Our Prophet and the Rightly Guided Caliphs have died. God makes victorious he who makes His faith triumphant. By God, I will not abandon this matter until I die. Whoever seeks the reward of heaven let him support it. Whoever desires war let him prepare for it." He stirred up the *murids*. Their zeal increased. It was as if the fire of the hypocrites' enthusiasm had been extinguished. He returned to his family, that is, to Ansal, and fasted for Ramadan there.

He got back to his house on the night of the 'Id.[47] When he went out before dawn to a community mosque to perform ablutions, he came upon a group of hypocrites who had lit a fire and were banging a drum. They danced and cursed the *murids*, even calling them "those who have sex with their mothers." They said, "Tomorrow we will drink wine, party, and dance. Then we will see how humiliated those *murids* will be."

Shamil was focusing on heading back [to his house at that moment] but said to himself, "If I leave here [now without doing anything], then I cannot claim to possess true faith." He pulled out his dagger and went after this group, saying literally, "God will make known who will conquer and who will be disgraced!" The group was seized with dread of him. They threw down their drum and all ran away. Some jumped in the water while others slipped through the crowd at the [mosque] gate.

Imam Shamil ripped off the drumskin. He broke its rim and threw it after those who had fled, saying, "Take this donkey skin of yours." Next to his house [there lived] a hypocrite—an ally of the Russians. They had set him up as Gimrah's headman in a house that Ghazi Muhammad had bought for Sheikh Muhammad Efendi al-Yaraghi. In the morning, those hypocrites [who had been celebrating during the night] came to that vile man's house to complain about Shamil. "He destroyed the drum that the judge had ordered nine of the village musicians to beat at dawn."

The village elders came to Shamil's door and yelled, "You are creating unrest. The likes of you are responsible for stirring things up and taking advantage of this!"

Shamil spoke [to them] from [the flat] roof of his house and raised his voice so that those who standing in front of this vile man's house [next door] could hear him. He said, "I found them saying various things. Let them do what they will. By God, I will not give up trying to stop forbidden actions and I will fight them. Even if I am alone, God is sufficient [for me]. Whoever wants to, let him believe; and whoever doesn't want to, let him not believe." His words were sharp and rough. Now humiliated, the group that had gathered at that evil man's house then dispersed.

Shamil spoke at the mosque in front of the congregation at a holiday prayer gathering. "Do you think that with the death of Ghazi Muhammad the *sharia* was weakened? By God, I will not let it falter [even] by small measures, but will strengthen it by large measures with God's help. You know that I have more knowledge, strength, and followers than he [did]. Let the opponents of *sharia* come forward in battle. 'The more honorable ones will expel the meaner ones from there.'"[48] Upon [hearing] this, the *murids'* leaders were bolstered, the people stood up to support the *sharia*, and Shamil's opponents grew less confident. The village headman [mentioned above] fled to the Russians on the pretext of a quarrel with [Shamil]. In Dhu'l-Qada [April] of this year [1248 AH/1833 CE], [a son named] Ghazi Muhammad was born to [Shamil]. (Praise God, Ruler of the two worlds!)

. . .

[The next section of the narrative described the brief career of Hamza (1832–1834) as the second imam. It then turned to events after Shamil became the movement's leader in 1834 when a group of Avar nobles closely related to Hadji Murat killed Hamza in Khunzakh. The text then focused on the conflict that arose between the villagers of Ansal and Shamil's followers from Gimrah around 1835 just as Shamil was planning to attack Khunzakh to avenge Hamza's killing.]

The beginning of Shamil's caliphate [*khilafa*] and other events

Hamza had [already] designated Shamil to be his successor as caliph and a group of notable clerics had accepted this. Shamil agreed to this [only] after refusing it until they were about to disperse without approving it. When Shamil heard that [Hamza] had been killed, the first thing he did was to execute [in retaliation] Sultanaw al-Rughchawi, who was in their jail. Then he headed to Ansal on his way to attack Khunzakh. He treated the people [there] politely and kindly. He said, "You are the leaders in these regions. There are those among you with learning, intelligence, and bravery. Be chiefs and leaders for this faith. Do not be [mere] followers, and God will not lay down His faith and His people." They showed [outward] obedience to him and came along with him, but sent a message to the Russians that they should hurry to Gimrah.

As Shamil was traveling with them, word came that the Russians had entered Gimrah. Shamil immediately went back [there]. Since Gimrah's bridge had been destroyed, he jumped into the river with about fifteen men and crossed to the Gimrah side. He and seven comrades charged at the Russian army from one direction. Rajabil Muhammad al-Chirkawi and Husayn ibn Ibrahim al-Gimrawi attacked from the other with seven [more] men. They fought hard and mowed down the [enemy]. A Russian senior officer was killed and the [Russian force] was put to flight. One 'Ashilta man was martyred.

Just as the women and children of Gimrah were being sent into the wilderness to protect them from the Russians, those who were in the village [then] saw [a group of] men approaching them. They were able to see because the trees and orchards around the village [of Gimrah] had already been cut down [by the Russians for better visibility]. When they looked over and [realized that] it was a group from Ansal, they ran up to them. Most of the Gimrah people came over to the Ansal force but a few men stayed with Shamil. The men from Ansal [then] cut down the orchards and trees of Gimrah on that side [of the town]. The Ansal force chose a skilled marksman to kill Shamil, but God would not allow this to happen. There were a dozen [of Shamil's] comrades barricaded behind a wall at the bridge who cursed at them and warned them. They coarsely told [the Ansal force], "Do whatever you can! Give it your best shot!" The [Ansal force] did not harm any of the women and children even though they were mixed in with them. Indeed, their location did not permit them to escape past Shamil's military camp and position.

That evening, al-Hajj Qibid's brother and Tahir, both from Ansal, claimed that everyone had turned against them [Shamil and his men] and that the men of Rughchah were coming and the Russians and Ulub [a local headman] would be coming back to attack them, too. They said, "The best idea for you is to go away from here to some fortified place so that the people can go back to their homes." They struck fear [in people] by [saying] this …

Shamil gestured to his comrades and said [to them], "Let's barricade ourselves in a house in Gimrah. We will stay there and fight them." They were not pleased to hear this, so he said, "Well, then let's go and fight them in some secure place in the forest." They were not happy to hear this [either]. Eventually, he ordered them to go to Rigil-Nukhu, where they stayed two or three days. Then they went back to the village [of Gimrah]. (Praise God, Ruler of the two worlds!)

The situation in Gimrah eventually led to a truce. They [began to] act according to the *sharia* in that village. The bulk of their foodstuffs and other property had been taken to Ansal. However, the [Ansal people] expropriated all of this, asserting that, "[the same amount that we] gave as security to Hamza, we have now taken back for ourselves because Shamil has weakened [us]. [To get it back,] pay us a fine."

Due to this standoff, the atmosphere in Gimrah became tense. Klugenau, the Russian commander of [Temir-Khan-]Shura [fort], sent them three groups of sixty donkeys carrying flour. (Praise God, hearts were turned around and affairs put in order!)

Then the people of Gimrah, its best and its worst, decided to pay the people of Ansal this fine, in the belief that what had been taken to Ansal was worth more than what was being demanded [as compensation for it]. Shamil lectured and admonished them at a meeting: "[Payment of] this fine will be a religious and wordly humiliation [for you]. You will never erase its mark." He swore that he would not give anything [to pay for this]. One by one, they stood up and all swore this [same] oath. When [the people of] Ansal found out about their decision, they gave their property back to them.

Then Klugenau invited Gimrah's judge Hasanal Muhammad al-Hariki to [visit] him, accompanied by some men. He set off with some rebels, *murids*, and Shamil's uncle Barti Khan. They came up to those who were obedient to Klugenau, praised his rule, and received gifts from him. They said, "This place lacks only the reciting of the [Muslim] testament of faith, but there is [material] abundance in his house here."

Barti Khan said, "We met a man from Qidhlar behind our cemetery." He told them boastfully that he was on a trip [to Shura] to sell them [the Russians] grapes [to make wine]. Then Shamil was informed that those hypocrites who were with him [Barti Khan] on the trip to Shura had gotten drunk and that the judge [of Gimrah who was leading the group] had said, "I do not command you and I do not forbid you."[49] Shamil got up, went into the judge's chamber and told him to prohibit their drinking, but [the judge did not see this] as his responsibility. He placed a book in Shamil's hand and said, "See here where it says that someone of the Shafi'i rite should not prohibit someone of the Hanafi rite from drinking."[50]

Shamil took the book and said, "See here where it says somewhat later that someone of the Shafi'i rite should punish the Hanafi wine drinker. Summon those drinkers tomorrow and punish them!" The judge was compelled to accept this and fell silent. He ran away to his house before morning [to avoid punishing them].

A story: At that time, Mahdi, son of the *shamkhal*, invited Shamil to meet with him, but Shamil refused. The people of Gimrah begged him to do it and pestered him about it, but he would not agree [to this]. A *murid* came and told [him], "They say that you are not going to that meeting because you are a coward."

Upon hearing that, Shamil stood up. Wearing a fur coat and a felt sleeping cap, he took a chamberpot but did not carry a gun or a sword out of the house.

It was as if he was going out alone to relieve himself. He arrived at the cemetery, put his fur coat on a wall, and hurried off to the meeting. The people of Gimrah followed him, asking him to stop so they could come with him. He did not stop but called out, "If you come, then I won't go with you."

Shamil came up to those who had gathered for the meeting. Among them were [Mahdi], son of the *shamkhal*, with nearly one hundred of his associates and servants. They got up as if startled. He had them sit down and sat down [himself] next to [Mahdi] ... He asked, "Tell me what you are talking about?" They demanded that he meet the *shamkhal* to honor and exalt him. "The people of the lowlands and the mountains will be guided by his signet ring and yours [Shamil's].[51]

The *shamkhal* had at that time a pregnant young wife and his region was very happy about this. Shamil said, "If you send that wife as a hostage to Qibid Muhammad, I will visit [the *shamkhal*]. If any treachery is committed against me, Qibid Muhammad will kill her like a pregnant dog." This meeting took place after Qibid Muhammad had killed some major criminals in his village. They said, "She cannot be a hostage." Shamil responded, "If you cannot send her as a hostage, then I cannot come." He got up and went back [to Gimrah]. They were left looking at his back. He ran into the men from Gimrah on the way back. He said to them, "Go on to see those people now. I told [them] what had to be said," he said. After that, he was asked, "What were you trying to do by risking death and going unarmed?"

Shamil replied, "I was put into a state of rage. If they had attacked me, I could have grabbed one of their weapons. [No matter what,] I would have resisted them." End [of story]. (Praise God, Ruler of the two worlds!)

Shamil's flight to 'Ashilta and what happened before and during this event

At that time, Klugenau [commander of the Temir-Khan-Shura fort] demanded that the people of Gimrah send him roughly five donkey-loads of grape vines and fruit. The men in Gimrah who had the power of "loosening and binding" [i.e., the village leaders] gathered at Barti Khan's house to discuss this and invited Shamil to meet with them. He asked them why they were meeting. They told him the news [about the Russian demand] and it seemed to him that they had resolved to send it. He asked, "If we—the ones who are here—send it, will anyone from our village not send it?"

"No," they said.

"Will anyone [from our village] send it if we don't?" he asked.

"No," they answered.

"Then you can't do this. It would create a bad precedent that would last for eternity." He admonished them, "Blessed is he who dies and whose sins die with him. Woe to him who dies but whose sins remain." He said, "I think that you should reject [this demand], explaining that you have already cut down most of the vineyards and orchards [i.e., most of the ripe grapes and fruit]. People from Ansal cut down what was left and you have nothing more to send this year. Say, 'you should request them from others this year and we will send [more] to you after ours grow back next year.' Perhaps God will create something after that [so that no delivery will ever have to be made]." The people of Gimrah fell silent and did not like what they heard. He left them there.

His cousin Ibrahim caught up with Shamil and told him that [the people of Gimrah] had condemned him by saying, "Look at him and what he is telling [us to do] at a time when none of the people can even defend their women from the Russians," and [that they had ultimately] decided to send [the loads to the Russians]. Shamil remarked, "Let them do what they wish." His heart shuddered and his feelings turned against them when they yielded to Klugenau.

A noteworthy remark: (Praise God that those who build up their worldly fortunes but tear down their faith will perish!) Those who had met there saw no improvement in their lives after that. Only a few of their people survived and their houses were burned up. Their dwellings were destroyed, but because Shamil persevered in faith, worldly fortune turned in his favor so he was able to travel around and was granted a long life. As some wise men have observed, "That which is for the good of mankind remains on the earth."[52]

Surprising events: Although the village of Gimrah burned three times, Shamil's house did not burn, even though there were great efforts to set it on fire. When 'Ashilta burned, his house [there] did not burn, either. His dwelling was also not [destroyed] when the Russians attacked Akhulgoh before the big battle [there]. May God give him success and lead us to faith!

That day, Shamil sent a courier to 'Ashilta to gather together a group of youths. About sixteen returned from there. He told no one his plan except his wife Fatima after the final evening prayer and she consented to it. They assembled their household belongings and furnishings, bundled them up, and handed them over to these youths after the morning prayer [on the next day]. [His sons] Jamal al-Din and Ghazi Muhammad were hoisted on the shoulders of some of the young men.

When Shamil came out [of the mosque] he addressed his household with the words, "I am leaving you since it is not possible for me to uphold the faith among you. After all, the best of God's creation, Muhammad, left the best of His land, Mecca, when it was no longer easy for him to maintain his faith [there].[53] If God wills [the faith] to be upheld in you, then I will return to you. If not, then what do you hold for me, you whose house walls have been smeared with the feces of [Russian] soldiers?"[54]

As he was leaving, he came upon his weeping mother. She asked, "Where are you going? How can you leave me behind?" He said, "I am not going far, only to your village, 'Ashilta. If you want, I will bring you there after I take the children." She was brought there and then returned to Gimrah, where she died. May God grant her mercy! [Shamil] stayed there [in 'Ashilta] for about two years. He found the people there to be like a herd of donkeys traveling on the steppe. When he preached to them and led them by "commanding and forbidding," they began to "hear and obey him."[55]

A boy whom he knew came there one night and told him, "In one woman's house, men and women are gathering together to strip grain off the stalks and sort it. You have already forbidden that."[56] He asked the boy to show him that house and he said that he would. Shamil got up, put on his weapon, and grabbed a thick staff. He came to the [house's] door and found it locked. He listened to those [inside] and recognized the voice of one of his relatives who was named "Inus." He cried out to him in a harsh voice, "Open the door!" Afraid and startled, the relative got up and opened it. [Shamil] went in, beat them with his staff, reprimanded them for their evil mixing, and berated them. They fled and there were only a few women left in the corners of the house. He asked, "Where is the mistress of this house?" A woman stood up and said, "Here I am. I offer myself to you as a sacrifice." Shamil vilified and berated her, and then left.

In the morning, he went after two men who had been involved in that activity but had refused to accept any punishment for it. The people tolerated them forcing this [refusal] on him. Shamil got up, put on his weapon, took the book [the *Quran*], and stood in front of the group. He took the book in his hands and said, "Today is the day to distinguish the *sharia*'s enforcers from its opponents. If you go and bring back these two wicked men, then it will be good for you [as those who defend the *sharia*]. Otherwise, I will go alone and fight them myself over this. Then I will seek help in surrounding areas and others will come to fight and destroy you. Do you think there is no one left to enforce the *sharia*? God does not abandon His faith and people but makes them victorious through His triumph!" Then they set like lions on those two men and punished them.

From that day onward, they complied with the *sharia*, but times were chaotic. There was such hatred and bitterness among the peoples of Daghestan that the glory of the *sharia* had diminished and the recalcitrance of hypocrites who raised their voices and carried their heads high was strengthened.

The people of Ansal attack Shamil

During that time, Ansal raised armies to fight Shamil three times, but God only increased their shame and disgrace when [they did] this. [Once] when they had united against him, Shamil wrote them a letter: "O people of Ansal, do not touch the rump of a bear. He will tear you apart." After they had been conquered and humiliated because of his power as a warrior, a hypocrite from the lowlands came upon this letter and said literally, "See how true that man's [Shamil's] word was. See how he sent them to destruction and finished them off!" On another of those occasions, forces from the Hindal area attacked 'Ish. They demanded that [the people of 'Ish] expel Shamil from their village and made them fear that they were going to attack their fields and crops. They begged him to go away then and return after those [Hindal forces] had left.

30

Shamil pointed to his big toe and swore, "Even if they asked me to move this toe for their sake, I would not budge it."

He went out with no more than ten men. He was armed and wore a helmet and chain mail as if covered in iron. He stopped on a hill some distance from the village of 'Ish in plain view of those who were attacking. A man who had known Shamil since his student days brought him a message from them: "They want you to leave this village and go somewhere nearby so that they can obey Ahmad Khan's orders. Then you may come back." Shamil cursed them and threatened them, speaking forcefully as if he were the commander of a great army.

He vowed not to move one finger. "Let the one who would force me to leave step forward. If you come back and tell me this again, I will shoot you in the middle of your forehead." When this messenger left, the [attacking] forces fell into a disgraceful retreat. Shamil and his followers pursued them [from one side] while young men from 'Ish came from the other direction and took much plunder from them.[57]

On another occasion, a group from Ansal attacked 'Ish, camped in its farms and orchards, and demanded that Shamil be sent away. They cut down crops there, burned them, and destroyed houses in the surrounding countryside. The people of 'Ish did not want to expel Shamil, but they had suffered because of what had been done to them on his account. One of them came to Shamil and told him, "Our judge, the scholar 'Ali al-Gulzawi, said at a meeting in front of all of us that you should leave our village for good in order to end all this strife." Shamil invited [the judge] to visit him. They sat on a bench and talked. Shamil asked, "What is all this that you have been quoted as saying?" [The judge] answered, "I did say it, because people are coming from over there in Khunzakh," pointing in one direction, "and from over there in Baqulal and here and there. This has produced strife and made the situation [here] trying. You have created difficulties."

Shamil calmly responded, "O judge, don't be so hasty. If the infidels were to overtake the people of Islambol [Istanbul], besiege them, and demand the expulsion of the sultan from their midst, would you issue a *fatwa* for his expulsion merely to calm things down and avoid having this confrontation [cause] any harm?"[58] The judge replied, "I would not issue such a *fatwa*."[59] Shamil said, "Well, if that's the case, then let's say that I am a leader [imam] like the sultan and this village is like Islambol [Istanbul]." The judge asked, "Are you accusing me of spreading sedition?" He replied, "In fact, I am saying that you are more than a spreader of sedition. You ought to be cut on your neck for spreading these sorts of lies." The judge left, ashen with fear.

Then [the men from] Ansal went back to Gimrah territory, intending to kill and capture some men there. They invited [the Gimrah men] to come over to them. Some of the men from Ansal were reciting the afternoon prayer led by a religious student while others were standing around behind the prayer group and talking with men from Gimrah. Suddenly there was a great commotion. That religious student stopped the prayer, got down from the high ground [where he had been

31

standing to lead the group], and ran away. The Ansal men killed one of [Shamil's] true *murids* and another man from Gimrah. The rest fled. Barti Khan was captured in the confusion. Some people shouted to their families around Gimrah that the Ansal men had killed such-and-such and so-and-so and captured such-and-such, so they should take precautions. The Gimrah people [there] ran away and barricaded themselves [against the Ansal attackers]. Since the [local] population was agitated, someone shouted in the Ansal dialect, "Whoever lives in this village is safe!"[60] The Ansal men moved against the village after nightfall. As the first of them came in, the young men of Gimrah confronted them, shouting, "The first of Shamil's comrades are here! He himself has crossed the bridge and is approaching. There is no power and strength save with God, the Exalted, the Great!"[61] The [Ansal] hypocrites were sent fleeing from there, throwing down their sacks of food on the village roads.

Some were captured, some killed, and others had plunder taken from them. They became scattered like the dispersed people of Saba so that they were not able to regroup that day.[62] They returned group by group to their home territory [of Ansal] in such a pitiful state that a woman from near their village met one of the groups and said, "It is a blessing that you [even] came back [alive]!" They did not say anything to her. She met another group and said the same thing and they gave no response. She met a third group and they did not answer. She said, "Let this mother [i.e., me] be a sacrifice for you so that [sin] would not fall upon you, even if you were found to be fearful [in battle]!" End [of story].

Shamil then traveled to Gimrah and remained there about a week. When 'Ali al-Gulzawi, the scholar and judge from 'Ish, realized what the hypocrites had been thinking and saw the effects of their words and deeds, he said to the people of 'Ish, "I said something that was not justified. I repent it and take it back. Shamil was created to do what he did and succeeded with God's help in doing it." He went to his house and resigned from his judgeship, as if he were ashamed, before Shamil came back to 'Ashilta.

The first conquest of Ansal during Shamil's administration

[Ansal] was [also] taken a second and third time. These two occasions would be "an exact recompense" for taking up arms against Shamil.[63] Sa'id al-Ihali had gone to Chechnia with some comrades to assemble an army and died there. They say he was poisoned. Hajj Tashaw al-Indiri then joined Shamil with about forty of his men. Shamil went with them and his [other] followers to the village of Chirqata. They submitted to him [as their leader] there after Basaw 'Illaw and his followers in the village and its surrounding areas decided to fight and resist [Shamil's forces]. Shamil and followers went to the village of Ihali and established authority over [its] people, then [they] continued on to Orota where there was great strife. The leader of [Shamil's] *murids* there was Aligul Husayn while Dibir Hajiyaw led its hypocrites. After about twelve of these hypocrites and eight *murids* were killed, Shamil arrived with about one hundred followers.

Hajj Nur Muhammad al-'Uruti and another man met him to request help. When he asked them to bring him into the village, they agreed and [all] went [together]. Everyone [in Orota] submitted to [Shamil], except Dibir Hajiyaw and his followers inside the fortress. [Shamil's army] attacked [this force inside] the fort as well as the Khunzakh hypocrites camped outside the village who had come to help their Orota allies. When darkness fell, Dibir Hajiyaw and his followers fled to Avar territory. He [Dibir] got away only because he was dressed in women's clothing.

[Shamil's men] stopped in the village of Khirik. Forces moved against them: from one side, troops from Khunzakh, and [a group of men from] 'Andal, Tah Nosalal and Jarbilil from the other. Shamil and his group pressed the attack against the Khunzakh group, while the Chechens led by Ghaziyaw al-'Andi fought the 'Andal troops. They all fled and dispersed. The coalition to oppose him had no success except for the Khunzakh force.

[Pressed by that Khunzakh force,] Shamil and his army then went down with axes into the orchards of Ansal on the road to Khirik. He threatened to cut down their trees, so [the village of Ansal finally] surrendered to him. He appointed the scholar Surkhai al-Kuluwi as their *naib* and judge.

The battle in Hutsal against armies from 'Andal and Khunzakh

Shamil and his *murtaziqs* moved against Butsun.[64] Its villagers prevented him from going into it. Then Shamil stayed with Murtaza Lasol Muhammad in 'Urkach. He and his followers held a meeting there and some of those with him wanted to go back to their homelands. He refused, saying "We will not go away like dogs chased away from the grindstone by the miller."

Shamil led his men from Hutsal to the bridge at Qaral. There, they seized a herd of cattle. He told the people that if they obeyed him and submitted to him, their cattle would be returned. They refused and appealed to their brothers for help. He offered to return cattle belonging to orphans if someone would come and identify them, but no one came. Infuriated at them, they slaughtered the cattle right in front of these [Qaral] people.

The men of 'Andal came up, led and urged on by the scholar al-Thughuri, son of the judge. They camped opposite the village of Hutsal. Khunzakh forces arrived and camped on another side [of the village]. The Russians camped with Klugenau and Ahmad Khan in the fields of Biri.

Shamil's force attacked the 'Andal men. The ['Andal force] pulled back, but the best of the *murids* were martyred [in that battle].

Klugenau wrote [Shamil] to ask him what he was doing. Shamil replied, "We will make peace and settle down when the *sharia* is followed among us Muslims [either] voluntarily or by compulsion. Whoever accepts it voluntarily—this will be good for them—but whoever refuses this, we will compel them to do it and fight them over this. You, Klugenau, if you agree to honor [an agreement that you sign with us], we will make peace and pledge to uphold it, but, if not, 'There is no power and strength save with almighty God.'"[65] Klugenau got angry [at this], threw the letter on the ground, and stomped on it.

Then Shamil's comrades attacked the camp of the Khunzakh force. They killed many soldiers and put them to flight. Ghaziyaw al-'Andi and another man each killed fifteen men. They say that Ghaziyaw had vowed to kill fifteen men from Khunzakh because they had killed *imam* Hamza. He fulfilled his vow there.

It is said that about a hundred men from the village of Avar and eight of Akalich's headmen who ruled according to the tribal customary law [*adat*] were killed. The scholar Muhammad, son of the judge of Avar, and the judge 'Umar al-Akalichi were captured. Shamil slapped 'Umar in the face and asked, "Do you not understand the meaning of God's words: 'And indeed we will make them taste penalties in this life short of the supreme penalty'?"[66] The men from 'Andal returned home with Klugenau and his whole army because their hopes had been dashed. (Praise God, Ruler of the two worlds!)

Shamil's mobilization to confront the Russians as they were going to Khunzakh and the battle of 'Ish against them

The people of Khunzakh feared that the imam's [Shamil's] state would turn against them, because the authority of religion and the people [who adhere to it] would be raised up. [They were also worried because of] what they had already done [i.e., killing Imam Hamza and fighting against Shamil]. They invited the Russians to build a fortress in their territory. They started the very process that would make them [their] servants. When Shamil found out about this, he left his family in 'Ashilta and went with his followers to raise an army, both by recruiting volunteers and forcing men from Baqulal, Agakhal, and other areas to join him. His plan was to stop the Russians in a mountain gorge and block them before they could reach the open area around Khunzakh. When he and his force reached the vicinity of 'Ish, its people put up strong opposition. [Shamil's] army escaped after the locals had killed, captured, and plundered [some of his force]. God saved Shamil just as he was about to be killed by letting his attacker be killed by one of his comrades.

Then Shamil stayed around Zunuh for about twenty days as he and his comrades starved, yet he got the people there mobilized. Then [Shamil] went back [to Khunzakh], but the Russians had already arrived there with their allies, who numbered not more than a hundred men, among whom were Hajj Tashaw and his Chechen comrades. When Shamil reached the village of Tsikal, the people of the Hid region attacked him there to prevent him from crossing their bridge. He crossed the river at Rihiq. Most of the people [of Rihiq] fought him, but some helped him.

Men from Qaralal came and built a bridge there. Shamil crossed over to them and traveled with them. He stopped at the entrance to the village of Tiklal. Muhammad Mirza Khan al-Ghumuqi [an ally of the Russians] was in the village of Sharakh with his army and the hypocrites of that region. He had sent envoys to Shamil to discuss a truce just as the Russians came up and surrounded them.

The *ghaza* in Tiliq and the Russian advance into 'Ashilta

Shamil and his volunteers proceeded into the village of Tiliq. The rest of his army fled to their native villages after the great hardships of that rainy night. The Russians attacked and besieged them [Shamil and his remaining forces] there.

The Russians were accompanied by the hypocrites and their followers from 'Andal and Guwal, who inflicted great harm on Shamil and his followers. Muhammad Mirza al-Ghumuqi and Ahmad Khan from the lowlands were also both there with their armies.

One night, the Russians sent a detachment to make an advance towards Haqlal. They attacked at dusk, killed [many soldiers in Shamil's] army, and plundered its things, leaving only a few remnants behind. The esteemed scholar Mulla Ramazan al-Chari was martyred that night. The [Russians] pressed them, destroying their fort and the raised building [inside it] with cannon-fire. Heads would have fallen down and hearts sunk had Shamil not persevered and forbidden [his followers] from communicating with those on the outside as they made a stand against the enemy there. Hajj Tashaw al-Indiri sent Ghaziyaw al-'Andi to Shamil. He told [Shamil], "Come on, let's leave this place. We will take the women and children of this village hostage until we can all escape from the enemy's siege. Otherwise, you must give me permission to leave or I will just go on my own." Shamil said, "By God, I will not leave here and no one here has permission to go. If anyone leaves without permission, I will put a bullet in the middle of his spine."

Ghaziaw al-'Andi came back and reported what Shamil had said. Hajj Tashaw was told, "Hold on and trust in God." He answered, "I do trust God, but my trust is compelled [by Shamil]." Russian units penetrated the outskirts of the village and the situation did not change for some forty nights. God removed the Russians from there through a truce by which Shamil's nephew, along with the son of Mirdai al-Tiliqi and the son of 'Abd al-Rahman al-Qarakhi were sent as hostages to Muhammad Mirza Khan.

Shamil met with them [his followers] and ordered them to uphold the *sharia* in their areas. The truce took effect when the hypocrites and the weak-willed ones believed that none of [Shamil's] followers who had been in Tiliq would last, due to the infidels' strength and their large number of allies. This happened at the end of Spring, 1253 AH [= 1837 CE]. I had blessed them with this poem:

O God, assist them in victory,
O Lord, grant Your assistance and gladden them.
Spread upon those servants,
The surplus of [Your] continuous help.
Send down Your presence amid the uproar,
And shake up the enemies and the tyrants.
Grant victory over those who abandoned You,
And give the spoils to those who acknowledged You.
Do not worry about those who oppressed them,
Send down on them the thunderbolts of destruction.
Answer the prayers of those in trouble,
Your faith, it is Your faith that we need.
If they forsake the community of the *sunna*,
The worship of the *sunna* will not be pure.[67]
To the one who came in victory and triumph,
I will send peace and prayer,
And also for his family and associates.
Blessed be the teacher and his companions!

As for Shamil's nephew, the Russians exiled him at that time, and he came back only after a long while, as will be related at the end of this book. As for the other two [the sons of Mirza and 'Abd al-Rahman], Muhammad Mirza Khan conveyed them by night to Kulasil and Batsadasil after some time and acted as if they had secretly escaped from him. Shamil went back to his family and found them in Chirqata. While he had been under siege [in Tiliq], the Russians had gone into 'Ashilta and its inhabitants had fled to Akhulgoh. They torched the village, but neither [Shamil's] house nor a house that his female relative had given him caught on fire. Then the Russians mustered their forces for the assault on Akhulgoh and the women and children there fled to Chirqata. The [Russians] attacked it and burned its houses except [Shamil's] house. Shamil's books almost fell into their hands but were rescued by the pious ascetic Muhammad al-'Ashilti.

Then the scholar Alibek ibn Khiriyasulaw, who was a judge in Irghin, and those with him from Baqulal and other regions made war against [the Russians]. They killed many of the enemy and prevented them from carrying out their plans. The Russians retreated [to their base]. News of this battle reached Shamil in Tiliq, but he paid no attention to it until the business there had been completed. Praise God, most Exalted! What was harder than that for which he [Shamil] was responsible and with which he was entrusted?

What happened between Shamil and the people of Chirqata when he was there

Shamil stayed in Chirqata while groups of *murids* from different regions came to see him. Twenty-three hypocrites from Chirqata gathered together and made an alliance to destroy the bridges and not leave the path open for outsiders to come to him, asserting that they would do against him what had to be done. Shamil was informed about this. His residence was at the entrance to the village at its highest point. He drew his sword, put it on his shoulder, and set out, accompanied only by his close companion Yunus, to see what they were doing and to threaten them with harsh words.

Shamil went to the door of the mosque and called for the judge to come out. He appeared, shaking with fear. [Shamil] saw that he was in league with them. He said to the judge, "I have heard about such-and-such and so-and-so. I know what the intentions and goals are [of these people]. If you plan to punish and imprison these men, then do it right now. Otherwise, I will do battle with any of them I meet, be they man or woman." The judge asked him to come into the mosque while he administered it [justice], but Shamil swore that he would not go in until the issue had been resolved. These men were then put in jail.

Upon that, Shamil entered the mosque and preached a sermon to the congregation after it had gathered. He sharply admonished them, saying "This faith [Islam] does not denigrate its people, but exalts them, despite the way its deniers reject it. The situation [here] is not as the hypocrites believe it is. By God, I will kill outright anyone who touches a bridge with anything but the soles of his feet." All opposition then quieted down.

A story: This incident happened while Nikolai the Russian was traveling in Daghestan.[68] Klugenau invited Shamil to a meeting while Shamil was living in Chirqata. He [Klugenau] came to it by way of the Gimrah mountain path with about fifteen companions and Shamil went with his comrades [too]. When they met, Klugenau extended his hand, but Shamil refused it, even though [Shamil's] comrades urged him [to take it]. They sat down. Klugenau asked him to come to meet their Nikolai, asserting that Nikolai would treat him with honor and dignity, appoint Shamil to administer the affairs of all the Muslims of Daghestan, and there would be no treachery from him. Shamil did not warm to this proposal. Suddenly, Akhbirdil Muhammad al-Khunzakhi sprang up with his comrades chanting, "There is no god but God!" The cursed one [Klugenau] was frightened and began to worry. He asked Barti Khan, "Isn't my fate in your hands?"

"Yes."

"Are you going to betray me?"

"No."

"Well, in exactly the same way, our Nikolai will not betray Shamil."

When they got up to leave, the cursed one offered his hand [once more], but Shamil refused it again. Akhbirdil Muhammad al-Khunzakhi stood between them to block the handshake. The cursed one showed anger at him, but not at Shamil. Shamil rebuked Klugenau and spoke sharply to him about this incident, saying, "Send this cursed one away from us." End [of story].

...

[After these negotiations broke down and hostilities resumed, the Russians sent a new commander, Pavel Grabbe, to mount a fresh offensive in the summer of 1839. The Russians defeated Shamil after an eighty-day siege at the fort of Akhulgoh, high in the northern Caucasus. In the end, they took Shamil's son Jamal al-Din as a hostage to allow Shamil to escape. By the winter of 1839, it appeared that the Russians had finally defeated his movement.]

The surrender of Shamil's son to the Russians as a hostage for a truce

When the cursed general [Grabbe] saw that he could not defeat them [Shamil's followers in Akhulgoh] or annihilate them, he invited them to make a truce. He requested Shamil's son as his hostage. Everyone with Shamil approved of this, but Shamil refused. "This will not benefit you and the cursed one will not leave you [in peace] because of this." [His followers] asked [him to meet Grabbe's demand] and he refused. They asked again and he refused. When they begged him once more and he saw that they were [too] weak and timid [to continue fighting], he granted their request. He gave his eight-year-old son Jamal al-Din to the [Russians] with a prayer: "Lord, You raised up Your prophet Moses (upon him be prayers and peace!) [when he was] in the hands of Pharaoh. This is my son. If I formally hand him over to the infidels, then he is under Your care and protection. You are the Best of guardians."[69]

Then the cursed one [Grabbe] requested that Shamil meet with his commander Pullo. Shamil ordered [his followers] to create the impression that he would not come because he was sick or something like that. He said, "If I come, perhaps he will demand from me what we cannot do."

The people wanted him [to go], but he refused until they began to attribute his refusal to cowardice. He got up angrily, and they all went to the meeting place [to see Pullo]. Women, children, and servants were sent out there so that a large group of people would be seen. They dressed women in young men's clothes and gave them hats and arms. When the *chalandar* [a Russian commander] saw their ranks,[70] he asked Yunus, "Who are those troops whom we have not seen until now?"

"That hill is as full of people as your tent is full of [Russian] soldiers."

When he saw people wearing hats but not turbans, [the Russian] remarked, "There are men among them who are not *murids*."

[Yunus] responded, "They are ours. The *murid* among us is the one who obeys God and adheres to his faith, not just those wearing turbans."

"Ah so," said the *chalandar*.

Shamil and his comrades found Pullo [at the stipulated place]. There were about one thousand officers and soldiers standing near him, [but at such a distance that] none of their guns would have hit Shamil if they were fired. Shamil sat next to Pullo. Pullo spread out a side of his cloak in front of Shamil, but he would not sit on it. Pullo started a long monologue. Acting [as if he were] proud and arrogant, Shamil [shifted around until he] was sitting on the edge of Pullo's uniform [so that Pullo couldn't stand up], lest the [Russians] treacherously try to kill him and ambush his comrades without them being able to get away. His comrade, the martyr Ghaziyaw al-'Andi, understood what was happening. He moved close to both of them and prepared to draw his weapon.

Pullo then came to the gist of his speech: "Your *adat* [custom] is that [you believe that] the best [course in life's] affairs is chosen by [each of] you [individually]. We only do what we are ordered to do and has been determined by the tsar. If a peace treaty and an agreement is to be concluded between us, it will be necessary for you to be presented to our general so that he can report to the tsar about this."[71]

Shamil, as if reprimanding and reproaching his comrades who had pressured him to come to this meeting, said in the Avar language, "Now, I'm caught. Now, I'm caught." Shamil's paternal uncle Barti Khan answered Pullo before Shamil could speak: "We are, as you say, free and independent spirits. One does something and another speaks against him. One agrees to something and another disavows it. We have scholars and wise men in the village who are not present here. We cannot make an [agreement] without consulting them."

Just then, Ibrahim al-Husayn gave the call for the midday prayer even though it was not yet time for this. Shamil stood up and said that there could be no discussion after the call to prayer, and they dispersed.

Then the [Russians] kept demanding that they send intermediaries. Shamil responded, "I will come armed with one hundred comrades. I will not be separated from my weapons. Let your general come with a thousand comrades, but leave his other soldiers behind and send them back [to their bases]." The [Russians] did not accept this but requested that Barti Khan come, but he refused. Then they demanded that [the families and] children [who were with Shamil] return to their native villages to guarantee the peace. He sent some families back to their homes in Chirqata and Gimrah, but this wasn't enough for the Russians.

Addendum: Shamil's comrade Yunus related that when Shamil decided to give [his son] Jamal al-Din as a hostage [to the Russians], they held a meeting to see who would accompany him and teach him the rules of the Islamic religion. No one felt obliged to do this. Then Yunus said to Shamil, "I do whatever you want. If you believe that I should go with him, then I will go." He made this clear to Shamil and went away with his son, carrying weapons.

When they arrived at the [Russian camp], they were treated with deference and respect. They were housed in the tent of the *chalandar*, who was the chief officer and director of all their affairs. One day, Yunus was summoned to the count's tent. The count praised him lavishly and observed, "Shamil heeds your words. If he joins our side, it will be good for him until the end of his days." Yunus replied, "He would not do that, but even if he were so inclined, there are those [of us] who would not let him."

"Go summon him," the count said, "maybe then he will come."

Yunus set off to Shamil and reported what the count had told [him].

Shamil said, "I knew before [we] sent my son to them [as a hostage] that they would not make peace with us. Now let them fight us wherever they want. They will get nothing from us except the sword." His comrades, among them Barti Khan and others, were not pleased with this answer. They wanted him to soften his words. He said, "It is useless for you to be gentle with them [the Russians]."

Yunus asked, "What should I say to him?" They did not find an answer. Yunus said, "I will say such-and-such."

They remarked, "That is the [right] approach." He returned to the *chalandar*'s tent towards morning, completed his morning prayer, and then slept until sunrise. The *chalandar* told him that he had been summoned by the count. He woke up Jamal al-Din, and they left [together].

At that very time, rows of soldiers were marching towards the count, while a big drum was being beaten as if they were being driven to their deaths.

The two came into his [tent]. Yunus was armed and did not put down his weapon or his turban.

"Well, what did Shamil say?" the count asked.

[Yunus] replied, "He decided that you could take his son to guarantee the peace agreement and you promised [him] that you would go away and not harm anything. Then you violated this [agreement] and ordered some of the families to be sent back to their homelands. You promised to make it possible for the rest [to leave] when they wanted to do so, but then you cheated them."

He mentioned a third [broken promise] and concluded, "We do not trust you after all this. You are treacherous, deceitful, and conniving."

The cursed one [the count] became agitated and said, "My business is not with Shamil and his speeches. We have been ordered to capture him and his family. We are sending them [the marching soldiers] to lay a bridge for that purpose."

Upon hearing these words, Yunus shuddered, he was thrown into a rage, and his hand reached for his dagger intending to kill the cursed one. But then he steeled himself, feeling pity for the child Jamal al-Din.

He thought to himself, "I will watch the situation. If [these Russians] do something hateful to Shamil, I will stay [true] to my belief in this affair, ready to attack suddenly and defy death." He cooled off. The cursed one realized that he had become unsettled and ordered the translator to take him out of the tent.

Yunus did not leave until he had poured out everything that was boiling inside him about [the Russians'] treachery and their violation of the agreements. Only then did he take Jamal al-Din to the *chalandar*'s tent. When he went into it, they stopped smoking out of respect for him.

Yunus said, "Do not stop doing anything for our sake, since we haven't stopped doing anything for your sake."

When the *chalandar* saw Yunus downcast, he slapped him on the back and said, "Don't be sad. Indeed, you are servants of God and people who obey Him. He will protect you and your Shamil and shield you from harm and suffering."

Yunus responded, "We believe that God decreed everything that happens in the world before He put it in place. We believe that He will not allow us to be

40

harmed by your great numbers and your might except as He has foreordained from eternity."

Thus armies of Russian soldiers, happy, laughing, and singing, returned back to the place where they had started [their campaign], because these cursed ones were glad about the peace agreement. As for the hypocrites from the villages and others like them, their faces darkened, their eyes overflowed with tears, and their hearts filled with fear upon hearing news of the peace. End [of story].

One day, after finishing the morning prayer, Yunus was still in the prayer position. The *chalandar* came up, performed seven [prayer] prostrations, and turned in prayer to God [himself]. Then he looked at Yunus and said, "Your worship of and obedience to God will bring rewards to you, but our submission to the tsar—there is no benefit in it [for us]." He continuously lectured [Yunus] like a Muslim preacher and calmed his [Yunus's] heart.

When Yunus realized with certainty that the Russians' only goal was to crush Shamil, he sought to find a trustworthy man to convey this information to him.

In a little while, the *chalandar* told him, "The count has ordered you to go get your wife and her household, along with the family of Murtaza 'Ali al-Chirkawi." Murtaza 'Ali was another man being held by them.

"There will be great wages and unceasing blessings from our tsar for you in this. Bring [others] with their families from there, too. Tell them that this [reward] can be theirs, too, with preference given to those who come first." He went on and on about this until Yunus clearly understood that they wanted to leave Shamil alone there.

Yunus invented a pretext to keep [the Russian] from guessing [that he understood] his [real] intentions. He said, "They won't let me come back."

"Messengers don't get arrested."

"But in truth, the boy will be lonely among you."

The *chalandar* summoned Murtaza 'Ali to join him. The two [Yunus and Murtaza 'Ali] said goodbye to each other and wept. Then Yunus set out, escorted by a group of officers. They saluted with a Russian bow when they joined him. He left them at the trenches [i.e., at the limit of the Russian encampment].

Then Yunus went to Shamil and told him this news in confidence. Only Tahir al-Ansali was present [during their discussion]. Shamil said, "I already knew [all this]."

Then word came that the *chalandar* had summoned Yunus back to the trenches. When he got there, Yunus found the *chalandar* talking with Barti Khan about sending Shamil [to the Russians]. But the call to afternoon prayer was sounded prematurely and Barti Khan went away, saying, "We will talk tomorrow." The chalandar said to Yunus, "Come here and we will go back [to the Russian camp]."

Yunus [declined] by offering the excuse that he had [to go back] and bring out [the people he had been sent to get].

The *chalandar* told him, "Tomorrow you can do that."

Yunus said, "Now [I will go], and I am taking my rifle."

"Well, return [soon]," remarked the *chalandar*.

Yunus went back to Shamil and asked permission to stay with him. Messenger after messenger came to Yunus from the *chalandar*. When the *chalandar* was informed that Yunus would not come, he kicked the ground and gave up on him. End [of story].

The [Russians] began to fight after they had been negotiating for about three days in this fashion. They saw that Shamil's comrades' bodies were thin, they were weak, their front lines were destroyed, and that they had other weaknesses. They were told about all this by hypocrites who had circulated among them [Shamil's forces] on behalf of the cursed one [the count], claiming to be intermediaries for peace negotiations.

The Russians hit them with great force, destroying all their reinforced positions with cannon-fire. Shamil's forces mounted great resistance to them over the course of a week, each night repairing, to the best of their abilities, what had been destroyed during the [previous] day. They grew weak and exhausted by this. They became so exasperated by the difficulties of this world that they competed to die. They became tired of this situation and began to look at dead men [with envy] as if they were entering paradise ...

On one of those days, Shamil sat in a conspicuous place in open view of the enemy. He sat his son Ghazi Muhammad down on his knee.[72] The dervish Nur Muhammad was with him, hidden behind the face of a cliff. Shamil envied his solitude, because he had no worries about a family. The dervish's relatives were [back] in their native villages. Shamil said to himself, addressing God, "O Lord, this [child] is the dearest spirit [in the world] to me. If my death comes from a bullet in the middle of my forehead, then [let it come in the same way] for my child."

He longed for a *halal* [religiously acceptable] death, but this would not happen except according to God's will and His plan for the two of them. God wanted both of them to live and get back to their tasks: vanquishing the fighting infidels, conquering the hypocrites, glorifying religion and putting the affairs of the Muslims in order, as we shall describe, God willing [later in this book]. As it is said, "that which is for the good of mankind remains on the earth."[73]

Shamil's departure from Akhulgoh and what he endured of hardship and ease after that time until he reached the village of Shubut

When God (May He be exalted!) wished to make manifest that which He had foreordained would truly happen: "the hole became wide for the one who was patching it," "the two rings of the camel's belly-girth met," and "one of the two saddlebags weighed heavily."[74]

The people stopped manning the outer defenses, gathering for battle, or showing up [at all at their posts]. Shamil stopped commanding and forbidding [i.e., administering justice and governing for the majority of his followers] there, since this was not having any effect on them. On the last day that they [his remaining supporters] gathered on the battlefield, Shamil headed there and resolved not to go back, but declared that he would be present with them to command and forbid [even if only for that small group, to the end]. [But] God saved him from that fate, along with men and women such as his sister, aunts and others. Then at night, [Shamil's followers] men, women, and children climbed into a ravine at the foot of the mountains. They pressed against one another. Some stepped on each others' feet and hurt each other. Shamil sent his son Ghazi Muhammad and his household after them, but he [stayed and] decided to seek martyrdom there [in Akhulgoh].

He asked his comrade Yunus what he was planning to do. [Yunus] replied, "I will do whatever you are going to do." Shamil ordered his servant Salih to kill his horse in the stable to keep the enemy from capturing it and walked away. When he drew near to the horse, it turned to him and whinnied. He showed mercy on it and could not kill it.

Shamil came out of his house equipped for battle. He left his books and other belongings there. He brought his hand down on one of his books, *Insan al-'Uyun*, that had been copied by the famous scholar Sa'id al-Harakani, and said, "Which enemy hands will you fall into?" God, with His radiant power, gave this book back to him after some time. May He be praised as the Wise Leader!

He went with less than ten men to a shelter on the battlefield that they had dug out during the night. Just then, Tahir al-Ansali came up to him and said, "We did not know what had happened to you until now. Many men there [in the ravine] are asking for you to come and will do whatever you do."

Shamil refused to do anything but stay there until God resolved the issue. [In a voice] full of thunder and lightning, Tahir said, "It would be best for you to do whatever you plan to do together with them, rather than completely by yourself." Shamil accompanied him to his house and met with him and Barti Khan there.

Barti Khan asked him, "What do you intend to do?"

Shamil said, "I will stay here and I won't climb down to the ravine to let the enemy kill us with stones and clods of dirt [that they throw down]."

Barti said, "[Then] I will go do that [i.e., go down]." He went into his house to prepare for [this trip].

Some young men from Nakhbakal got Shamil to go down and visit the place where the families [were] and he went. They all stayed there for about three days, but the enemy was [now] above and below them. Shamil and his comrades could not travel together in one group and could not relieve their hunger.

One day, Shamil dozed off and dreamed that his wife Jawhara had fallen on the ground. His son by her, Sa'id, who was about two years old, was crawling on top of her. He interpreted his dream to mean that [his wife] had died from a head wound, which actually did happen. She was lying infirm [in Akhulgoh] for about three days after Shamil had departed from there.

She kept asking Tahir al-Ansali to get her some water. Right up until she died, she was chewing on fried bits of grain that she had sewn into the borders of her veil for her son. Afterwards, the son was crawling on her. He called out, first to his father, Shamil, and then to his mother, Jawhara.

A story: Shamil came there again after some time had passed. Someone pointed out the place where Jawhara had fallen. They found her covered with rocks and wet clay deposited by the river's floods and drifts. Her body and clothing remained so unchanged that even her lips were still moist as they rested evenly over her teeth like those of a live person. They buried her in Akhulgoh.

Another [story]: A [dead] man was found there in a mountain cave, his body and clothing perfectly preserved until that date of 1272 AH [= 1855/56 CE]. Anyone who went there could see him.

Another [story]: It was related that a decrepit old man from the village of Ur said that he came to Akhulgoh about twenty-five years after the battle there. He saw a woman who had fallen as a martyr there clutching the two sides of her veil. On one side of it there was some wheat and on the other, some salt. Her corpse had withered.

Another [story]: About twenty men began to dig fields and gardens for a man from 'Ashilta near the gravesites of the Akhulgoh martyrs and all their hands suddenly became dry. End [of story].

In the end, it was true that Shamil had commanded his people and family to fight to the last ounce of their strength and told the wounded to jump in the river in order to avoid capture. When Shamil, grieving the martyrdom of his uncle Barti Khan, said to those offering condolences, "God will unite you with him [i.e., Barti Khan]." That was how much Shamil was finished with this earthly realm and longed for death.

Then one night, [he and his followers] moved stealthily up a long, dry creek bed to the heights of a mountain in order to get out of that ravine into open territory. But there were Russian forces ahead of them [there at the summit].

[Shamil] looked for someone who would carry his son Ghazi Muhammad up the creek bed for a large sum of money. No one would do it, so Shamil carried him up on his own back. He put Ghazi Muhammad on his back, tied him [in place], and carried his shoes in his mouth.

He climbed up the creek bed first and was followed by some of his companions. He stopped at the top of the hill and refused to go any further until Musa al-Balagini and some other comrades caught up with him. He sent eight others, one after another, for his family. Ghaziyaw al-'Andali asked him to go to an open area nearby, because, he said, "where we are stopped here is too narrow for those climbing up." Just as they came out into the open area, Shamil saw something black and whispered to Ghaziyaw, "What is that black thing over there? Is it the shape of a man or something else?" Suddenly, a volley [of shots] from soldiers' rifles rang out around them. He said, "Let's go and attack [them]. They have discovered [our] maneuver [here] and we can no longer hide."

They attacked and opened fire on the [Russians]. The [Russian] soldiers who had been in front of them were put to flight. In [those first few moments of] the attack, Shamil fired five shots. They told him that [another] large force was coming to attack them from the front. He ordered them to stay quietly near some rocks until these troops' rifles had rung out [indicating that they were near]. His companions stood behind him and Sultan Bek al-Dilimi stood in front of him, concealing him. They then attacked that [Russian] army. [Sultan Bek] al-Dilimi was martyred there.

The Russians were driven off to one side. Shamil and his comrade Akhbirdil Muhammad proceeded to follow them. Muhammad called another comrade to come over to him and swore in front of him, "By God, you [Shamil] will not die tonight!"

They asked him later why he had said that. He answered, "I had a vision that a great stream rushed over Akhulgoh and drowned everyone in it, but Shamil, a few of his comrades, and I rushed away from there to the mountain paths of Chiriq without being harmed by it. I interpreted this to mean that we would be saved but that place destroyed."

As [Shamil] traveled with his comrades, a piece of frozen ground flew by his head and hit his neck. He fell on the ground. One of his comrades asked him, "Where were you wounded?"

"I was not wounded," he replied. He stood up and shook off the dirt. They encountered a second group of soldiers and then a third, but God did not allow the [Russians] to defeat [them]. They went around the camps of the Russians and their allies with ease and came to a body of water. Shamil started to go back from there to see about his family but they held him back.[75] His companion Yunus got up and said, "I will go do this [instead]." Soon after that, news came that [Shamil's] son Ghazi Muhammad and his mother Fatima had escaped [from the mountain] and were coming to meet them. End [of story].

Addendum: This youth, his son Ghazi Muhammad who was seven years old [at that time], rode on a man's back as they were passing right through the middle of the Russian armies. [Suddenly] a soldier [attacked,] thrust his bayonet into his leg, and injured him. Keeping in mind his father's instructions [to avoid being captured], he told the man carrying him, "Throw me in the river, throw me in the river!"

As for Shamil's wife Jawhara and her son Sa'id, they stayed there, as was mentioned. As for his sister, she was heavy [so climbing was not possible for her]. When the Russians came to capture the women and children there, [the sister] wrapped her veil over her face and threw herself in the river. End [of story].

Six of the thirty who had climbed up to the top of the hill with Shamil were martyred there. After that event, [those who survived] said, "Well at last we are safe from the Russians." This saddened Shamil. He wept and blamed them. "You did not let me fight *ghaza* [holy war] there until I died. Where will we seek refuge and settle down now? In this world there are only those who hate us and are our enemies." They went along the river like sheep emaciated by starvation. When they had to take off their shoes to go in the water, Shamil commanded them to perform ritual ablutions for the morning prayer.

As they finished praying, some Gimrah thugs came up across from them to do battle with [Shamil] and stop him. A large river separated the two groups. When they fired weapons [at Shamil's group], he recognized these men and their

45

ringleaders. He pulled out his sword, raised it over his head, and swung it so that they could see it.

He shouted, "Hey so-and-so and so-and-so! This is my left-handed sword and it won't take more than three months to stab you [with it], God willing." These words struck great terror in their hearts. Their evil leaders had meant to round up everyone who did not agree with them in Gimrah about corrupting the *sharia*, and arrest them and send them to the Russians, but these words made them fear that the situation might turn against them [so they fled]. They [Shamil's group] went along in that way until it had turned hot and they all fell down in a heap, exhausted by weakness, hunger, and lack of sleep.

When it became known that Shamil and his followers had escaped from the mountain, Ahmad Khan al-Sahali [i.e., from the lowlands] and Hadji Murat al-Khunzakhi [i.e., Tolstoi's Hadji Murat] went after Shamil with an army of hypocrites seeking to capture him. When they drew close to where [he was], God closed their eyes and deterred their hearts before they could fire one shot. They went back home.

Then Shamil and his comrades got up and moved on like a herd of starving sheep. [Having moved far away from water by then,] they became so thirsty that they started drinking from the hoofprints of animals on the mountain paths. Shamil hired two men at a high price to go and fetch some water for them. They went and got some. One of them brought some of it to the group that was in front with Ghazi Muhammad and the other carried the rest of it to the group with Shamil. They [all] drank [their fill]. When the trailing group caught up with the leading group that was sitting and resting, they found [Shamil's son] Ghazi Muhammad sitting on a little rise off to the side of the others.

Shamil came up to him and asked, "Well, how are you? Did you drink enough water?" He answered in a sad voice, "They did not give me water." [Shamil] spit and cursed at them for this.

He was kind and gentle to his son. He told him, "We will get to some water soon—we will give you your fill of food and drink then. Let's go." His son stood up. His legs were unsteady under him. He almost fell. [Shamil] lifted him up onto his shoulders. His son's head banged into his own head. [The son] said, "My neck isn't strong enough to support my head." He had become worn out because of the injury he had suffered, as well as his other difficulties and troubles. They went on that way all night.

The next evening as they headed to the crest of the mountains, Ghazi Muhammad became sad and began to complain to Shamil that he would die of hunger. [At the time,] he was riding on someone else's back [not Shamil's]. Shamil pointed to the top of the mountains in the darkness. He asked, "Do you see that? When we get there, we will feed you bread and fill you up." They did the morning prayer before going up it. They climbed up it as the sun was rising.

Just then, they noticed a rider heading towards them. When he saw them, he stopped and rode back in the direction that he had just come. Shamil yelled, "Shoot him, shoot him!"

46

He turned around and asked, "Is it really you?" When he recognized them, he rejoiced. He said, "I thought that you were a group of enemies." He was carrying a saddlebag full of bread and cheese, hoping to encounter and feed the people who had escaped from the mountains. He fed Ghazi Muhammad his fill and the others all ate theirs, too.

Shamil ordered this kind man, whose name was 'Isa Hajiyaw al-Chirkawi, to carry Akhbirdil Muhammad on his horse because he was exhausted and injured. He carried him away [and then returned]. [Shamil] ordered him to carry another wounded man and he took him, too. Then he went off to a distant sheep pasture [where provisions were stored] and came back with flour for them. May God bless him for it! This is a summary of what happened in Akhulgoh. A detailed account of the events there would fill a thick book, which to read would consume one's heart in flames and bathe one's eyes in tears.

Jawad Khan al-Darghiyyi, who used to work for the Russians, said that once, while he was at the Qidhlar fort, he read in a chronicle that 33,000 Russians died [there]. Why wouldn't this be true, when it is said that 5,000 of them were killed in one day alone [in Akhulgoh]? They say that the accursed Pullo returned from [Akhulgoh] with only two men left in his army, but God knows best!

More than three hundred men were martyred there. The first was Murtaza 'Ali al-Chirqawi. Among the community leaders and religious scholars [who were martyrs there] ... Alibek al-Khunzakhi, Shamil's uncle Barti Khan, the emigrant scholar Surkhai al-Kuluwi, the steadfast ... Khiz al-Chirqawi, and the brave Bala li-Muhammad al-Birguni—a man they say killed one hundred enemy soldiers in a day ... The Russians captured around 600 (some even say 700) of the men, women, and children of Akhulgoh as well as its scholars, among them their judge, Silikul Muhammad al-Tanusi, who died in captivity ... May God reward their efforts with goodness and may He impose on them and on us the word of piety and allegiance!

Addendum: In which the kindness of God (May He be exalted!) is related: From the day when Shamil was saved from the disasters of that summit, the world has not stopped raising his standing and pouring favor and grace on him until our time. It has showered favor and grace on him until the present day. This is all from the blessings of God upon him and upon his people, but most of them do not know it. Let us hope to God that the world continues in this way until his [Shamil's] government and his holy campaigns [ghazawat] lead to the appearance of Muhammad al-Mahdi at the end of time.[76] Since God, May He be exalted!, did say, "That which is for the good of mankind remains on the earth,"[77] how can we not be hopeful?

The blessed news of his ghazawats [holy campaigns] reached the two holy sanctuaries [Mecca and Medina] as well as Balkh and Bukhara [in Central Asia]. Shaykhs there started praying for his victories, conquests, and long life in their sermons, just as we noted. Hajj Di'in 'Ali al-Chari recounted that when he fled from Siberia and came to Bukhara, he learned that its sultan visited the tomb of Shaykh Muhammad Naqshbandi (May God bless his secret!) each afternoon and

47

prayed there for Shaykh Shamil. The people [following his lead] said "Amen," even those in the bazaars ... End [of story].

[*The Shining of Daghestani Swords* now returned to the discussion of events after the conclusion of the Akhulgoh siege.]

[Shamil and his followers] continued along until they stopped to camp in a sheep pasture. There they met a young man they knew whose father had been martyred near them on the hill [at Akhulgoh]. [The youth] honored his father by entertaining them and slaughtering sheep for them. He treated them with honor. They saw the first new moon of Rajab, 1255 [= September, 1839] there at the time of two seasons [i.e., Indian summer]. They set out at nightfall and heard the sound of men coming towards them. Each group asked the other: "Who are you?"

Then they recognized each other. It turned out that this was a group of *murids* from the village of Artlukh who had set out to meet Shamil. They brought him to their region, hiding him from the sinners of their village. One [of these *murids*] came with bread, another with cakes, another with cheese, and another with meat. They hosted him and honored him. At that time, Imanqalaw al-Jirfati, having seen some of them [Shamil's group] there, and having heard that Shamil and his comrades had been driven out and chased away with curses, announced to the villagers of Artlukh, "Whoever takes the property of one of them [i.e., Shamil's followers] will not [have to] give it back to him." End [of story]. This man was later executed for hypocrisy by order of the martyred *naib* Hitin al-Danukhi. He deserved it. End [of story].

They traveled away from there by night until they reached the village of Almakhal in the morning just as the muezzin was calling people to prayer. However, they passed through there secretly without telling anyone, lest [its people] be harmed by sinners from neighboring large villages who might have attacked them had they allowed [Shamil's group] to stay with them.

[Shamil's men] went down to the water to do ritual ablutions. The judge, notables, and ordinary people [of Almakhal] came running up to them, begging them to come back and accept the village's hospitality. When [Shamil] explained to them why [his group] would not camp in their village, they swore that they would not let [his men] leave without offering them hospitality and that they would burn [with shame if their guests did not accept this].

Shamil said, "Well, if that's the case, then let's stay there." One person came with food and another brought something else until they had all treated their guests with honor and given them the sweetest and tastiest morsels to eat. They gave them provisions and had them rest until noon. Then they moved on.

A story: Shamil and his comrade Yunus were traveling ahead of their comrades on this trip. They passed the headman of Zandiqi [a Chechen village] as he lay sleeping in some grass and sat down beside him.[78] He woke up. Shamil asked of his comrade, "Don't you have something you can give him to eat?" He took out a piece of goat meat. The headman asked them about Shamil. Shamil told him that he supposedly had been robbed, shot, and killed. This headman wept, moaned, and fell down as if he had fainted. They got up and left him there. Then the other comrades passed by him [a little while later]. He then asked them for more news about Shamil. When they told him, "Shamil was one of the two men who just passed by you," he ran after them. The two of them had stopped to rest and saw an old man coming towards them with nothing covering his head. It was that *shaykh* who had fallen on Shamil's lap weeping profusely—this was how much the news [of Shamil's supposed death] had saddened him.

They entered the village of Tattakh between the two evening prayer times. They were hosted there for about three days. One man, having earlier made a vow, slaughtered a bull and prayed over it that Shamil would be saved from any bad luck caused by the enemy. He fed them and the others. Then they moved on and camped in the village of Bayan where they were made welcome and honored. Shamil stayed with someone who had [even] come [earlier] to Tattakh to invite him to be his guest.

Muhammad Shafi, Shamil's son, was born there on the 20 Rajab [= 29 September, 1839] and before the seventh day [an animal] was sacrificed in his honor. Then they moved to the village of Vedan where they saw the first moon of the month of Sha'ban [= 10 October, 1839]. Shamil left his family there and went with his companions to look for an appropriate place to stay and settle down [for a longer time]. They found the most suitable place for that to be Gharashkiti in the region of Shubut. Shamil stayed there as the honored guest of a man who had come to meet them as they were leaving Vedan. Then his host went away [again, still] during Sha'ban and came back with Shamil's family after the tenth day of the month. When the followers who had planned to return home left, eight of his close followers stayed with him: his faithful companion Yunus, his servant Salih, the injured Khudanatil Muhammad, Biladi, Himmat al-Hutsaliyun, the wounded Nur Ali, Murtaza 'Ali al-Haradarikhiyan, and the wounded Musa al-Balatkini. As Shamil was passing through Bayan and Vedan, the famous and brave warriors Shuayb al-Tsamuturi and Jawad Khan al-Darghiyyi met with him. At this meeting, Javad Khan said to Shamil, who was depressed about what had happened to him, "Don't be distressed about the dispersion and destruction of your old comrades. Indeed, a new group of more than three thousand of your old followers will gather here again for you. I am your servant. Your wish is my command. Order whatever you want and I will follow your instructions." May God bless him!

Shamil appointed them both as *naibs* to govern those two areas. He ordered them to seize whatever they found in the hands of someone who had come from Ma'arukh to do harm if that man had claimed to be a *murid* or a villager, but if he didn't [make this claim], then he should be let go. They used to confiscate the horses of those who had come to Chechnia from 'Andal, Baqulal and Karalal to look for provisions [to take away]. Several of Shamil's companions joined them in this action, among them the immature boy, Murtaza, son of the martyr Murtaza Lasol Muhammad al-Urgahi, and others. They calmed those areas down through such actions until their inhabitants began to obey his authority. End [of story].

[Shamil] stayed there like a discarded rag. No one noticed or cared about him. Once, a woman from Chirkah named Azizay came to complain to him that she was being sold into slavery there. He explained to her that he did not have the power to free her …

[Over the decade following his severe 1839 Akhulgoh defeat, Shamil slowly rebuilt his forces and carried out intermittent raids against the Russians in Chechnia and Daghestan. The next selection captures the flavor of such encounters in its description of the encounter at Shamkhal Birdi. In 1847, Vorontsov decided to deny Shamil the use of rich farmlands in central Daghestan. He attacked Shamil's forts at Saltah, Girgil, and Chokha. After capturing Saltah in 1847 and destroying Girgil in 1848, the Russians were repulsed by Shamil's forces at Chokha in 1849. The following excerpts chronicle four encounters between Shamil and the Russians: the battles at Shamkhal Birdi, the fortress of Saltah, the fortress of Akhdi, and Chokha. These passages show how Shamil came back from his massive defeat by the Russians in 1839 by mounting a series of limited attacks against Russians designed to wear them down.]

The battle at Shamkhal Birdi

When [a Russian force] had stopped there [at Shamkhal Birdi], the imam's troops surrounded them and held them under siege for several days. The Russians dug in there and along the road with every good heavy cannon and other weapon [they had]. [Shamil's men] were attacking them from all sides, but the [Russians] could not mount any resistance and could not defend themselves [because of their lack of munitions and supplies]. Cannon-fire killed one of their commanders there in his tent.

Vorontsov wept again, but [one of his officers] Ilya consoled him just as he had done earlier when he had cried three times [over their situation]. The Russian troops experienced such powerful hunger and thirst that it almost destroyed them. [Soldiers] began to suck on trees to get water. They say that a [Muslim] hypocrite who was there offered a soldier an ear of corn for fifteen rubles [i.e., an exorbitant price]. He literally answered, "[Why not?] What am I going to do with fifteen rubles after I die?"

A story: They say that Vorontsov had a cow with him for milk. Jawad Khan, son of Mustafa Khan al-Shirvani, stole it because he was so hungry. Jawad Khan had about a hundred servants with him as he marched. One night, some people slaughtered and ate that cow, and buried its bones under Jawad Khan's tent. When morning came, they looked for the cow to milk. When it didn't turn up, they began to search the troops' [belongings] and any suspicious places. Then they came across a large pile of buried bones. When these were brought to

50

Vorontsov, he demoted [Jawad Khan] to the ranks and ordered him banished from there. The shunned Jawad Khan hired a Chechen guide for one hundred coins. He traveled on a difficult and dangerous road with them [Jawad and his servants] until he brought him [Jawad Khan] to [Temir-Khan-]Shura after many of his servants had perished.

As the imam was laying siege to them, the news came that his wife Fatima had died. (May God have mercy upon her!) He sent a man to [look after] this while he himself remained there [at the siege]. His *naibs* came up and asked him to return to his home. They declared that they would be able to defeat the besieged enemy force there [by themselves]. Imam [Shamil] then did go back [to his home].

War had worn out his *naibs* and troops. They were so hungry that they grilled the corpses of dead Russian horses and ate them. When the cursed [Russians] found out that the imam had left, they celebrated by banging drums and playing pipes. In the morning, a relief force with provisions came to them from the town of Gurzal [Awul, just to the north on the Aqsay river]. The road was cleared between the two [Russian forces], and the [relief force] finally broke through to them. A force of about one thousand guarded the [relief force] from behind so that it couldn't be attacked from that direction. The men of this force didn't budge from their positions even as they were killed to the last man.

They say that they all would have converted to Islam to follow the imam [Shamil], if they had stayed under that siege for one more day, given how thirsty and weak they were. They report that when Vorontsov was rescued [from there], he counted up how many of his troops were left. When he found that he had lost thirteen thousand soldiers, he wept and remarked, "This Satan Shamil threatened me and events turned out just as he said they would."

One Christian with them there, who later accepted Islam and became a good Muslim, said, "Indeed, I would not be lying if I swore that three hundred thousand men had gone there with Vorontsov and that, when he returned, he was told that only a quarter of those who had been sent to fight alongside him from local [Muslim] areas that were allied with him came back alive." (Thanks be to God, Ruler of the two worlds!) ...

The battle at Saltah fort

At the end of spring, 1263 AH [= 1847 CE], Idris, the imam's *naib* in Girgil, requested his assistance and reported that the Russians were moving against the fort [there]. [Shamil] set out with material and equipment. When he reached the Khunzakh plateau, Qibid Muhammad al-Tiliqi and Ghazi Muhammad al-Tiliqi met him. They told him that they had not heard about any news about what was happening. [Shamil] kept going until he reached the plains of the village of Quruda. When he heard the sound of guns, he flew [like a bird] and went up Ifuta mountain. He found the Russians retreating from the fort after having assaulted it with siege ladders. The cursed Vorontsov withdrew from there with

51

heavy losses to his army. When he saw how the fort endured and how many had died in the heat from sickness, he fled with his armies and to camp on Durchali mountain.

Word reached the *imam* that Vorontsov was moving against the Saltah fort. [Shamil] went up there with his comrades and camped near [the village of] Darada. The *naibs* and their groups returned to their home areas.

After Vorontsov had stayed there about a month, he attacked the Saltah fort. The imam called his *naibs* and their troops back. He stationed two *naibs* inside the fort, each accompanied by half of their armies, and set up the others outside in order to protect the road—to fight the enemy from the rear and on the flanks, on the inside and the outside. The infidels launched an attack from each flank on the fortress and from above with shells that destroyed roofs and blew holes in the earth. Those inside held out against them, battling and killing many of them. Even some of their notables and leaders were among the dead and wounded.

Some Christians and others in Vorontsov's force were saying among themselves said that not one of the [Russian] soldiers' hundreds of guns hit its target, but that [the Muslims'] guns did not miss [nor did their bullets] fall on the ground. This happened with God's help.

A story: The tsar wrote a letter to Vorontsov in Saltah: "I am sending you a youth who is one of my truest companions and most beloved friends, so that he can acquire a high rank and an eminent title under you. Give him an honorable dwelling and preserve his dignity." Vorontsov ordered three thousand of his best cavalrymen to meet and escort him. They met him at Qidhlar and returned with him and his servants, enjoying themselves and having a good time until they arrived on the Saltah plain. Despite the fact that they rode with him in the center and with cavalry surrounding him on all four sides, a small, weak bullet struck behind the ear of that young boy and he fell down. They carried him to Vorontsov and he died. They took out his organs, dressed [the area] with preservatives, and sent his corpse back. Praise God, Lord of the two worlds!

When Vorontsov saw the strength of those in the fort and the severe losses that his forces had suffered, he sent troops to cut off the road to the fort. They secured the road only after a fierce battle. It reached the point that there was no way in or out except by breaking through the barricades of the infidels and the ranks of their armies. Despite that, the [forces inside] kept causing so many [Russian] losses that that they had to dispatch first aid [convoys] for the wounded every three days.

The cursed Argutinskii was hit in the face by a bullet. (How many of their aristocrats and great leaders were wounded and killed there!) The powerful Vorontsov wept three times and tore his hair in remorse, but he drove his troops against the fort nearly sixteen times.

A great sickness [cholera] broke out on both sides, but then the infidels resorted to a trick. They built a fortified turret outside the fortress that towered over the turrets inside. The [Russians] dug holes under the fortress and put gunpowder in them. They lit them to blow up and smash [the walls] of the

52

fortress. When even this measure did not weaken [the besieged force, though], the [Russians] began, God forbid, to make the [fort's] water unclean by throwing corpses and animal dung in it. The imam ordered [troops stationed] outside [the fort] to attack [the Russians] from all directions—not to leave them in peace and at leisure in their camps—so that the enemy would become so weary and discontented that its fighting spirit and zeal against [the Muslims] would wither.

After this grinding siege had dragged on about three months for those inside the fortress, they [started] one night to abandon the fortress without the imam's permission. He had issued them equipment and provisions on that very same night. The imam said to a group of his *naibs* and followers in the morning, "In fact, this cursed Vorontsov has not defeated us, we have defeated him. No one realizes this except him and me." End [of story].

This is confirmed by the story that as [Russian] forces in the village of Uhlib prepared to fire their cannons according to their *zakon* [regulations] while Vorontsov advanced, they had fired them only once when his adjutant came running up, signaling them to stop.

When he approached them, he said, "Vorontsov forbids this." He was asked why, and said "What is Vorontsov supposed to be joyous and happy about? Don't you see them?" He pointed to the first aid [convoy] for the wounded. One end of it had gotten to Uhlib, but the other end had still not left [the village of] Tsadaqar.

He said, "In truth, those *murids* are not leaving the Saltah fort because we defeated them in battle. In fact, they are going away [only] because its water has been polluted and they cannot perform their religious duties [i.e., ablutions] there." It was reported that the [Russians] lost seventeen thousand [regular soldiers] in Saltah in addition to [the irregular forces] from various regions who were killed and those who died from sickness. (Praise God, whose reign has no decline and no end!) ...

The attack on Akhdi

In the fall of that year [1848], the imam sent out armies and artillery with their equipment and soldiers, all led by Daniyal Sultan. He captured the fortress of Nichik and those in it: three hundred hypocrites and their leaders. When the imam caught up with that force, he freed those prisoners and sent their leaders to the fortress at 'Irib. The forces stopped in Akhdi and found the population there, even the women and children, overjoyed at the imam's approach and burning with desire to meet him. [Shamil's force] laid siege to the fort there and attacked it. [Among the imam's forces,] the men of Akhdi were among those who fought most intensely there and many were killed. Some hypocrites from that place [Akhdi] were in the fort alongside the Russians.

On one of those days, Hajj Yahya al-Chirkawi hit the powder magazine of the fortress with a cannon-ball. This set it on fire and the magazine exploded. The fortress wall next to the magazine collapsed. Nothing prevented the *naibs* from going into the fortress except their slowness and procrastination. No one rushed to storm it [, though,] except Misigulaw al-'Andi, but the defenders were already filling the breach [in it] with bags of provisions [grain]. [The defenders] became very thirsty during the siege.

Then those under siege [accidentally] set the artillery shells [stored] in one of their towers on fire, which burned up a few of their soldiers. The imam ordered [his men] to put gunpowder under a wall on another side of the fortress. The powder caught fire [and] the wall was split in half. The inner half stayed up but the outer half crashed down. The situation for the defenders was thrown into confusion. They fled from their battle stations to houses located inside [the fortress]. [Again,] no one stormed into the fortress except for the naib Qadi al-Ishichali by himself.

Just as they were laying siege and fighting there, the [Russian] commander Argutinskii appeared with a great army on the side of a mountain coming from the direction of Shirakhal and began to attack them. People's faces changed color, their hearts dropped, their mouths dried out, and their voices fell silent. The enemy fired cannons down that slope and those laying siege to the fortress returned to the village. Those inside it [the besieged] came out and threw themselves in the water because they were so thirsty. The only thing left for those [who had been laying siege] to do was to escape.

This was the situation when two messengers came to the imam from one of his naibs who had been stationed to guard the Hazra side of [the fortress] with a cavalry detachment of less than five hundred. They reported, "We encountered a detachment of [enemy] forces there. We put them to flight, killed some of them, captured some, and plundered their things." End [of story].

A story: A Christian, who had been captured in that battle, had [later] accepted Islam, and had become a good Muslim, reported that almost five hundred [Russian] cavalry troops had been there. Hypocrites and Christians had gathered [there] from the region of Qubah. They were camped, waiting for Argutinskii to fire a blank into the air as the signal for a simultaneous attack from two directions against the forces of the imam.

They were eating and drinking. Nothing in the sky or on the ground gave them the impression that they were about to be attacked. Their horses were scattered around [the camp]. Some of these [soldiers] were bathing, some were asleep, and some were sitting, not paying any attention to their weapons. At first a soft, pleasant breeze blew on them, but then a group of riders surrounded them. They saw that there [were so many of them,] it was as if they covered the face of the earth. There was a multitude of painted and white flags among them. [Shamil's forces] took some of the [Russians] prisoner, plundered some others, and [let] a few others escape, although they forced them to surrender their weapons and mounts.

When the two messengers arrived [with this news], the hearts of [Shamil's followers] became calmer, their souls felt encouraged, their spirits were lifted, and they raised their voices. The imam ordered the one-eyed Muhammad

Efendi al-Humi to go after the enemy with twenty of the imam's comrades to do battle with them and hold them back. The people [of the village], even its women and children, moved against [the enemy, too]. They fought them and put them to rout. The [Russian] commanders began to go back up the mountain. [The imam's forces] attacked from behind them, advancing until they reached the summit of the mountain. Those who had been in the fortress retreated back into it, fortified themselves in it, and were again under siege [as before]. The next morning, [the fort's] *nachal'nik* [commander] sent the hypocrites from Akhdi who were there in the fortress back to their village, saying that the fortress would be conquered the next day [anyway]. When these [hypocrites] arrived back [in Akhdi village], the imam sent them and some others from there to the 'Irib fort as hostages. Among them was the village scholar, the poet Mirza Ali.

The next day, Argutinskii came from the direction of Hazra. The armies met each other on the open plain and did battle. The wise and brave *naib* of 'Iri, 'Uthman; its *mufti*, the scholar Muhammad ibn Ma'ruf al-Nuqushi; as well as the two emigrant scholars, Hajiyaw ibn al-Tsitawi al-Huchuti and Muhammad ibn 'Abd al-Latif al-Ilisuwi ... were martyred. Then the [imam's forces] fled and the enemy attacked them from behind, plundering their things as well as capturing and killing some of them. The whole group fled and the imam returned [to Akhdi]. The men of Akhdi did not attack them from behind like other hypocrites [had].

The imam stationed watchmen from among his followers at narrow places on the roads. They were to confiscate anything that had been taken from the people of that area's villages and give it back to [its rightful owners]. Among those taken prisoner [by the Russians] in that battle, some died in their hands while others were exchanged for hostages held there and in Nichik. Most of those taken prisoner or killed there were Daniyal Sultan's people. To console him on his return, I wrote him a letter containing these two couplets:

> What good is regret, when things are foreordained?
> Indeed, we strive to achieve only that which is predestined.
> The Lord decrees and upon the servants [mankind]
> Is the duty to be content. All of them shall be rewarded ...

The battle at Chokha fort

In 1265 AH [= 1849 CE], when the cursed Argutinskii moved against the fortress at Chokha and began to widen the road to it, the imam mustered his forces on the plain of Hutub. He convened a council there of his *naibs* and summoned the *naib* of that fortress, Hajj Musa to it. He [Shamil] had told him [Hajj Musa] in secret that the enemy was going to attack two mountains: first the mountain of Sughur and then a mountain to its right, 'Ali Mamad. The imam ordered them to dig earthworks on those two hills and barricade themselves in trenches.

They came in the afternoon to do this and started working after nightfall. The imam spent the night between the two hills, [supervising their work] and keeping them from falling short in this task. In the morning, he assigned each *naib* to a battle station and they prepared themselves as necessary.

On the third day after this, the cursed Argutinskii came down with his Satanic retinue [of troops]. Some men went out to do battle with him there. The Russians then set up large cannons one cannon-shot away from the fort and equipped them with trenches and overhangs. They began firing heavy artillery at soldiers all around the area. This caused so much damage that the imam's tent was moved three times [to protect it].

Then [the Russians] (May God abandon them!) captured a mountain in front of the fort and a mountain behind it. They kept on firing until they had destroyed most of the fort's walls, its buildings, and the tower that stood on top of it. They forced those inside the fort to take cover so that they could no longer fire back at [those attacking] them. When matters came to such a state, the *naibs* lowered their heads, people's resolve was weakened, their fortitude diminished, and their strength dissipated.

The imam gathered together all his *naibs*, including the commander of the fort. He first criticized them but then offered some encouragement. He said, "Those Russian commanders are working day and night to establish themselves [here] and promote their authority. They follow their *zakon* [law] with their arms, legs, knees, and teeth.[79] You do not hold fast to the religion of God, who is your Lord and your Creator, except with the two sides of your little finger and thumb, thus." He made a circle with those two fingers.

[Despite their initial successes in these battles against Shamil, the Russians ultimately did not capture the Chokha fort. They pulled back after this failed series of assaults, but Shamil's forces continued intermittent attacks on the Russian positions in their vicinity. The next selection includes al-Qarakhi's most detailed account of Hadji Murat. Its negative portrait of him differed dramatically from Tolstoi's depiction. *The Shining of Daghestani Swords* clearly contrasted Shamil's honorable son Ghazi Muhammad with the untrustworthy Hadji Murat, depicted in this section as a traitor to Shamil's cause.]

The first *ghaza* at Shali

At the beginning of winter in the year 1266 [AH= 1849 CE] the Russians came with a large group to cut down the forest there. The imam assembled an army and set out with cannons, equipment, and soldiers. They were cutting down trees there and burning them every day from morning to night. Shamil's men would fight them them from the rear and also attack them with cannons and guns from the front, depending on what they were able to do. The situation continued in this way until the end of winter. Then they [the Russians] left, having suffered many losses. They [the imam's forces] returned [home, too]. Among the martyrs there were the scholar and *naib* Turach al-Karati as well as the courageous *naib* Murtaza 'Ali al-'Uruti (May God bless them!) In this year, a gunpowder factory was built at the water [i.e., to use the river's current to run its machinery] and all of its equipment and supplies were set up.

The appointment of Shamil's son
Ghazi Muhammad as a *naib*

When Turach, the *naib* of Galalal, was martyred, the imam consulted learned men and notables about naming his son Ghazi Muhammad as [Turach's] successor. He ordered scholars and followers of the path [i.e., Sufi leaders] to seek the best course [in this matter]. This negligent transmitter [i.e., al-Qarakhi, the author of the work] saw the office of *naib* written down for [Ghazi Muhammad] in a book.

That winter was when I began to live with the imam in Darghiyya. He renamed me "Muhammad Tahir." My name had been Muhammad Tilaw. After that, I stayed with him season upon season [i.e., continuously] until my father died, which happened between the time when his son Jamal al-Din came back [i.e., March, 1855] until the Russians climbed up to Burtinah to build a fort there [in December 1857]. [80]

The [scholars] approved of that [appointment of his son] after some consideration and deliberation. When [Ghazi Muhammad] was chosen, he was eighteen and had not reached full maturity. He studied there in Karata with several teachers. They guided him to the best policies and educated him in the best principles of leadership. When he assumed this position, he continued to be distinguished by insight [*hilm*] and wisdom as well as to be marked by kindness, mercy, and respect for eminent people. He did not dwell on things or act arrogantly, and did other things appropriate for a leader and a *naib* [of Shamil] by attempting to promote religion, guard [the community], and act with caution, while demonstrating courage, horsemanship, and skill. (May he continue to be like this until the coming of the *Mahdi* on the Day of Judgment and may he continue to increase his capacity for knowledge and justice, as well as his happiness through piety and kindness!) He has never held himself back from thanking the One [God] who offers much grace.

The second, third, and fourth *ghazas* at Shali

At the beginning of the winter of 1267 AH = [1851 CE], the infidels came there [to Shali] again with more equipment and greater forces than before in order to cut down trees. [81] The imam came out [to engage them] with his army, as in the first engagement [there]. [The imam's forces] fought [with the Russians] in this manner until the end of winter, enduring great hardships and marches on horseback under very difficult conditions. They would come out of their night bivouac every morning into [conditions of] extreme winter cold and travel to distant battlefields through the deep Chechen mud, returning after sunset. In these circumstances, they inflicted casualties [on the Russians] and suffered casualties [themselves]. (Praise God, Lord of the two worlds!) This was the great battle of Shali. Two smaller battles took place there in the eighth and ninth years [i.e., in 1268 and 1269 AH = 1851 and 1852 CE].

The second, third, and fourth military raids at Qaytaq and Tabarsaran

Numerous messages and messengers began to arrive from those places [Qaytaq and Tabarsaran], asking him to send a *naib* with an army there to govern them according to the *sharia* and unite them under its rule, so they could act as one against the ill-fated Russians. Shamil sent his troops and equipment there at the beginning of the summer of this seventh year [i.e., 1267 AH = 1850/51 CE]. They set up camp on the mountain of Rughchah. He sent his *naib* 'Umar al-Salti with two other *naibs*, Qadi al-Ishichali and Nur Muhammad al-Qarakhi, accompanied by their followers and other men: about three thousand [troops in all]. He ['Umar] turned back on the road [though], so Shamil dismissed him and his two commanders.[82]

The *naib* Hadji Murat al-Khunzakhi [i.e., Tolstoi's Hadji Murat] asked Shamil to send him [in their place] accompanied by five hundred horsemen, including the *naib* Husayn al-Girgili, Shan Kiray, deputy of the *naib* Ibrahim al-Gimrawi, and the *naib* Batir al-Mililti, along with their retinues. Then the imam went away and camped in the village of Bukhdah. He moved on to stop at the mountain of Durchali and the Russians attacked his army there. A new *naib*, the scholar Muhammad al-'Uradi al-Hidali, was among the martyrs in that battle.

As others were fleeing, the imam's son Ghazi Muhammad, still a callow youth and not yet fully mature, held his ground with about six followers. Many of those who ran away were saved because he himself had stood firm against the attackers. This was his first battle after he had been made a *naib*. (Praise God (May He be exalted!), for giving him success and setting him on the right course!)

Hadji Murat went with his followers to mount an attack in the village of Buynakh on the house of Shahwal Khan, the paternal uncle of Abu Muslim Khan Shamkhal. They killed him and captured his sons and wife, who was the sister of Jamaw Khan al-Khaydaqi. They seized the weapons, valuables, and other things that they found in his house. The brave *naib* Batir al-Mililti was injured there and died in Tabarsaran. They departed with the prisoners and property. When they reached Qaytaq, its people asked them to release the women and children and they would get her brother Jamaw to make peace with them. Hadji Murat would not agree to this and paid [them] no attention.

The imam had sent [Hadji Murat and his men] there to establish themselves in a secure location, to build a strong fortress, and to govern the people of those regions so that they would be led to oppose the enemy and obey him. However, Hadji Murat did not follow this plan, but went his own way. He kept on attacking and raiding here and there [i.e., everywhere].

They would drag those prisoners with them wherever they went, like a mother cat carrying her kittens. They did this for some time. The people of these regions did not come to terms with him [Hadji Murat] and did not join forces with him. They went back to fighting among themselves. That woman [the wife of the *shamkhal*'s uncle] escaped on the road during an incident in which that courageous emigrant Shan Kiray and others were martyred. When Hadji Murat returned [from his campaign], the imam also returned and dismissed him.

Addendum: Hadji Murat's dismissal weighed on him and he became quite depressed and upset. He and his followers secretly tried to corrupt the people of Khunzakh against their *naib* and against the imam, forcing most of its notables to follow Hadji Murat's orders, renounce their loyalty to the imam, and abandon their pact with the *naib*. When this became obvious, some of the imam's troops moved against them. They gathered in the village of Raqahchi for the battle.

After all this, the people disavowed Hadji Murat, but he remained under the imam's authority and Shamil forgave him. After that, no house [there] would receive [Hadji Murat] as a guest, and there was no dwelling where he could be at ease. Most of the things in his house were destroyed due to his bad behavior. It is said that because he feared being denounced [to the imam], he fled to the Russians with some cash.

His followers and family remained behind in that area, and most of his places for hiding his treasure were uncovered. During the time when the imam was at the battle of Shali during the eighth year [i.e., 1268 AH= 1851/52 CE], Hadji Murat was staying in the [Russian] fortress at the Sunja [river, i.e., *Groznaia* (modern Groznyi)].

[Hadji Murat] sent Shamil a message, asking him to let his children [join] him, but [Shamil] did not answer. He [sent another message] asking again. The imam literally replied, "O you fool who has forsaken Islam! I am not such a fool like you that I would let them be sent there to abandon it [Islam] like you." Then Hadji Murat went to the fortress of Char.[83] They say that he regretted having fled [to the Russians]. I, Muhammad Tahir, was told this by a reliable source who had been with him in the fortress of Char. It was said that [Hadji Murat] would not eat or drink with them [there] and finally went to the village of Nukhuh. He got into a quarrel with a headman there while walking in a field and talking with him. [Hadji Murat] killed [the man] and most of his comrades. He fled with seven of his comrades in the direction of Ilisu and was killed there. (Praise God, Lord and Creator!)

...

[During this long period of intermittent attacks on Russian outposts, Shamil had captured some Georgian noble women and girls to trade for his son Jamal al-Din: an exchange that ultimately did take place.]

The return of Shamil's son, Jamal al-Din, to him

The imam provided for those [young] women and those who were with them [i.e., the Georgian noble women and their servants]. There were some twenty-odd individuals in the women's section of his house. He treated them as is customary [according to Islamic practice]: veils covered their faces, and they were shown honor, esteem, and respect. Messengers came constantly from their families, demanding the release of these women in exchange for [some kind of] ransom. After about nine months, the long and short of it was that Jamal al-Din was exchanged for the commander of the Tsuntiya fortress, and those women were released for thirteen and a half weights of silver. Other prisoners were exchanged one for one. They designated a place for this [exchange] at a site between Muhras Shu'ayb and the Uysunghur fortress.

The imam arrived there with his *naibs*, their followers, his son Ghazi Muhammad, his comrades, the [captured] commander [who was to be exchanged], some other captives who were with him, and those young women, who were riding in a wagon. They camped on the banks of the Michik River. [The Russians] arrived and set up camp on the opposite side [of the river].

They went from one side to the other in small groups. Word came from the Baron, in whose hands the matter rested [on the Russian side], for them to send the imam's son Ghazi Muhammad with about twenty of his companions to see him and meet his brother [Jamal al-Din]. The imam said, "Let him go, if he wishes, trusting in God."

Ghazi Muhammad set out with thirty riders. They crossed the river and stopped on a hill, where they lined up in a row facing them [the Russian forces]. Some [Russian] commanders came up to them with a row of infantry soldiers standing behind them. The Russians stopped in front of them and formed lines, with Jamal al-Din in the middle of their formation. Ghazi Muhammad pointed to Jamal al-Din and greeted him. Jamal al-Din would have joined Ghazi Muhammad's group, but Ghazi Muhammad ordered him to stay in their ranks until the [appropriate] time.

The cursed deserter Butay and his son were alongside the Russians. He began to greet the *murids*, but not one of them even looked at him. No one answered him or showed him and his son any courtesy. That bothered Butay and weighed on him.

Ghazi Muhammad sent [a message] to the imam that he should have those [Georgian] women brought [to him], so [Shamil] sent them on their wagon. When they came up behind Ghazi Muhammad, the Russians brought three wagons filled with silver and prisoners for the exchange.

Yunus took the son of Chavchavadze, who was seated on a horse, and gave him back to [his father] as the fulfillment of his promise to him. Ghazi Muhammad commended [the prisoners] and told them, "Our son has returned because of you." He literally said to the infidels, "We have not harmed your children. We are not people of treachery and forbidden behavior [*haram*]. We are warrior true believers." Then their spokesman said to Ghazi Muhammad, "Don't fire any cannons and rifles here in celebration, in order not to frighten these women and children of ours." He agreed and ordered them to bring their wagons of silver to other side of the river.

Earlier, the imam had ordered them to take off Jamal al-Din's clothes and to dress him in our clothes [as soon as he was exchanged]. Having moved the people [i.e., the *murids* and exchanged prisoners] to the side away from Jamal al-

Din, Ghazi Muhammad ordered him to change clothes. Then, when they had moved away from [the Russians], people began to crowd around Jamal al-Din to look after him and greet him. When they had crossed the river, those who were in the wagons full of silver began to throw out bags of silver, saying, "This is for you, this is for you," but the people [there] didn't pay any attention and didn't care about anything but Jamal al-Din.

This [scene] increased his standing in the infidels' eyes. Two of their [Russian] officers came with them and praised the imam for how well he had raised those children and treated them with respect. They left after embracing Jamal al-Din.

One fifth of the silver was set aside [for the imam's administration] and the remainder was divided among those who had participated [in the capture of enemy prisoners to be held as hostages]. Then they all moved on.

When they were all camped in one place, the *naibs* formed up their men into ranks and he had them go around with Jamal al-Din, passing the units rank by rank so that they could have their fill of looking at him. They rejoiced in God's blessing and glory. They fired their weapons to show happiness [on his return] and anger at [their] enemies. As for the imam, he sat under a tree—crying, humbling himself before God, thanking Him, and saying, "Praise God and exalt Him!" He asked me, "Did you not see what your Lord did with what was given by you [to Him] as a trust and charge [i.e., Jamal al-Din]?"

Conclusion: See how God caused the return of the one He had been given as a trust and charge [Jamal al-Din] from the hands of His manifest enemy, the cursed Russian tsar! [Shamil] had raised him for sixteen of his years and had taught him knowledge that would benefit Islam and Muslims. [The tsar] had given him valuable gifts and had bestowed all sorts of precious and suitable items on him. (See how his father's trust in God bore fruit that all was excellent, dear, and wonderful! This came only from God, the Powerful, the Wise! There is no power and strength save in God!)

...

[After Jamal al-Din had been sent back, Shamil's military situation soon deteriorated. The end of the Crimean War in March 1856 finally allowed the Russians to break a stalemate that had continued between them and Shamil in the Caucasus for almost fifteen years. In the summer of 1856, the Russian army began a series of intensive campaigns in Daghestan that took place over the next three years and finally resulted in the capture of Shamil's capital at New Darghiyyah in April 1859. Shamil himself did not actually surrender to the Russians until September 6, 1859, after they had cornered him on the Ghunib plateau, as described in the next excerpt.]

The great disorder and upheaval all over Daghestan during which Shamil fell into Russian hands

In the spring of 1275 AH [= 1859 CE], when it became known that the Russians had made up their minds and were heading against Ma'arukh, they [the imam's forces] burned down the villages of 'Andal and Baqulal [to force their inhabitants] to move to the mountain of Kalal. The approaches to it were reinforced with great effort. [Shamil's] equipment, consisting of gunpowder, cannons, and baggage belonging to him and those with him, was transported to that mountain.

His most valuable property was located in Inkhub. A severe famine there had grown worse after a two-year drought and an epidemic among its livestock. Its population became weaker and weaker because of all this and because of how difficult it was to do work, both in places already mentioned and in various other areas not discussed.

[Shamil] was not safe on the mountain [of Kalal] and during the first part of 1276 AH [= late summer and fall of 1859 CE], a [Russian] general came down with a vast army from the mountains of 'Andal to the plains of Tandub. This terrifying force along with their hypocrite helpers advanced down the Irghin river and crossed over a small bridge. Every regional Russian commander had come out from his area with his own detachment of troops, and they [the Russians] carried loads of "red and white" [i.e., copper and silver coins] to win the hearts of simple people and make slaves out of freemen. End [of story].

The men of Baqulal and 'Andal conveyed Shamil, his bearers, and his soldiers, together with their children and most valuable goods, to Karata. Then they went back to their homes and left him there. (May God reward them well!) By order of the imam, the *naib* Qadi al-Ishichali burned the tools that they left on that mountain and destroyed the cannons. Some men, especially those who had been [the imam's] comrades [only] during the prosperous times, looted the wealth and property of Shamil that had been left there. [Still] other men, some of his closest friends and esteemed *naibs* in particular, hurried to join the Russians, offering "hearing and obedience" [to their commands].

Shamil left Karata with his son Ghazi Muhammad and those in their retinue, [carrying] their baggage and most valuable property. They had burned Ghazi Muhammad's house in Karata with the intention of climbing up to the Ghunib plateau.

The people [must] have been jealous of them, considering what this group endured. When they got to the mountains of Rughchah and Guwal, [people] blocked [their passage]. They passed through the Bizu' river valley to the area of Buq Muhammad. That country was a place inhabited by emigrants from Tumal. On the second night there, Shamil and Ghazi Muhammad climbed up [to Ghunib] with their families [to escape] from the battles [against them], attacks [on them], and pillaging of their belongings. Some of his comrades climbed up there with them, leaving their families behind, but some stayed behind while their families climbed up. The imam's entire treasury, his treasurer Hajiyaw al-'Uruti, and the majority of his soldiers stayed behind in that area.

One night, the treasurer, those with him who were commanders of the artillery, and the soldiers—Isbahi al-Chirkawi, the *naib* Dibir al-'Andi, and others—set out for the 'Irib fort to see Daniyal Sultan. Qurbanli Muhammad al-Batsadi, the *naib* of Qaralala, went with them, along with his comrades, among whom were Hajiyaw ibn Hajj Dibir al-Qarakhi, who had been separated [from them] when they left Ishchali. Rebels gathered from the three villages of the Qarakh valley and met them in the forest of Bizuʿ. Most of the comrades of that [Qaralala] *naib* then joined up with these rebels, who stole the large amounts of cash and valuable property on hand.

Hajiyaw al-Qarakhi "roared thunder and raged lightning" to prevent them from doing this, but his injunctions had no effect on them. Those brigands gained nothing from their robbery, since this property had not been blessed as theirs by law, and they fell into misfortune. Then the treasurer and those traveling with him stayed in the village of Tsurib, a place inhabited by refugees from Akhdi that was located between Qinsir and Qaralala. (Praise the Exalted One!) How much had the imam collected over the course of ten years for his personal treasury and collection of valuables! God did what He did when the people became envious that it [the treasury] had been locked up and their hearts shuddered and grew foul with unclean [greed].

The first part of this chapter about the beginning of the unrest skipped over the fact that the imam had already ordered his treasurer not to hold back [these valuables: i.e., Shamil refused to keep the public treasury for himself]. End [of story].

They [the treasurer and his group] stayed about three nights in Tsurib. Daniyal Sultan sent [a message] to them: "Come to us or return to Qarakh, so the criminals don't attack us again." They returned to Qarakh. The treasurer stayed with a host there in the village of Qurush with all that remained of the imam's books and other things. This host and the judge [of Qurush] took out [for themselves] what they thought were the best books [God's power, [though,] came down on them for that and they later repented. The judge gave some of these books to this author [me]. I brought some to the imam's son Ghazi Muhammad and some to my son. Among these works was the *Meccan Bestowal* written by al-Quduqi.

Then Murtaza ʿAli, the brother of Qibid Muhammad al-Tiliqi, came with some comrades. He was a *naib* from the Russian side. He took all that they [the treasurer and his group] had with them of treasuries, belongings, and soldiers and conveyed them to Tiliq. The Russian commander allowed Qibid Muhammad and Murtaza ʿAli to keep all of those belongings and treasuries, but combined these soldiers with their soldiers. The road was left open for those [traveling] with these goods [to go wherever they wanted]. The treasurer Hajiyaw al-ʿUruti was detained by them for some time.

There were no forts left, except the ones that had surrendered to them [the Russians] and not a single *naib*, except those who had hung their heads and given in to them. Daniyal Sultan surrendered the fort of ʿIrib near Qinsir with all its stores of gunpowder, shells, cannons, rifles, and so forth. But he himself set out with his comrades to see the general in Tandub, claiming that he had been invited by him. He was ordered to send his family and belongings to Chartalah. He was given about one hundred backs [i.e., porters] to carry them there.

63

Then the Russians took up positions around the plateau of Ghunib. They set up camp on the Kahal mountain next to Ghunib. *Naibs* and other [former Shamil followers] were with them, both eminent and ordinary men.

Shamil had with him [only] such notables as the talented emigrant scholar Hajj Ibrahim al-Chirkisi, the emigrant scholar Hajj Nasrullah al-Qabiri al-Kurali, and the tough-minded scholar Ghalbaz al-Karati who was depressed by being dismissed as a *naib* and by his son's death in some incident. It was said that he literally told them at a meeting about truce negotiations, "Our fathers used to say, 'You (meaning the Russians) have sweet tongues and great wealth. At first, these two things weigh little, but later, they become heavy. We do not want peace with you.'" End [of story].

The gentle scholar and brave teacher Hajiyaw al-Qarakhi who had been dismissed as a *naib*, two other *naibs*—the eloquent scholars al-'Andali and al-Khunzakhi, as well as the son of his [Shamil's] paternal uncle Ibrahim al-Gimrawi, the consummate gentleman Milrik Murtaza 'Ali al-Chirkawi al-Mugharrib, the *naib* Murtaza al-'Urkachi al-Mugharrib, and the *naib* Ghursh al-Sughuri were there among the nearly two hundred people on the battlefield. All of those in Ghunib, men or women, defended its roads and borders according to their strength. Then the Russian general, the Baron, summoned the blind Muhammad Efendi al-Huyami who had lived in Qarakh near Shamil, as well as Muhammad Tahir [the author of this work] and his student Hajiyaw al-Qarakhi, to visit him. He sent them to the imam to negotiate a peace agreement.

When they reached the fort at Ghunib, the imam would not let anyone enter it except those who would agree to stay with him there. So Efendi and Muhammad Tahir went back, while Hajiyaw went into it and remained with him. For this reason, he fell into severe trouble for some period of time after that with [the Russian] administration and was enslaved [by them], but then was set free. End [of story].

A group of Russians climbed up to Ghunib in Safar 1276 AH [= September, 1859 CE] from a place that had been overlooked by the guards. Their leader, Amirasol Muhammad al-Kudali, was killed there and his comrades were taken prisoner. All of the guards who had been [assigned to] various areas of the Ghunib [plateau] gathered in the village. Some men and women from Ghunib, as well as other outsiders like the scholar Nasrullah and the emigrant Kamal al-Ghuludi, were martyred there. The [Russian] general, their commanders, our [Muslim] notables who had become their allies, and their troops moved up to [Ghunib]. Shamil gathered the men there in the mosque [inside the fort]. At that time, the scholar Dibir ibn Inkachilaw al-Khunzakhi and his family went away from there out into the countryside. He was led away from the right course by that, but then was brought back. They drew close to him [again] by making him a *naib*. End [of story].

[Shamil] pleaded with, cajoled, and admonished those gathered in the mosque, together and individually. He called each of them by name, summoning them to the struggle, to die for the faith, and to seek out death in battle. No one, however, displayed any eagerness for this, even his two sons, with the excuse that [they wanted] to be merciful to their children. Intermediaries came to him [Shamil] from them [the Russians] demanding [that he sign] a peace agreement and come to the [Russian] general. Daniyal went with this [proposal] to his son-in-law Ghazi Muhammad. It is said that [Shamil] yielded to this only because [Ghazi Muhammad] urged him on. He agreed only on the conditions that he and his comrades could still bear arms when they met the general and that the general would permit him to go on the pilgrimage to the *Bayt al-Haram* [in Mecca] accompanied by those who wanted to join him.

They agreed among themselves that, if the Russians [were to try to] separate them from Shamil or if they tried to take away their weapons, they would begin fighting and would seek their own deaths in combat against them. With this settled, they set out. Nevertheless, the Russians moved between Shamil and his comrades and took Shamil's weapons, claiming that the general was afraid of armed men.

God the Wise and Mighty (May He be exalted!) did not allow what had been agreed upon to happen. It is said that Murtaza al-'Uruti protested about this at the time but Ghalbaz put him off. End [of story]. Someone who had been with the Russians there later reported that if [Shamil's followers] had begun to fight right then, they could have killed most of the [Russian] commanders and notables.

People [allied with the Russians] seized and plundered the property, weapons, and horses that had belonged to Shamil, his two sons, and their followers. When all of the [local] infidels and the Muslims became mixed together there, our notable men who had previously made peace with the Russians began to talk quietly among themselves, ashamed [of what they had done] in Shamil's presence. From among them, the judge Aslan al-Tsadaqari said, "If a frog falls in a hole, he won't clean off the dirt. Let's [just] pass on by him," and they went away.

They allowed the people there to return to their home territories, but Shamil and his two sons were taken with their families to a [Russian] camp on the mountain at Kahal, and from there to the fortress at [Temir-Khan-]Shura accompanied by an armed guard.

Shamil, accompanied by his experienced [personal] secretary 'Abd al-Karim al-Chirkawi, his son Ghazi Muhammad, and two colleagues, the scholars Hajiyaw ibn Ghaziyaw al-Karati and Tush al-Karati, was sent to visit the tsar in two expensive carriages with an honorable and distinguished cavalry escort ...
[When Shamil surrendered, he was sent to meet Tsar Alexander II in St. Petersburg.]

Imam Shamil's journey to the great tsar

In 1277 AH [= 1860–1861 CE], an imperial edict came by telegram from the city of St. Petersburg summoning him there. We traveled [there] with [Shamil]. Captain Runovskii and an imperial agent from St. Petersburg were with us to accompany the imam on the trip. This type of agent was the tsar's special ambassador, urgently dispatched for special important missions. The imam rode with his most beloved son in one magnificent carriage and we traveled in another until we reached Moscow. From there, we took a train. After we had gotten off of it, we met a man at the outskirts of the city of St. Petersburg who would become one of the imam's friends: an intelligent, quick-witted man who served as our interpreter and now lives in the well-protected domains of Islambol [Istanbul] at the side of the great *padishah* [the Ottoman Sultan]. He is Colonel Boguslavskii, who can speak and translate Arabic, Persian, Turkish, English, French, and other European languages. At that time, he was the adjutant to the duty officer: a general who is the assistant to the tsar's minister who supervises all Russian military affairs.

[Boguslavskii] was a man of true and penetrating intellect, brimming with intelligence. Hence, he was asked repeatedly to translate between the imam and the great tsar, and also between the imam and the general. We found at our disposal another magnificent carriage prepared for the imam. This colonel came up to him, greeted him, welcomed him, and offered him hospitality. He spoke with him in Arabic and how skilled he was! O how incredibly skilled!

...

[The next passage provides al-Qarakhi's impressions of an observatory in St. Petersburg that he also visited on this trip. His reactions conveyed ambivalence about the relationship between science and devout faith.]

The wonders of St. Petersburg

When we were there, they took us once to a place where there was a group of astrologers and seers. They had so many books that you couldn't count them and a very long telescope through which they could see stars, even at noon.

Is it surprising that with this telescope they can see any star they want and in any place in the sky by studying the science of the stars, prohibited among us to investigate, or that the one person who has figured this out, is [now] looking for ways to use this [knowledge]? The first argument [against it] is that much of what the astrologer tells us will frighten most people. The ignorant man who is weak in his faith wrongly believes that he cannot know about the transcendental [i.e., God]. [That man's] heart is troubled, which leads him to associate things [with God] that he should not.[84] Indeed, nothing is concealed from Him on the earth or in the sky. "He knows what is seen and what is not. He is the Great, the most High."[85] The second argument [against it] is that because the knowledge of [when] an ill-fated or lucky star will rise gives an advantage to travelers, soldiers, and those with some other goal, permitting them either to pursue a desired activity or to refrain from it by looking at their star. However, this is legitimate. What benefits man should not be forbidden (*haram*). "For each one, there is a goal to which God turns him."[86] God is most knowing about the truth of things. This is the end of what I, that is Muhammad Tahir, have gathered together as a detailed summary of Shamil's circumstances and it concludes here ...

[The final section of *The Shining of Daghestani Swords* discussed events that took place after al-Qarakhi had left Shamil, culminating in Shamil's death during his pilgrimage trip to Mecca. The final section of *The Shining of Daghestani Swords* presented here described Shamil's last days, and marked the actual end of the earliest 1872 manuscript of the text.]

Addendum about the time when Shamil was bathed in all blessing

On 22 Safar, 1286 AH [= June 4, 1869 CE], [Shamil] set out to travel with his family to God's Sacred House [Mecca] but they kept his son, the esteemed Ghazi Muhammad, and his wife from joining him. Shamil asked for Ghazi Muhammad to come with him, but they would not permit it. Two hours after the noon prayer on that day, Shamil boarded a ship leaving from Anapa [a Black Sea port]. News of this event was sent on the long thread known as "the tele-graph." [That report] reached [Temir-Khan-]Shura about four hours after the noon prayer. Praise [God,] who makes [some of] what is created serve [other parts of] creation! What is stranger, the arrival of that news from Anapa to [Temir-Khan-] Shura in [just] two hours, while the journey takes two months by trade caravan, or the fact that the tsar sent Shamil just like that on the *hajj* pilgrimage?

The poet said: "If the Merciful One [God] honors a slave with His power, then no [other] creature can ever humiliate him." (Praise the Lord, powerful Ruler of all creation! Peace be upon the prophets! Praise God, Lord of the two worlds!) End [of story].

Another poet said, "When the Ruler of the realm [God] helps his slave, his orders must be carried out [even] by free [people]."

It was reported in the Russian newspaper that when Shamil's ship came to Islambol [Istanbul], he sent two comrades who were traveling with him to the *padishah* of Islam [the Ottoman sultan] to request him to allow [Shamil] to go ashore there. He gladly and nobly permitted this. When he disembarked, he was met by such a large crowd of notables and great men that most of them were only able to shake the hands of people who had shaken Shamil's hand. Food was prepared for him by the Russian tsar's representatives there as a way to show him hospitality and he was asked to accept it. He told them, "Your ruler has treated me with hospitality and has honored me with the best treatment so far. Now I am the guest of the Ottoman sultan," and praised them.

When Shamil stayed in Istanbul, he was given a great welcome. The great imam prepared a house for him that he had bought for 6,500 piasters. While Shamil was staying there, they brought him five gold coins each day.

They showed him the rarest treasures of the *padishah* of Islam [the Ottoman sultan]. The most surprising thing he saw was a millstone that turns around and pours out many small, delicate, sharp needles with eyes in them. Then they took him out onto the sea to a Mahmud ship.[87] He thought that it looked like a decorated piece of cotton cloth with many points because of [the light that] fell on the [patched] holes that had been caused by iron [cannonballs]. When Shamil saw it with everything that was on it, he observed, "This is not a ship, but a village! How can you fight on it when you can't see the shore?"

Then the ship began to rumble with a "karkar" sound and raised up so that the shore was visible. Shamil said to those with him quite sincerely as it rose up, "They are throwing us in the sea!"

It was reported that he was asked there, "Of what you have seen in your life, what compares best with this?" He answered, "I would compare this with the brave warriors whom I left behind among the people of the mountains of Daghestan. One of them could resist an entire enemy army." This [account] was confirmed by a report that when the Russian tsar was traveling to Ghunib, many of the mountain peoples' leaders and notables met him on the imperial iron bridge. The tsar praised them by saying, "Shamil was pleased with you and I am pleased with you." End [of story].

A follower of Shamil who had been with him on that trip told us: "When Shaykh Shamil was staying in Istanbul, a Daghestani scholar settled there [in Istanbul], who was angry about what Shamil had been doing, came to visit him. We were sitting and talking with Shamil, who told us, "Go and bring him in." The man came in to discuss what his problem was. This scholar said that Shamil had killed men and taken away property. Shamil answered by [showing him] the justifications for what he did in [Islamic legal] books. He silenced the man who had come for this discussion, so he went away."

Shaykh Shamil knew that the *padishah* of Islam [the Ottoman sultan] was equipping an army to fight Ismail Pasha of Egypt, who had rebelled by refusing to turn over the big cannons that [the sultan] had demanded [from him].[88] Shamil asked that this matter be put off until he had presented himself to [Ismail] Pasha. [The sultan] agreed to his request.

When [Shamil] presented himself to [Ismail], [Ismail] showed him great respect, came off of his throne, and seated Shamil on it. Shamil then spoke with him about this matter and told him: "It would not be fitting for a fight to break out between the two of you that would delight the infidels."

Ismail Pasha said to Shamil, "I will do what you command in this affair."

Shamil said, "I think that you need to send your son to him." When he sent his son [to the sultan], everyone rejoiced and showed their joy by firing a great number of rifle shots. The *padishah*'s daughter was sent to marry that son [of Ismail], for which happiness was shown in Egypt in the same way [i.e., by firing shots in the air].

One day, one of their scholars came to him and spoke with him about that killing [in Daghestan mentioned above]. Shamil said, "We acted according to the books of *sharia* in all situations." He replied, "If that's true, then good for you." Shamil ordered [Islamic legal] books to be brought. Two men brought them out in a sack. Shamil showed the justification for what he had done. The scholar accepted this and was convinced by it.

As his departure was approaching, Ismail Pasha showed his goodwill to [Shamil] and gave him abundant gifts. When the ship came one night to a place where a pharaoh had once drowned, the waves of the sea rose up.[89] The ship's captain complained to Shaykh Shamil. [Shamil] gave a note to one of his comrades and told him to throw it in the sea without having it touch the ship. He threw it in and [the sea] calmed down. We found that news of this [event] had reached Alexandria and the *sharif* [governor] of Mecca before Shamil left the ship. This is the end of what his associate told us. God, may He be exalted, is most-knowing!

Shaykh Shamil had stayed six months in Istanbul during his *hajj* pilgrimage, waiting for the great imam [the Ottoman sultan] to invite him [for a visit] and to say goodbye [to the sultan] when he saw [him]. When six months passed and he wanted to visit the holy house of God [Mecca], Shamil went to take his leave. When [Shamil] came to him, the great imam shook [Shamil's] hand. Russian notables say that this had not happened before and would not happen after that. The *shaykh al-Islam* or mufti of the [great] imam was there and was skeptical of [Shamil's] level of [religious] knowledge.[90] He examined him and did not find him [deficient] as he had feared. The imam gave Shamil 3,000 piasters for his travel expenses. There were 500 pilgrims and 16 servants traveling with Shamil. Two of his wives joined him [for this trip]: Zahida, daughter of Jamal al-Din al-Ghazi-Ghumuqi, and Shawana the Christian, accompanied by four daughters and a young son named Muhammad Kamil.

They prepared a good ship for him that is called a "steamer." He was visited on this ship by the *shaykh al-Islam* and other notables from the [Ottoman] court. Those in his retinue there said that he was planning to return to radiant Medina and live there until his death, instead of going back to Istanbul or to Russia, but this never passed his lips [i.e., he never actually said this]. This is the end of what the Russian newspapers tell us.

He is now, that is in Sha'ban, 1287 AH [= November, 1870 CE], in radiant Medina according to what we have heard. May God provide for us and for him a good end [to life]! In this year, 1287 AH [= 1870 CE], the Russian tsar allowed Shaykh Shamil's son Ghazi Muhammad to visit his father [in Medina] and the sacred house of God [in Mecca] for a period of seven months. It was not suitable for Ghazi Muhammad to go to see his father [directly] from Istanbul, because of Arab brigandage on the routes between there and radiant Medina. So he went to noble Mecca [instead].

The notables accompanying Shamil found the climate unhealthy in Medina and his two daughters died there. They kept asking him if they could go back to Istanbul, but Shaykh Shamil would literally reply, "I want one thing for myself: I want to die here. Why would I move anywhere else?" He took sick for a while and in Dhu al-Hijja on 1278 AH [*sic*: should be 1287 AH], Shaykh Shamil passed away with the grace of God. May He be exalted! He was buried with honor and praise in the garden of Baqiyya [in Medina] among the honored shrines near the shrine of al-'Abbas.[91] News of his death reached Ghazi Muhammad while he was in honored Mecca the venerated. He recited the phrase "We are from God and it is to Him we return," and wept until his eyes became red and swollen. He then arranged a meal for all the Daghestani pilgrims there as a charitable offering [in memory of Shamil] and literally said to them, "My father once governed [your] area. When you arrive back in your homeland, ask its people to say a funeral prayer for him, and request that they forgive him and pardon whatever he did that caused them harm." He added, "I am a prisoner of the Russian tsar. Pray for me that God (May He be exalted!) releases me from captivity."

Ghazi Muhammad then came to radiant Medina. He visited the shrines there before coming to his father's tomb. It is reported that he now intends to move his father's family to Mecca the venerable in accordance with an order from the *sharif* of Mecca, since Shamil had entrusted the care of his family to him. Then Ghazi Muhammad returned to the Russian tsar's custody, as the two of them had arranged. The tsar sent his [Ghazi Muhammad's] family to serve his father's family.

They report that the tsar gave him four young men and four young women as servants for his wife and that he [the tsar] sends a large stipend to him and to the family of his father, set at 300,000 piastres for him and 300,000 for his family. At present in 1289 AH [= 1872 CE], he is in Istanbul with his family and his father's family, honored and esteemed in the presence of the great notables there.

[At this point, the earliest manuscript of the work ends. The other manuscripts continue for two or three more pages, but the story really ends here with Shamil's death.]

Notes

1 Al-Qarakhi, Muhammad Tahir, *Khronika Mukhammeda Takhira al-Karakhi*, edited and translated by A. M. Barabanov and I. Iu. Krachkovskii (Moscow: Akademia Nauk SSSR, 1941, 1946), Introduction, 8. The Russian translation was published in 1941, the Arabic original in 1946. All references to these texts will first indicate the Russian, then the Arabic text page numbers.

2 Ibid.

3 Muhammad Tahir Qarahi, *Kafkasya Mucahidi İmam Şamil'in Gazavatı*, ed. Tahir Olgun and Tarik Cemal Kutlu (Istanbul: Gözde Kitaplar Yayınevi, 1987).

4 All phrases and sentences in brackets [ ] have been added to clarify the meaning of the text.

5 Most subsequent repetitions of this standard ritual Muslim praise of God that follow the divine name throughout the text have been left out of this translation. Many less common expressions of religious praise have been retained and enclosed by parentheses, though, to provide a sense of how the original text was structured.

6 Muhammad's family and companions are viewed in the Islamic world as the most faithful Muslims.

7 This phrase derives from the rule stated in the Quran that Islamic leaders should "promote the good and prohibit the evil." (See, for example, Quran 3:104, 3:110.)

8 "Customary law" (often called *adat* in the nineteenth-century Caucasus) refers to man-made rules not based on God's revelation. Thus, it was the exact opposite of the *sharia*: the Islamic holy law based on God's revelation through the Quran and the

words and deeds of the prophet Muhammad. See Moshe Gammer, *Muslim Resistance to the Tsar: Shamil and the Conquest of Chechnia and Daghestan* (London: Frank Cass, 1994), pp. 42–43.

9 Al-Qarakhi criticized revering rulers like the tsar as idols. Idol worship is a clear sign for Muslims that men are not obeying God's law. Rulers act like idols when they make their own laws. Imperial monarchs were suspect because they claimed legitimacy to rule that belonged to God alone. Al-Qarakhi called the tsar *padishah*, alluding to the pre-Islamic imperial Persian monarchs often regarded as illegitimate by devout Muslims.

10 Ghazi Muhammad was the first imam (religious leader) who led resistance to the Russians between 1829 and 1832.

11 Hamza Bek, the second imam, succeeded Ghazi Muhammad in 1832 but was killed in 1834.

12 Shamil led the resistance from 1834 until 1859 as the third imam. Al-Qarakhi mentioned Mecca and Medina, the two holiest places in Islam, as well as Balkh (in Afghanistan) and Bukhara (in Central Asia) to convey the extent of Shamil's reputation across the Muslim world.

13 Considerable debate continues about the nature of this resistance movement: how much was it a typical Sufi project and to what extent was it something new, labeled "muridism" by some scholars? See the discussion in Part III "War of Worlds" below to further explore this question.

14 All dates in the original Arabic text were given in *hijri* years (AH): the 354-day lunar calendar that began with Muhammad's *hegira* (flight) to Medina on July 16, 622 of the common era (CE). They are followed in this edition by CE years in brackets.

15 A typical eulogy for Sufi leaders.

16 Muslim writers often contrast the illegitimacy of *adat* (customary law) with the legitimacy of *sharia* (holy law), because only holy law comes from God. Although Muslim theologians generally do not oppose customary law that agrees with *sharia*, they agree that customary precedent is an inferior source of law to divine revelation. In nineteenth-century Daghestan, customary law endured in particular through each local group's distinct succession rules. See Anna Zelkina, *In Quest for God and Freedom* (New York: New York University Press, 2000), pp. 14–15.

17 Kawthar is the fountain of redemption in paradise.

18 The Ka'ba in Mecca is the holiest site in Islam, near the place where, according to Muslim belief, Abraham tried to sacrifice his son Ishmael (Isma'il).

19 The Hashimis were members of Muhammad's subtribe in Mecca.

20 The *shamkhal* was the hereditary ruler of a Turkic group in the eastern Caucasus. Since the late eighteenth century, *shamkhals* had generally allied with the Russians, most recently since 1818.

21 These two scholars were masters of the Khalidi branch of the Naqshbandi Sufi order to which Shamil belonged. Both Shamil and Ghazi Muhammad had been initiated into this order by Jamal al-Din, who began to preach in the Caucasus in the 1810s. Shamil continued to consult Muhammad Efendi as a Sufi leader throughout his own career.

22 Quran 39:18

23 Quran 77:39.

24 Based on Quran 37:177.

25 Quran 2:279.

26 Based on Quran 32:21.

27 Quran 3:139.

28 The *fatiha* is the opening chapter of the *Quran*, memorized by all Muslims as a catechism of faith.

29 This sentence refers to the five religious obligations known as the "pillars of Islam": prayer, reciting the "Testament of Faith," maintaining a daytime fast during the month of Ramadan, making a pilgrimage to Mecca (the *hajj*) once in life, and giving charity. Muslim legal scholars do not agree on any number of grave sins, but it is clear that this author wanted to promote a fairly encompassing definition of sin by choosing such a large number. S.v. *Encyclopedia of Islam* (2nd edition), article "Khatia."

30 This refers to Sa'id Efendi al-Harakani, an alim who had declared jihad against the Russians in 1819 but later opposed the Naqshbandis. See Gammer, *Muslim Resistance to the Tsar*, p. 43.

31 Consumption of alcohol is forbidden by the Quran.

32 Khunzakh was the capital of the hereditary rulers of the Avar people, who generally allied with the Russians and opposed the movement of Ghazi Muhammad, Hamza, and Shamil. At this time, Pakhu Bike was the Avar regent for her infant son and was the daughter of Umma Khan.

33 The implication was that God was admonishing Muslims through natural portents like earthquakes.

34 This is the night of the holiest Islamic celebration, when sheep are slaughtered to celebrate how God allowed Abraham not to sacrifice Ismail.

35 Indiri and Targhu were both Chechen villages near the Russian forts *Vnezapnaia* ("sudden") and *Burnaia* ("stormy") built respectively in 1820 and 1821 to complement the first Russian defensive fort in Chechnia: *Groznaia* ("menacing") which had been built in 1819 (the site of modern Groznyi).

36 Quran 12:18. The implication is that the woman knew for certain that her children would enter paradise as martyrs in holy war.

37 Muhammad Efendi al-Yaraghi was a learned Muslim scholar in the Avar area who belonged to the chain of Naqshbandi Sufi *shaykhs*. He had been Hamza Bek's *shaykh* and spritiual teacher in the village of Chokha, beginning in 1801. See Zelkina, *In Quest for God and Freedom*, 102–103, 160.

38 Buraw was the Daghestani name for the Russian fort at Vladikavkaz.

39 Hasan and Husayn were Muhammad's two grandsons. Their names were often used together in Muslim names.

40 Quran 2:156.

41 Quran 3:178.

42 Muhammad is considered by Muslims to be the last prophet of God, so this is about the highest praise that a devout Muslim could give someone and not be considered blasphemous.

43 *Kashf* is a technical Sufi term to describe mystical knowledge of the world beyond everyday phenomena, akin to knowledge of Plato's *noumena* ("things as they are") but in an Islamic religious mystical context.

44 Here Shamil alluded to Quranic descriptions of heaven, in which beautiful maidens (*houris*) attend martyrs.

45 In the late summer of 1831, Ghazi Muhammad and his disciples (probably including Shamil) had attacked Russian forces several times in Chechnia.

46 Various versions of the phrase "hearing and obedience" provide a formula for how Muslims ought to follow Islamic law.

47 The 'Id al-Fitr is a major Muslim holiday which marks the end of Ramadan, the holy month of fasting and contemplation in daylight and nighttime celebration for Muslims.

48 Quran, 63:8. This is an ironic Quranic passage since it cites hypocrites wrongly referring to themselves as more honorable than Muhammad.

49 The implication is that he had abdicated his responsibility as an Islamic leader to command what is good and forbid what is bad.

50 The Hanafi and Shafi'i rites are two of the four schools of Islamic legal interpretation among Sunni Muslims. They are named for their founders. They differ slightly on how to interpret specific aspects of law, but not on basic prohibitions such as the ban on drinking alcohol. Al-Qarakhi was trying to show how this judge attempted to cite a specious religious technicality to argue that one Muslim rite's judge could not punish sins committed by another rite's follower. He had Shamil respond that all Muslims regardless of rite must uphold basic Islamic law.

51 The implication here is that Shamil and the Shamkhal would both recognize each other's authority in their respective domains: the Shamkhal in the lowlands and Shamil in the mountains.

52 Quran 13:17.

53 Shamil compared his situation to that of Muhammad when he had to make the hegira (flight to Medina). In 622, Muhammad fled from Mecca, the city where he had begun to receive divine revelations in 610 CE, to Medina because of a plot against him.

54 Russian soldiers apparently defecated in houses when they captured villages, just as in *Hadji Murat* they were said to have fouled a well.

55 Here are two stock descriptions of an effective Islamic government, in which the ruler commands what is obligatory and forbids what is prohibited while the people "hear and obey" what he says.

56 Men and women engaging in such activity together would have seemed questionable to Shamil given how Islamic injunctions against inappropriate mixing of the sexes were traditionally interpreted.

57 According to Islamic law, it is legitimate to take plunder from an enemy in battle under strict constraints.

58 Islambol, which in Turkish means "full of Islam," was an Islamic alternative developed during the Ottoman era to the actual name of the city Istanbul, which apparently comes from a Greek phrase meaning "to the city."

59 A *fatwa* is a judicial opinion issued by someone regarded as knowledgeable about Islamic law.

60 I.e., to imply that those who stayed peacefully inside their houses would not be hurt. The Ansal group was trying to tell the people that they were only after Shamil's *murids*.

61 I.e., to bolster their own spirits against the attackers.

62 The people of Saba (called Sabaeans and recognized in the Quran as legitimate monotheists) were members of a pre-Islamic civilization that flourished in Yemen but was later broken up into small tribal groups.

63 Quran 78:26.

64 The *murtaziqs* were a standing cavalry army who were excused from regular labor for military service under the command of Shamil's *naibs*. Every group of ten households in territories controlled by Shamil was obliged to pay for an armed horseman who was called a *murtaziq*. See Gammer, *Muslim Resistance to the Tsar*, pp. 228–229.

65 In other words: "if you follow agreements you have made, then we will conclude one with you, but if not, then God knows what will happen."

66 Quran 32: 21.

67 The term *sunna* refers to "the words and deeds of Muhammad", the second most important component of the sharia after the Quran. "Sunni" is the adjective of this word.

68 This probably referred either to Leontii Pavlovich Nicolai or his brother Aleksandr Pavlovich Nicolai, both important Russian commanders in the Caucasus.

69 The story of Moses and the Exodus is mentioned in the Quran, along with accounts of many other Jewish and Christian prophets in the Abrahamic tradition.

70 Barabanov translates *chalandar* as "field officer." Its meaning is not clear.

71 The word translated here as commander is *sardal*, a variant of the term *sardar* used in *Hadji Murat*. See, for example, p. 112
72 As noted earlier, Shamil had named one of his sons for the first imam Ghazi Muhammad.
73 Quran 13:17.
74 These three Arabic proverbs are used to describe situations that have become severe and distressing. See E. W. Lane, *Arabic–English Lexicon* (Cambridge: Islamic Texts Society, 2000), volume 1, 221, 728.
75 Shamil had become separated from his family when he went to fight the Russians, apparently in the action referred to above in which Sultan Bek al-Dilimi was martyred.
76 Muhammad al-Mahdi is the messiah believed to be coming to mankind on Judgment Day.
77 Quran 13:17.
78 A footnote in one version of *The Shining of Swords* identified Zandiqi as a Chechen village.
79 Here al-Qarakhi used the Russian word for law (*zakon*) to emphasize its infidel and illegitimate character. The use of this term parallels al-Qarakhi's many references to the *adat*: the customary law of the Muslim mountaineers that Shamil and his followers also did not consider legitimate, because the only legitimate law was the *sharia* (holy law).
80 Al-Qarakhi thus indicated that he lived continuously with Shamil from 1849 until at least 1855 and therefore was an eyewitness to the events of that time period.
81 Clearcutting forests was a major component of the Russian campaign in the mountains. This deprived the native forces of cover, disrupting their ability to move stealthily. In this way, it hindered their ability to take advantage of mobility and surprise, two of the most important aspects of their guerilla war against the larger, better supplied Russian army units.
82 Umar apparently retreated after a skirmish with the Russians on the way to Qaytaq and Tabarsaran.
83 That is, the Russian fort at Zakartalah.
84 "Associating" other things or beings with God (in Arabic, *shirk*) is a grave sin for devout Muslims, because this denies his transcendence and his oneness. For them, God is one being and transcends all creation.
85 Quran 13:9.
86 Quran 2:148.
87 This presumably refers to one of the newer Ottoman sailing vessels acquired during the reign of Sultan Mahmud II (ruled 1808–1839).
88 In the summer of 1869 when this story was taking place, Ismail Pasha, the khedive of Egypt (ruled 1863–1879) had just opened the Suez Canal: a sign that he was beginning to assert some independence from the Ottoman Sultan, who was still regarded as his sovereign. Al-Karakhi was trying to show Shamil's standing as an Islamic diplomat by demonstrating how he tried to make peace between these rulers.
89 This is a reference to the biblical and Quranic story of the Pharaoh who drowned with his army in the Red Sea while pursuing Moses.
90 This refers to the chief Ottoman religious official: the *shaykh al-Islam*. The term imam here refers to the Ottoman sultan.
91 Shamil died in March 1871 CE which corresponds to Dhu al-Hijja 1287 AH, not 1278 AH.

Part II

INTRODUCTION

> The hero of my tale, whom I love with all the powers of my soul,
> whom I have tried to reproduce in all his splendor, and who
> always was, is, and will be beautiful—is Truth.
>
> Lev Tolstoi

> Their god is freedom, their law is war.
>
> Mikhail Lermontov on the Chechens (1832)

The tragic drama of Chechen and Daghestani resistance to Russian military conquest in the nineteenth century is the inspiration for Hadji Murat, *the last work by one of the greatest novelists in the history of world literature. Lev Tolstoi was close to seventy years old when the project that became* Hadji Murat *began to gestate in his creative consciousness. The full mastery of his powers is still evident in his penetrating characterizations and his deft imparting of mood and scene. It is an astonishing accomplishment.*

Tolstoi labored over this task for eight years, finishing it in 1904. It was not published until after his death in 1910. It is worth noting that ten drafts of the novel exist and that an "authoritative version based on Tolstoi's manuscripts was established only in 1950 for the ninety-volume Jubilee edition of the author's works."[1] This final, posthumous work of the great master is, we feel, unjustifiably obscure in the West. This no doubt stems from the fact that the commonly available English translation by the English adept of Tolstoi, Aylmer Maude, is seriously flawed as a translation project and is based on an earlier, incomplete draft of the novel. There is no need to cite chapter and verse of the shortcomings of Maude's translation in this Introduction, but a brief example will give a sense of the problem. Maude translates the Russian word buket, *which is a direct transliteration of the French original* bouquet, *as "nosegay." More serious than the many, to our ears, odd examples of early twentieth-century British that are peppered throughout his translation are his renderings of conversations, which frequently are quite meaningless.[2] A far cry from Tolstoi's Russian original, which is in the words of one critic, "Crystal-clear, exciting and supremely well narrated, it has claims to belong to that category of universal literature which Tolstoi prized so highly in his treatise* What is Art?; for ... its pathos is grounded in what Tolstoi called 'those very simple, everyday feelings* *accessible to all'—the feelings of family solidarity and of compassion for human life."* [3] *It is this Tolstoi that we have sought to capture in our translation.*

Here, in sharp contrast with The Shining of Daghestani Swords, *the narrative structure matters a great deal. As the existence of ten drafts indicates, Tolstoi was not rendering a "true" historical narrative of the defection of Hadji Murat, the sometime naib of Shamil, to the Russians and then his attempt to return to the "mountain" side of the conflict. What we have is a carefully structured and meticulously researched and written tale, expressive of the tortured, anti-imperialist conscience of Tolstoi. R. F. Christian has noted that the action moves from inanimate nature, through the lower ranks of the Russian social hierarchy to the imperial chambers in St. Petersburg and back down again to the natural setting of Hadji Murat's death and the ploughed fields of the narrator's setting. This is not the place to discuss Tolstoi's philosophy of history, but, as the reader will see, Tolstoi believed that imperial power corrupted the very souls of the ruling classes. Meanwhile, the common people—for example, Hadji Murat's messenger Bata and the common Russian soldier Avdeev—can and do have much in common. Whether Tolstoi's moral universalism and his effort to salve his tormented conscience would have been received sympathetically by the Chechens and other mountain peoples who fell under Russian rule is one of the questions for the reader of these texts to resolve.*

One of our goals in presenting these works is to present them to the reader in as direct and unfiltered a way as possible, so we will end these introductory remarks by mentioning the two central metaphors of Hadji Murat. *The first is the "beautiful raspberry thistle in full flower—the kind our folk call 'Tatar,'" the pointless destruction of which inspires the narrator to tell his tale. The other is the Tavlinian tale of the captured falcon, which attempted to return to its own kind, but was rejected by them, because it still wore the fetters and bells of its captivity. Using these two literary devices, Tolstoi presents the fates of both the mountain peoples in general and of Hadji Murat in particular to the reading public in the linear and secular fashion characteristic of the European novelistic tradition for much of the nineteenth century. This is a profoundly different mode of presentation and matrix of understanding of what the conflict represented than that offered in al-Qarakhi's* The Shining of Daghestani Swords. *The reason we have put these two texts together is so that the reader can decide whether Tolstoi's empathetic understanding of the conflict from, he thinks, the perspective of the mountain peoples is actually shared by them or whether the radically different presentation and focus of al-Qarakhi's work constitute a root-and-branch rejection of all Russian points of view, however sympathetic. If you will, whether Harold Bloom is right, when he asserts that "Tolstoi holds Hadji Murad in his hands, as if indeed he held the man, and not a fiction."* [4] *Regardless of how the individual reader resolves those questions, we hope that we have succeeded in translating for the English-speaking reading public "the greatness," again in Bloom's words, "almost beyond the reach of art, of* Hadji Murad." [5]

HADJI MURAT

Lev Tolstoi
(translated and annotated
by Thomas Sanders and Gary Hamburg)

I was returning home by way of the fields. It was the very middle of summer. The meadows had been harvested, and the peasants were just beginning to mow the rye. In that season of the year there is a delightful variety of flowers: red, white, and pink, scented tufty clover; milk-white "he loves me-he loves me not" daisies with bright yellow centers and a pleasant spicy smell; yellow honey-scented canola blossoms; tall standing lilacs with white, tulip-shaped little bells; creeping sweet peas; yellow, red and pink scabious; plantains with their faintly but pleasantly scented, pink-tinged blossoms; cornflowers, bright blue in the sunshine and while still young, but growing paler and redder towards evening and as they age; and delicate, almond-scented dodder with its quickly fading blossoms.

I gathered a large bouquet of flowers and was heading home when I noticed a beautiful raspberry thistle in full flower—the kind our folk call "Tatar" and carefully avoid when mowing, but when they do unintentionally cut it down, the balers remove it from the straw so as not to prick their hands. It occurred to me to pick this thistle and place it in the middle of my bouquet. I climbed down into the ditch, and, after driving away a velvety bumblebee that had gotten itself deep into the flower and had there fallen into a sweet, lazy slumber, I set to work picking the flower. But this proved a very difficult task. Not only did the stalk prick me even through the handkerchief I had wrapped around my hand, it was so terribly sturdy that I fought with it nearly five minutes, as I broke its long fibers one by one. After I had finally torn off the bloom, the stalk was all in shreds, and the flower itself no longer seemed so fresh and beautiful. Moreover, because of its coarse, primitive features, it did not go with the delicate blossoms of my bouquet. I regretted needlessly destroying a flower that had looked beautiful in its proper place, and I threw it away. "But what energy and life force!" I thought to myself, recalling the effort it had cost me to pick the flower. "How intensely it defended itself and how dearly it sold its life!"

The way home led through bare, freshly ploughed black-earth fields. I meandered at my own pace along the dusty, black-soil path. The ploughed field was a nobleman's, so vast that on either side and ahead of me to the top of a hill nothing could be seen except black, evenly furrowed, still unsown earth. The land was well tilled, and nowhere was there a single plant—not so much as a blade of grass—to be seen; it was entirely barren. "Ah, what a destructive creature is man … How many different animals, how many plants, he annihilates to support his own existence!" I thought, involuntarily searching for some living thing in this lifeless black field. In front of me, to the right of the road, a familiar-looking little bush made itself visible. On approaching, I recognized it as the same kind of "Tatar" thistle as that whose flower I had vainly plucked and thrown away.

This particular plant had three stalks. One had been torn, and, like the stump of an amputated arm, its remains protruded from the plant. The other two stalks each bore a flower. At one time these flowers had been red, but now were black. One stalk had been broken; half of it hung down with a dirty flower at its tip. The other, though also covered with black mud, still stood erect. Evidently, a cartwheel had run over it, and then the stalk had righted itself and now stood twisted to one side, yet still upright. It looked to me as if a piece of the bush's body had been torn away, as if its bowels had been ripped out, an arm had been wrenched off, and one of its eyes plucked out. And yet it still stands firm and will not surrender to man, who has destroyed all its brothers around it.

"What energy!" I thought. "Man has conquered everything, he has annihilated millions of plants, and this one still won't submit."

Then I remembered an incident in the Caucasus of long ago, an incident part of which I myself had seen, part of which I had heard from other witnesses, and part of which I myself had imagined. That story as it took shape in my recollections and my imagination follows.

I

It was late in the year 1851. On a cold November evening Hadji Murat rode into Makhket, an unpacified Chechen *awul*, that exhaled the pungent smoke of burning dung. The strained singing of the *muezzin* had just faded away, and through the clear mountain air that had become saturated by the odor of dung smoke there could clearly be heard—above the lowing of the cattle and the bleating of the sheep that were dispersing among *saklyas*, nearly conjoining yet still separate from one another like the cells of a honeycomb—the guttural voices of arguing men, and women's and children's voices from down near the fountain.

This Hadji Murat was Shamil's deputy, famous for his exploits, who formerly never rode out without his banner and in the company of some dozens of *murids*, caracoling and cavorting around him. Now, wrapped in a hood and felt cloak from under which protruded a rifle, he rode with only a single *murid*, trying to attract as little attention as possible and peering with his quick black eyes into the faces of the inhabitants he met along the road.

Having entered into the center of the *awul*, Hadji Murat did not take the road leading to the square, but turned to the left down a narrow lane. On reaching the second *saklya*, which was cut into the side of a foothill, he stopped and looked around. There was no one beneath the overhang in front of the *saklya*; but on the roof itself, behind the freshly plastered clay chimney, there lay a man covered with a sheepskin coat. Hadji Murat touched the man with the handle of his whip and clicked his tongue. From under the sheepskin, there rose an old man, wearing a nightcap and a torn, threadbare cotton dressing gown shiny from wear. The old man's lashless eyes were moist and red, and he blinked to get them unstuck. Hadji Murat said the customary "Seliam aleikum!" ["Peace be upon you!"] and uncovered his face.

"Aleikum seliam!" ["Upon you be peace!"] said the old man, smiling with toothless mouth. Having recognized Hadji Murat, he rose on his thin legs and began to lower them into the wooden-heeled shoes that were standing by the chimney. Once his shoes were on, he unhurriedly slipped his arms into the sleeves of the worn, wrinkled sheepskin and climbed backward down the ladder that leaned against the roof. Both while dressing and descending, the old man kept shaking his head on his thin, wrinkled, sunburnt neck and didn't stop mumbling with his toothless mouth. Reaching the ground, he hospitably grasped the reins and right stirrup of Hadji Murat's horse. But, swiftly dismounting his horse, Hadji Murat's strong, agile *murid* motioned the old man aside and took his place.

Hadji Murat got off his mount and, limping slightly, walked under the overhang. Out of the door to meet him quickly strode a fifteen-year-old boy who fixed on the arrivals glittering eyes, dark as ripe currants.

"Run to the mosque and call your father," ordered the old man, and, moving ahead of Hadji Murat, opened for him the light, creaking door of the *saklya*. Just as Hadji Murat entered the outer door, there exited a thin, spare, middle-aged woman wearing a red blouse, yellow cotton dressing gown and light blue wide-legged pants, and carrying pillows.

"May your arrival bring good fortune!" she said and, bending over double, began arranging along the front wall pillows for the guests to sit on.

"May your sons live long!" answered Hadji Murat, who, having taken off his felt cloak, rifle and sword, handed them to the old man.

The old man carefully hung the rifle and sword on a nail next to the master of the house's weapons, which were suspended between two large washbasins that stood out against the smoothly plastered, carefully whitewashed wall.

Hadji Murat adjusted the pistol behind his back, went up to the pillows spread out on the floor and, wrapping his Circassian coat more tightly about him, sat down on them. The old man squatted alongside on bare heels, closed his eyes, and raised his hands, palms upward. Hadji Murat did the same. Having prayed, each man then stroked his face, passing his hands downward till the palms met at the end of his beard.

"*Ne habar?*" ["What's the news?"] Hadji Murat asked the old man.

"*Habar yok*," ["No news,"] replied the old man, looking with his red, lifeless eyes not at Hadji Murat's face, but at his chest. "I live at the apiary and only came here today to see my son. He will know."

Hadji Murat understood that the old man did not want to relate what he knew and what Hadji Murat needed to know, and, slightly nodding his head in assent, did not ask him any more questions.

The old man started to speak again. "There is no good news. The only thing new is that all the rabbits are conferring with each other about how to drive the eagles away. But the eagles ravage first one, then another of them. Last week the Russian dogs burned the hay over in the village of Michit. May their faces be torn apart," he added, hoarsely and angrily.

Hadji Murat's *murid* entered the room and, treading softly on the earthen floor with the long strides of his strong legs, he took off his felt cloak, rifle and sword, just as Hadji Murat had done. Keeping with him only dagger and pistol, he hung them on the very same nail from which Hadji Murat's rifle hung.

"Who's he?" the old man asked Hadji Murat, indicating the newcomer.

"He's my *murid*. Eldar's his name," said Hadji Murat.

"Good," said the old man, indicating to Eldar a spot on the strip of felt next to Hadji Murat.

Eldar sat down, crossed his legs, and silently fixed his handsome, ram-like eyes on the face of the old man, who was talking. The old man related how two local boys had trapped two Russian soldiers the week before; one they had killed and the other they had sent to Shamil in Vedeno. Hadji Murat listened absent-mind-edly, glancing at the door and listening to the sounds coming from outside. Under the overhang in front of the *saklya* steps sounded, the door creaked, and the master of the house came in.

The master of the house, Sado, was around forty with a small beard, long nose, and eyes as dark, though not quite so shining, as those of the fifteen-year-old boy, his son, who had run after him and who had entered the *saklya* together with his father and sat down by the door. Taking his wooden shoes off by the door, the master nudged to the back of his unshaven head, with its abundant black hair, a worn old Caucasian fur cap, and then he immediately squatted on his haunches in front of Hadji Murat.

Exactly as the old man had done, he closed his eyes, lifted his hands, palms upward, recited a prayer, stroked his face with his hands, and only then began to speak. He told Hadji Murat that Shamil had ordered him captured, dead or alive, that Shamil's messengers had only left the day before, that the people were afraid to disobey Shamil, and that therefore it was necessary to be careful.

"In my house," Sado said, "while I'm alive, no one will do harm to my friend. But how will it be out in the open fields? This we must think about."

Hadji Murat listened attentively and nodded his head approvingly. When Sado had finished speaking, he said: "Good. Now I must send a man to the Russians with a letter. My *murid* will go, only he needs a guide."

"I will send brother Bata," said Sado. He turned to his son: "Call Bata."

The boy, as if on springs, leapt to his nimble feet and, swinging his arms, quickly left the *saklya*. Some ten minutes later he returned with a dark, sunburnt, wiry, short-legged Chechen wearing a tattered yellow Circassian coat with torn, fringed sleeves and with black leggings dragging at half-mast. Hadji Murat greeted the newcomer and immediately, again without wasting a single word, asked, "Can you lead my *murid* to the Russians?"

"I can," Bata answered cheerfully. "I can do anything. Other than me not a single Chechen can get through. Another might try, promising everything, but he won't succeed. I can do it."

"All right," said Hadji Murat. "For your trouble you'll get three," holding up three fingers.

Bata nodded his head to show that he understood, but added that it was not the rubles he valued: for honor's sake alone he was ready to serve Hadji Murat. Everyone in the mountains knew of Hadji Murat, how he had fought the Russian pigs.

"Good," said Hadji Murat. "A rope is good when long, a speech when short."

"Well, then I'll shut up," Bata said.

"Where the Argun River turns, opposite the cliff, there is a glade in the woods with two haystacks. Do you know the place?"

"I know it."

"My three horsemen wait for me there," said Hadji Murat.

"*Aiya*," said Bata, nodding his head.

"Ask for Khan-Mahoma. Khan-Mahoma knows what to do and what to say. Lead him to the Russian commander, to Vorontsov, the prince. Can you do it?"

"I'll lead him there."

"Lead him there and bring him back. Can you do that?"

"I can."

"You'll lead him there, you'll bring him back to the forest. And I will be there."

"I will do it all," said Bata, who rose, placed hands on his chest, then left.

"Another man must be sent to Gekhi," Hadji Murat said to his host, when Bata had left. "In Gekhi, here's what must ..." he started to say, grabbing one of his cartridge pouches, but, on seeing two women enter the *saklya*, he immediately dropped his hand and fell silent.

One was Sado's wife, that same thin, middle-aged woman who had arranged the pillows. The other was a very young girl in red, wide-legged trousers and green cotton dressing gown, with a necklace made of silver coins covering her whole chest. At the end of the medium-length, thick, black braid resting between the shoulder blades on her slender back, a silver ruble was suspended; the very same currant-black eyes as those of her father and brother gaily glittered in her young, would-be stern face. She did not look at the guests, but it was obvious that she felt their presence.

Sado's wife brought in a low, round little table, on which were tea, stuffed pastries, pancakes in butter, cheese, thin, rolled-out bread, and honey. The young girl brought in a basin, ewer, and towel.

Sado and Hadji Murat both kept silent the whole time, while the women, who moved quietly in their red, soft, thin-soled slippers, arranged the items they had brought the guests. Eldar, having fixed his ram-like eyes on his own crossed legs, was motionless as a statue the whole time that the women were in the *saklya*. Only when the women had left and their soft steps had completely died out beyond the door did Eldar begin to breathe easily, and then Hadji Murat grabbed one of the cartridge pouches, pulled out a shell-casing, removed from it the bullet, and from under the bullet pulled out a rolled note.

"Give this to my son," he said, indicating the note.

"Where should the reply be sent?" asked Sado.

"To you, then you will convey it to me."

"It will be done," Sado said, placing the note in his own cartridge pouch. Then, taking the ewer in his hand, he moved the basin toward Hadji Murat. Hadji Murat rolled the sleeves of his dressing gown onto his muscular arms, which were white above the wrists, and he held them under the stream of cold, clear water that Sado poured from the ewer. Wiping his hands on the clean, brown towel, Hadji Murat turned to the food. Eldar did exactly the same. While his guests ate, Sado sat opposite them and several times thanked them for the visit. Seated by the door, the boy, never taking his eyes off Hadji Murat, smiled as if confirming with his smile his father's words.

Although it had been over twenty-four hours since Hadji Murat had eaten, he ate only a little bread and cheese, and, having pulled a small knife out from under his dagger, he got some honey and spread it on bread.

"Our honey is good. This year above all other years the honey is abundant and good," said the old man, obviously gratified that Hadji Murat was eating his honey.

"Thanks," said Hadji Murat and turned away from the food. Eldar wanted to eat more, but he, following his *murshid*'s example, moved away from the table and passed Hadji Murat the basin and ewer.

By receiving Hadji Murat, Sado knew he had risked his life, for, after Shamil's quarrel with Hadji Murat, it had been announced to all inhabitants of Chechnia that, on pain of death, they were not to receive Hadji Murat. Sado knew that any minute the inhabitants of the *awul* might discover the presence of Hadji Murat in his house and might demand his surrender. Yet this did not bother Sado, it actually pleased him. Sado considered it a sacred obligation to defend his guest, even though it should cost him his life, and he was pleased with himself, proud of himself, for behaving as he was supposed to.

"While you are in my house and my head is on my shoulders, no one will harm you," he repeated to Hadji Murat.

Hadji Murat looked into Sado's glittering eyes and, understanding that this was true, declared rather ceremoniously, "May you receive joy and long life!"

Sado silently laid his hands upon his breast as a sign of gratitude for these kind words.

Having closed the shutters and prepared kindling in the fireplace, Sado in an exceptionally happy and animated mood left the guestroom where his friend was staying and entered the portion of the *saklya* where the entire family lived. The women were still not asleep and were talking about the dangerous guests spending the night in the other room.

II

That same night fifteen versts from the *awul* in which Hadji Murat was spending the night, three soldiers, and a non-commissioned officer marched out of the advance fort Vozdvizhensk through the Shahgirinskii Gates. After the fashion of Russian soldiers in the Caucasus in those days, the men wore thigh-length sheep-skin coats, fur hats, woolen cloaks rolled across their shoulders, and tall boots reaching above their knees. Shouldering their arms, the soldiers first walked along the road, then, after having gone about five hundred paces, they turned off it and, rustling the dry leaves with their boots, moved about twenty paces to the right, then stopped at a fallen sycamore whose black trunk was visible even in the darkness. This sycamore was the usual station for ambush parties.

The bright stars that had seemed to run along the tops of the trees as the soldiers walked through the woods, now stood still, shining brightly through the bare branches of the trees.

"Thanks a lot," Sergeant Panov said dryly, as he slipped from his shoulders a long bayonet rifle and leaned it, with a clatter, against the tree trunk. The three soldiers did the same.

"Looks like I lost it!" Panov muttered angrily. "Either I forgot it or it popped out of my pack along the way."

"What are you looking for?" asked one of the soldiers in a bright, cheery voice.

"My pipe. The devil knows where it's gone."

"The stem there?" asked the bright voice.

"The stem's right here."

"Why not stick it right into the ground?"

"What you mean? Where?"

"We'll make it work great in no time."

It was forbidden to smoke on ambush, but this ambush hardly deserved the name: it was more like an advance guard sent out to prevent the mountaineers from approaching unobserved with cannon the way they used to, and firing on the fort, so Panov did not feel it necessary to deny himself tobacco and therefore went along with the suggestion of the cheerful soldier. The cheerful soldier took a penknife out of his pocket and began to dig at the ground. Having dug a hole, he smoothed it, fit the stem into it, then filled it with tobacco, packed the tobacco down, and the pipe was ready. A sulfur match flared illuminating for an instant the high-cheeked face of the soldier lying on his belly. The pipe stem whistled, and Panov savored the pleasant odor of burning rough tobacco.

"Did I get it to work or what?" he said, rising to his feet.

"And how!"

"Terrific, Avdeev! Let someone else have a puff. How 'bout it?"

Avdeev pushed himself over on his side, making room for Panov and letting smoke escape from his mouth.

When they had finished their smoke, the soldiers started to talk.

"They say the company commander has dipped into the till again," one of them said in a lazy voice. "He's lost at cards again, see."

"He'll pay it back," said Panov.

"Everyone knows he's a good officer," Avdeev affirmed.

"A good one, a good one," the soldier who had begun the conversation repeated gloomily. "If you ask me, the company oughtta talk to him—'If you took money, tell us how much and when you'll pay it back.'"

"The company should be the judge," said Panov, tearing himself away from his pipe.

"Of course. The group should decide," Avdeev agreed.

"Yeah, but there'll be oats to buy and boots to get towards spring. We'll need the money, and what if he swiped it?" insisted the dissatisfied soldier.

"I'm saying the company should decide," Panov repeated. "This isn't the first time: he borrows money; he pays it back."

At that time in the Caucasus, each company was practically self-supporting. It received money from the state treasury at the rate of 6 rubles 50 kopecks per man and supplied its own provisions: it planted cabbages, mowed hay, maintained its own wagons, and showed off its well-fed horses. Company money was kept in a chest, the key to which was held by the commander, and it often happened that the company commander borrowed from the chest. The sullen soldier Nikitin wanted an accounting from the commander, but Panov and Avdeev thought it wasn't necessary.

After Panov had his smoke, Nikitin had one too and then, having spread out his cloak, sat down on it, leaning against the tree. The soldiers fell silent. The only sound was the wind rustling through the crowns of the trees above their heads. Suddenly, above this incessant low rustling, there rose the howling, squealing, weeping, and laughing of jackals.

"Listen! Those damned creatures, what a racket they make!" said Avdeev.

"They're laughing at you, 'cause your mug's crooked," said the thin, Ukrainian peasant voice of the fourth soldier.

Once again everything quieted down, with only the wind swaying the branches of the trees, now revealing the stars, now covering them up again.

"Hey, Antonych," the cheerful Avdeev suddenly asked Panov. "You ever get bored?"

"What you mean 'bored?'" Panov asked reluctantly.

"Sometimes I get really bored, so bored I can't control myself."

"Listen to you!" Panov responded.

"That time I drank up all the money, that was all from boredom. It came over me, just came over me. I thought to myself: 'I'll get good and stinking drunk!'"

"That happens, but it's even worse with wine."

"I've got drunk on wine, too. Can't help myself."

"How come you're bored?"

"Me? I miss home."

"Why? Your folk rich?"

"Not rich, but we lived alright."

And Avdeev began to recount what he had already related many times to this same Panov.

"See, I took my brother's place as a soldier," Avdeev related. "He's got five kids, and my folks had just married me off. My mother started begging. I think, what's it matter to me, maybe they'll remember me well. I went to our *barin*. We have a good *barin*. And he says, 'Good man! Off you go, then!' So I went in my brother's place."

"Well, that's good." Panov said.

"Yeah, but can you believe it, Antonych, now I'm bored. And mostly I'm bored because of that. I say to myself, 'Why'd you go instead of your brother?' 'He lives like a king now, and here you're suffering.' And the more I think, the worse it gets. It's a sin, right?"

Avdeev fell silent.

"Want to smoke again?" Avdeev asked.

"Okay, set it up."

But the soldiers were not to have their smoke. No sooner had Avdeev begun to set up the pipe again, when, above the rustling of the trees, footsteps sounded on the road. Panov grabbed his rifle and nudged Nikitin with his foot. Nikitin got to his feet and picked up his cloak. The third soldier, Bondarenko, also stood up, saying "What a dream I was just having, brothers ..."

Avdeev shushed Bondarenko, and the soldiers froze in place, listening. The soft footsteps of men not wearing boots approached. Ever more clearly the crackle of leaves and dead branches could be heard through the darkness. Then conversation in that special, guttural language which the Chechens speak could be heard. Now the soldiers not only heard but saw two shadows passing through the space between the trees. One shadow was shorter, the other taller. When the shadows drew even with the soldiers, Panov, rifle in hand, stepped with his two comrades onto the road.

"Who goes there?" he yelled.

"Chechen, unarmed," said the one who was a bit shorter. This was Bata. "Rifle *yok*, sword *yok*!" ["No rifle, no sword!"] he said, pointing to himself. "Need parince."

The taller one silently stood alongside his comrade. He didn't have a rifle either.

"A go-between," Panov said, explaining things to his comrades. "He wants to see the colonel."

"Parince Vorontsov much need! 'portant business!" Bata said.

"Ok, Ok! We'll lead you there," Panov said. "You take him," he turned to Avdeev, "You and Bondarenko. Hand them over to the duty officer, then come back here. And look," he said to Avdeev, "be careful. Make them walk in front of you. If they're shaveheads, they're tricky."

"And what's this?" Avdeev said, making a move with his rifle and bayonet, as if stabbing someone. "I'll just stick 'em a time or two and let the air out of them."

"What good'll he be, if you run him through?" said Bondarenko.

"Alright, march!"

When the footsteps of the two soldiers and the go-betweens had died away, Panov and Nikitin return to their post.

"It's the devil brings them out at night," Bondarenko remarked.

"I guess so, Panov said. "It's got nippy," he added and, unrolling his cloak, put it on and then sat down against a tree.

After about two hours Avdeev and Bondarenko came back.

"Well, d'you hand 'em over?" Panov asked.

"Yeah. They were still up at the colonel's. We took 'em straight to him. Listen, brother, those shaveheads are great guys," Avdeev continued. "Lord! I had quite a talk with them!"

"You sure love to talk," Nikitin remarked disapprovingly.

"Really, they're just like Russians. One's married. 'You hitched?' I say. 'Yeah,' he says. "Got a kid?' I go. 'Kids.' 'A couple?' 'A couple,' he goes. That's how we talked. Great guys."

"Right, great guys." said Nikitin. "Just get caught alone with him, he'll slit your gut."

"It'll be light soon," said Panov.

"Yeah, the little stars are fading," Avdeev said, sitting down and getting comfortable.

And the soldiers again fell silent.

III

The windows of the barracks and soldiers' houses had long been dark, but in one of the best houses of the fortress lights still shone through all the windows. The house was occupied by the Kurinskii Regiment's commander, son of the army commander-in-chief, imperial aide-de-camp Semyon Mikhailovich Vorontsov. Vorontsov lived with his wife, Mar'ia Vasil'evna, the famous St. Petersburg beauty, and he lived in the small, Caucasian fortress more luxuriously than anyone had ever lived there before. Vorontsov and especially his wife thought their lifestyle modest, even deprived, whereas local inhabitants were stunned by its unexampled opulence.

Now, at midnight, in the large drawing room where a carpet covered the entire floor and heavy curtains hung across the doorways, around a formal wooden game table lit by four candles, hosts and guests sat playing cards. One of the card players was the master of the house himself, a long-faced, fair-haired colonel, wearing the monogram and gold shoulder knots of an imperial aide-de-camp. His partner, a graduate student from St. Petersburg University whom the princess had recently enlisted to tutor her young son by her first husband, was a shaggy-headed youth of gloomy appearance. They played against two officers: the first was company commander Poltoratskii, a broad-faced, ruddy-complex- ioned transfer from the imperial guard; the other was the regimental adjutant, who sat bolt upright on his chair with a cold expression on his handsome face. The princess herself, Mar'ia Vasil'evna, a large-boned, black-browed beauty, sat alongside Poltoratskii, touching his leg with her crinoline and peeking at his cards. In her words, in her glances and smile, in the movements of her body and in the scent of perfume emanating from her, there was something that rendered Poltoratskii oblivious to everything except an awareness of her proximity, so he made mistake after mistake, each error irritating his partner more than the preceding one.

"No! That can't be! Again, you've wasted your ace," the adjutant muttered, flushing all over when Poltoratskii threw down his ace.

As if just awakened from slumber, Poltoratskii uncomprehendingly turned his kind, wide-set, dark eyes toward the dissatisfied adjutant.

"Do forgive him!" Mar'ia Vasil'evna said, smiling. "See, I told you," she continued, turning to Poltoratskii.

"But that's not what you said at all," Poltoratskii said, smiling too.

"Oh, wasn't it?" she asked and smiled back. And that answering smile so terribly agitated and delighted Poltoratskii that he blushed a deep red and, gath- ering up the cards, began to shuffle them.

"It's not your deal!" the adjutant said sternly, and with his white, pearl-ringed hand he began to deal the cards as if he wanted only to get rid of them as quickly as possible.

The prince's valet entered the drawing room and announced that the prince was being summoned by the duty officer.

"You will excuse me, gentlemen," the prince said, speaking British-accented Russian. "You play for me, Marie. Sit in."

"Everyone agreed?" the princess asked, quickly and lightly rising to her full, imposing height, rustling her silks, and smiling the radiant smile of a happy woman.

"As always, I'll agree to anything," said the adjutant, very glad that the princess, who could not play at all, would now be on the other team. Poltoratskii simply spread his hands out, smiling helplessly.

The rubber had ended by the time the prince came back to the drawing room. He returned especially happy and animated.

"Do you know what I shall propose?"

"Well?"

"Let us drink some champagne."

"For that I'm always ready," Poltoratskii said.

"Excellent. That would be lovely!" the adjutant added.

"Vasilii! You deal!" the prince said.

"Who summoned you?" the princess asked.

"The duty officer and someone else."

"Who? On what business?" Mar'ia Vasil'evna asked in a rush.

"I musn't say," Vorontsov said, shrugging his shoulders.

"You musn't say?" Mar'ia Vasil'evna repeated. "We'll see about that."

Servants brought in the champagne. The guests drank it by the glassful, and, having finished gambling and settling their debts, they began to take their leave.

"Isn't your company on duty tomorrow in the forest?" the prince asked Poltoratskii.

"Yes, mine ... Why?"

"Then we shall be seeing each other tomorrow," the prince said, smiling slightly.

"I'm very glad, sir," said Poltoratskii, not fully understanding what Vorontsov was saying to him and concerned only that he would soon be pressing Mar'ia Vasil'evna's large white hand.

As always, Mar'ia Vasil'evna firmly grasped Poltoratskii's hand and vigorously shook it. Then, having reminded him once more of his mistake when he led with diamonds, she—or so it seemed to Poltoratskii—graced him with a radiant, tender, and meaningful smile.

Poltoratskii went home in the kind of ecstatic mood that can only be understood by people like him, people raised and educated in high society who suddenly, after months of isolated military life, meet a woman from their former social circle, particularly a woman like Princess Vorontsova.

When he got to the little house where he lived with a fellow officer, he pushed on the front door, but the door was locked. He knocked; the door didn't open. He grew irritated, then began to drum on the locked door with his foot and his sword. From the other side of the door footsteps became audible, and finally Vavilo, Poltoratskii's house serf, undid the little hook that held the door closed.

"Where did you get the bright idea to lock the door? Moron!"

"How can you say that, Aleksei Vladimir ..."

"Again, you're drunk. Here, let me show you how I can say ..." Poltoratskii wanted to hit Vavilo, but changed his mind.

"Oh, the hell with you! Light a candle!"

"Right away."

In fact, Vavilo had been drinking, but he drank because he had attended a name-day party at the sergeant quartermaster's. Once home, he fell to thinking about his life compared to that of Ivan Matveevich, the sergeant quartermaster. Ivan Matveevich had a good income, was married, and hoped in a year to retire from military service. Vavilo had still been a boy when he had been "taken upstairs," that is, taken into the service of the masters. Now he was nearly forty, he hadn't married and was living on the road with his slovenly master. The master was good enough, he didn't beat Vavilo much, but what kind of a life was this? "He has promised to free me when we return from the Caucasus, but where will I go with my freedom? A dog's life!" thought Vavilo. And he had wanted to sleep so badly that, fearing someone might break in and steal something, he had latched the door and dozed off.

Poltoratskii entered the bedroom he was sharing with his comrade Tikhonov.

"Well, how did it go? Did you lose?" Tikhonov asked, waking up.

"No, in fact, I won seventeen rubles, and we drank a bottle of Cliquot."

"And you gazed at at Mar'ia Vasil'evna?"

"Yes, I gazed at Mar'ia Vasil'evna." Poltoratskii repeated.

"Soon we have to get up," Tikhonov said. "We take the field at 6 o'clock."

"Vavilo!" Poltoratskii shouted. "See that you wake me up promptly at 5 a.m."

"How can anyone wake you, when you're so drunk?"

"I'm telling you, wake me up! Hear?"

"I hear."

Vavilo carried away Poltoratskii's boots and clothes.

Then Poltoratskii lay in his bed smiling, smoked a cigarette, and extinguished the candle. In the darkness before him he saw the smiling face of Mar'ia Vasil'evna.

The Vorontsovs did not sleep right away either. After the guests had left, Mar'ia Vasil'evna went up to her husband and, stopping right in front of him, said sternly:

"Eh bien, vous allez me dire ce que c'est?"

"Mais, ma chère …"

"Pas de ma chère! C'est un émissaire, n'est ce pas?"

"Quand même je ne puis pas vous le dire."

"Vous ne pouvez-pas? Alors c'est moi qui vais vous le dire."

"Vous?"

["Very well, now, are you going to tell me what happened?"

"But, my dear …"

"'My dear' nothing! It's an emissary isn't it?"

"Even if there were an emissary, I cannot tell you so."

"You can't? Well, then I'll tell you."

"You?"]

"It was Hadji Murat, wasn't it?" said the princess, having heard for several days already about negotiations with Hadji Murat and having presumed that the man her husband had met was Hadji Murat himself.

Vorontsov could not deny this, but he disappointed his wife by telling her that the man was not Hadji Murat himself, just a messenger announcing that Hadji Murat would come tomorrow to the place where an expedition had been sent out to fell the forest.

Mired in the monotonous life of the fortress, the young Vorontsovs, husband and wife, were delighted over this event. Having discussed how pleasant the news would be to his father, husband and wife went to bed after two o'clock in the morning.

IV

After three sleepless nights spent fleeing Shamil's *murids*, Hadji Murat dozed off as soon as Sado left the *saklya*, scarcely having wished him a good night. He slept

89

clothes on, head on hand, elbow sinking into the red feather pillow Sado had laid out for him. Close by, next to the wall, slept Eldar who lay on his back, his strong, young limbs extended, so that his muscular chest, covered by black cartridge pouches and white Circassian coat, was higher than his freshly-shaven, blue-shadowed head which had fallen from the pillow. His child-like, protruding, lightly down-covered upper lip made sipping sounds as it contracted and expanded. He slept just like Hadji Murat: fully clothed, with pistol and dagger in his belt. In the *saklya*'s hearth the fire had burned down and in a niche above the stove a night candle guttered faintly.

In the middle of the night the door of the guest quarters squeaked, and Hadji Murat immediately sprang up and grabbed his pistol. Stepping lightly on the earthen floor, Sado entered the room.

"What's wrong?" Hadji Murat asked, as if he had not been to sleep at all.

"There's a problem," Sado said, sitting down in front of Hadji Murat. "A woman watching from her rooftop saw you ride into town," he said. "She told her husband, so now the whole *awul* knows. The neighbor just rushed up to my wife; she says the elders have gathered in the mosque, and they want to detain you."

"We must ride," Hadji Murat said.

"The horses are ready," Sado said and quickly left the *saklya*.

"Eldar," Hadji Murat whispered, and Eldar, on hearing his name and—the main thing—his master's voice, leapt to his strong legs and straightened his fur hat. Hadji Murat put on his rifle and felt coat. Eldar did the same, and both quietly left the *saklya*, exiting from beneath the overhang.

The dark-eyed boy brought up the horses. At the sound of hooves on the hard-beaten surface of the street, someone's head popped out of the door of the neighboring *saklya* and, his wooden shoes clattering, a man ran up the hill toward the mosque.

There was no moon, only the stars shone brightly in the black sky; in the darkness hovered the outlines of the *saklya* roofs and, on the *awul*'s promontory, above the other buildings stood the mosque with its minaret. From the mosque the rumbling of voices echoed ominously down the village lanes.

Hadji Murat, quickly seizing his rifle, put his foot in the narrow stirrup and, soundlessly, in a flash, vaulted onto his mount, landing in the high cushion of the saddle.

"May God reward you," he said to his host, his right foot feeling instinctively for the other stirrup, and then, ever so lightly, he touched the shoulder of the boy holding his horse, thereby signalling the lad to step aside. The boy stepped aside, and the horse, as if she already knew what to do, trotted briskly out of the narrow lane onto the main road. Eldar rode behind him. Sado, clad in a sheepskin coat and rapidly waving his arms, moved rapidly behind them, almost running, crossing first to one side and then to the other of the narrow lane. Blocking the village exit, in the center of the road, there suddenly appeared a moving shadow, then another as well.

"Halt! Who goes there? Stop!" shouted a voice, as several men obstructed the path.

Instead of stopping, Hadji Murat drew a pistol from beneath his belt and, spurring on his horse, rode directly at the knot of people trying to block the road. The people standing in the road scattered, and Hadji Murat, without looking back, briskly descended from the village. Eldar followed at a sharp trot. Two shots cracked behind them; two bullets whistled by without hitting either Hadji Murat or Eldar. Hadji Murat continued riding at the same pace. Having covered about three hundred paces, he stopped his lightly panting horse and listened. From ahead of him down the hill came the sound of rapidly flowing water. Behind him from the *awul*, roosters called to each other. Over these sounds, clattering hooves and men's voices drew near from behind. Hadji Murat touched his horse and rode on at the same steady pace.

The galloping pursuit soon overtook Hadji Murat. There were about twenty men on horseback. They were inhabitants of the *awul* who had decided to capture Hadji Murat or at least to clear themselves with Shamil by making a show of trying to capture him. When they had gotten close enough to be seen in the darkness, Hadji Murat stopped, dropped the reins, and, with a practiced motion, undid his rifle case and with his right hand pulled out a rifle. Eldar did the same.

"What do you want?" Hadji Murat cried, "To capture me? Just try!"

And he raised his rifle. The men from the *awul* came to a halt. Rifle in hand, Hadji Murat left the road, descending into a nearby ravine. Without coming any closer, the horsemen rode after him. When Hadji Murat had crossed over to the other side of the ravine, the riders following him shouted that he should hear what they had to say. In response, he fired his rifle and spurred his horse into a gallop. By the time he reined her in, his pursuers could no longer be heard; nor could the roosters of the *awul* be heard, whereas the murmuring of running water and the sporadic cries of a large owl struck his ears more clearly than ever. The black wall of the forest was quite near. This was the very wood where his *murids* awaited. On reaching the outskirts of the woods, Hadji Murat stopped, and, filling his lungs with air, he whistled once, then fell silent to listen. After a minute an identical whistle sounded from inside the forest. Hadji Murat turned off the path and rode into the woods. When he had gone about a hundred paces, through tree trunks he spied a campfire, shadows of people sitting around the fire and, half-illuminated by the campfire, a horse, hobbled but still saddled. Three men sat near the fire.

One of the men sitting around the fire sprang up and walked toward Hadji Murat, taking hold of his horse's bridle and stirrup. The man was Hadji Murat's blood brother, the person who managed his household affairs.

"Put out the fire," Hadji Murat said, getting down off his horse.

The men began scattering the fire and stomping out the burning branches.

"Has Bata been here?" Hadji Murat asked, going over to a felt cloak that had been spread out on the ground.

"Yes. He left long ago with Khan-Mahoma."

"By what road?"

"That one," answered Khanefi, pointing in the opposite direction from the one Hadji Murat had come.

"Alright," Hadji Murat said and, unslinging his rifle, began reloading it. "We have to keep watch. They're chasing me," he said to the man who was putting out the fire.

That man was the Chechen Gamzalo. Moving toward the felt cloak, Gamzalo took a rifle from its case and quietly walked to the edge of the clearing near the spot where Hadji Murat had ridden in. Eldar, after dismounting his own horse, took Hadji Murat's horse and, stretching high each horse's head, tied them to a tree. Then, as Gamzalo had done, rifle on shoulder, he took a position on the far side of the clearing. The fire was extinguished, the forest no longer seemed as dark as it had earlier, and in the sky stars still shone, albeit faintly.

Glancing up at the stars, at the hundred-fired Pleaides, which had already ascended halfway to the zenith, Hadji Murat calculated that it was well past midnight, long since time for his evening prayers. He asked Khanefi for the ewer that they always carried in one of their packs and, putting on his felt cloak walked down to the nearby stream.

Having removed his shoes and performed his ritual ablution, Hadji Murat stepped barefooted onto his felt cloak, knelt down, sat back on his calves, and then, having first covered his ears with his fingers and closed his eyes, he recited his customary prayers, facing to the east.

When he had finished his prayers, he returned to the spot where his saddle-bags lay, and, sitting down on his felt cloak, he rested his elbows on his knees, cleared his head and fell deep into thought.

Hadji Murat had always trusted in his own destiny. In any undertaking, he was firmly convinced of success from the outset, and up to now fate had smiled on him. This was how it had been, with rare exceptions, throughout the course of his stormy military life. Now, he hoped, things would also turn out well. He pictured to himself how, with the army that Vorontsov would give him, he would march against Shamil, take him prisoner, take revenge on him; then Hadji Murat pictured how the Russian tsar would reward him, and how he would once again rule Avaria, and how all Chechnia would submit to him. With these thoughts in his head, he did not notice when he fell asleep.

In a dream he saw himself and his brave men singing a religious song and crying, "Hadji Murat is coming!", then flying at Shamil, seizing him and his wives, and listening to Shamil's wives crying and sobbing. Then he awoke. The song "There is no God but God," the shouts "Hadji Murat is coming!" and the cries of Shamil's wives turned out to be the howling, crying, and laughter of jackals that had awakened him. Hadji Murat raised his head, glanced at the eastern sky, which through tree trunks was already showing light, and asked one of his *murids* about Khan-Mahoma. Learning that Khan-Mahoma had not yet returned, Hadji Murat cleared his head of all thoughts and instantly nodded off again.

He was awakened by the bright voice of Khan-Mahoma, returning with Bata from their mission. Khan-Mahoma immediately sat down next to Hadji Murat and began to tell him how the soldiers had met them and escorted them straight to the prince, how he had spoken with the prince himself, how pleased the prince had been, and how the prince had promised to meet them that very morning at the site where the Russians would be cutting down the forest—on the other side of Michik in the Shalin clearing. Bata interrupted the speech of his companion from time to time, adding his own details.

Hadji Murat questioned them carefully concerning the precise words with which the prince had responded to his offer to defect to the Russians. Khan-Mahoma and Bata answered with one voice that the prince had promised to receive Hadji Murat as a guest and to make sure that he was well treated. Hadji Murat asked next about the route to the clearing, and, when Khan-Mahoma assured him that he knew the route well and would lead him straight there, Hadji Murat got out his money and gave Bata the promised three rubles. Then he ordered his *murids* to take from his saddlebags his gold-embossed weapons, fur cap and turban, and to clean them so that he would arrive among the Russians in excellent form. By the time they had polished the weapons, cleaned saddles and harnesses, and brushed down the horses, the stars had faded, it had become quite light, and there was a gentle draft from an early morning breeze.

V

Early in the morning, while it was still dark, two companies under Poltoratskii's command marched out carrying axes to a spot ten versts beyond the Shahgirinskii Gates and, having positioned a perimeter line of sharpshooters, began at dawn's light to fell trees. By eight o'clock, the fog, which had mingled with the thick smoke from hissing and crackling green branches in the bonfires, had begun to lift, and the loggers, who before then had not been able to see five paces in front of themselves and had only heard each other working, began to discern both the bonfire and the road through the forest made by felled trees; the sun alternately appeared as a bright spot in the fog, then hid itself again. In a clearing not far from the road, on top of signal drums sat Poltoratskii, his subordinate Tikhonov, two officers of the 3rd Company, and Baron Friese, a friend of Poltoratskii's from the Corps of Pages and former officer of the Horse Guards who had been reduced to the ranks for dueling. Scattered around the drums were cigarette butts, bottles, and scraps of the paper used to wrap small snacks. The officers had drunk vodka, eaten breakfast, and were now drinking porter ale. The drummer was opening their eighth bottle. Although he had not had enough sleep, Poltoratskii was in that state of heightened mental acuity and good, carefree gaiety that he always felt among his troops and fellow officers, even when there was the possibility of danger.

The officers carried on a lively conversation over the latest news, the death of General Sleptsov. No one saw this death as the most important moment in the general's life, the moment of its ending and return to the source from which it sprang; instead they saw in it the valor of a dashing officer who had hurled himself with his sword drawn at the mountaineers and had desperately cut them down in swaths.

Although everyone, particularly officers who had been in action, knew if they opened their eyes that, neither in the current Caucasus war, nor for that matter in any war anytime or anywhere, had there occurred that sort of cutting down the enemy in hand-to-hand combat that is always assumed to have occurred and is actually described as having taken place (indeed, if such slashing with swords and bayonets does happen, then those being slashed and stabbed are only helpless runaways), this fiction of hand-to-hand combat was nevertheless avowed as truth by those very officers and lent them the quiet pride with which they—one in a dashing, the other in a very modest pose—sat on the drums, smoked, drank, and joked, not worrying about death, which could take any one of them at any moment, just as it had Sleptsov. Indeed, as if in confirmation of their expectations, in the middle of their conversation they heard to the left of the road the brisk, pleasing sound of a sharply snapping rifle shot, then somewhere in the fog a bullet flew past, whistling merrily, and crashed into a tree. Several low-pitched thunderous retorts from the soldiers' weapons answered the unfriendly fire.

"Aha!" Poltoratskii shouted in a merry voice. "Our boys are returning fire. Say, brother Kostia," he said, turning to Friese, "here's your chance to redeem yourself. Join the company. We'll arrange a charming little battle here, then we'll concoct a flattering report for you."

The demoted baron jumped to his feet and went at a quick pace to that place in the smoke where he had left his company. Poltoratskii's little Kabarda bay was brought to him. He mounted and, having formed up his company, led it to the line in the direction of the shots. The line of sharpshooters stood at the edge of the forest in front of a treeless, downward-sloping ravine. The wind was blowing toward the forest, and not only the near slope of the ravine was clearly visible, but the other side of it as well.

As Poltoratskii approached the line, the sun broke through the mist, and, about two hundred yards away, on the opposite side of the ravine where new forest was cropping up, several riders became visible. These Chechens were the ones who had followed Hadji Murat, wanting to witness his arrival among the Russians. One of them fired on the line. Several soldiers from the line fired back. The Chechens retreated, and the firing ceased. But when Poltoratskii arrived with his company, he ordered them to fire, and scarcely had the word been passed, when up and down the whole line there erupted a continuous, cheerful, invigorating crackle of arms, accompanied by pretty little bursts of smoke that dissolved into the air. The troops, glad for the diversion, hurried to reload and fired off round after round. The Chechens evidently felt the sense of excitement, too, and one after another dashed forward on his horse and fired several rounds at the soldiers. One of those rounds wounded a soldier. He was the same Avdeev who had been on ambush duty the night before. When his comrades came up to him, he was lying on his back, face upward, holding a wound in his stomach with both hands, rocking himself rhythmically and moaning softly.

"I'd just started to reload my gun. I hear—'click,'" said a soldier who had been on the line with him. "I look, and he'd dropped his gun."

Avdeev was a member of Poltoratskii's company. Seeing a small knot of soldiers gathered together, Poltoratskii rode up to them.

"What is it, brother? You hit? Where?" he asked.

Avdeev did not answer.

"I'd just started to reload, Your Honor," said the soldier who was Avdeev's line mate. "I hear something—a click. I look, and he'd dropped his gun."

"Tse, tse," Poltoratskii clicked his tongue. "Does it hurt much, Avdeev?"

"Doesn't hurt, but I can't walk. A little shot of vodka, please, Your Honor."

Vodka, or rather the grain alcohol drunk by the soldiers in the Caucasus, was found, and Panov, frowning severely, brought Avdeev some in a canteen lid. Avdeev started to sip, but immediately pushed the lid away with his hand.

"My soul won't accept it," he said. "You drink it."

Panov drank down the alcohol. Avdeev tried to raise himself again, and again he sank back. The soldiers spread out a cloak and laid Avdeev on it.

"Your Honor, the colonel is coming," the sergeant-major said to Poltoratskii.

"Well, then, you boys deal with the wounded man," Poltoratskii said, and, flicking his whip, he set off at a brisk trot to meet Vorontsov.

Vorontsov rode a chestnut-colored thoroughbred English stallion; he was accompanied by the regimental adjutant, a Cossack, and a Chechen interpreter.

"What's going on here?" he asked Poltoratskii.

"From over there a raiding party attacked our advance line," Poltoratskii answered.

"Come, come, now. You started the whole thing yourself."

"Oh, no. Not me, prince," Poltoratskii said, smiling. "They snuck down on their own."

"I heard they wounded a soldier?"

"Yes, a shame. A good soldier."

"A serious wound?"

"Apparently, serious. In the stomach."

"And I, do you know where I am heading?" Vorontsov asked.

"No idea."

"You can't even guess?"

"No."

"Hadji Murat is defecting, and we are going to meet him right now."

"That can't be!"

"His emissary came to my house yesterday," Vorontsov said, with difficulty holding back a smile of joy. "Right now he should be waiting for me at Shalin glade; so spread sharpshooters out from here to the glade, then come along with me."

"Understood, sir!" Poltoratskii said, lifting his hand to his cap; then he rode off to his company. He himself led a column of troops on the right side; he ordered the sergeant-major to watch the left side. Meanwhile, four soldiers transported the wounded man to the fortress.

Poltoratskii was already on his way back to rejoin Vorontsov, when he noticed several horsemen overtaking him. He stopped and waited for them.

In front was an imposing man riding a white-maned horse and wearing a white Circassian coat, a turban, and bearing weapons with gold work on them. This man was Hadji Murat. He rode up to Poltoratskii and said something to him in Tatar. Raising his eyebrows, Poltoratskii spread his hands as a sign that he did not understand, then he smiled. Hadji Murat answered with a smile of his own, and this smile struck Poltoratskii with its childlike geniality. Poltoratskii never expected to see such geniality from a fearsome mountaineer. He had expected to see a dark, cold, alien character, yet there was before him the simplest of men, smiling such a good-natured smile that he seemed like a friend of long acquaintance. Only one thing about him was exceptional: the wide-set eyes which looked attentively, penetratingly, yet calmly into the eyes of others.

Hadji Murat's retinue was composed of four men. Among them was that same Khan-Mahoma who had been to Vorontsov's the night before. He had a round, ruddy face with lively, dark, almost lidless eyes, whose beaming expression was full of the joy of life. There was also a thickset, hairy man whose eyebrows grew together. He was the Tavlinian Khanefi, who took care of Hadji Murat's belongings. He led a pack horse bearing tightly packed saddle bags. Two members of the retinue particularly stood out. One of them was young, thin as a woman in the waist, but broad-shouldered, his face sporting a short, light-brown beard, a handsome young man with ram-like eyes: this was Eldar. The other man was blind in one eye and lacking both eyebrows and lashes; he had a trim reddish beard and a scar across his nose and face. This was the Chechen Gamzalo.

Poltoratskii pointed Hadji Murat toward Vorontsov, who had just come into view on the road. Hadji Murat headed over to the prince, pulled his horse up, placed his right hand on his breast, said something in Tatar, then waited for an answer. The Chechen interpreter translated:

"He says: 'I surrender to the will of the Russian tsar. I want,' he says, 'to serve him. I have wanted to for a long time, but Shamil wouldn't allow it.'"

Having heard out the interpreter, Vorontsov extended his hand in its suede glove to Hadji Murat. Hadji Murat looked at this hand, hesitated for a second, then firmly grasped it and once again said something, glancing now at the interpreter, now at Vorontsov.

"He says, he did not wish to surrender to anyone but you, because you are the son of the *Sardar*, the commander. He has respected you greatly."

Vorontsov inclined his head to indicate gratitude. Hadji Murat said something else, pointing to his suite.

"He says that these men, his *murids*, will do as he does; they will also serve the Russians."

Vorontsov glanced at them and bowed his head to them as well.

The happy, dark-eyed, lidless Chechen, Khan-Mahoma, also bowing his head, must have said something funny to Vorontsov, because the hairy Avar bared his teeth in an ivory-white smile. The red-headed Gamzalo briefly flashed his good eye at Vorontsov, then returned his gaze to the ears of his horse.

While Vorontsov, Hadji Murat and his retinue rode back to the fortress, the Russian soldiers, called back from their lines, gathered in groups and made their own comments:

"How many good folk that damned moutaineer has killed! Now they'll probably give him a medal," said one.

"Yeah, probably. He was Shamil's right-hand man. Now, all of a sudden ..."

"But he's a helluva fighter. What they call a '*dzhigit*.'"

"But the red-haired one. That red-haired one's an animal, he'd cut you to pieces."

"A real bastard! Has to be."

Everyone took special notice of the red-haired one.

Where the woodcutting was going on, the soldiers along the road ran up to take a peek. An officer yelled at them, but Vorontsov stopped him.

"Let them look at their old acquaintance. Son, do you know who this is?" Vorontsov asked a soldier who was standing nearby, pronouncing the words slowly with his English accent.

"Haven't a clue, Your Excellency."

"Hadji Murat ... Heard of him?"

"How could a person not hear of him, Your Excellency. We've beaten him many times."

"Yes, well, and we've got it from him, too."

"Exactly right, Your Excellency," the soldier answered, pleased with his luck at getting to talk with the chief.

Hadji Murat understood that they were talking about him, and a bright smile shone in his eyes. In the sunniest of moods Vorontsov returned to the fortress.

VI

Vorontsov was very pleased that he and no one else had succeeded in arranging the defection to the Russian side of a powerful adversary, second in importance only to Shamil. The one unpleasant aspect of the affair was that General Meller-Zakomel'skii was the designated army commander in Vozdvizhensk, so the entire business ought to have been handled through him. Vorontsov had acted outside of channels, so he might face a reprimand. And the thought rather soured his pleasure.

When they reached the fortress, Vorontsov turned Hadji Murat's *murids* over to the regimental adjutant; he himself escorted Hadji Murat home.

Princess Mar'ia Vasil'evna, elegantly attired and smiling, together with her son, a handsome, curly-haired six-year-old boy, met Hadji Murat in the drawing room; Hadji Murat pressed his hand to his chest and, through the accompanying interpreter, he declared somewhat solemnly that he considered himself the prince's friend, since the prince had welcomed him into his own home; further-more, the prince's entire family was just as sacred to him as the prince himself. Mar'ia Vasil'evna liked both Hadji Murat's appearance and his manners. That he blushed red when she extended to him her large, white hand inclined her all the more in his favor. She suggested he have a seat, asked him whether or not he drank coffee, and then ordered some brought. Hadji Murat, however, declined the coffee when they brought it to him. He understood a little Russian but could not speak it, so, when he didn't understand, he smiled, and his smile pleased Mar'ia Vasil'evna just as it had Poltoratskii. Mar'ia Vasil'evna's curly-headed, bright-eyed little son, whom she had affectionately nicknamed Bul'ka, did not take his eyes off of Hadji Murat, whom he had always heard described as a great warrior.

Leaving Hadji Murat with his wife, Vorontsov went to his office to draft a report notifying the general command of Hadji Murat's defection. Having duly notified the commander of the left flank, General Kozlovskii, in Groznyi, and having sent a letter to his father, Vorontsov hurried home, fearing the displeasure of his wife for having imposed on her this strange, terrifying man with whom one had to deal gingerly, so as neither to give offense nor show favoritism. But his anxiety was misplaced. Hadji Murat was sitting in an armchair, holding Bul'ka on his knee, his head inclined, listened attentively to the interpreter's translation of the laughing Mar'ia Vasil'evna's remarks. Mar'ia Vasil'evna was saying that, if Hadji Murat gave to every friend the things that the friend praised, then he would soon be walking around naked as Adam.

When the prince entered the room, Hadji Murat took the surprised and now offended Bul'ka off his knee and stood up, immediately replacing the playful expression on his face with one that was stern and serious. He sat down only after Vorontsov had taken a seat. Continuing the conversation, he answered Mar'ia Vasil'evna that it was the mountaineers' custom to give to a friend what-ever the friend likes.

"Your son, *kunak*," he said, patting the curly head of the boy, whom he had seated once again on his knee.

"He's charming, your brigand," Mar'ia Vasil'evna said in French to her husband. "Bul'ka admired his dagger, so he gave it to him."

Bul'ka showed the dagger to his father.

"*C'est un objet de prix*," said Mar'ia Vasil'evna

"*Il faudra trouver l'occasion de lui faire cadeau*," Vorontsov replied.

["That's a valuable object."

"We will have to find an occasion to give him a gift."]

Hadji Murat sat with lowered eyes and, patting the boy on the head, kept repeating, "*Dzhigit, dzhigit*."

"A marvelous dagger, marvelous," Vorontsov said, pulling the sharpened, rippled steel blade half way out of its scabbard. "I thank you."

"Ask him how I may be of service to him," Vorontsov said to the interpreter.

The interpreter conveyed the question, and Hadji Murat immediately answered that he needed nothing, but then asked to be taken to a place where he could pray. Vorontsov summoned a valet and ordered him to carry out Hadji Murat's instructions.

As soon as Hadji Murat was alone in the room to which they led him, his face changed: the expression of pleasure, tenderness, and solemnity disappeared and a worried look came over him.

The reception that Vorontsov had given him was much better than he had expected. But the better that reception, the less Hadji Murat trusted Vorontsov and his officers. He feared everything: that they would seize him, shackle him, and banish him to Siberia or simply kill him, and therefore he was on his guard.

When Eldar entered the room, Hadji Murat asked him where the *murids* had been quartered, where the horses were, and whether the *murids'* weapons had been taken from them.

Eldar reported that the horses were in the prince's stables, that the men had been quartered in the barn, that they still had their weapons, and that the interpreter was providing them with food and tea.

Puzzled by this, Hadji Murat shook his head and, taking off his things, began his prayers. When he had finished, he ordered his silver dagger brought to him, and, having put his things back on and fastened his belt around his waist, he sat with his feet on an ottoman to await what was to be.

Shortly after four o'clock he was summoned to dine with the prince.

At dinner, Hadji Murat ate nothing except pilaf, which he served himself from the very same part of the dish where Mar'ia Vasil'evna had taken her serving.

"He is afraid that we are going to poison him," Mar'ia Vasil'evna said to her husband. "He takes his food from the place I took mine." And she immediately asked Hadji Murat through the interpreter, when he would pray again. Hadji Murat held up five fingers and pointed to the sun.

"That means soon."

Vorontsov pulled out his pocket watch and pressed a lever on it. The watch struck 4.15. The chimes obviously surprised Hadji Murat, so he asked the prince to ring it again and to show him the watch.

"*Voila l'occasion! Donnez-lui la montre,*" Mar'ia Vasil'evna said to her husband.

["Here's the occasion! Give him the watch."]

Vorontsov immediately offered the watch to Hadji Murat. Pressing his hand to his chest, Hadji Murat took the watch. Several times he pressed the lever, listened, and nodded his head approvingly.

After dinner a valet announced the arrival of General Meller-Zakomel'skii's adjutant.

The adjutant informed the prince, that the general, having heard about Hadji Murat's defection, was very displeased that it had not been reported to him, and he demanded that Hadji Murat be delivered to him immediately. Vorontsov said that the general's order would be carried out at once; then, through the interpreter, he informed Hadji Murat of the general's demand and requested that he accompany him to see Meller.

When she found out why the adjutant had come, Mar'ia Vasil'evna immediately understood that some unpleasantness might take place between the general and her husband and, despite all her husband's attempts to dissuade her, insisted on accompanying him and Hadji Murat to the general's.

"*Vous feriez bien mieux de rester; c'est mon affaire, non pas la vôtre.*"

"*Vous ne pouvez pas m'empêcher d'aller voir madame la generale.*"

["It would be much better for you to stay here. This is my business, not yours."

"You can't stop me from visiting the general's wife."]

"You could do it another time."

"But I want to go now."

There was nothing to be done about it. Vorontsov agreed, so all three of them went to the general's.

When they arrived, Meller with morose civility conducted Mar'ia Vasil'evna to his wife and ordered his adjutant to show Hadji Murat into the waiting room and not to let him go anywhere without orders.

"Please," he said to Vorontsov, opening the door to his study and letting the prince enter first. Entering the study, he stopped in front of the prince and, without asking him to sit down, said: "I am the military commander here and therefore all negotiations with hostile elements must be conducted through me. Why did you not notify me of Hadji Murat's defection?"

"An emissary came to me and announced Hadji Murat's desire to surrender to me," the prince answered, growing pale with excitement and expecting a rude outburst from the enraged general and at the same time becoming infected with the same rage.

"I am asking why you did not notify me."

"I intended to do so, baron, but ..."

"I am not 'baron' to you. My title is 'Your Excellency.'"

And here the baron's pent-up resentment suddenly erupted. He now gave vent to long-accumulated frustrations.

"I have not served my sovereign for twenty-seven years so that people who entered the service yesterday, taking advantage of their family connections, should give orders under my very nose about matters that do not concern them."

"Your Excellency, I beg you not to speak unjustly," Vorontsov interrupted him.

"I'm speaking the truth, and I will not allow ..." the general said even more angrily.

At that moment, her skirts rustling, in came Mar'ia Vasil'evna followed by a slight, modest woman, Mrs. Meller-Zakomel'skii.

"Oh, come, come, General. Simon did not intend to cause you difficulties," Mar'ia Vasil'evna began.

"Princess, I was discussing a business matter ..."

"Well, you know, it's best to leave it at that. You know: a few harsh words are preferable to genuine bad blood. That's what I say," and she began to laugh.

Then the angry general succumbed to the enchanting smile of the beautiful woman. Beneath his mustache a smile was briefly visible.

"I admit that I was out of line," said Vorontsov, " but ..."

"And I got myself worked up," Meller said, and gave his hand to the prince.

A truce was concluded, and it was decided to leave Hadji Murat with Meller, then to send him to the commander of the left flank.

Hadji Murat sat in the next room and, although he did not understand what was being said, he did understand what he needed to understand: that they were quarreling about him; that his defection from Shamil was a matter of enormous importance to the Russians; that, if only they did not banish him or kill him, he could demand a lot from them. Hadji Murat also grasped that although Meller-Zakomel'skii was the army commander, he did not have as much influence as his subordinate Vorontsov, so Vorontsov was important and Meller-Zakomel'skii was not. Therefore, when Meller-Zakomel'skii summoned Hadji Murat for an interview, Hadji Murat behaved in a proud and dignified manner, saying that he had left the mountains to serve the White Tsar and he would give an account about everything only to his *Sardar*, that is, to the commander-in-chief, Prince Vorontsov senior, in Tbilisi.

VII

They took the wounded soldier Avdeev to the hospital, which was located in a small house with plank roofing at the entrance to the fortress, and put him in one of the empty beds in the common ward. There were four patients in the ward: one was tossing about with typhoid fever; another—pale-faced, with blue circles beneath his eyes, feverish—gasped for air between paroxysms of coughing. The other two had been wounded in a raid three weeks earlier: one, hit in the arm, was up and walking around, the other had a shoulder wound and was sitting on a bed. Everyone except the typhus victim gathered around the newly arrived patient and asked questions of those who had brought him in.

"Sometimes they fire as if they are sprinkling peas over you, and nothing happens. And here they fired five shots total," one of those bringing him in commented.

"Each man gets what's ordained to him."

"Ow!" Avdeev cried loudly, as they began to put him on the bed, trying to hold in the pain. When they had laid him on the bed, he frowned and stopped groaning, but continued moving his feet around. He clasped both hands over his wound and stared fixedly straight ahead.

The doctor came in and ordered the wounded man turned over so that he could see whether the bullet had gone out the other side.

"What are these?" the doctor asked, pointing at the large, crisscrossed white scars on his back and buttocks.

"Those are old, Your Honor," mumbled Avdeev with a groan.

They were the marks of his punishment for drinking up the company's money.

The orderlies turned Avdeev back over, and for a long time the doctor rummaged with a probe in Avdeev's stomach, finally found the bullet but couldn't remove it. After closing up the wound and plastering on a bandage, the doctor left. Throughout the whole process of probing and bandaging the wound, Avdeev lay with his teeth clenched and his eyes closed. When the doctor had gone, he opened his eyes and looked around in astonishment. His glance was directed at the patients and the orderly, but it was as if he didn't see them but saw something else that surprised him.

Avdeev's comrades Panov and Seregin came in. Avdeev lay in the same position, staring straight ahead. For a long time, he failed to recognize his comrades, even though his eyes looked right at them.

"Hey, Pyotr, would you like word or something sent home?" Panov asked.

Avdeev didn't answer, although he was looking right at Panov's face.

"I said, would you like word or something sent home?" Panov asked again, touching Avdeev's cold, big-boned hand.

Avdeev seemed to come to. "Ah, Antonych has come."

"Yes, I'm here ... I've come. Do you want to send a letter home? Seregin will write it."

"Seregin," Avdeev said, with difficulty shifting his gaze. "Seregin will write it? Good. Write this: 'Your son, your Petrukha,' tell them, 'orders you to live a long life.' ... Til now I always envied my brother. I was just now talking to you about that. No more. I'm happy. Happy he's still alive. God grant him long life. I'm happy. Write that!"

Having spoken, he was silent for a long time, his eyes still fixed on Panov.

"Hey, you find your pipe?" he asked suddenly.

Panov didn't answer.

"Your pipe, your pipe, I say. You find it?" Avdeev repeated.

"It was in my bag."

"There you are. See? Could you pass me a candle? I'll die soon," Avdeev said.

At that moment, Poltoratskii came in to check on his soldier.

"How's it going, son? Bad?" he asked.

Avdeev closed his eyes and shook his head "no." His face with its high cheekbones was pale and severe. He didn't answer at all, just repeated to Panov: "The little candle; I'm going to die."

They put a candle in his hand. But his fingers wouldn't close around it, so they put it between his fingers and held his hands together for him. Poltoratskii left, and five minutes after his departure the orderly put his ear to Avdeev's chest and said that he was dead.

The report to Tbilisi described Avdeev's death in the following manner: "On November 23 two companies of the Kurinskii Regiment went out from the fortress to fell trees. At mid-morning a large gang of mountaineers suddenly attacked the woodcutters. The line began to fall back, but at that moment the Second Company attacked with bayonets and threw back the mountaineers. In this skirmish, two privates were lightly wounded and one was killed. The mountaineers themselves lost about one hundred men, killed and wounded."

VIII

On the same day that Petrukha Avdeev lay dying in the hospital in Vozdvizhensk, his old father, the wife of the brother for whose sake he went off to be a soldier, and the daughter of the oldest brother—an unmarried maiden—were threshing oats on the hard-frozen threshing room floor. The day before a deep snow had fallen, and toward morning the temperature had plunged far below zero. The old man awakened only with the roosters' third crowing. After seeing the bright light of the moon in the frozen window, he had crawled off the stove shelf, drawn on his shoes, put on his fur coat and hat, and gone to the barn. Having worked there for two hours, the old man went back into the *izba*, then woke his son and the women. When his wife and the teenage girl entered the barn, the threshing floor had been cleaned. In the shifting white snow a wooden shovel stood straight up; a broom, its bristles pointing up, stood alongside it; meanwhile, sheaves of oats were spread out in two rows, laid ear to ear on the threshing floor, so that together they resembled a long thick rope. Each person chose a flail and began to thresh, carefully timing their three blows. The old man struck hard with his heavy flail, breaking the straw, the young maiden struck the tops of the sheaves with measured blows, while the daughter-in-law turned the oats over with her flail.

The moon had set, dawn's light had to begun to break, and they had already finished one line of sheaves when the older son, Akim, in sheepskin coat and hat, came out to the threshers.

"What are you loafing about for?" shouted his father, pausing in his work and leaning on his flail.

"The horses had to be seen to."

"The horses had to be seen to," mimicked his father. "The old woman will see to that. Grab a flail. You've gotten awfully fat, you drunk!"

"What? Have you ever given me anything to drink?" the son mumbled.

"What's that?" the father, frowning and missing a beat with his flail, asked threateningly.

Without saying anything, the son picked up a flail, and the work went on, now with four flails.

"Trup, ta-ta-TRUP. Trup, ta-ta-TRUP!" the old man's flail came down hard after the three lighter blows.

"The back of your neck is clean and white, just like a fine gentleman's! Meantime, I'm working so hard my pants won't even stay up on me," the old man grumbled, skipping his stroke and just swinging the flail in the air, so as to not break his rhythm.

They finished that line of sheaves, and the women began to separate the straw with rakes.

"Petrukha was a fool to go in your place. They'd a beat the nonsense out of you in the army, and he was worth five of the likes of you here at home."

"There now, Papa, why don't you let it be," the daughter-in-law said, removing the broken sheaf bindings.

"Yes, it takes six to feed you, but you don't do one man's share of work. Petrukha, now, he did the work of two men, and not this ..."

Along the narrow tamped-down snow path from the farmyard came the old man's wife, her new bast shoes tied over thick-wrapped leggings. The men raked the unwinnowed grain into piles; the married women and young girl swept up.

"The village elder came by. As our labor dues for the master, everyone is to haul bricks," the old woman said. "I got breakfast together. You're going, right?"

"Harness the roan and ride it," the old man said to Akim. "And watch out so that I don't have to answer for you like the other day. Think how Petrukha would have done it."

"When he was here, you used to swear at him," Akim snapped back at his father. "Now, he's not here, you chew me out."

"Means you deserve it," his mother retorted just as angrily. "We'd never trade Petrukha for you."

"Oh, alright," said the son.

"Some 'alright.' You drank up all the grain, now you say 'alright.'"

"You don't know what you've got til it's gone," said the daughter-in-law, then, after storing the flails, everyone walked back toward the house.

The trouble between father and son had begun a long time earlier, almost from the time Peter went into the army. Even then the old man felt that he was trading a hawk for a cuckoo. Of course, the law, as the old man understood it, specified that a childless man had to go in place of one with children. At the time Akim had four children, Peter none. Still, Peter was the same kind of worker as the old man: skilled, quick on the uptake, strong, durable, and, most importantly, industrious. He was always working. If he happened to pass by where people were working, then, just like his father would have done, he immediately jumped in and helped—he'd take a turn or two with a scythe, or load a wagon, or cut down a tree, or chop some wood. The old man regretted his absence, but there was nothing to be done about it. Being a soldier was like being dead. A soldier was cut off from his family for good, and remembering him just tore at the heart to no purpose. Only rarely, to take a dig at the older son, did the old man recall Peter, as he had just now. The mother, though, often thought of her younger son and long ago, the second year he'd been gone, had asked the old man to send dear Petrukha a little money. But the old man had made no reply.

The Avdeevs' household was wealthy by peasant standards, so the old man had managed to stash some money away, but until now he would never have even considered touching his savings. When the old woman heard him mention his younger son that day, she decided to ask him again, after the oats had been sold, to send her boy something—if only a ruble or two. And she did just that. When she was alone with her husband after the young people had gone to the master's to perform their labor obligations, she talked her husband into sending Petrukha a ruble from the oat money. So when from the piles of winnowed oats twelve *chetverts* had been loaded onto sacking in three carts and the sacking had been securely fastened with pins, she gave the old man a letter dictated by her to the church sacristan; the old man promised to put a ruble in the letter in town and to mail it off.

Dressed in a new fur coat and kaftan and in warm, white, woolen leg wrappings, the old man took the letter, put it in his bag, and, having said a prayer, got into the lead cart and drove to town. His grandson rode in the last cart. In town, the old man ordered the caretaker of the inn to read it to him, and he listened attentively and approvingly.

In the letter, Petrukha's mother sent him first of all her blessing, secondly greetings from everyone else, word of the death of his godfather, and only at the end the news that Pyotr's wife Aksinia "didn't want to stay with them and had gone to town to work. People say she lives well and honestly." The letter referred to the inn, to the ruble, and then there was added, word for word and straight from her heart, what the old woman, overcome with sadness and with tears in her eyes, had ordered the sacristan to write: "And one more thing, my darling child, my little dove, my Petrushenka. I've cried my eyes out over you. I miss you so much. Light of my eyes, will I never see you again? Why have you left me?" At that point, the old woman began to sob and cry, and she said: "Leave it at that!"

And it was left like that in the letter, but Pyotr was not fated to get the news that his wife had left home, nor the ruble, nor his mother's last words. The letter and the money came back with the news that Pyotr had been killed in the war, "defending tsar, fatherland and the Orthodox faith." That was what the army clerk wrote.

When this news reached her, the old woman wailed aloud for as long as time permitted, and then she went back to work. The very next Sunday, she went to church, had the requiem service performed, entered Peter's name in the list of deceased to be remembered in prayers, and she distributed pieces of specially blessed communion bread to "good people in the memory of God's servant, Pyotr."

The soldier's wife, Aksinia, also wailed when she learned about the death of her "beloved husband" with whom she "had lived only one short year." She mourned both her husband and her own wasted life. As she wailed, she remembered "Pyotr Mikhailovich's brown locks and his love, and her bitter life with her orphaned son Van'ka"; and she bitterly reproached "Petrusha for taking pity on his brother and not on her with her bitter wandering life among strangers."

But in the depths of her soul, Aksinia was glad about Pyotr's death. She had gotten pregnant by the assistant in the shop where she lived and worked, and now no one could curse her, and the assistant could marry her the way he said he would when inclining her to make love with him.

IX

Vorontsov, Mikhail Semyonovich, educated in England as the son of the Russian ambassador there, was a rarity among the Russian higher officials at the time by virtue of this European education: he was ambitious, gentle, and affectionate in dealing with his subordinates and a refined courtier in relations with his superiors. He could not understand life without power and submission. He owned all the higher ranks and decorations and considered himself an accomplished soldier, the victor over Napoleon in the battle of Krasnoe. In 1851, he was over seventy but was still quite spry and physically vigorous. Most importantly, he was still in full possession of a subtle and agreeable intellect, which he dedicated wholly to maintaining his own authority and to shoring up and spreading his own popularity. He controlled vast wealth—both his own and that of his wife (*née* Countess Branitskaia), in addition to the enormous salary he received as imperial viceroy, and he spent a large part of his means on the construction of a palace and gardens on the southern coast of the Crimea.

On the evening of December 4, 1851 a courier's troika drove up to his palace in Tbilisi. Weary and black with dust, an officer, who brought news from General Kozlovskii about Hadji Murat's defection to the Russians, stretched his legs, then walked past the guards stationed on the wide front steps of the viceroy's palace. It was six o'clock in the evening, and Vorontsov was going to dinner when they announced to him the courier's arrival. Vorontsov received the courier without delay and therefore was several minutes late for dinner. When he entered the drawing room, the dinner guests, some thirty in all, who were either seated around Princess Elizaveta Ksaver'evna or standing in groups by the windows, now rose and turned toward him. Vorontsov was in his usual black military frock-coat, with half-shoulder straps but without epaulettes, and with the white cross around his neck. His clean-shaven volpine face smiled pleasantly, and his eyes narrowed as he glanced at those gathered around.

Entering the drawing room with soft, hurried steps, he apologized to the women for being late, greeted the men, and, going up to the Georgian Princess Manana Orbeliani, a tall, full-figured, beautiful forty-five-year-old woman of Oriental type, gave her his arm so that he could escort her to the table. Princess Elizaveta Ksaver'evena for her part offered an arm to a newly-arrived ruddy-complected general with a bristly mustache. A Georgian prince gave his arm to Countess Choiseuil, a friend of the hostess. Doctor Andreevskii, the adjutants and others—some with ladies, some without—followed behind these first couples. Footmen in kaftans, knee-breeches, and dress shoes pulled out chairs, then pushed them in for the guests as they took their seats. With a flourish the *maître d'hôtel* ladled steaming soup out of a silver tureen.

Vorontsov sat at the middle of a long table. Opposite him sat his wife alongside the general. To his right sat the beauty, Princess Orbeliani; to his left was a shapely, dark, rosy-cheeked daughter of a Georgian prince, brilliantly adorned and continuously smiling.

"*Excellentes, chère amie,*" ["Excellent, my dear,"] he answered to his wife's question about what kind of news he had gotten from the courier. "*Simon a eu de la chance.*" ["Our son Semyon has had a stroke of luck."]

And he began to relate, in such a way that all those sitting at the table could hear, the stunning news—for him alone it wasn't completely news, since the negotiations had already been going on for some time—that the famous Hadji Murat, Shamil's bravest lieutenant, had handed himself over to the Russians and would be brought to Tbilisi in two days.

All the guests, even the young adjutants and officials seated at the far end of the table who till then had been laughing to themselves about something, grew quiet and listened.

After the prince had finished speaking, the princess asked of her neighbor, the ruddy-faced general with the bristly moustache, "And you, general. Have you ever encountered this Hadji Murat?"

"More than once, princess."

And the general related how in 1843, after the mountaineers had captured Gergebil'e, Hadji Murat had stumbled upon General Passek's detachment and how he had almost killed Colonel Zolotukhin before their very eyes.

With a pleasant smile on his face Vorontsov listened to the general's story, evidently pleased that the general had involved himself in the conversation. But suddenly Vorontsov's face took on a vacant, dejected expression.

The general, having warmed to the topic, had begun to tell how he had run up against Hadji Murat on another occasion.

"Why, he was the same one," the general said, "if it will please Your Excellency to remember, who ambushed the biscuit expedition, just before the rescue."

"Where?" asked the count, narrowing his eyes.

What the brave general called the "rescue" was the unfortunate Dargo campaign, in which Prince Vorontsov's entire detachment would surely have perished had suddenly approaching troops not rescued them. Everyone knew that, under Vorontsov's command, the entire Dargo campaign, in which the Russians lost many men killed and wounded and several pieces of artillery, had been an embarrassment, and, therefore, if anyone spoke at all of that campaign under Vorontsov, they spoke of it only in the way that Vorontsov had characterized it in his report to the tsar—namely, as a brilliant feat of Russian arms. The very word "rescue" indicated that it was not a brilliant achievement, but a mistake that cost many lives. Everyone understood this, so some acted as if they didn't understand the significance of the general's words, while others nervously waited to see what would happen next; still others, smiling, exchanged glances. Only the ruddy-faced general with the bristly mustache noticed nothing and, carried away by his story, calmly answered, "Before the 'rescue,' Your Excellency."

And once launched on his favorite subject, the general related in detail how "this Hadji Murat so deftly cut the detachment in two that, had the rescue unit

not arrived"—he seemed to take special relish in repeating the word "rescue"—
"the entire detachment would have perished on that very spot, because ..."

The general did not manage to finish his story, because Manana Orbeliani,
having grasped what was happening, interrupted him, asking him about the
comfort of his quarters in Tbilisi. The general, astonished, looked at everyone
around the table and at his aide-de-camp at the end of the table, who was
looking back at him with a fixed and meaningful stare—and suddenly he understood. Without answering the princess, he frowned, fell silent, and began
hurriedly eating, without chewing, the delicacy that lay on his plate, the appearance and even the taste of which were incomprehensible to him.

The situation had become awkward for everyone, but the awkward situation
was relieved by the Georgian prince seated on the other side of Princess
Vorontsova. A very stupid man but an exceptionally delicate and artful flatterer
and courtier, he began, as if noticing nothing, loudly to relate the tale of Hadji
Murat's abduction of the widow of Akhmet Khan of Mekhtulina: "He entered
the village at night, grabbed what he wanted, and galloped off along with his
entire party."

"What exactly did he want with that particular woman?" the princess asked.

"Well, he was an enemy of her husband; he tracked him but never caught
him, so when the khan himself died, he took vengeance on the widow."

The princess translated this into French for her old friend Countess Choiseul,
who was seated beside the Georgian prince.

"*Quelle horreur!*" ["How terrible!"] said the countess, closing her eyes and
shaking her head.

"Oh, no," Vorontsov said, smiling, "They tell me that he treated his prisoner
with chivalrous respect and later freed her.

"Yes, for a ransom."

"Well, of course, but nevertheless he acted nobly."

These words of the prince set the tone for further stories about Hadji Murat.
The courtiers understood that the more significance they attributed to Hadji
Murat, the more pleasant it would be for the prince.

"The astounding daring of the man! A remarkable fellow!"

"I'll say! In '49, in broad daylight, he burst into Temir-Khan-Shura and plundered the shops."

Sitting at the end of the table, an Armenian who had been in Temir-Khan-
Shura at the time, related that exploit of Hadji Murat in detail.

Almost the entire dinner passed in conversation about Hadji Murat. Everyone
without exception praised his bravery, his intellect, his magnanimity. Someone told
how he had ordered the execution of twenty-six prisoners; even that elicited the
same reaction: "What's to be done? *À la guerre, comme à la guerre.*" ["War is war."]

"He is a great man."

"Had he been born in Europe, he perhaps might have been a new
Napoleon," said the stupid Georgian prince who had the gift of flattery.

He knew that every reference to Napoleon, for victory over whom Vorontsov wore the white cross of St. George on his neck, was pleasant to Vorontsov.

"Well, perhaps not Napoleon, but a dashing cavalry general, at any rate," said Vorontsov.

"If not Napoleon, then Murat."

"And look: his name is Hadji Murat."

"Hadji Murat has defected; this is the end for Shamil," someone said.

"They feel that now" (that "now" meant "under Vorontsov") "they can't hold out," someone else said.

"*Tout cela est grâce à vous*," ["All of this is thanks to you,"] Manana Orbeliani said to Vorontsov.

Prince Vorontsov tried to moderate the waves of flattery, which had already begun to flood over him. But it was pleasing to him, and in the very best of moods he led his wife to the drawing room.

After dinner, when coffee was brought to the drawing room, the prince was particularly amiable with everyone and approached the general with the bristly red mustache to try to show him that he had not noticed the general's *faux pas*.

Having made a round of all the guests, the prince sat down to play cards. He played only the old-fashioned game of bridge. The prince's partners were: the Georgian prince; the Armenian general, who had learned his bridge from the prince's valet; and Doctor Andreevskii, a first-rate player.

Laying beside him a gold snuff box with a portrait of Alexander I, Vorontsov tore open a pack of satin-surfaced playing cards and was about to shuffle them, when his valet, the Italian Giovanni, entered with a letter on a silver tray.

"Another courier, Your Excellency."

Vorontsov put down the cards and, having excused himself, broke the seal on the letter and began to read.

The letter was from his son. He described the surrender of Hadji Murat and the conflict with Meller-Zakomel'skii.

The princess approached and asked what their son had written.

"It's all about this same business. *Il a eu quelques désagréments avec le commandant de la place. Simon a eu tort.* But all is well that ends well," ["He had some disagreements with the commandant of the place. Simon was at fault. But all is well that ends well,"] he said, handing the letter to his wife, then, turning to his partners who were waiting deferentially, asked them to draw their cards.

When the first hand had been dealt, Vorontsov opened the snuff box and did that which he was in the habit of doing when he was in a particularly good mood: taking a pinch of French snuff in his aged, wrinkled white fingers, he lifted it to his nose and released it.

X

The next day, when Hadji Murat arrived at the Vorontsovs' palace, the waiting room was full of people. Here, in full dress uniform and medals, was yesterday's old, bristly-moustached general, who had come to take his leave; here too was a regimental commander, who faced the threat of court-martial over misuse of the regimental mess fund; here was a wealthy Armenian, a protégé of Doctor Andreevskii, who held a state license to sell vodka in the region and was now petitioning for renewal of his contract; also here, dressed in black, was a slain officer's widow who had come to request a pension for housing her children at public expense; here in magnificent Georgian attire was a penniless Georgian prince who was trying to obtain for himself an estate that had been confiscated from the church; here was a police official holding a bulky file containing a new plan for subjugating the Caucasus; here finally was a khan who had shown up only so that he could tell the people at home that he had been at the prince's palace.

They all waited their turn, and one after the other were shown into the prince's office by the handsome, fair-haired young aide-de-camp.

When Hadji Murat entered the room striding briskly despite his limp, all eyes turned to him, and he heard his name pronounced in whispers from various parts of the room.

Hadji Murat was dressed in a long, white Circassian coat over a brown cotton dressing gown with a delicate, silver lace around the collar. He wore black leggings and soft shoes of the same color, which were stretched like gloves over his instep. On his head was a Caucasian fur cap and a turban, the very same turban for which he, after being denounced by Akhmet-Khan, had been arrested by General Klugenau and which had been the reason he joined Shamil. Hadji Murat walked quickly across the parquet floor of the anteroom, his entire thin figure swaying from the slight lameness in one leg, which was slightly shorter than the other. His widely-spaced eyes calmly looked straight ahead and, it seemed, saw no one.

Having greeted him, the handsome aide-de-camp asked Hadji Murat to have a seat, while he announced his arrival to the prince. But Hadji Murat declined to sit down and, placing his hand on his dagger and moving one foot back a bit, disdainfully looked around at all those present.

The interpreter, Prince Tarkhanov, went up to Hadji Murat and struck up a conversation. Hadji Murat responded reluctantly and tersely. A Ghumuq prince came out of the office, where he had lodged a complaint against a police official, and behind him came the aide-de-camp who summoned Hadji Murat, led him to the office door and showed him in.

Vorontsov received Hadji Murat standing at the corner of his desk. The old white face of the commander-in-chief was not the smiling face of the day before, but a rather stern and solemn one.

Entering into the large room with its enormous desk, large windows, and green Venetian blinds, Hadji Murat placed his small, sunburned hands on his chest at the spot where the lapels of his white Circassian coat overlapped, and, using the Ghumuq dialect that he spoke well, he declared unhurriedly, distinctly, and respectfully: "I surrender to the exalted protection of the great Tsar and yourself. I sincerely pledge to serve the White Tsar to the last drop of my blood, and I hope to be useful in the war against Shamil, my enemy and yours."

Having heard out the interpreter, Vorontsov looked at Hadji Murat and Hadji Murat looked into the face of Vorontsov.

The eyes of the two men met and said to each other much that was inexpressible by words, something entirely different from what the translator said. Directly and without words, the eyes communicated to the other party the whole truth. Vorontsov's eyes said that he did not believe a single word that Hadji Murat had spoken, that he knew Hadji Murat was the enemy of every Russian and always would be, and that Hadji Murat was submitting to them now only because he had been forced to do so. Hadji Murat grasped this and nevertheless made assurances of his loyalty. Meanwhile, Hadji Murat's eyes were saying that an old man ought to be thinking about death, not about war; and that he, although aging, was still cunning, and so must be dealt with cautiously. Vorontsov understood this and, in spite of it, related to Hadji Murat his conditions for concluding the war successfully.

"Tell him, son," Vorontsov said to the interpreter (he used the informal "you" with the young officer), "that our sovereign is as gracious as he is mighty, and that, most likely, if I so request, the tsar will pardon him and take him into his service. Did you tell him that?" he asked, looking at Hadji Murat. "Until such time as I shall receive the gracious decision of my sovereign, tell him that I take it on myself to receive him and to make his stay with us pleasant."

Hadji Murat once again placed his hands on the center of his breast and then spoke with animation.

He said through the translator that even before this occasion, in 1839 when he governed Avaria, he had faithfully served the Russians and never would have betrayed them had his enemy, Akhmet-Khan, who wanted to destroy him, not slandered him to General Klugenau.

"I know, I know," said Vorontsov (although if he ever had known this, he had long since forgotten it). "I know," he said, sitting down and gesturing toward the ottoman that stood by the wall. But Hadji Murat did not sit down, shrugging his powerful shoulders as a sign that he could not bring himself to sit in the presence of such an important man.

"Akhmet-Khan and Shamil, both are my enemies," he continued, turning to the interpreter. "Tell the prince that Akhmet-Khan is dead, so I cannot revenge myself on him, but Shamil is still alive, and I will not die without having paid him back," he said, knitting his brows and clenching his jaws tightly.

"Yes, yes," Vorontsov said calmly. "How exactly does he want to pay Shamil back?" he said to the interpreter. "And tell him that he can sit down."

Hadji Murat again declined to sit and, in answer to the question, said that he had gone over to the Russians precisely to help them destroy Shamil.

"Fine. Fine," said Vorontsov. "What exactly does he want to do? Sit down, boy. Sit down."

Hadji Murat sat down and said, that if they would only send him to the Lezgian front and give him some troops, that he would guarantee to raise the whole of Daghestan and Shamil would not be able to hold out.

"That's good. That could be done," Vorontsov said. "I'll need to think a little about it."

The interpreter translated Vorontsov's words for Hadji Murat. Hadji Murat pondered them for a moment.

"Tell the *Sardar*," he added, "that my family is in the hands of my enemy; and as long as my family is in the mountains, my hands are tied and I cannot serve him. Shamil will kill my wife, kill my mother, kill my children, if I come out openly against him. If the prince will only rescue my family, exchange some prisoners for them, then I shall die or destroy Shamil."

"Good, good," Vorontsov said. "We will think about it. Right now have him go to the chief of staff and lay out in detail to him his situation, intentions, and requests."

Thus ended the first meeting between Hadji Murat and Vorontsov.

Later on that same day, in the evening, in the new theater that had been decorated in the Oriental style, there was an Italian opera. Vorontsov was in his loge, while in the parterre there appeared the striking figure of the limping Hadji Murat replete with turban. He entered with Vorontsov's aide-de-camp, Loris-Melikov, who had been assigned to accompany him, and he took a seat in the front row. With Oriental, Muslim dignity that expressed not wonder but studied indifference, Hadji Murat sat through the first act, then rose to his feet and, calmly glancing over the audience, left the theater, attracting to himself the attention of the entire audience.

The next day was a Monday, the day of the Vorontsovs' weekly dinner party. In the large, brightly-lit hall, music carried discreetly from an artificial winter garden. Young and not so young women in dresses that revealed their necks and arms and nearly bared their bosoms twirled in the embrace of men in colorful uniforms. At the mountainous buffet footmen in red frock coats, knee breeches, and polished shoes poured out champagne and carried around candies for the ladies. The "*Sardar*'s" wife who, despite her advanced years, was also half-naked, circulated among the guests, smiling warmly; she even said through the interpreter several kind words of welcome to Hadji Murat, who looked around at the guests with the same indifference that he had exhibited the evening before at the theater. Following the hostess's example, other women in revealing attire also approached Hadji Murat, and each of them stood in front of him without feeling any shame and smilingly asked him the very same question: How did he like what he saw? Vorontsov himself, in gold epaulettes and gold aiguillettes and with his white cross and ribbon around his neck, went up to him and asked him the same question, evidently certain, as were all those who asked, that Hadji Murat could not help but like what he saw. And Hadji Murat responded to Vorontsov the same way he responded to all the others: that among his people there was nothing like this, but without indicating whether it was good or bad that they did not have this among his people.

Hadji Murat made an effort right there at the ball to start a conversation with Vorontsov about the business of ransoming his family, but Vorontsov, acting as if he did not hear the words, walked away from him. Loris-Melikov himself later told Hadji Murat that a ball was no place to discuss business.

When it struck 11 o'clock and Hadji Murat had checked the time on the watch given to him by Mar'ia Vasilievena, he asked Loris-Melikov if he could leave. Loris-Melikov said that he could, but that it would be better to stay. In spite of this, Hadji Murat did not stay and drove off in the carriage placed at his disposal to his assigned quarters.

XI

On the fifth day of Hadji Murat's stay in Tbilisi, Loris-Melikov, the viceroy's aide-de-camp, came to see him at the commander-in-chief's direction.

"With my head and my hands, I am happy to serve the *Sardar*," Hadji Murat said, with his usual diplomatic expression, bowing his head and placing his hands on his breast. "I await your command, young man," he said, looking gently into Loris-Melikov's face.

Loris-Melikov sat down in the armchair next to the desk. Hadji Murat lowered himself onto a low ottoman opposite the armchair and, propping his arms on his knees, inclined his head and began attentively to listen to what Loris-Melikov was telling him. Loris-Melikov, speaking in fluent Tatar, said that the prince, although he already knew about Hadji Murat's past, wanted to hear the whole story from Hadji Murat himself.

"Kindly tell it to me," Loris-Melikov said, "and I'll write it down, translate it into Russian later, and the prince will send it to the tsar."

Hadji Murat sat silent for a moment. (He not only never interrupted another's conversation, but also always waited to see whether his interlocutor had something further to say.) Then he raised his head, and having pushed the turban back on his head, he smiled that peculiar, childlike smile that had captivated Mar'ia Vasil'evna.

"That I can do," he said, evidently gratified by the thought that his story would be read by the emperor.

"You tell it to me," Loris-Melikov said, using the informal "you," since Tatar does not have the formal "you," "from the beginning without hurrying." Meanwhile, he produced a notebook from his pocket.

"I can do that, only there is a great deal, a very great deal, to tell. Many things have happened," said Hadji Murat.

"If you don't manage it all in one day, you may finish the story another day," Loris-Melikov said.

"Start from the beginning?"

"Yes, from the very beginning. Where were you born? Where did you live?"

Hadji Murat lowered his head and sat like that for a long time. Then he took a stick that was laying on the couch, drew from beneath his dagger an ivory-handled knife decorated with gold and having a razor-sharp damask steel blade, and began to whittle the stick with it and at the same time to tell his story.

"I was born in Tsel'mes, a small *awul*, 'the size of an ass's head,' as we say in the mountains. Not far from us, about the distance of two rifle shots, was Khunzakh, where the khans lived. And our family was close to theirs. My mother nursed the oldest khan, Abununtsal-Khan, and for that reason I also became close to the khans. There were three khans: Abununtsal-Khan, who was 'milk brother' of my brother Osman; Umma-Khan, my blood brother; and Bulach-Khan, the one Shamil threw off the cliff. But that was later.

"I was about fifteen when the *murids* began coming around the *awuls*. They beat on stones with wooden sabers and cried: 'Muslims, a holy war!' All the Chechens had joined the *murids*, even the Avars were beginning to join them. At that point I was living in the palace. I was like a brother to the khans: what I wanted to do, I did, and I had become rich. I had horses, and weapons and money. I lived a life of pleasure, not a thought in my head. That was how I lived until Kazi-Mula was killed and Hamza took his place. Hamza sent the khans emissaries to say that, if they did not accept the holy war, he would destroy Khunzakh. Now for the first time I was forced to think. The khans were afraid of the Russians, they were afraid to join the holy war, so the *khansha* sent me and her second son, Umma-Khan, to Tbilisi to request help against Hamza from the Russian chief commander. The chief commander was Rozen, a baron. He wouldn't see me or Umma-Khan. He passed word that he would help us, but he did nothing. Only his officers started visiting us and playing cards with Umma-Khan. They got him drunk on wine, they took him to sinful places, he lost to them at cards everything he owned. He was strong in body, like a bull, and brave as a lion, but in soul he was weak as water. He would have lost his last horses and his own weapon if I had not led him away. After Tbilisi my thinking changed, so I tried to persuade the *khansha* and the young khans to join the holy war."

"Why did your thinking change?" asked Loris-Melikov. "Did you not like the Russians?"

Hadji Murat fell silent for a moment.

"No, I did not like them," he said forcefully and then closed his eyes. "And then there was an incident that made me want to accept the holy war."

"What sort of incident?"

"Near Tsel'mes the khan and I ran across three *murids*: two escaped, but I killed the third with my pistol. When I went to take away his weapon, he was still alive. He looked at me. 'You,' he says, 'have killed me. All is well with me. But you are a Muslim, you are young and strong, so join the holy war. God commands it.'"

"So then you joined it?"

"No, I didn't join it, but I began to think," said Hadji Murat, and he continued his account. "When Hamza approached Khunzakh, we sent him old men as emissaries and commanded them to say that we would agree to the holy war if only he would send us a learned young man to explain how we should undertake

114

it. Hamza commanded his forces to shave the old men's moustaches, to pierce
their nostrils, affix to their noses tablets of submission, and send them back. The
old men said that Hamza was prepared to send us a spiritual instructor to teach
us how to undertake the holy war, but only if the *khansha* would send her younger
son to him as a hostage. The *khansha* trusted Hamza and sent him Bulach-Khan.
Hamza received Bulach-Khan with respect and then asked us to send him the
older brothers as well. He commanded the emissaries to say that he wished to
serve the khans just as his father had served their father. The *khansha* was a
woman – weak, stupid and impulsive, like all women are when they live without a
man's guidance. She was afraid to send both her older sons and sent only Umma-
Khan. I rode with him. A verst outside of the village we were met by *murids* who
sang, shot their weapons, and cavorted around us. And when we rode up, Hamza
came out of this tent, walked up to the side of his horse and welcomed Umma-
Khan as royalty. He said: 'I have not done your house any harm and do not wish
to do any in future. You have only not to attack me and not to hinder my effort to
lead the people on a holy war. Then I shall serve you with all my forces, just as my
father served yours. Permit me to live in your house. I shall offer you my counsel,
and you may do what you wish.' Umma-Khan was obtuse in speech. He did not
know what to say, so he remained silent. Then I said that if that were Hamza's
intention, we should permit him to ride to Khunzakh. The *khansha* and khan
would receive him with honor. But they did not allow me to finish speaking, and
here for the first time I encountered Shamil. He was there also, next to the imam.
'They do not ask you, but the khan,' he said to me. I fell silent. While Hamza
escorted Umma-Khan to the tent I rode off for Khunzakh. Then emissaries
began to implore the *khansha* to send the eldest son to Hamza. I saw the treachery
and warned the *khansha* not to send her remaining son. But a woman has as much
intelligence as an egg has hair. The *khansha* trusted Hamza and commanded her
son to go. Abununtsal did not want to go. Then she said; 'It is clear that you are
afraid.' Like a bee, she knew where to sting him. Abununtsal lost his temper,
stopped speaking with her, and commanded his horse to be saddled. I rode with
him. Hamza received us even more warmly than Umma-Khan. He himself rode
out to meet us with two rifle shots from the mountain. Behind him rode mounted
cavalry with banners; they sang, 'There is no god but God!'; they shot their rifles
and cavorted. When we rode up to camp, Hamza led the khan into the tent.
Meanwhile, I stayed with the horses. I was at the foot of the mountain when the
shooting began in Hamza's tent. I rushed toward the tent. Umma-Khan lay on
the ground in a pool of blood, while Abununtsal fought with the *murids*. Half his
face had been cut off and hung suspended by the remaining skin. He held it with
one hand, and with the other used his dagger to slash anyone who came near
him. After I arrived, he cut down one of Hamza's brothers and had lunged
toward another before the *murids* shot him, and then he fell."

Hadji Murat stopped talking, his sunburned face flushed angrily, and his eyes
filled with blood.

"Terror seized me, and I ran away."

"Can that be?" said Loris-Melikov. "I thought you have never been afraid of anything."

"After that, never; from that moment I have always remembered my shame, and when I have remembered it, then I am no longer afraid."

XII

"Enough for now! I must pray," Hadji Murat said. From the inside pocket of his Circassian coat he pulled the Breguet watch Vorontsov had given him, carefully pressed the spring and, having tilted his head to the side while repressing a child-like smile, he listened. The watch chimed out twelve and a quarter.

"A present from *Kunak* Vorontsov," he said, smiling. "Good man."

"Yes, he is a good man," Loris-Melikov said. "The watch is also good. Now, you pray. I'll wait until you're finished."

"*Iakshi*." ["Good."] Hadji Murat said and went to his bedroom.

Left alone, Loris-Melikov transcribed into his notebook the most important points of Hadji Murat's narrative, then lit a cigarette and began to pace back and forth across the room. When he reached the door opposite Hadji Murat's bedroom, Loris-Melikov heard the animated voices of people rapidly speaking in Tatar. He guessed that the voices belonged to Hadji Murat's *murids* and, opening the door, he entered their room.

In the room hung that sour, leathery smell peculiar to mountain folk. On a *burka* on the floor next to the window sat one-eyed, red-haired Gamzalo in a torn, dirty *beshmet* plaiting a bridle. He was speaking heatedly in his hoarse voice, but on Loris-Melikov's entry, he immediately fell silent and, taking no notice of the interloper, continued what he was doing. Opposite him stood the merry Khan-Mahoma; baring his white teeth and flashing his black lashless eyes, he was repeating the same phrase over and over. Handsome Eldar, sleeves rolled up on his powerful arms, was rubbing down the girths of a saddle suspended from a nail. Khanefi, the chief worker and the manager of the household, was not in the room. He was cooking dinner in the kitchen.

"What were you arguing about?" Loris-Melikov asked Khan-Mahoma, after he had greeted them.

"Oh, he keeps praising Shamil," Khan-Mahoma said, offering his hand to Loris. "He says Shamil is a great man. He's learned, a man of God, and a *dzhigit*."

"How is it he left Shamil but still praises him?"

"Left, but praises," muttered Khan-Mahoma, baring his teeth and flashing his eyes.

"What about you, lad? Do you think Shamil is a man of God?" Loris-Melikov asked.

"If he wasn't a man of God, the people would not listen to him," said Gamzalo quickly.

"Shamil is no man of God, but Mansur was," Khan-Mahoma said. "He was a true man of God. When he was imam, the whole people was different. He

rode on horseback from *awul* to *awul*, everyone came out to kiss the hem of his
Circassian coat, they repented their sins and vowed to live right. Old men claim
that in those days everybody lived as God intended – nobody smoked, nobody
drank, nobody skipped prayers, everyone forgave insults even when blood had
been spilled. In those days, lost money and belongings, as soon as they had been
found, were tied to a staff and left by the side of the road. In those days, God
smiled on the entire people; things were different then," Khan-Mahoma said.

"But today in the mountains people still don't drink or smoke," Gamzalo said.

"Your Shamil is a *lamora*," Khan-Mahoma said, winking at Loris-Melikov.

"*Lamora*" was a contemptuous epithet, meaning "rock dweller."

"A 'rock dweller' is a true mountain man," Gamzalo replied, "And mountains
are the eagles' home."

"Well said, youngster! You cut me to the quick!" Khan-Mahoma said, baring
his teeth and enjoying his opponent's skillful retort.

Eyeing the silver cigarette case in Loris-Melikov's hand, Khan-Mahoma asked
for a smoke. When Loris-Melikov said that a Muslim shouldn't smoke, Khan-
Mahoma winked, nodded toward Hadji Murat's bedroom, and said that it was
all right, so long as the authorities didn't notice. At once he lit up without
puffing, awkwardly pursing his red lips while releasing the smoke.

"That is wrong!" Gamzalo said sternly and left the room. Khan-Mahoma
winked again and, cigarette in mouth, began to question Loris-Melikov about
the best place to buy a silk *beshmet* and a white Causcasian fur cap.

"What, lad? You think you've got enough money?"

" 'Course I do," Khan-Mahoma answered, winking.

"Ask him where he got the money," Eldar said, turning his handsome smiling
face toward Loris.

"I won it gambling," Khan-Mahoma quickly replied, relating how yesterday,
walking around Tbilisi, he had happened on a small cluster of men—Russian
day laborers and Armenians—pitching coins. The pot was big: three gold coins
and a pile of silver ones. Khan-Mahoma immediately got the game's drift, and,
jingling the copper coins in his pocket, stepped into the middle of the circle and
said that he'd bet the whole pot.

"The whole pot? You have that much?" Loris-Melikov asked.

"All I had on me was twenty kopecks, total," Khan-Mahoma said, showing his
teeth.

"What if you'd lost?"

"Then, this." And Khan-Mahoma indicated his pistol.

"You'd have traded your gun?"

"Why trade? I'd have run for it; anyone tried to stop me, I'd 've killed him. I'd
have done it, too."

"But you won."

"Yep! I grabbed the stakes and took off."

Loris-Melikov understood Khan-Mahoma and Eldar completely. Khan-
Mahoma was a happy-go-lucky type living fast and loose, not knowing what to

do with his high spirits, always cheerful but heedless, someone gambling with his own life and the lives of others, a man willing to risk his life today by defecting to the Russians and just as willing to risk it again tomorrow by going back to Shamil. Eldar was also an open book: a man completely devoted to his *murshid*, a man calm, strong, and firm. The only one Loris-Melikov couldn't understand was red-headed Gamzalo. He could see that this man was not only devoted to Shamil, but felt an insurmountable repugnance, contempt, disgust, and hatred toward all Russians; for this reason Loris-Melikov could not grasp why Gamzalo had defected to the Russians. Loris-Melikov had been wondering, as had several other leading officials, whether the desertion of Hadji Murat and his stories of enmity with Shamil were deceptions, whether he had defected only to scout out the Russians' weaknesses and whether, after escaping into the mountains, he would then direct Chechen forces against the Russians' vulnerable spots. With every fiber of his being Gamzalo seemed to confirm this hypothesis. "Hadji Murat and the others know how to conceal their true intentions," Loris-Melikov thought to himself, "but this one betrays himself by his unconcealed hatred."

Loris-Melikov tried to engage Gamzalo in conversation. He asked whether he was bored. Without putting down his work, Gamzalo glanced sideways out of his one good eye at Loris–Melikov and growled: "No, I'm not bored."

He answered all Loris-Melikov's other questions the same way.

While Loris Melikov was in the bodyguards' room, there entered Hadji Murat's fourth *murid*, the Avar Khanefi, a man with a hirsute face and neck, his barrel chest shaggy, as if overgrown with moss. A robust, uncomplaining worker who was always engrossed in some activity, he was, like Eldar, unconditionally obedient to his master.

When Khanefi entered the bodyguards' room looking for some rice, Loris-Melikov stopped him and asked where he was from and whether he had been with Hadji Murat a long time.

"Five years," Khanefi replied to Loris-Melikov's question. "We are from the same *awul*. My father killed his uncle, so his family plotted to kill me," he said, looking calmly into Loris-Melikov's face from beneath his thick eyebrows. "That was when I asked him to accept me as a brother."

"What does that mean: 'to accept as a brother?'"

"I didn't shave my head for two months, didn't cut my nails, and I went to them. They let me in to see Patimat, his mother. Patimat received me with open arms, so I became his brother."

Hadji Murat's voice sounded in the next room. Eldar immediately recognized his master's summons; having wiped his hands, he briskly strode into the drawing room.

"He is asking for you," he said on returning. Having passed a cigarette to the happy-go-lucky Khan-Mahoma, Loris-Melikov went to the drawing room.

XIII

When Loris-Melikov entered the drawing room, Hadji Murat greeted him with a smiling face.

"So, to continue?" he said, taking a seat on the low divan.

"Yes. Absolutely," Loris-Melikov said. "I just went to see your bodyguards and had a nice talk with them. The one is a cheerful fellow," he added.

"Yes, Khan-Mahoma, he's friendly," Hadji Murat said.

"But I liked the young, handsome one."

"Ah, Eldar. That one's young, but tough as nails."

They fell silent.

"So, to go on?"

"Yes. Yes."

"I told you how they murdered the khans. After killing them, Hamza entered Khunzakh and settled in the khans' palace," Hadji Murat began. "The *khansha* was still alive. Hamza summoned her. She began telling him off. He motioned to his *murid* Asel'der, and he struck her from behind, killed her."

"Why did he have to kill her, too?"

"Why do you think? You start something, you finish it. They had to finish off the whole clan. So they did. Shamil killed the youngest son, threw him off a cliff."

"All Avaria was submitting to Hamza; only my brother and I decided not to submit. We had to have his blood to avenge the khans. So we pretended to submit but thought only how to spill his blood. We talked it over with grandfather and decided to wait until Hamza came out of his palace, then we'd ambush him and kill him. Someone overheard us, told Hamza, so he summoned grandfather and said: 'See here, if it's true your grandsons are plotting to do me harm, I'll hang you and them together from the same rafter. I'm doing God's work, so it's wrong to get in my way. Go home, old man, and remember what I said.'

"Grandfather came home and gave us the message. Then we decided not to wait, but to move on the first day of holiday at the mosque. Our comrades refused to help; that left me and my brother. We each took two pistols, put on our felt cloaks, and went to the mosque. Hamza came in with thirty *murids*. They were all carrying drawn swords. Next to Hamza was Asel'der, his favorite *murid*, the same one who'd cut off the khansha's head. When he spotted us, he shouted at us to remove our felt cloaks, then he came at me. I had my dagger in my hand, so I killed him and threw myself at Hamza. But my brother, Osman, had already shot him. Hamza was still alive, he lunged toward my brother, but I cut off his head. There were thirty *murids* against us two. They killed my brother Osman, but I beat them back, jumped out a window and escaped.

"When people learned that Hamza had been killed, the whole population rose up, the *murids* fled, and those that didn't were killed."

Hadji Murat stopped and took a deep breath.

"That was all good," he continued, "later it all went bad. Shamil took Hamza's place. He sent envoys to me to say that I should join him against the

Russians; if I refused, he would destroy Khunzakh and kill me. I told him I wouldn't join him and wouldn't let him near me."

"Why didn't you join him?" Loris-Melikov asked.

Hadji Murat frowned and didn't answer immediately.

"It would have been wrong. The blood of my brother Osman and of Abununtsal-Khan was on Shamil. I didn't join him. Rozen, the general, sent me an officer's commission and ordered me to take command of Avaria. That would have been alright, but Rozen had already appointed Kazi-Ghumuq Khan Mahomet-Murzu and Akhmet-Khan. That one hated me. He had promised his son to the *khansha's* daughter, Saltanet. The *khansha's* family would not give Saltanet to him, and he thought I was to blame for this. He came to hate me and sent his men to kill me, but I evaded them. Then he lied about me to General Klugenau, saying that I refused to order the Avars to give firewood to the soldiers. He also said that I wore a turban, this very one," Hadji Murat said, indicating the turban on his Circassian cap, "and said this meant I had joined Shamil. The general did not believe this lie, so he did not arrest me. But after the general left for Tbilisi, Akhmet-Khan did what he pleased; a company of his soldiers seized me, put me in irons and tied me to a cannon.

"Six days and nights they kept me like that. On the seventh day they untied me and took me to Temir-Khan-Shura. Forty soldiers with loaded rifles escorted me. My hands were bound, the soldiers had orders to kill me if I tried to escape. I knew that. When we began our approach, alongside the Moksokh River the path was narrow, on the right was a cliff that dropped over a hundred feet. I moved to the right, away from my escort toward the edge of the cliff. A soldier tried to stop me, but I jumped over the edge and pulled him along with me. The soldier died in the fall, but I survived. My ribs, arms, legs—all were broken and my skull was cracked. I tried to crawl, but couldn't. My head began to spin, I passed out. Woke up soaked, in a pool of my own blood. A shepherd spotted me. He called for help, people carried me into the *awul*. My ribs and head mended; my leg mended too, only shorter."

And Hadji Murat extended his crooked leg.

"Still serves me well," he said. "When people found out what happened, they visited me. I healed up, moved to Tsel'mes. Again, the Avars asked me to rule them," said Hadji Murat with calm, assured pride. "I agreed."

Hadji Murat rose quickly; taking a letter pouch out of his saddlebag, he pulled out two yellowed letters and handed them to Loris-Melikov. The letters were from General Klugenau. Loris-Melikov read them through. In the first letter, Klugenau wrote:

"Ensign Hadji Murat. You served under me. I was satisfied with you and considered you a good man. Not long ago Major-General Akhmet-Khan informed me that you are a traitor, that you have donned the turban, that you are in communication with Shamil, that you have instructed the people not to obey Russian authorities. I ordered you arrested and brought to me. You fled. I don't know whether this is for the best or not, because I don't know whether you are guilty or not. Listen to me now. If your conscience is clean before the great tsar, if you are innocent, come to me. Fear nothing; I am your defender. The khan will not harm you; he is under my command. Therefore, you have nothing to fear."

Klugenau added that he always keeps his word and is just; again he exhorted Hadji Murat to come to him.

After Loris-Melikov had finished the first letter, Hadji Murat opened the second letter, but before handing it to Loris-Melikov, he related how he had answered the first letter.

"I wrote him that I wear the turban not for Shamil, but to save my soul; that I don't want to join and cannot join Shamil, because my father, brothers, and other relatives were killed through him; I wrote I couldn't come over to the Russians either, because they had dishonored me. In Khunzakh, when I was tied up, some bastard sp ... spit on me. So I can't join you until this man has been killed. Mainly, though, I fear that liar Akhmet-Khan. Then the general sent me this letter," said Hadji Murat, handing Loris-Melikov the other yellowed piece of paper.

"You answered my letter. Thank you," Loris-Melikov read. "You write that you are not afraid to change your allegiance, but the dishonor inflicted on you by an infidel forbids it. I assure you Russian law is just, and with your own eyes you will see the punishment of the man who dared to insult you. I have already ordered an investigation. Listen, Hadji Murat. I have the right to be dissatisfied with you, because you doubt me and my honor, but I forgive you, knowing the mistrustful character of most mountain folk. If your conscience is clean, if you really donned the turban to save your soul, then you are a righteous man and can look the Russian government and me in the eye; those who disgraced you, I assure you, will be punished, *your property will be returned to you,* and you will see for yourself what Russian justice can do. Anyway, Russians look at things differently; in their eyes it does you no discredit that some pig disgraced you. I myself have permitted the Gimrintsy to wear the turban and judge their actions as appropriate; consequently, I repeat, you have nothing to fear. Come to me with my envoy; he is loyal to me, *he is not a slave of your enemies,* but the friend of a man who enjoys the government's special trust."

In closing, Klugenau again urged Hadji Murat to join him.

"I did not trust the letter," Hadji Murat said, when Loris-Melikov had finished reading, "so I did not join Klugenau. For me, the main thing was to take revenge on Akhmet-Khan, and I couldn't do that through the Russians. Around then, Akhmet-Khan had surrounded Tsel'mes and wanted to capture or kill me. I didn't have enough men; I couldn't beat him back. Just then, an envoy from Shamil brought me a letter. Shamil promised to help me beat back Akhmet-Khan, to kill him, and to give me all Avaria to oversee. I thought it over for a long time and joined Shamil. Since then I have not stopped fighting the Russians."

Here Hadji Murat related all his military exploits. There were very many of them, and Loris-Melikov knew them in part. All his campaigns and raids were striking for the exceptional speed of his marches and the daring of his attacks, which were always crowned with success.

"There was never friendship between Shamil and me," Hadji Murat concluded his tale. "He feared me and needed me. Then somebody asked me who would be imam after Shamil. I said that the imam would be the one who had the sharpest sword. They reported this to Shamil, so he decided to get rid of me. He sent me to Tabasaran. I went and carried off a thousand sheep and three hundred horses. Then he said that I had not followed orders, he took away my rank of *naib*, and demanded that I turn over all my money. I send him a thousand gold pieces. He sent his *murids* and took all my property from me. He demanded I come to him; I knew he wanted to kill me, so I did not go. He sent men to take me; I fought them off, then joined Vorontsov. Only I didn't bring along my family. My mother, my wife, and my son are in Shamil's hands. Tell the *Sardar*: as long as my family is there, I can do nothing."

"I shall tell him," Loris-Melikov said.

"Do everything you can. Try. What's mine is yours, only help me with the prince. My hands are tied, and the end of the rope is in Shamil's hands."

With those words, Hadji Murat ended his story to Loris-Melikov.

XIV

On December 20, Vorontsov wrote the following to War Minister Chernyshev. The letter was in French.

"I did not write you at once, esteemed prince, since I wanted first to decide what we should do with Hadji Murat, and since I have felt indisposed for two or three days. In my last letter I notified you of Hadji Murat's arrival here; he came to Tbilisi on the 8th; I met him the next day; then over the next eight or nine days I entered into talks with him and pondered what he might do for us in the future, but especially I pondered how we should treat him now, since he is distraught over his family's fate and says, with every appearance of candor, that so long as his family is in Shamil's hands, he is paralyzed, powerless to help us and to show his gratitude for the kind reception and pardon afforded him. Anxiety over his dear ones has put him in a feverish state; the personnel designated by me to live with him here assure me that he does not sleep nights, eats almost nothing, prays constantly, and only requests permission to go riding with a guard of several Cossacks—this is his only mode of recreation and exercise, something essential to him after years of routine. Every day he has come to me to find out whether I have any news about his family, and he has begged me to order that all the prisoners at our disposal on the various fronts be gathered together for exchange to Shamil, to which exchange he would add a little money. There are people who will give him money for this purpose. Over and over he has implored me: 'Rescue my family, then give me the chance to serve you (the best place would be on the Lezgian front, in his opinion), and, if I have not rendered you great service in a month, punish me as you wish.'

"I have answered him that to me all this seems quite fair, and that among us are very many people who will never trust him so long as his family remains in the mountains rather than with us as hostages; I said that I shall do everything in my power to collect the prisoners along our frontiers and that, not having the right, according to our regulations, to provide him with additional money for the ransom, I may nevertheless find another way to help him. Having said this, I frankly stated my opinion that under no circumstances will Shamil return his family, that he probably will say as much, then promise him a complete pardon and restoration of his previous offices, but will threaten, if he does not return, to kill his mother, wife, and six children. I asked him if he can say in all honesty what he will do if he receives such a declaration from Shamil. Hadji Murat raised his eyes and arms toward heaven and said to me that all is in the God's hands, but he will never surrender himself to his enemy, because he is certain that Shamil will not pardon him and so he will not long remain among the living. As regards the extermination of his family, he did not think that Shamil would behave so thoughtlessly: 1) so as to not make his enemy even more desperate and dangerous; and 2) because there are many people in Daghestan, even some very influential ones, who would dissuade him from that. Finally, he repeated to me several times, that, no matter what God's will for the future might be, at this moment he thinks only about ransoming his family; he implores me, in the name of God, to help him and allow him to return to the Chechnia region where, through our commanders and with their permission, he might communicate with his family, learn their whereabouts, and discover how to liberate them; he says that many people and even several *naibs* in that hostile region are obliged to him to a greater or lesser degree, and that living among the whole population of people under Russian control or neutral to it, he will easily be able, with our help, to make arrangements to achieve the objective that haunts him day and night, the fulfillment of which will relieve his anxiety and will enable him to act in our interest and to earn our trust. He requests that we send him back to Groznyi with a convoy of twenty to thirty brave Cossacks, who will serve him as a defense against his enemies and serve us as guarantee of the truth of his stated intentions.

"You will grasp at once, esteemed prince, why all this has so preoccupied me, for no matter what I do, a heavy responsibility rests on my shoulders. It would be in the highest degree naïve to trust him completely; but if we had wished to deny him the means to flee, then we would have had to lock him up; however, in my opinion, that would be both unfair and impolitic. Such a step, news of which would quickly spread throughout Daghestan, would do us great harm there by discouraging all those—and they are many—disposed to move overtly or covertly against Shamil and who are keenly watching how we treat the imam's bravest and most enterprising lieutenant, a man who saw himself forced to place himself into our hands. If we begin to treat Hadji Murat as a prisoner, then the favorable impact of his desertion from Shamil will be immediately dissipated.

"Therefore, I think that I could not have acted differently than I have, and yet I sense that I may be accused of a great blunder if Hadji Murat should take it into his head to desert us anew. In the field and particularly in such tangled affairs, it is difficult if not impossible to find a straight path toward one's objective without risking mistakes and without exercising one's discretion; but once the road seems straight, it must be taken, come what may.

"I ask you, esteemed prince, to turn this matter over to His Majesty, the Emperor, for consideration; I shall be grateful if our August Sovereign deigns to approve my action. Everything that I have written to you above I have also written to Generals Zavadovskii and Kozlovskii, to guide Kozlovskii in dealing with Hadji Murat; the latter I have warned to do nothing without prior approval and I have forbidden him to travel anywhere at all. I told him that it will be better for us if he rides with one of our convoys, but I also said he must be aware that Shamil will begin to put out the story that we are keeping Hadji Murat under guard; I also extracted from him a promise that he will not ride to Vozdvizhenskoe, since my son, to whom he first surrendered and whom he considers his *kunak*, is not the commander of that place, so misunderstandings might result. By the way, Vozdvizhenskoe is too close to numerous hostile villages; and in any case, for the communications he desires with his compatriots, Groznyi is suitable in every respect.

"Besides the twenty hand-picked Cossacks who, by his own request, do not move so much as a step away from him, I have sent with him Captain Loris-Melikov—a worthy, excellent and very intelligent Tatar-speaking officer who knows Hadji Murat well and who, it seems, also possesses his complete confidence. During the ten days that Hadji Murat has spent here, by the way, he has lived in a house with Lieutenant-Colonel Tarkhanovyi, the commander of Shushinskii military district, who is here on official business. He is a thoroughly reliable man, and I trust him completely. He, too, has earned Hadji Murat's trust, and through him alone, as he speaks excellent Tatar, we have discussed the most delicate and secret matters.

"I consulted with Tarkhanovyi concerning Hadji Murat, and he completely agrees with me that either we should act as I have been doing or we must lock Hadji Murat in prison and guard him under the strictest regime possible, because once we treat him badly, he will not be easy to guard—either that or we must remove him completely from his native territory. But these last two measures would not only forfeit every advantage accruing to us as a result of the falling out between Hadji Murat and Shamil, but would also inevitably put a halt to any development of disaffection among the mountaineers and would obviate the possibility of a revolt by them against Shamil's government. Prince Tarkhanovyi told me he thinks Hadji Murat has been telling us the truth and that Hadji Murat has no doubt that Shamil will never forgive him and will order him executed, despite any promised pardon. The only thing that bothered Tarkhanovyi in his dealings with Hadji Murat is his attachment to his religion, and Tarkhanovyi does not hide that Shamil may work on him from that angle. But, as I said above, Shamil will never convince Hadji Murat that he will not take his life, either immediately on his return or after some time has elapsed.

"That is all, esteemed prince, that I wish to say to you concerning this episode in our local affairs."

XV

This report was dispatched from Tbilisi on December 24. On New Year's Eve, a military courier, having exhausted ten horses and bloodied ten drivers, delivered it to then Minister of War Prince Chernyshev.

On January 1, 1852 Chernyshev carried Vorontsov's report, along with a number of other items, to a briefing of Emperor Nicholas.

Chernyshev envied Vorontsov because of the universal respect Vorontsov enjoyed, because of his enormous wealth, because Vorontsov was a real aristocrat while Chernyshev was only a *parvenu*, and, most importantly, because of the special favor the emperor showed Vorontsov. For these reasons, Chernyshev took every opportunity to do Vorontsov harm. In his last report on affairs in the Caucasus, Chernyshev had succeeded in eliciting Nicholas's dissatisfaction with Vorontsov on the ground that, owing to the high command's carelessness, a small Russian army detachment had been virtually wiped out by the mountaineers. Now he intended to present in an unfavorable light Vorontsov's orders concerning Hadji Murat. He intended to insinuate to the sovereign that Vorontsov, who was always protecting and even indulging the locals at the Russians' expense, had acted imprudently by leaving Hadji Murat in the Caucasus; that Hadji Murat in all likelihood had defected only to observe the Russian defenses, and so it would be better to transfer Hadji Murat into central Russia and to make use of him only after his family had been rescued from the mountaineers and his loyalty could therefore be assured.

Chernyshev's plan misfired because, on that New Year's morning, Nicholas was especially irritable and, out of contrariness, was disinclined to listen to any suggestion whatsoever, regardless of the source. He was even less inclined to heed Chernyshev, whom he tolerated only because he considered him temporarily indispensable, but whom he considered an absolute scoundrel, because of Chernyshev's efforts to discredit Zakhar Chernyshev by implicating him during the investigation of the Decembrist uprising so as to confiscate his estate. So, thanks to Nicholas's foul mood, Hadji Murat remained in the Caucasus and his fate was not altered as it might have been had Chernyshev delivered his report at another time.

It was 9.30 when, through the impenetrable twenty-degree-below zero chill, Chernyshev's fat, bearded coachman, wearing a sharp-cornered, sky-blue velvet cap and sitting on the coach seat of a little sleigh identical to the one Emperor Nicholas Pavlovich rode, drove up to the entrance of the Winter Palace and gave a genial nod to his friend, Prince Dolgorukii's driver, who, having dropped off the prince some time ago, was waiting at the palace entrance with the reins stuffed up under his fat, padded bottom and was rubbing his frozen hands together.

Chernyshev wore an overcoat with a fluffy, gray beaverskin collar and a tricornered hat with gamecock feathers as if it were part of his uniform. Removing a bearskin cover, he slowly extricated from the sleigh his frozen feet which were not covered by overshoes (he was proud that he didn't wear overshoes) and then, taking courage and shuffling awkwardly, he crossed the welcome carpet to the door, which was respectfully opened for him by a doorkeeper. In the entranceway, after dropping his overcoat into the arms of an old court lackey who had come scurrying up, Chernyshev approached the mirror and carefully lifted the hat off his curled wig. Having glanced at himself in the mirror, he twisted the curls at the temples and on the top of his head with an accustomed movement of his aged hands, then straightened his service cross, shoulder-braids, and large, monogrammed epaulettes, and, scarcely controlling his recalcitrant old man's legs, he undertook to climb the sloping, carpeted stairs.

Passing by the ceremonially-uniformed footmen who were standing at the door and who bowed obsequiously to him, Chernyshev entered a reception room. The duty officer—a newly appointed aide-de-camp, resplendent in a new uniform, epaulettes and shoulder braids, with a reddish, not-yet wrinkled face, a thin dark mustache and hair combed forward on the sides just like Emperor Nicholas Pavlovich wore it—deferentially greeted him. Prince Vasilii Dolgorukii, assistant minister of war, with a bored expression on his vacant face, also adorned with exactly the same sideburns, mustache, and hairstyle as Nicholas, rose to greet Chernyshev.

"*L'Empereur?*" Chernyshev addressed the aide-de-camp, indicating the study door with a questioning glance.

"*Sa Majesté vient de rentrer,*" ["His Majesty has just returned,"] the aide-de-camp said, obviously enjoying the sound of own voice, and then, stepping so smoothly that a full glass of water placed on his head would not have spilled, he pressed on the soundlessly opening door and, indicating with his whole being respect for the place he was entering, disappeared behind it.

During this interval, Dolgorukii opened his brief case and checked the papers inside it.

Chernyshev himself, frowning, paced back and forth stretching his legs and remembering everything that he needed to report to the emperor. Chernyshev was right beside the door when it opened again and through it came once again, even more resplendent and solicitous than before, the aide-de-camp, who with a gesture invited the minister and his assistant into see the emperor.

After a terrible fire, the Winter Palace had long ago been reconstructed, but Nicholas was still living on its upper floor. The study, in which he received reports from ministers and other high officials, was a very tall room with four huge windows. A large portrait of Emperor Alexander I was hanging on the main wall. Two desks stood between the windows. Along the walls there were several chairs, in the middle of the room an enormous writing table, by the table Nicholas's armchair and chairs for those he was receiving.

Behind the writing table Nicholas sat in a black frock coat without epaulettes, clad in narrow suspenders, his massive torso thrown back in the chair, his skin distended over his considerable paunch, his lifeless, immobile eyes studying everyone who entered. His long, white face—with its enormous receding fore-

126

head showing itself from beneath tufts of hair artfully smoothed forward and joined with his wig to cover the bald spot—was today especially cold and immobile. His eyes, always lackluster, looked even more lackluster than usual, his compressed lips visible beneath his upturned mustache, his fat oily cheeks, set off by a high collar and freshly shaved without touching his symmetrical, baby-sausage-shaped sideburns, his fat chin squeezed down toward the collar—gave his face an expression of dissatisfaction, and even anger. The cause of his bad mood was fatigue. The cause of the fatigue was that, the night before, he had been at a masquerade ball where, as he strolled the floor in his horseguard's uniform and feathered helmet among the public that first crowded up to him, then timidly made way for his massive, self-assured figure, he had again encountered a masked woman, who at the previous masquerade had aroused his aging desires by the whiteness of her skin, her marvelous figure, and her tender voice, and who had promised to meet him again at the next masquerade. At last night's masquerade she had come up to him, and this time he had not let her go. He had taken her to the special loge kept ready so that he might be alone with his lady. Going silently up to the door of the loge, Nicholas looked around, seeking to catch his orderly's attention, but the orderly was nowhere to be seen. Nicholas frowned, then he himself pushed open the door of the loge, letting the lady enter in front of him.

"*Il y a quelqu'un!*" ["There's someone here!"] she said, stopping. The loge was in fact occupied: on a small velvet couch sitting side by side were a cavalry officer and a rather young, rather pretty, fair-skinned, curly-haired woman in a hooded cape with her mask off. Seeing the angry figure of Nicholas drawn up to his full height, the white-skinned woman hurriedly covered her face with her mask. The cavalry officer himself, struck dumb with horror, stared fixedly at Nicholas without getting off the couch.

No matter how accustomed he was to the terror he inspired in people, that terror was still pleasant to Nicholas, and he liked sometimes to impress those he had terrified by addressing them in gentle words. That is what he did on this occasion.

"Well, brother, since you are younger than me," he said to the officer, who was rigid with fear, "you can yield your spot to me."

The officer jumped up and, blanching and blushing at the same time, bowed and scraped his way silently out of the loge with his young woman, so that Nicholas was left alone with his lady.

The masked woman turned out to be an attractive, twenty-year-old, innocent girl, the daughter of a Swedish governess. This girl told Nicholas how, already as a young child, she had fallen in love with him from his portraits, how she had adored him and had decided to get his attention, no matter what it took. Well, now she had gotten it, and, as she said, she did not need anything more. The young maiden was then taken to the place where Nicholas usually had his rendezvous with women, and Nicholas spent more than an hour with her.

When he had returned to his room that night and had lain down on the hard, narrow bed of which he was so proud and had covered himself with the cloak that he regarded (and even publicly described) as being as famous as Napoleon's hat, he couldn't sleep for a long time. He would visualize the frightened and rapturous expression on the white face of the young maiden, he would contemplate the full, powerful shoulders of his long-time lover Nelidova, then he would compare the one with the other. That such dissipation on the part of a married man is morally wrong never entered his mind; indeed, he would have been very surprised had anyone condemned him for it. Even though he was sure that he had comported himself properly, a certain moral uneasiness remained; to stifle that uneasiness he turned to an idea that never failed to calm his nerves: the idea of his own greatness.

Although he had gone to bed late, he rose, as always, at 8.00 and, having performed his morning toilet, having rubbed down with ice his large, well-fed body, and having prayed to God (he recited the same prayers he had been saying since childhood—the Hail Mary, the Apostles' Creed and the Lord's Prayer— without attributing any significance whatsoever to the words he was uttering), he exited the palace through a small portico emerging onto the embankment. He was wearing an overcoat and military hat. In the middle of the embankment he ran into a student who was just as tall as he was and who wore the full uniform and hat of the School of Jurisprudence. Recognizing the uniform of that school, which he disliked for its freethinking ways, Nicholas Pavlovich frowned, but the height and the painstaking nature of the student's coming-to-attention and the exaggeratedly extended elbow of his salute softened the emperor's displeasure.

"Your family name?" he asked.

"Polosatov, Your Imperial Majesty."

"Good man!"

The student still stood with his hand raised to his hat in salute. Nicholas stopped.

"Lad, do you want to enter the army?'

"By no means, your Imperial Majesty."

"Moron!" With that, turning on his heels, Nicholas walked on, exclaiming loudly the first words that came to him, "*Koperwein, Koperwein.*" Several times he repeated the name of yesterday's young maiden. "Foul, foul." He was not thinking about what he was saying, but he managed to master his emotions by suddenly paying attention to the words he was muttering. "Yes, what would Russia be without me?" he asked himself. Then, sensing the return of his dissatisfaction, he asked again: "Yes, not just Russia alone, but Europe too, what would they be without me?" He then remembered his brother-in-law, the Prussian king, and on recalling the king's weakness and stupidity, shook his head.

Walking back toward the portico, he caught sight of Elena Pavlovna's carriage, which with its red-liveried footman was approaching the Saltykov entrance. Elena Pavlovna was to him the personification of those empty people who render judgments not only about the sciences and poetry but also about politics, in the mistaken belief that they might be able to govern themselves better than he, Nicholas, could govern them. He knew that, no matter how many times he had suppressed these people, they had resurfaced. Then he remembered his recently deceased brother Mikhail Pavlovich. A feeling of depression and sadness enveloped him again. He frowned darkly and again began to whisper the first words that came to him. He stopped whispering only when he had entered the palace. On entering his rooms, he looked into the mirror, smoothed down his sideburns and the hair over his temples and set his wig over his bald spot; he then curled the ends of his mustache and went directly into his study, where briefings were delivered.

First, he received Chernyshev. Chernyshev immediately understood from the emperor's face and especially from his eyes that the tsar was particularly out of sorts today and, knowing about the previous evening's liaison, understood whence came that mood. Having coldly greeted Chernyshev and invited him to be seated, Nicholas fixed his lifeless eyes upon the minister.

The first point in Chernyshev's briefing was a case of theft by army quartermasters; next was the issue of re-deploying troops on the Prussian border; next was the selection of several people who had been nominated to receive service awards at New Year but who had been passed over on the original list; next came Vorontsov's report on Hadji Murat; and finally there was the unpleasant case of a student from the medical academy who had tried to kill a professor.

Silently pursing his lips, Nicholas ran his large white hands, one bearing a wedding band on the fourth finger, over a stack of papers, and he listened to the report on the theft without ever dropping his eyes from Chernyshev's forehead and the tuft of hair above it.

Nicholas was certain that everyone steals. He knew that he would have to punish the quartermasters and had decided to send them all to serve in the ranks, yet he also knew that this punishment would not hinder those who would replace the cashiered officers from doing the same thing. It was the very nature of officials to steal, his duty was to punish them, and, no matter how fed up with it he was, he conscientiously did his duty.

"Apparently, there is only one honest man in Russia," he said.

Chernyshev immediately grasped that this single honest man in Russia was Nicholas himself, so he smiled approvingly.

"It must be so, Your Majesty," he said.

"Leave it; I'll write down my decision later," Nicholas said, taking the paper and placing it on the left side of the table. Next, Chernyshev began to report on the awards and the troop relocation. Nicholas read through the list, crossed out several names, then tersely and decisively he gave orders to move two divisions toward the Prussian border.

In no way could Nicholas forgive the king of Prussia for granting a constitution during the period after 1848 and, therefore, while conveying to his brother-in-law the most amicable feelings in letters and in conversations, he deemed it essential to station troops on the Prussian border just in case. These troops might be needed to defend the throne of his brother-in-law, should there be popular unrest in Prussia (Nicholas saw everywhere an inclination to revolt.), just as he had used troops to defend Austria against the Hungarians. Besides, these troops on the border were needed to lend more weight and significance to advice he offered the Prussian king.

"Yes, what would have happened with Russia by now, if not for me," he thought again.

"Well, what else?"

"A courier from the Caucasus," Chernyshev said, and he began to summarize Vorontsov's despatch about Hadji Murat's surrender.

"There, see!" Nicholas said. "A good start."

"Obviously, the plan put together by Your Majesty is beginning to bear fruit," said Chernyshev. Such praise of his strategic abilities was especially pleasing to Nicholas, because, even though he had boasted publicly of his strategic acumen, in the depths of his soul he had always known he had none. So now he wanted to hear in greater detail this praise.

"How do you mean?" he asked.

"I mean that if we had long ago adopted Your Majesty's plan of gradually, painstakingly, moving forward, cutting down the forests and destroying the enemy's reserves, the Caucasus would long ago have been subjugated. Hadji Murat's defection I attribute solely to your plan. He understood that they can no longer hold out."

"True," Nicholas said.

Even though the plan of slow encroachment into enemy territory by felling forests and destroying food supplies was the brain child of Ermolov and Vel'iaminov, a plan diametrically opposed to Nicholas's own, which had aimed simultaneously to capture Shamil's stronghold and to extirpate that nest of bandits and which had been implemented in the 1845 Dargo campaign that had cost so many lives, nonetheless Nicholas still regarded himself as originator of the plan of slow movement, systematic felling of woods, and destruction of food supplies. Perhaps if Nicholas meant to claim credit for the plan of slow movement, felling of forests, and destruction of food supplies, he should have hidden his role in the completely contradictory military operation of '45. Yet he made no effort to hide that role, choosing to pride himself on the plan for the 1845 expedition as well as on the plan of slow movement forward, even though these plans plainly contradicted each other. His entourage's flattery—constant, brazen, and flying in the face of all empirical evidence—had led him to the point where he no longer saw his own contradictions, where he made no effort to match his words and deeds to reality, to logic or even to simple common sense, but was completely sure that all his orders, no matter how senseless, unfair and inconsistent, became sensible, fair, and consistent simply because he had issued them.

An example was his decision concerning the student from the Medical-Surgical Academy, the subject of the next report after the one on the Caucasus.

The facts were the following: a young medical student, having twice failed an exam, took it a third time, and, when the examiner again failed him, the neurotic student, perceiving in this an injustice, grabbed from the table a penknife and, in an apparent fit of frenzy, threw himself on the professor and inflicted on him several trifling wounds.

"What's his family name?" asked Nicholas.

"Brzezowski."

"A Pole?"

"Of Polish descent and a Catholic," Chernyshev answered.

Nicholas frowned.

He had done much harm to the Poles. To justify that harm, he had to be certain that all Poles were worthless villains. Nicholas deemed them such, and he hated them in direct proportion to the harm he had done them.

"Wait a moment," he said and, closing his eyes, lowered his head.

Having heard this expression more than once from Nicholas, Chernyshev knew that, when the emperor had to decide some kind of important question, all he had to do was to concentrate for a few moments and an inspiration would come to him, a suitable decision would take shape of its own accord, as if some inner voice was whispering to him what to do. Nicholas took the report and at the bottom of it wrote in his large handwriting:

"He deserves the death penalty. But, thank God, we don't have the death penalty in Russia. And it is not for me to introduce it. Make him run twelve times a gauntlet of a thousand men ... Nicholas." He signed with his unnaturally large flourish.

Nicholas knew that twelve thousand blows of the rod were not only certain, excruciating death but also cruel and unusual punishment, since five thousand blows would suffice to kill the strongest of men. He enjoyed being implacably cruel but still found it pleasant to imagine that we have no death penalty in Russia.

Having signed his decision concerning the student, he pushed it across the table to Chernyshev. "Here," he said. "Read it."

Chernyshev read it and, to betoken respectful awe over the decision's wisdom, he bowed his head.

"And bring all the students onto the parade ground to be present at the execution," added Nicholas.

"It will do them good. I shall exterminate this revolutionary spirit, extirpate it by the roots," he thought.

"I hear and obey," Chernyshev said and, pausing a bit and adjusting his wig, he returned to the report on the Caucusus.

"What orders do you wish me to convey to Mikhail Semyonovich?"

"Adhere strictly to my system of destroying villages, of wiping out food supplies in Chechnia, and of harassing them with raids," said Nicholas.

"And Hadji Murat? What are your orders concerning him?" asked Chernyshev.

"Well, Vorontsov writes that he wants to make use of him in the Caucasus."

"Isn't that risky?" Chernyshev said, avoiding Nicholas's gaze. "Mikhail Semyonovich is, I fear, too trusting."

"What do you think, then?" Nicholas asked sharply, having taken note of Chernyshev's intention to put Vorontsov's decision in an unfavorable light.

"Well, I would have thought it safer to send him to central Russia."

"You would have thought," Nicholas said sarcastically. "Well, I don't think so. I agree with Vorontsov. Inform him."

"I hear and obey," said Chernyshev and, having risen to his feet, the minister started to take his leave.

Also taking his leave was Dolgorukii, who during the briefing had said only a few words in response to questions from Nicholas about the redeployment of troops to the Prussian border.

After Chernyshev Nicholas received Bibikov, the governor-general of the Western district, who had come for instructions before returning to his post. Approving the measures Bibikov had already taken against rebellious peasants who had refused to convert to Orthodoxy, Nicholas ordered him to try in military courts all those who had disobeyed. This would mean sentencing peasants to run the gauntlet. In addition, the emperor ordered Bibikov to conscript into the army a newspaper editor who had disclosed the news that several thousand state peasants would soon be reclassified as crown peasants.

"I do this, because I regard it as necessary," the emperor said. "I shall not permit any public discussion of it."

Bibikov understood the profound cruelty of the decision affecting the Uniate peasants and the deep injustice in transferring state peasants, the country's only free men and women, to the status of crown peasants—that is, making them into serfs of the royal family. Yet he could not bring himself to object. To refuse an order from Nicholas would be to forfeit the brilliant position that had taken him forty years to acquire and that he now so much enjoyed. So Bibikov humbly bowed his dark, graying head to signify his submission and willingness to carry out His Majesty's cruel, senseless, and dishonorable will.

After dismissing Bibikov, Nicholas rose to his feet feeling well satisfied over having done his duty, then glanced at his watch and went to change into his parade uniform. Having put on the uniform replete with epaulettes, medals, and a ribbon, he walked into the reception hall where more than a hundred people— men in uniforms and women in elegant, low-cut dresses, all standing in their appointed places—tremblingly awaited his entrance. With lifeless gaze, puffed-out chest, and stomach so tightly girded by a waist-sash that it bulged out above and below it, he went out to meet the expectant group and, on feeling all faces turn to him with quivering servility, he assumed an even more triumphant air. On encountering the eyes of his acquaintants, he remembered who was who, stopped and spoke to them a few words—sometimes in Russian, sometimes in French—then, as he pierced them with his cold, lifeless gaze, he listened to their responses.

Having received their congratulations, Nicholas entered the chapel.

God greeted and praised Nicholas through His clergy, just as the laity had done, and although he was sick of it, the emperor accepted these congratulations and this praise as his due. Everything was as it should be, because on him depended the welfare and happiness of the entire world, and, although he was growing weary of it, he could not deny the world his help. When, at the end of the service, the majestic, immaculately clad deacon intoned "Many Years," and the choir with its wondrous voices warmly seized on and repeated these words, Nicholas glanced around and spied near the window his mistress Nelidova and her splendid shoulders, he resolved in her favor the comparison with last night's young woman.

After the service, he went to the empress's chambers and spent several minutes in the family circle, joking with his children and his wife. Then he went through the Hermitage to meet Court Minister Volkonskii, and, among other things, he instructed the minister to pay out of his special fund an annual pension to the mother of last night's Swedish girl. Leaving Volkonskii, he departed on his customary carriage drive.

Dinner that day was in the Pompei Hall; aside from his younger sons Nikolai and Mikhail, the guests included Baron Lieven, Count Rzhevskii, Dolgorukii, the Prussian ambassador, and the aide-de-camp of the Prussian king.

While they waited for the emperor and empress to make their entrance, an interesting conversation arose between the Prussian ambassador and Baron Lieven concerning the latest disturbing news from Poland.

"*La Pologne et le Caucase, ce sont les deux cautères de la Russie,*" ["Poland and the Caucasus, those are Russia's two sore spots,"] Liewen said. "*Il nous faut cent milles hommes à peu près dans chacun de ces deux pays.*" ["We need close to 100,000 men in each of those countries."]

The ambassador feigned surprise that it should be so.

"*Vous dites, la Pologne,*" ["You say, Poland."]

"*O, oui, c'était un coup de maître de Metternich de nous en avoir laissé l'embarras.*" ["Oh, yes. It was a master stroke by Metternich to have left us that problem."].

At that point in the conversation the empress entered with her trembling head and frozen smile, and Nicholas entered behind her.

At dinner Nicholas spoke of Hadji Murat's defection and asserted that the war in the Caucasus would soon be coming to an end as a result of his orders to hem in the mountaineers by felling trees and building a system of fortresses.

The ambassador, having glanced at and immediately broken eye contact with the Prussian aide-de-camp, with whom only that morning he had spoken about Nicholas's unfortunate proclivity to consider himself a great strategist, now warmly applauded that plan on the ground that it proved again Nicholas's great strategic abilities.

After dinner, Nicholas went to the ballet, where hundreds of scantily-dressed women paraded about in tights. One in particular caught his fancy, and, having summoned the ballet master, Nicholas thanked him and ordered he receive in reward a diamond ring.

The next day during Chernyshev's briefing, Nicholas again confirmed his orders to Vorontsov that, since Hadji Murat had defected, now was the time to intensify the harassment of Chechnia and to tighten the cordon around it.

Chernyshev drafted a despatch to Vorontsov, then another military courier, riding horses into the ground and pummeling his drivers' faces, galloped off toward Tbilisi.

XVI

In January 1852, in immediate response to Nicholas Pavlovich's instructions, the authorities organized a raid deep into Chechnia.

The detachment detailed for the raid consisted of four infantry battalions, two companies of Cossacks, and eight cannon. The column proceeded along a road. On both sides of the column, in an unbroken chain moving first up, then down gullies, marched riflemen in high boots, sheepskin coats, and Caucasian fur hats, their rifles on their shoulders and cartridges in their bandoliers.

As always, the detachment moved through enemy territory observing strict silence. Only occasionally, as they bumped across ditches, their guns jingled, or an artillery horse, not understanding the order for silence, snorted or neighed, or an angry commander in hoarse but restrained voice shouted at his men that the line was too extended or was too close to or too far from the column. Only once was the silence broken when there bounded out of a small briar patch that fell between the line and column a white-bellied, gray-backed female goat and an identically-colored ram with small horns sweeping back toward his spine. The beautiful, startled creatures, curling their front legs up against their chests, flew in huge bounds so close by the column that several soldiers, shouting and laughing, ran after them intending to stick them with their bayonets, but the goats reversed directions, bounded back across the line, then, followed by several cavalrymen and company dogs, hurtled themselves away into the mountains.

Although it was still winter, the sun had already begun to climb higher in the sky; by noon, when the company, which had set out early in the morning, had already covered about three miles, the air had warmed up considerably, and the sun's rays were so bright that it hurt one's eyes to look at the steel of the bayonets or at the bright spots that suddenly flared up, like little suns, on the bronze of the cannons.

Behind the troops was the clear, rapid stream the detatchment had just crossed, ahead were tilled fields and meadows intersected by shallow gullies, even further ahead were mysterious black mountains covered with forest, while beyond the black mountains were jutting rock faces, and on the lofty horizon were eternally wondrous, eternally changing snow-capped peaks dancing in the shifting light like uncut diamonds.

Leading the Fifth Company, in a black uniform and Caucasian fur cap, with his sword slung across his shoulder marched a recent transferee from the Guards Regiment, the tall and handsome officer Butler, who at that moment was feeling

134

acutely the joy of life but also the proximity of death, the desire for action and the consciousness of belonging to an enormous whole directed by a single will. Now going out on his second mission, Butler rejoiced to think that any minute now the enemy would open fire and that he would neither duck his head to avoid the incoming cannon-ball nor pay attention to the whistle of the bullets, but rather, as he had previously done, would raise his head higher and with a smile in his eyes would glance around at his fellow officers and soldiers and would start talking about something unrelated.

The detachment had turned off the good road onto a little-used path running through a field of corn stubble, then began to approach a wood when, from whence it could not be determined, an ominously whistling cannon-ball flew past and landed near the middle of the wagon train, next to the road in the corn field, its detonation showering him with dirt.

"It's starting," Butler said to his fellow officers, smiling happily.

And sure enough, right after the cannon shot, there appeared from the forest a thick crowd of mounted Chechens with colors unfurled. In the middle of the group there was a large green banner, and the old sergeant-major of the company, who had very good eyes, informed the near-sighted Butler that this must be Shamil himself. The party rode down the hill, appeared on the high bank of the nearest gully on the right, then began to descend into the gully. A little general clad in a warm, black uniform and wearing a white high-peaked Caucasian fur cap rode on his ambler toward Butler's company and ordered him to move to the right against the descending cavalry. Butler quickly led his company in the direction ordered, but he had not managed to reach the gully before he heard two cannon shots, one after the other, behind him. He looked around: two clouds of blue-gray smoke rose over two guns and drifted along the small gully. The Chechen horsemen, evidently not expecting artillery fire, rode back up the hill. Butler's company opened fire on and gave chase to the mountaineers; meanwhile, the entire hollow was hidden in gun smoke. Only above the hollow could it be seen how the mountaineers hastily retreated, firing back at the pursuing Cossacks. The detachment continued to pursue the mountaineers, and on reaching the high bank of the second gully an *awul* opened up before them.

Butler and his company entered the *awul* on the run, following the Cossack cavalry. None of the inhabitants were there. The soldiers were ordered to burn the grain, the hay, and the *saklyas*. Acrid smoke spread across the entire *awul*, and through this smoke soldiers darted about, dragging from the *saklyas* whatever they found inside; mainly, they caught and shot chickens that the mountaineers had not managed to carry away. The officers sat at a distance from the smoke, ate breakfast and had a drink. The sergeant-major brought them a board laden with several honeycombs. There was no sign of the Chechens. A little after noon the order was given to move out. Outside the *awul* the company formed up in a column, and Butler took his assigned place in the rear guard. As soon as they set out, some Chechens appeared and, moving behind the detachment, they escorted it down the mountain with rifle shots.

When the detachment came out onto a clearing, the mountaineers fell back. None of Butler's men had been wounded, so he returned in the happiest, brightest frame of mind.

When the detachment, having forded the little stream it had crossed in the morning, had spread itself out over the corn fields and meadows, the company singers came forward and songs rang out. There was no wind, the air was fresh, clean and so transparent that the snow-capped mountains standing hundreds of miles away seemed quite close, and, when the singers fell silent between songs, the regular tramp of feet and the rattle of weapons sounded like a background against which the songs sprang up and died down. The song they sang in Butler's Fifth Company had been composed by a cadet in the regiment's honor and was sung to a dance tune with the refrain "Better by far, better by far, the marksmen are! The marksmen are!"

Butler was riding alongside his immediate commander, Major Petrov, with whom he shared quarters, and he couldn't help but rejoice over his decision to leave the guards and come to the Caucasus. The main reason for his transfer from the guards was that he had lost so much at cards in Petersburg that he had nothing left. He was afraid that, if he stayed in the guards, he would be unable to resist gambling, yet he had no more money left to lose. Now all that was behind him; there was a different life after all, one both fine and dashing. He now forgot both his ruin and his unpaid debts. And the Caucasus, the war, the soldiers, the officers, the drunken, but good-hearted and brave Major Petrov—all seemed to him so fine that sometimes he could not bring himself to believe that he was not in Petersburg, not in a smoke-filled room thumbing cards and laying bets, hating the banker and feeling an oppressive ache in his head, but here in this marvelous country, among these brave Caucasians.

"Better by far, better by far, the marksmen are! The marksmen are!" the singers chimed. His horse stepped a happy pace to the music. The company's shaggy, gray dog Trezorka, swaggering like an officer, with tail tucked tight and a preoccupied air ran in front of Butler's company. Butler's spirit was invigorated, calm, and cheerful. To him war represented only the opportunity to subject himself to danger, to the possibility of death and, by doing so, the chance to earn awards and the respect of his Caucasian comrades and his Russian friends. The other side of war—the killing and maiming of soldiers, of officers, of mountaineers—strangely never entered his imagination. In order to preserve his poetic image of war, he had never, even accidentally, looked at dead or wounded men. So it was now: we had sustained three dead and twelve wounded. He passed by a corpse lying on its back, and only out of the corner of one eye did he spy the somehow contorted position of the waxy arm and the dark red spot in the head, but he did not stop to examine the body more carefully. He regarded the mountaineers only as dashing horsemen against whom he had to defend himself.

"This's how to live, old man," said the major during a pause in the singing. "It's not like you live in Piter: 'Dress, right dress!' 'Dress, left dress!' Here we've done a little work, then we're home. Mashurka will serve us some pirogis now, and good cabbage soup. Real life! Isn't it? You bet!" Then he called for his favorite tune, "As the Sun Was Rising."

The major lived as man and wife with a paramedic's daughter, at first known as Mashka, but later as Mar'ia Dmitrievna. Mar'ia Dmitrievna was a beautiful, fair-haired, freckle-covered, thirty-year-old, childless woman. Whatever her past had been, she was now the major's faithful companion, looking after him like a nanny, and the major needed her care since he often drank himself unconscious.

When they arrived at the fort, everything was as the major had foreseen. Mar'ia Dmitrievna fed her tasty, satisfying dishes to him, Butler, and two other officers he invited from the detachment, and the major ate and drank till he couldn't talk, then went to his room to sleep. Butler, also tired, but feeling contented and a bit too full of the *chikhir* wine, went to his little room and had scarcely managed to get undressed before, palm under his handsome, curly head, he fell into a deep sleep, dreamless and untroubled.

XVII

The *awul* destroyed in the raid was the same one in which Hadji Murat had spent the night before defecting to the Russians.

Sado, at whose house Hadji Murat had stayed, had gone with his family into the hills as the Russians approached the *awul*. Returning to the *awul*, Sado found his *saklya* in ruins: the roof had caved in, the door and the posts supporting the balcony had been burned, the interior had been fouled. His son, that same handsome sparkling-eyed boy who had gazed so reverently at Hadji Murat, had been carried dead to the mosque on a cloak-covered horse. He had been run through by a bayonet in the back. The fine-looking woman who had waited on Hadji Murat during his visit, now in torn blouse ripped open at the front and revealing her old sagging breasts, her hair wildly disheveled, stood over her son scratching her face till it bled and wailing ceaselessly. Sado and some relatives took pick and shovel to dig a grave for his son. Old grandfather sat on the *saklya*'s collapsed wall sharpening a stick and staring vacantly straight ahead. He had just returned from his beehives. Two stacks of hay there had been burned; the apricot and cherry trees he had planted and nursed had been broken and set to the torch; most importantly, all the hives and their bees had also been burned. The wail of women could be heard in all the houses and in the square, where two more bodies had been deposited. Little children howled along with their mothers. Howling too were the hungry cattle, to whom there was nothing to give. The older children were not playing; instead they looked with frightened eyes at their elders.

The soldiers had fouled the fountain, obviously deliberately, so that water could not be taken from it. The mosque had also been defiled in the same way, so the mullah and his young pupils were cleaning it. The old men who were heads of household gathered on the square and, squatting down, discussed their situation. About hating the Russians no one said even a single word. The feeling gripping every Chechen from the youngest to the oldest was stronger than hatred. The feeling was not hatred but a refusal to recognize these Russian dogs as human beings, a feeling of such revulsion, disgust, and incomprehension in the face of these creatures' senseless cruelty that the desire to exterminate them, like the desire to exterminate rats, poisonous spiders, and wolves, was just as natural a feeling as the instinct for self-preservation. ✳

The inhabitants had a choice: to stay there and restore by dint of terrible effort all that had been built up by great labor and that had been so easily and senselessly destroyed, meanwhile expecting at any minute a repetition of the same destruction, or, contrary to the laws of their religion and to their sense of revulsion toward and suspicion of the Russians, to submit to their adversaries. After praying, the elders unanimously agreed to send Shamil a messenger asking for his help, then they immediately set about rebuilding the destroyed village.

XVIII

Not early in the morning on the third day after the raid, Butler went out the back porch onto the street, intending to go for a walk and get some fresh air before taking the breakfast tea he usually had with Petrov. The sun had come out from behind the mountains, so it hurt to look at the brightly illuminated white adobe walls on the right side of the street, but, as always, it cheered and relaxed him to look left at the forest-covered black mountains receding into the distance and growing ever taller as they did so, and to look across the ravine at the opaque chain of snow-covered peaks that now, as always, strove to assume the guise of clouds.

Butler looked at these mountains, filled his lungs with air, and rejoiced that he was alive and alive in this beautiful place. In addition, he rejoiced that he had conducted himself so impeccably yesterday both during the assault and especially during the retreat when things were a bit hot; he also rejoiced on remembering how yesterday, on their return from the expedition, Masha, rather Mar'ia Dmitrievna, Petrov's mistress, had fussed over everyone and had treated everyone so simply and sweetly but had been, he thought, especially affectionate toward him. Mar'ia Dmietrievna with her thick braid of hair, her wide shoulders, her high bosom and with the radiant smile on her kind, freckled-covered face magnetically attracted the strong, young single male in Butler, and it even seemed to him that she desired him. But he supposed that reciprocating that desire would offend his kind, simple-hearted comrade at arms, so he observed with Mar'ia Dmitrievna the simplest, most respectful relations and was pleased with himself for doing so. At the moment this feeling of self-satisfaction was what occupied him.

He was distracted from these thoughts by many horses' hooves rapidly clattering on the road in front of him, the clatter suggesting that several men were approaching at a gallop. He raised his head and spied at street's end an approaching group of horsemen. In front of twenty or so Cossacks rode two men: one in a white Circassian coat and high Circassian hat with a turban; the other an officer in the Russian forces, dark, hook-nosed, clad in blue uniform with an abundance of silver on his clothes and weapons. Under the rider in the turban was a handsome, chestnut paint horse with a small head and beautiful eyes; under the officer was a tall, dandified Karabakh horse. Butler, a horse-lover, immediately appreciated the vigorous strength of the first horse and stopped to find out who these people were. The officer spoke to Butler.

"This commanding officer home?" he asked, betraying by ungrammatical speech and accent his non-Russian origins, and gesturing with his whip toward Ivan Matveevich's house.

"The very one," Butler said.

"And who is that?" Butler asked, coming closer to the officer and indicating with his eyes the man in the turban.

"Hadji Murat that. Here came, here guest will be at military commander," the officer said.

Butler knew about Hadji Murat and about his defection to the Russians, but he had never expected to see him here, in this tiny fort.

Hadji Murat looked at him amiably.

"Greetings, *koshkol'dy*," Butler said, repeating a Tatar greeting he had learned.

"*Saubul*," Hadji Murat answered, nodding his head. He rode up to Butler and offered his hand, whip dangling from two fingers.

"Commander?" he asked.

"No, the commander's in there. I'll go call him," Butler said, addressing the officer, then mounting the porch and pushing on the door.

But the door of the "parade entrance," as Mar'ia Dmitrievna called it, was locked. Butler knocked, but, not getting an answer, he went around to the other side. Having called his orderly and having received no answer and not finding either of the other two orderlies, he went into the kitchen. Mar'ia Dmitrievna, hair wrapped up in a scarf, face flushed, sleeves rolled up on her plump white arms, was slicing rolled-out dough that was just as white as her arms, into small pieces for pirogis.

"Where've the orderlies gone?" Butler asked.

"Gone to get drunk," Mar'ia Dmitrievna said. "What's it to you?"

"Unlock the door; you've got a whole crowd of mountaineers at the door. Hadji Murat's here."

"Tell me another fib," Mar'ia Dmitrievna said, smiling.

"I'm not kidding, it's the truth. They're by the porch."

"You're joking, right?" said Mar'ia Dmitrievna.

"Why would I make it up? Go look for yourself, they're by the porch."

"Well, that's something!" said Mar'ia Dmitrievna, rolling down her sleeves and fumbling for the hairpin in her thick plait. "I'll go wake up Ivan Matveevich," she said.

"No, I'll go," Butler said. "Hey, Bondarenko, go unlatch the door."

"Fine by me," said Mar'ia Dmitrievna, returning to her work.

Having been informed that Hadji Murat was on the way to the fort and having heard earlier that Hadji Murat had come as far as Groznyi, Ivan Matveevich was not at all surprised to learn of the arrival, so, propping himself up a bit, he rolled a cigarette, lit up, then started to dress, hacking loudly and grumbling at his superiors for sending him "this devil." After he had finished dressing, he demanded some "medicine" from his orderly. The orderly, knowing that "medicine" meant "vodka," gave him a drink.

"There's nothing worse than mixing," Ivan Matveevich muttered, drinking down the vodka and then chewing some black bread. "Yesterday I drank some *chikhir*, so my head aches. Okay, ready now," he stood up and entered the sitting-room into which Butler had already shown Hadji Murat and the officer escort.

The officer accompanying Hadji Murat conveyed to Ivan Matveevich the left flank commander's orders to accommodate Hadji Murat and, while permitting him to have contact with the mountaineers through envoys, to prohibit him from leaving the fort without an escort of Cossacks.

Having read the written order, Ivan Matveevich stared intently at Hadji Murat and then thoroughly studied the order again. After several times moving his glance from the papers to Hadji Murat and back, he finally rested his eyes on Hadji Murat and said, "*Iakshi, bek, iakshi.* Let him stay here. Tell him I have orders not to let him out alone. Orders are holy writ. So we'll put him—what do you think, Butler?—we'll put him up in the office?"

Butler did not manage to answer before Mar'ia Dmitrievna, coming in from the kitchen and standing in the doorway, said to Ivan Matveevich:

"Why there? Put him up here. We'll give him the *kunak* room and pantry, too. That way we can keep our eyes on him," she said, and having glanced at Hadji Murat and caught his eyes, she quickly looked away.

" Know what? Maybe Mar'ia Dmitrievna is right," Butler said.

"You crazy? Leave the woman out of it!" Ivan Matveevich said, frowning.

During the entire conversation Hadji Murat sat still, hand tucked behind the handle of his dagger, a faintly contemptuous smile on his face. He said he didn't care where he lived. The only thing he needed was what the *Sardar* had promised—that he be in contact with the mountaineers, so he insisted they be allowed to visit him. Ivan Matveevich said it would be done, then asked Butler to entertain the guest while they brought him something to eat and prepared his rooms; he himself would go to the office to fill out the necessary papers and to issue the necessary orders.

Hadji Murat's relations with his new acquaintances immediately took very clear shape. From the first, Hadji Murat felt disgust and contempt for Ivan Matveevich and always behaved haughtily toward him. To Mar'ia Dmitrievna, who prepared and brought his food to him, he took a special liking. Her liked her for her simplicity, for what to him was her exotic foreign beauty, and for her attraction to him, which she unconsciously transmitted to him. He tried not to look at her, not to speak to her, but his eyes involuntarily turned toward her and followed her movements.

With Butler himself, Hadji Murat became friendly from their very first meeting; he willingly chatted with him a great deal, asking him about his life and relating his own story, reporting to him the news that his messengers brought concerning his family, and even asking Butler's advice about what he should do.

The news the messengers brought him was not good. In the course of the four days he spent in the fort, the messengers came to him twice, and both times the news was bad.

XIX

Soon after his desertion to the Russians, Hadji Murat's family was taken to the *awul* of Vedeno and detained there to await Shamil's decision. The women—his aged mother Patimat, his two wives—in addition to their five little children, lived under guard in the *saklya* of headman Ibrahim Rashid. Hadji Murat's son, eighteen-year-old Yusuf, had been placed in a "dungeon"—that is, in a pit more than seven feet deep, along with four criminals who were also awaiting a decision on their fates.

No decision had been forthcoming because Shamil had been away. He was on campaign against the Russians.

On January 6, 1852 Shamil was returning home to Vedeno after a battle with the Russians in which, according to the Russians, he had been defeated and forced to flee to Vedeno but in which, according to Shamil and all his *murids*, he had achieved victory and had routed the Russians. In this battle, he himself fired his rifle, which rarely occurred, and, snatching out his sword, would have launched his horse straight at the Russians but had been restrained from doing so by his accompanying *murids*. Two of them were killed right next to Shamil.

It was midday when Shamil approached his residence surrounded by a party of *murids* who caracoled around him, fired their rifles and pistols and sang out ceaselessly "*La ilaha illa Allah!*" ["There is no god but God!"]

The entire population of the large *awul* of Vedeno stood in front of their houses and on the roofs to greet their master, and, in a sign of triumphant celebration, they fired a salute from their guns and pistols. Shamil rode a white Arab steed that pulled happily at the reins as it neared home. The horse had the plainest of gear without gold or silver ornamentation: a finely-worked red bridle with a stripe down the middle; metallic, cup-shaped stirrups; a red blanket that was visible from under the saddle. The imam wore a full-length sheep-skin coat covered on the outside with brown cloth and with black fur fringes showing at the collar and at the sleeves; meanwhile, stretched across his long, thin torso was a black leather halter holding a dagger. On his head he wore a tall Circassian fur cap, flat on the top with a black tassel; around his head was a white turban the end of which hung down his neck. He wore green leather slippers on his feet, and his calves were wrapped in black leggings, edged with plain braid.

In fact, the imam wore nothing glittering, no gold nor silver, yet his tall, ramrod-straight, powerful, simply-clothed figure, surrounded by *murids* whose clothes and weapons were festooned with gold and silver decorations, conveyed the very aura of majesty that he so desired to foster and that he had contrived to purvey among the people. His cement-colored face, set off by the red close-cropped beard and bordering the beady constantly-squinting eyes, was completely motionless, as if made of stone. As he rode through the *awul,* he felt thousands of eyes fixed on him, but his own eyes never rested on any man. Hadji Murat's wives and children, like all the other residents of his *saklya,* went out onto the balcony to watch the imam's arrival. Only the aged Patimat, Hadji Murat's mother, did not go out but remained sitting on the floor of the *saklya,* her gray hair loosened and unkept, her long arms clasping her thin knees, her fiery black eyes blinking as she stared at the smoldering branches in the fireplace. Like her son, she had always hated Shamil; now even more than formerly, so she had no desire to see him.

Nor did Hadji Murat's son witness Shamil's triumphant entrance. From his dark, fetid pit all he could do was listen to the shots and to the singing, so he suffered as only a vital young man deprived of freedom can suffer. Sitting in the stinking pit and seeing the familiar faces of his unfortunate, dirty, emaciated fellow prisoners who mostly hated one another, he passionately envied those *murids* who, enjoying fresh air, light, and freedom, caracoled on dashing mounts around the leader, firing their weapons and happily singing "*La ilaha illa Allah.*"

Having passed through the *awul,* Shamil entered a large courtyard that communicated with the inner courtyard where his seraglio was located. Two armed Lezgians greeted Shamil at the first courtyard's open gates. The courtyard was packed with people. Here were people who had come on business from distant places; here were petitioners; here, too, were those summoned by Shamil himself for trial and sentencing. As Shamil entered on horseback, everyone in the courtyard stood and respectfully greeted the imam, placing their hands to their breasts. Some knelt down and stayed on their knees the whole time that Shamil was crossing the courtyard from the outer gates to the inner ones. Although Shamil recognized among those waiting both many people he disliked and many boring petitioners who would demand his attention to their concerns, he rode past them with the same, stony expression, and, after entering the inner gates, he dismounted near the balcony of his residence, to the left of the gates.

After the tension of the campaign, which was taxing not so much physically as emotionally since Shamil, in spite of his public claim that the campaign had brought victory, knew well that the expedition had been a failure, that many Chechen *awuls* had been burned and destroyed, that this fickle, superficial people, the Chechens, were wavering, and that some of them, closest to the Russian-held territory, were on the verge of defecting to the Russians—all of which was depressing and would require counter-measures, Shamil felt momentarily that he wished neither to do nor to think about anything. He wanted only one thing now: relaxation and delight in the conubial caresses of his favorite wife, the eighteen-year-old, dark-eyed, quick-footed Christian, Aminet.

142

But it was not only impossible even to think about seeing Aminet, who was just on the other side of the fence running through the inner courtyard and separating the wives' quarters from the men's areas (Shamil was sure that even now, as he got down from his horse, Aminet and the other wives were watching through a chink in the fence), not only could he not go to her, he could not even lie down on a mattress and rest from his labors. He would first have to perform the midday prayer ritual, something he had not the slightest inclination to do now, but that was inconceivable not to perform, given his role as his people's religious leader, and that for Shamil himself had become as essential as his daily bread. So he completed his ablutions and prayers. After having finished his prayers, he summoned those who had awaited him.

The first to come to him was his father-in-law and teacher, a tall, gray-haired, immaculate old man with a beard white as snow and a flushed red face, Jamal Edin, who, after praying quickly, started to question Shamil about the events of the campaign and to report to him what had transpired in the mountains during his absence.

Among all kinds of matters—murders prompted by bloodfeuds, thefts of livestock, accusations of failure to observe the *sharia*'s prohibitions against smoking and drinking alcohol—Jamal Edin reported that Hadji Murat had despatched men to carry off his family to the Russians, but that this plot had been exposed and the family brought to Vedeno where its members now lived under guard, awaiting the imam's decision. In the adjoining guest room the elders had been assembled to discuss all these matters; Jamal Edin advised Shamil to dismiss them that same day, since they had already been waiting for him for three days.

After he had eaten the dinner brought to him by Zaidet, a sharp-nosed, dark-complexioned, unpleasant-looking woman whom he did not love yet was his first wife, he walked into the guest room.

Six men comprising his council stood to greet him: elders with grizzled gray and red beards, some heads in turbans and some not but all surmounted by high Circassian fur caps, torsos clad in new *beshmets* and Circassian coats girded by leather belts holding daggers. Shamil was a head taller than the others. Just as he did, they all raised their hands, palms upward, and, closing their eyes, they prayed, then moved their hands down their faces to the points of their beards until their palms met. After this, they all sat down, Shamil in the middle on a higher pillow, and they began to discuss all the current business.

Cases involving those accused of crimes were decided according to the *sharia*: for stealing two men were condemned to having a hand severed; another was sentenced to beheading for murder; three were pardoned. Then the elders came to the main item on the agenda: consideration of measures to combat Chechen defections to the Russians. To counteract such defections, Jamal Edin had composed the following proclamation:

"I wish you the eternal peace of Almighty God. I hear that the Russians sweet-talk you and call on you to submit to them. Do not trust them; do not submit: hold out. If you are not rewarded in this life, then you will receive your reward in the next life. Remember what happened before when they confiscated your weapons. If God had not brought you to your senses then, in 1840, you would long ago have become imperial soldiers and would have been walking about with muskets instead of your daggers, and your wives would have been walking about without veils and would have been dishonored. Judge the future by the past. It is better to die in enmity with the Russians than to live with the infidels. Hold out a bit longer, then, with *Quran* and saber, I shall come to lead you against the Russians. Right now I sternly command you to entertain neither the intention nor even the thought of surrendering to the Russians."

Shamil approved the proclamation and, having signed it, ordered it sent out.

After these issues had been disposed of, the case of Hadji Murat was discussed too. This matter was very important to Shamil. Although he did not want to admit it, he understood that if Hadji Murat, with all of his cunning, daring, and bravery, had been on his side, then things would not have gone the way they were going now in Chechnia. To make peace with Hadji Murat and enjoy his services again would have been good; since that was out of the question, however, Shamil could not afford to permit Hadji Murat to assist the Russians. Hence, in any case, it would be necessary to entice him back to Chechnia, and, having enticed him, to kill him. The way to kill him was either to send a man to Tbilisi who would kill him there or to entice him to Vedeno and murder him here. The bait to lure him back was his family, principally his son whom, Shamil knew, Hadji Murat passionately loved. Therefore, Shamil would have to work through the son.

When the councilors discussed this, Shamil closed his eyes and fell silent.

The councilors knew this meant that he was listening to the Prophet's voice speaking to him and indicating what had to be done. After a solemn, five-minute silence, Shamil opened his eyes and, squinting harder than usual, said: "Bring me Hadji Murat's son."

"He is here," Jamal Edin said.

And, in fact, Yusuf, Hadji Murat's son, thin, pale, tattered, and fetid, but still handsome in face and figure, with the same fiery, black eyes as his grandmother Patimat, was already standing at the gates of the outer courtyard awaiting a summons.

Yusuf did not share his father's feelings toward Shamil. He did not know the whole past history, or knowing it but not having lived through it, did not understand why his father so stubbornly opposed Shamil. To him who only wanted one thing—namely, the continuation of that wild and easy life that he, as the son of the *naib*, had lived in Khunzakh—it seemed completely unnecessary to be at odds with Shamil. As a rebuff to his father and to contradict him, he loudly praised Shamil and manifested toward him the exultant submissiveness that was widespread in the mountains. Yusuf entered the *kunak* room with a peculiar sense of anxious reverence for the imam and, stopping at the door, met Shamil's unyielding, flint-eyed gaze. He hesitated several moments, then went up to Shamil and kissed his large, long-fingered white hand.

144

"Boy, you are Hadji Murat's son?"

"I am, imam."

"You know what he has done, boy?"

"I know, imam, and I regret it."

"Can you write?"

"I studied to be a *mullah*."

"Then write your father that, if he returns to me now, before Bairam, I shall pardon him and all will be as before. If not and he stays with the Russians, then," Shamil frowned threateningly, "I shall send your grandmother and your mother to different *awuls;* as for you, boy, I shall cut off your head."

Not a muscle in Yusuf's face quivered, and he bowed his head to signify that he understood Shamil's words.

"Write it down and give it to my envoy."

Shamil fell silent and looked at Yusuf for a long time.

"Write that I have taken pity on you and shall not kill you, but shall put out your eyes, as I do the eyes of all traitors. Go."

Yusuf appeared calm in Shamil's presence, but when they had led him out of the *kunak* room, he threw himself on his escort and, having pulled the escort's dagger out of its sheath, tried to slit his own throat; but they grabbed him by the arms, tied him up, and carried him back to the pit.

That evening when prayers had been said and it had grown dark, Shamil donned his white full-length coat, walked behind the fence to that part of the courtyard quartering his wives, and headed for Aminet's room. But Aminet was not there. She was with the older wives. Then Shamil, trying not to be noticed, stood by the door of her room, waiting for her. But Aminet was angry at Shamil, because he had given silken fabric not to her but to Zaidet. She had seen him come out of his quarters and enter her room in search of her, so she deliberately stayed away from her room. She stood for a long time in the doorway of Zaidet's room and, smiling quietly, she glanced at the white figure, now entering, now exiting her room. Having waited for Aminet in vain, Shamil returned to his own room in time for midnight prayer.

XX

Hadji Murat had spent a week at the fortress in the home of Ivan Matveevich. Although Mar'ia Dmitrievna had quarreled with the hirsute Khanefi (Hadji Murat had only brought two men with him, Khanefi and Eldar) and had once shoved him out of the kitchen for which he had nearly knifed her, she obviously nurtured special feelings of respect and sympathy for Hadji Murat. She now no longer served him his meals, having handed that concern over to Eldar, but she took advantage of every opportunity to see him and to please him. She also participated in the liveliest manner in his parlays about his family; she knew how many wives he had, how many children and what their ages were; and after every visit by emissaries she quizzed everyone she could about the results of the discussions.

Butler himself became friends with Hadji Murat during that week. Sometimes Hadji Murat came to his room, sometimes he came to Hadji Murat's. Sometimes they spoke through an interpreter, sometimes through their own devices, through hand signals and most of all through smiles. That Hadji Murat liked Butler was evident from the way Eldar treated Butler. When Butler entered Hadji Murat's room, Eldar greeted Butler, baring his brilliant teeth in a joyous smile, hastily putting down cushions for him to sit on, and taking his sword, if he had it with him.

Butler also got to know and befriend the shaggy Khanefi, Hadji Murat's blood-brother. Khanefi knew many mountain songs and sang them well. For Butler's entertainment Hadji Murat would call Khanefi and order him to sing, naming those songs he considered the best. Khanefi's voice was a high tenor, his singing was extraordinarily clear and expressive. One of the songs, a favorite of Hadji Murat's, affected Butler with its majestically sad melody. Butler asked the interpreter to relate its gist, then he copied it down.

The song dealt with a blood-feud, such as the feud that had existed at one time between Hadji Murat and Khanefi.

The song went as follows:

> The earth on my grave will dry,
> You will forget me, mother of mine.
> Grass will overgrow my grave, father of mine,
> The grass will smother your grief.
> Tears will dry in your eyes, sister of mine.
> Out of your heart will fly your grief.
> But don't you forget me, elder brother of mine.
> Till you avenge my death.
> Don't you forget me, second brother of mine.
> Till you, too, lie under earth.
> Hot-blooded bullet, you bring me death.
> Were you once my faithful slave in need?
> You cover me over now, black earth,
> Didn't I trample you with my steed?
> Cold, cold you are, death.
> My faithful slave you were of nigh.
> Now my body belongs to the earth,
> My soul to the vaulting sky.

Hadji Murat always listened to this song with his eyes closed and, when it ended on a drawn-out, dying note, always said: "A good song, a wise song."

The poetry of the exotic, vigorous mountain life captivated Butler more profoundly than ever after Hadji Murat's arrival, so Butler naturally grew close to him and the *murids*. He started wearing *beshmet*, Circassian coat and leggings; he imagined himself as a mountaineer living life just as the mountaineers live it.

146

On the day of Hadji Murat's departure, Ivan Matveevich gathered several officers to see him off. The officers were sitting—some at a table where Mar'ia Dmitrievna was pouring tea, others at another table with vodka, *chikhir* brandy, and snacks—when Hadji Murat, dressed for the road and bearing arms, came limping into the room with quick, soft steps.

They all stood and shook hands with him in turn. Ivan Matveevich invited him to sit on the sofa, but Hadji Murat, thanking him, sat instead on a chair near the window. The silence that reigned during his entrance evidently did not bother him in the least. He glanced attentively at all the faces and looked indifferently at the table laden with samovar and hors d'oeuvres. Petrovskii, a lively officer who was seeing Hadji Murat for the first time, asked him through the interpreter whether he liked Tbilisi.

"*Aiya!*" he said.

"He says 'yes,'" said the interpreter.

"What did he like in particular?"

Hadji Murat answered something.

"He liked the theater best of all."

"And did he like the ball at the commander-in-chief's?"

Hadji Murat frowned.

"Each people has its own ways. Our women do not dress like that," he said, glancing at Mar'ia Dmitrievna.

"So, he didn't like it?"

"We have a saying," he said to the interpreter. "A dog fed meat to a donkey, and the donkey fed hay to the dog: both went hungry." He smiled. "To each people its own customs are good."

The conversation went no further. Some officers began to drink tea, others to eat hors d'oeuvres. Hadji Murat took the cup of tea offered to him and set it on the table in front of him.

"Like cream? Or a roll?" Mar'ia Dmitrievna asked, offering them to him.

Hadji Murat bowed his head.

"So, it's good-bye!" Butler said, touching him on the knee. "When will we meet again?"

"Good-bye, good-bye!" Hadji Murat said in Russian, smiling. "Butler—*kunak*. Strong *kunak*. Time—I go!" he said, motioning with his head in the direction he had to travel.

At the doors of the room Eldar appeared, carrying something large and white across his shoulder and holding a saber in his hand. When Hadji Murat beckoned, Eldar strode with his long strides up to Hadji Murat and gave him a white *burka* and the saber. Hadji Murat stood up, took the *burka* and, draping it across his arm, gave it to Mar'ia Dmitrievna, saying something to the interpreter. The interpreter said:

"He said, 'You praised the *burka*; take it.'"

"Oh, but why?" Mar'ia Dmitrievna said, blushing.

"It must be so. Our custom," said Hadji Murat.

"Well, thank you," said Mar'ia Dmitrievna, taking the *burka*. "May God grant that your son be rescued," she added. "*Ulan iakshi*," ["The son is good,"] she said. "Tell him I want him to rescue his family."

Hadji Murat looked at Mar'ia Dmitrievna and approvingly nodded his head. He then took the saber from Eldar's hands and gave it to Ivan Matveevich. Ivan Matveevich took the saber and said to the interpreter:

"Tell him to take my brown gelding; I have nothing else to give him."

Hadji Murat waved his hand in front of his face to indicate that he did not need anything and that he wouldn't accept the gelding, and then, pointing first to the mountains and then toward his heart, he moved toward the exit. Everyone followed him. The officers, who stayed inside, took the saber out of its scabbard, examined the blade and decided that it was a real Gurda.

Butler walked out with Hadji Murat onto the porch. But here something happened that no one had expected and that might have ended in Hadji Murat's death were it not for his fast reflexes, decisiveness, and agility.

The common residents of the Ghumuq *awul* Tash-Kichu, who nurtured a deep respect for Hadji Murat and who had visited the fortress many times just to catch a glimpse of the famous *naib*, had sent representatives to Hadji Murat three days before his departure, inviting him to their mosque for the Friday prayer service. On learning of this invitation, the Ghumuq princes from Tash-Kichu who hated Hadji Murat and had a blood feud with him, announced to the people that they would not admit Hadji Murat into the mosque. At this, the common people grew agitated, and a pitched battle broke out between them and the princes' supporters. The Russian authorities pacified the villagers and sent word to Hadji Murat that he could not visit the mosque. Hadji Murat did not go to the mosque, and everyone thought that that was the end of the matter.

Now, at the very moment of Hadji Murat's departure, as he came out onto the porch and as the horses stood at the steps, there rode up to Ivan Matveevich's home an acquaintance of Butler and Ivan Matveevich, the Ghumuq prince Arslan-Khan.

Catching sight of Hadji Murat, he snatched a pistol from his belt and pointed it at him. But before Arslan-Khan had managed to pull the trigger, Hadji Murat, despite his lameness, sprang cat-like off the porch at Arslan-Khan. Arslan-Khan fired but missed. Meanwhile, with one hand Hadji Murat had grabbed Arslan-Khan's horse by the reins, and the other hand had drawn his dagger, shouting something at him in Tatar.

Butler and Eldar dashed up to the enemies at the very same moment and grabbed them both by the arms. At the shot Ivan Matveevich rushed out, too.

"Arslan, how dare you start this crap at my house!" he said, when he learned what had happened. "You lost your mind? Outside the fortress you two 're free to go at it, but at my place there'll be no killing."

Arslan-Khan, a small man with a black mustache, his face all pale and quivering, dismounted his horse, sent a spiteful glance at Hadji Murat, and went with Ivan Matveevich into his quarters. For his part, Hadji Murat went back to the horses, breathing heavily and smiling.

"Why'd he try to kill you?" Butler asked through the interpreter.

"He says it is our law," the interpreter translated the words of Hadji Murat. "Arslan-Khan has to revenge himself on Hadji Murat for spilt blood. That's why he tried to kill him."

"And what if he overtakes him on the road?" Butler asked.

Hadji Murat smiled.

"If he kills me, that is Allah's will. So, good-bye," he said again in Russian and, grasping the horse by the mane, he took in with his eyes all those who were accompanying him and tenderly met the glance of Mar'ia Dmitrievna.

"Good-bye, little mother," he said, addressing her. "Thanks."

"God bless you and grant your family be rescued," Mar'ia Dmitrievna repeated.

He did not understand the words, but he understood her concern for him and nodded his head in reply.

"Look, don't forget your *kunak*," Butler said.

"Tell him, I am a true friend to him. I shall never forget," he answered through the interpreter. And, despite his crooked leg which barely touched the stirrup, he quickly and lightly raised his body into the high saddle and, having adjusted his saber and pistol with a practiced movement, he assumed that peculiar, proud military bearing characteristic of mountaineers on horseback and rode off from Ivan Matveevich's house. Khanefi and Eldar also mounted their horses and, bidding friendly farewells to their hosts and to the officers, trotted after their *murid*.

As always, talk flew about the man who had just departed.

"What a man!"

"He threw himself at Arslan-Khan like a wolf. His whole face changed."

"Yeah, but he's a liar. A real schemer, has to be," Petrovskii said.

"God grant us a few Russian schemers just like him," Mar'ia Dmitrievna suddenly interrupted with annoyance. "He stayed with us for a week, and we saw nothing but good from him," she said. "He's polite, smart, fair."

"How d'you know?"

"Guess I just do."

"Fallen for him, eh?" Ivan Matveevich said as he left. "That's the story."

"So I fell for him. What's it to you? Only why put down a good man. He's a Tatar, but he's a good man."

"You're right, Mar'ia Dmitrievna," said Butler. "Good you stood up for him."

XXI

For the inhabitants of the forward forts on the Chechen line life had returned to normal. There had been two more alarms against which the infantry companies had mustered out at a run and the militiamen had galloped out, but on neither occasion had they managed to catch the tribesmen. The mountaineers had melted away into the hills, and, once, near Vozdvizhensk the mountaineers had driven off eight Cossack horses from a watering hole and had killed a Cossack. There had been no more raids since the last one when the *awul* was destroyed. Action was suspended in expectation of a major expedition into Chechnia following the appointment of Prince Bariatinskii as the new commander on the left flank.

As soon as he had arrived in Groznyi, the new left flank commander Prince Bariatinskii, a friend of the heir to the throne and a former commander of the Kabardinskii Regiment, put together a detachment to continue executing the imperial strategy laid out by Chernyshev in his order to Vorontsov. Having assembled in Vozdvizhensk, the detachment departed the fortress to assume a position near that of the Kurinskii Regiment. On finding its post, the troops halted and started cutting trees.

The younger Vorontsov was quartered in a magnificent linen tent; his wife, Mar'ia Vasil'evna, visited the camp and often stayed the night. The relations between Bariatinskii and Mar'ia Vasil'evna were an open secret, so those officers and soldiers having no attachment to the court cursed her crudely because, owing to her presence in camp, they were sent out on night watches. The mountain tribesmen routinely brought up artillery and fired shells into the camp. The shots generally missed, and ordinarily the Russians took no measures against the bombardment; yet in order to stop the tribesmen from moving up guns and scaring Mar'ia Vasil'evna, soldiers were sent out on night watches. To go out on watch every night to prevent a lady being frightened was insulting and offensive, so the soldiers and officers who were not accepted into high society honored Mar'ia Vasil'evna with coarse words.

Butler came on leave from his outpost in order to visit with his classmates and regimental comrades-in-arms from the Corps of Pages who served in the Kurinskii regiment as the commander's adjutants and staffers. From the outset he enjoyed his visit immensely. He stopped by Poltoratskii's tent and there he found many acquaintances who greeted him joyously. He also visited Vorontsov whom he knew slightly, since they had once served in the same regiment. Vorontsov received him warmly, introduced him to Prince Bariatinskii, and invited him to a farewell dinner he was giving Bariatinskii's predecessor as left flank commander, General Kozlovskii.

The dinner was magnificent. Six tents were carted in and set up in a row. Down their whole length ran a table covered with place settings and bottles of wine. Everything was reminiscent of life in the St. Petersburg guards regiments. At two o'clock the guests were seated. At the center of the table sat Kozlovskii on one side and Bariatinskii on the other. To the right of Kozlovskii sat Prince Vorontsov, to the left Princess Vorontsova. The whole length of the table on both sides sat officers of the Kabardinskii and Kurinskii regiments. Butler sat next to Poltoratskii; they chattered merrily and drank with the officers around them. When it came time to eat the roasted meat and the orderlies had started to pour champagne by the bottle, Poltoratskii said to Butler, with genuine anxiety and regret:

"He'll disgrace himself, our 'you know.'"

"What d'you mean?"

"He has to make a speech, right? How'll he manage?"

"Look, it's not the same as taking a rampart under hostile fire."

"But he's got the lady beside him and these society people."

"True, it is painful to watch him," the officers agreed among themselves.

But here came the solemn moment. Bariatinskii rose to his feet, lifted his goblet, and addressed a short speech to Kozlovskii. When Bariatinskii had finished, Kozlovskii rose and in a fairly firm voice began speaking:

"By the supreme will of His Majesty, I leave you, part with you, fellow officers," he said. "But consider me always—you know—with you. You, gentlemen, are familiar—you know—with the truth that an individual alone in battle is not a real soldier. Therefore, everything that in my service—you know—I have been awarded, everything—you know—that has been showered on me by the great generosity of our Sovereign the Emperor—you know—all of my position—you know—and my good name, everything, literally everything—you know," here his voice began to quiver, "for everything I am obliged to you and you alone, my friends!" And his heavily-lined face wrinkled even more. He sobbed, and tears sprang to his eyes. "From the bottom of my heart I give you—you know—my sincere, heartfelt gratitude …"

Kozlovskii could say no more and, since he remained standing, he began to embrace his fellow officers as they came up to him one by one. Everyone was touched. The princess covered her face with her handkerchief. Prince Semyon Mikhailovich, his mouth twisted, blinked his eyes. Tears came to the eyes of several officers. Butler, who scarcely knew Kozlovskii, couldn't hold back the tears either. He found all this very moving. At that point toasts were drunk to Bariatinskii, to Vorontsov, to the officers, to the soldiers, so when the guests finally left the dinner, they were drunk on wine and *esprit de corps*, to both of which they were so susceptible.

The weather was splendid, sunny, calm; the fresh air was invigorating. All around bonfires crackled and singing resounded. Everybody seemed to be celebrating something. In the happiest, most exhilarated of moods Butler went to Poltoratskii's. There officers had gathered, a card table had been opened up, and the aide-de-camp had laid down a hundred rubles as the bank. Twice Butler left the tent, his hand in his pants pocket gripping his wallet, but in the end he couldn't hold himself back and, despite the promise he had made to himself and to his brother not to play cards, he began to gamble.

Less than an hour had passed before Butler, red-faced, sweating, hands messy with chalk dust, sat, elbows on the table, recording his wagers from crumpled ledger cards. He had lost so heavily that he was afraid to add up his total. Without adding, he knew that, even if he signed over in advance his pay and the value of his horse, he nevertheless could not pay the sum that the unknown aide-de-camp had written down next to his name. He would have continued to play, but the stern-faced aide-de-camp with the clean, white hands had laid down his cards and begun to tote up the chalk columns recorded by Butler. The embarrassed Butler asked to be excused, because he could not immediately pay his losses in full, and he said that he would have it sent from home, and, when he had said that, he noticed that everyone began to feel sorry for him and that everyone, even Poltoratskii, avoided his gaze. This was his last night on leave. He ought not to have played but should have gone to the Vorontsovs, where he had been invited, and "everything would have been alright," he thought. But now it was not only not alright, it was horrible.

Having taken leave of his comrades and acquaintances, he went home, and, arriving there, he immediately lay down and slept eighteen hours straight, as people generally do after losing heavily. Because he had asked her for a fifty-kopeck piece to tip the Cossack who had accompanied him home, and judging by his sad expression and curt answers, Mar'ia Dmitrievna guessed that he had lost at cards, and she had jumped all over Ivan Matveevich for letting him go on leave.

The next day Butler woke up at noon and, on remembering his situation, he would have liked to plunge back into the oblivion from which he had just emerged, but he couldn't do so. Steps had to be taken to repay 470 rubles that he owed to a complete stranger. One of those steps consisted of writing to his brother, confessing his sin, and begging him for the last time to send him 500 rubles against the mill, which they still jointly owned. Then he wrote a miserly female relative, asking her to lend him at whatever rate of interest she wanted that same 500 rubles. Next, he went to Ivan Matveevich, knowing that he—or rather, Mar'ia Dmitrievna—had money, to ask him for a loan of 500 rubles.

"I'd give it to you," Ivan Matveevich said. "I'd give it to you right away, but Mashka won't. These women are so damn tight-fisted, the devil alone can figure them out. But you've got to get out of this fix, damn it. What about that bastard storeowner, doesn't he have money?"

But there was no point trying the storeowner. So Butler's salvation could only come from his brother or his stingy female relative.

XXII

Not having achieved his goal in Chechnia, Hadji Murat returned to Tbilisi, where every day he visited Vorontsov's office, and, when he was admitted, implored the general to collect all imprisoned mountain tribesmen and to exchange them for his family. He said again that, without his family, his hands were tied and he couldn't serve the Russians and annihilate Shamil, as he wanted to do. Vorontsov vaguely promised to do what he could, but he was delaying action until General Argutinskii had come to Tbilisi and they had discussed the matter. Then Hadji Murat started to implore Vorontsov to permit him to go for a time to live in Nukha, a small settlement in the Transcaucasus where, he claimed, it would be easier for him to carry on negotiations over his family with Shamil and Shamil's loyalists. Besides, Nukha was a Moslem town with a mosque where he could more readily perform the prayers required by Islamic law. Vorontsov wrote to St. Petersburg about this, and in the meantime he allowed Hadji Murat to go to Nukha.

For Vorontsov, for the St. Petersburg authorities, and for most Russians familiar with the Hadji Murat affair, that affair represented either a happy turn in the Caucasian wars or simply an interesting incident; but for Hadji Murat himself it was, especially in recent days, a terrible turn in his life. He had fled the mountains partly to save himself, partly out of hatred of Shamil, and, despite a difficult flight, he had achieved his goal, and, at first, he had rejoiced over his success and had actually devised a plan of attack on Shamil. But it turned out that his family's rescue, which he had thought would be easily arranged, was more complicated than expected. Shamil had seized his family and, keeping them prisoner, had threatened to send the women to different *awuls* and to blind or kill his son. Now Hadji Murat was riding to Nukha to try, with the aid of his supporters in Daghestan, to rescue his family by guile or by force. The last emissary to visit him in Nukha had reported that Avars loyal to him were promising to abduct his family and come over to the Russians with them, but that the number of people ready to participate in the abduction was too few to carry out the plot at the family's place of imprisonment in Vedeno, so they would attempt the rescue only if the family were moved from Vedeno elsewhere. In that case, they resolved to seize the family during transit. Hadji Murat ordered his friends to be notified that he was pledging 3000 rubles for his family's rescue.

In Nukha Hadji Murat was allotted a small, five-room house not far from the mosque and the khan's palace. In that same house lived his officer escorts, an interpreter, and his bodyguards. Hadji Murat's life was spent waiting for and receiving emissaries from the mountains and taking rides permitted him on the outskirts of Nukha.

Returning from an outing on 8 April, Hadji Murat learned that, in his absence, an official from Tbilisi had arrived. In spite of his desire to discover what news the official had brought, before going to the room where a police officer and the official awaited him, Hadji Murat first went to his own quarters where he said his midday prayers. When he had finished his prayers, he went into the adjoining room that served as living room and a reception area. The official who had come from Tbilisi, a rotund state councillor named Kirillov, transmitted to Hadji Murat Vorontsov's request that he come to Tbilisi on April 12 for a meeting with Argutinskii.

"*Iakshi*," said Hadji Murat angrily.

He did not like State Councillor Kirillov.

"Did you bring money?"

"I brought it."

"It's two weeks late now," said Hadji Murat and showed ten fingers and then four more. "Give it here."

"We'll give it to you right away," the official said, getting his money purse out of travelling bag. "And what does he need money for?" he asked in Russian, assuming that Hadji Murat didn't understand, but Hadji Murat did understand and looked angrily at Kirillov. While fetching the money, Kirillov tried to strike up a conversation with Hadji Murat to have something to report to Prince Vorontsov on his return, so he asked Hadji Murat through the interpreter if living in Nukha wasn't boring. Hadji Murat glanced scornfully out of the corner of his eye at the small, fat man dressed in civilian clothes and without a weapon, and made no response. The interpreter repeated the question.

"Tell him that I don't want to talk with him. Let him give me the money." And, having said this, Hadji Murat sat down again at the table intending to count the money.

When Kirillov had drawn out the gold coins and arranged them in seven stacks of ten gold coins each (Hadji Murat received five gold coins a day), he pushed them toward Hadji Murat. Hadji Murat swept the gold into the sleeve of his Circassian coat, stood up, quite unexpectedly slapped the state councillor on his bald pate, and started to leave the room. The state councillor jumped to his feet and ordered the interpreter to tell Hadji Murat that he mustn't dare strike a state councillor whose rank was equivalent to an army colonel's. The police officer confirmed this. Hadji Murat nodded his head as a sign that he was aware of that, and left the room.

"What can you do with him," the police official said. "He'll stick a dagger in you, that's all. With these devils you can't reason. I see he's already turning into a wild beast."

As soon as dusk fell, two emissaries, hoods pulled down to their eyes, came in from the mountains. The police official led them inside to Hadji Murat. One of the emissaries was a fleshy, dark Tavlinian, the other a gaunt old man. The news they brought Hadji Murat was not good. His friends, who earlier had promised to rescue his family, now flatly refused the attempt, fearing Shamil, who had threatened the most severe punishments of those who helped Hadji Murat. Having heard the emissaries' report, Hadji Murat propped his arms on his crossed legs and, bowing his turbaned head, remained silent for a long time. Hadji Murat was thinking and thinking decisively. He knew that he was thinking for the last time, and it was essential to make a decision. Hadji Murat raised his head and, getting out two gold pieces, gave one to each of the emissaries and said: "Go."

"What will the answer be?"

"The answer will be what God wills. Go."

The emissaries rose to their feet, then exited the room; meanwhile, Hadji Murat continued sitting on the rug, propping his elbows on his knees. He sat that way and thought a long time.

"What to do? Trust Shamil and return to him?" Hadji Murat thought. "He's a fox, he'll lie to me. Even if he weren't lying, I can't surrender to him, to a red-headed liar. I can't, because now, after I've been with the Russians, he'll never trust me," Hadji Murat thought.

Then he recalled a Tavlinian tale about a falcon that had been captured, had lived with men, and had returned to its mountain home and to its own kind. The falcon returned but in fetters, fetters with small bells attached to them. The other falcons wouldn't accept him as one of their own. "Fly," they said to him, "to that place where they put the silver bells on you. We have no bells, no fetters." The falcon didn't want to abandon his homeland, so he stayed. But the other falcons refused to have him, and eventually they pecked him to death.

"They'll peck me to death the same way," thought Hadji Murat.

"Stay here? Conquer the Caucasus for the Russian tsar? Earn glory, titles, wealth?"

"That's possible," he thought, remembering his meeting with Vorontsov and the prince's flattering words.

"But I must decide immediately, or Shamil will destroy my family."

That entire night Hadji Murat stayed awake thinking.

XXIII

Toward the middle of the night his decision came together. He decided that he must flee to the mountains and, together with the Avars loyal to him, burst into Vedeno and either die or free his family. Whether to bring his liberated family back to the Russians or to flee with them to Khunzakh and fight Shamil from there, Hadji Murat had not resolved; he only knew that right away he would have to flee the Russians for the hills. So at once he began to put his decision into effect. He pulled his black, quilted *beshmet* from under his pillow and went to his retinue's quarters. His men were staying just across the hall. As soon as he entered the hallway with its door open to the outdoors, he was enveloped by the dewy freshness of the moonlit night, and his ears were struck by the simultaneous whistling and trilling of several nightingales in the garden adjoining the house.

Crossing the hall, Hadji Murat opened the door to his retinue's room. In the room there was no light, save from the new moon in its first quarter shining through the window. A table and two chairs stood to the side; four of his men lay on rugs and *burkas* on the floor. Khanefi was sleeping outside with the horses. Hearing the door squeak, Gamzalo got up, glanced at Hadji Murat and, recognizing him, lay back down. But Eldar, who was lying next to Gamzalo, jumped up and donned his *beshmet* in expectation of receiving orders. Kurban and Khan-Mahoma continued to sleep. Hadji Murat put his *beshmet* on the table, and the *beshmet* knocked on the wood of the table with the sound of something hard. The hard substance was gold rubles stitched into its lining.

"Sew these in, too," Hadji Murat said, giving Eldar the gold he had received that day.

Eldar took the gold and, moving quickly to a place where he could see, drew a small knife from under his dagger and began to unstitch the *beshmet*'s lining. Gamzalo raised himself up and sat with his legs crossed.

"And you, Gamzalo, tell the boys to look after their rifles and pistols, to ready the ammunition. Tomorrow we're going on a long ride," said Hadji Murat.

"There's bullets, there's powder. It will be ready," Gamzalo said and muttered something unintelligible.

Gamzalo understood why Hadji Murat had ordered the guns loaded. From the start—and the longer they stayed, the more the desire grew—he had wanted only to kill and slash as many Russian dogs as possible before fleeing to the hills. And now he saw that Hadji Murat wanted precisely that, so he was satisfied.

When Hadji Murat had left, Gamzalo woke his comrades, then all four spent the night looking over the rifles, pistols, gunpowder charges and flints, replacing the defective ones, sprinkling fresh powder on the pans, plugging up each firing packet with a bullet and a measured charge of gunpowder wrapped in a piece of oiled rag, sharpening sabers and daggers, and greasing the blades with fat.

Before dawn Hadji Murat went into the hallway again to get water for his ablutions. From the passageway, the nightingales, who burst into song at the coming light of dawn, could be heard even more distinctly than during the night. From his retinue's room issued the regular hiss and whistle of iron on stone made by a dagger being sharpened. Hadji Murat had dipped some water out of the barrel and had gotten as far as the door to his room, when he heard from his *murid*'s room, alongside the sound of sharpening, Khanefi's thin voice singing a familiar tune. Hadji Murat stopped and began to listen.

The song told how the *dzhigit* Hamza and his boys wrestled a herd of white horses from the Russians, how a Russian prince overtook them beyond the Terek river, and how the prince surrounded them with an army as great as a forest. Then the song told how Hamza had slaughtered the horses and, having entrenched himself with his men behind a bloody rampart of dead horses, how they had fought the Russians so as long as there were bullets in their rifles, daggers in their belts, and blood in their veins. But before he died, Hamza spied some birds flying in the sky and shouted to them: "You, migrating birds, fly to our homes and tell our sisters, our mothers and our fair maidens that we all died for the *ghazwa*. Tell them that our bodies won't lie in graves, but savage wolves will drag our bones away and devour them, and black crows will pluck out our eyes."

The song ended with these words, and to those last words sung in a mournful melody were added the brisk voice of the cheerful Khan-Mahoma, who shouted at the very end of the song "*La ilaha illa Allah!*" and let loose a piercing cry. Then everything quieted down, and again there could be heard nothing but the nightingales' clucking and whistling from the garden and the regular hiss and occasional whistle of iron slipping quickly across whet stones on the other side of the door.

Hadji Murat was so lost in thought that he failed to notice that he had tipped over a pitcher and water had poured out of it. He shook his head at himself and went back into his room.

Having finished the morning prayer, Hadji Murat looked over his weapons and sat on his bed. There was nothing more to do. To ride out of town, he would still have to ask permission of the police official. But his courtyard was still dark, and the police official was still asleep.

Khanefi's song reminded him of another song composed by his mother. The song told of things that had actually happened when Hadji Murat was born and which his mother used to recount to him.

The song went as follows:

> Your damask steel dagger pierced my white bosom, but I pressed my little sunflower, my boy, against it; I washed him with my warm blood, and my wound healed over without grasses and roots. I was not afraid of death, and my *dzhigit* son will not fear it either.

The words of the song were addressed to Hadji Murat's father, and the meaning of the song was that at the same time that Hadji Murat was born, the *khansha* also gave birth to her second son Bulat-Khan. The *khansha* demanded that Hadji Murat's mother, Patimat, who had nursed her older son Abununtsal-Khan, come and serve as wet nurse. But Patimat did not want to leave her son and said that she would not go. Hadji Murat's father got angry and ordered Patimat to obey. When she again refused, he struck her with a dagger and would have killed her if relatives had not dragged her away. In the end, she stayed with her son and nursed him: that incident was the subject of her song.

Hadji Murat remembered his mother as she put him down to sleep next to her under a fur cover on the *saklya* roof, as she sang him that song, and as she was when he had asked her to show him the place on her side where the mark of the wound still remained. He vividly pictured in front of himself his mother— not the wrinkled, gray-haired, gap-toothed woman he had recently left behind, but the one that was young, beautiful, and so strong that, when he was already five years old and heavy, she had carried him on her back in a basket over the mountains to his grandfather's.

And he remembered his wrinkled, gray-bearded grandfather, the silversmith, how he had hammered silver with his sinewy hands and had made his grandson say prayers. He remembered a fountain down the mountain, where he, holding on to the leg of his mother's wide trousers, had gone with her to get water. He remembered the skinny dog that licked his face, and the special smell of smoke and sour milk when he went with his mother to the barn, where she milked the cows and heated the milk. He remembered how it was the first time she had shaved his head, and how he had gazed wonderingly into the bright, bronze wash basin hanging on the wall at the image of his own round, blue-veined head.

And having remembered himself as a small child, he then remembered his beloved son Yusuf, whose head he himself had shaved for the first time. Now this Yusuf was already a young, handsome *dzhigit*. He remembered his son as he had seen him the last time. That had been on the very day he had ridden out of Tsel'mes. His son had brought him a horse and had asked permission to accompany him. Yusuf had been dressed and armed and had held his own horse by the reins. Yusuf's handsome, young, ruddy face, his tall, thin figure—he was taller than his father—breathed the courage of youth and the joy of living. Yusuf's shoulders, broad despite his youth, his very wide, youthful hips, his long, thin torso, his long, powerful arms, the strength, suppleness, and agility of his movements always gladdened his father, so the father had always taken pride in his son.

"It's better that you stay. You are the only man in the house now. Protect your mother and your grandmother," Hadji Murat had said.

And Hadji Murat remembered the expression of pride and spirit with which Yusuf had, blushing with pleasure, said that, as long as he lived, no one would harm his mother or grandmother. Nonetheless, Yusuf had mounted his horse and accompanied his father as far as the stream. At the stream, he had turned back, and since that moment Hadji Murat had not seen wife, mother or son again.

And this was the very son that Shamil wanted to blind! What Shamil would do to Hadji Murat's wife—that he did not even want to think about.

These thoughts so agitated Hadji Murat, he couldn't sit any longer. He jumped up and, limping quickly, went to the door, opened it, and shouted for Eldar. The sun had still not risen, but it was completely light. The nightingales had not stopped singing.

"Go tell the police official that I want to take a ride, then saddle the horses," he said.

XXIV

Throughout this period Butler's sole consolation was the poetry of military life to which he surrendered himself not only while on duty, but also in private life. Dressed in Circassian clothes, he rode his horse in the *dzhigit* manner and twice went out with Bogdanovich on ambush, although on neither occasion was anybody captured or killed. Such daring and his friendship with the brave Bogdanovich seemed to Butler somehow pleasant and stimulating. Meanwhile, he paid off his debt by borrowing money from a Jew on prohibitive interest— that is, he bought time and put off his day of financial reckoning. He tried not to think about his situation and, in addition to losing himself in combat, he sought oblivion in wine. He was drinking more and more, and so, from one day to the next, he fell deeper into moral decline. He no longer played the noble Joseph to Mar'ia Dmitrievna; on the contrary, he began to make vulgar advances to her, although, to his surprise, he was firmly rebuffed, which deeply embarrassed him.

In late April, there arrived at the fort a detachment designated by Bariatinskii to spearhead a new drive into what had previously been considered the impenetrable heart of Chechnia. Here were two companies of the Kabardinskii Regiment, and, according to the custom established in the Caucasus, these companies were received as guests by the companies already stationed in Kurinsk. Simple soldiers were assigned to various barracks where they were treated not only to a supper of cooked grain and boiled beef but also to vodka, while officers were billeted with their fellow officers, and again, following custom, the local officers hosted the new arrivals.

The partying ended in a drinking bout and ribald singing, and Ivan Matveevich —very drunk, no longer ruddy-cheeked but pale-gray—sat on a chair as if on a horse, and, having grabbed a sword, slashed at his imaginary foes with it, alternately swearing, laughing, embracing someone, and dancing to his favorite song: "Shamil started a revolt in years gone by, Try-rye-Ra-ta-tye, in years gone by."

Butler was at the party, too. He kept unsuccessfully trying to see even in this the poetry of military life, yet, though he felt dreadfully sorry for Ivan Matveevich, he could do nothing to put an end to his antics. So Butler, feeling tipsy, quietly slipped away and set off for home.

The full moon shone on the little white houses and on stones in the road. It was so bright that every pebble, straw, and piece of dung on the road could be seen. On approaching home, he encountered Mar'ia Dmitrievna, a shawl covering her head and neck. After Mar'ia Dmitrievna's rebuff, his conscience slightly pricked, Butler had been avoiding her. Now, intoxicated by moonlight and wine, he rejoiced to see her and felt the urge to wheedle himself into her affections again.

"Where're you headed?" he asked.

"Just checking on my old man," she answered genially. She had sincerely and firmly rebuffed Butler's advances, but it bothered her that recently he had been avoiding her.

"Why check up on him? He'll be coming along."

"Under his own power?"

"If not under his own power, they'll carry him."

"Either way, it's bad news," said Mar'ia Dmitrievna. "So I shouldn't go after him?"

"No, there's no point. Let's head home instead."

Mar'ia Dmitrievna turned about and walked toward home alongside Butler. The moon was shining so brightly that, as their shadows danced on the roadside, there danced around their heads shimmering halos. Catching sight of the shimmering, Butler wanted to tell Mar'ia Dmitrievna that he still had feelings for her, but he didn't know how to start. Meanwhile, she was waiting to hear what he would say. In silence they had walked almost all the way home, when from around the corner horsemen galloped. An officer was leading a convoy.

"Who in God's name is that?" Mar'ia Dmitrievna said, jumping to the side.

The moon was shining from behind the approaching riders, so that Mar'ia Dmitrievna did not recognize the officer until he had almost drawn even with them. The officer, a man named Kamenev, had previously served with Ivan Matveevich, so Mar'ia Dmitrievna knew him.

"Pyotr Nikolaevich, is that you?" Mar'ia Dmitrievna asked him.

"The one and only," said Kamenev. "Hey, Butler, hello. Not asleep yet? Strolling with Mar'ia Dmitrievna? Watch out, Ivan Matveevich'll give you hell. Where is he?"

"Hear that?" said Mar'ia Dmitrievna, pointing in the direction from which came the sound of the music of a big, bass drum and singing. "The boys're getting smashed."

"Who is? Your unit?"

"No, troops just came in from Khasav-Iurt, so we're throwing them a party."

"Ah, that's nice. Look, I'm in a hurry. I need to see him for just a minute."

"What's up? Something important?" Butler asked.

"A minor little matter."

"Good or bad?"

"Depends. For us it's good; for a certain somebody it's pretty awful." And Kamenev broke into laughter.

At that moment, the two on foot and Kamenev reached Ivan Matveevich's house.

"Chikhirev!" Kamenev shouted to a Cossack, "Come on over here!"

A Don Cossack broke formation and rode up. He had the usual Don Cossack uniform, the high boots, the overcoat, and over his saddle were slung saddlebags.

"Well, get the thing out," Kamenev said, sliding down off his horse.

The Cossack also dismounted, then grabbed out of his saddlebags a sack with something inside. Kamenev took the sack from the Cossack and plunged his hand inside it.

"So, shall I show you a surprise? Promise you won't get scared?" he asked Mar'ia Dmitrievna.

"What's to be afraid of?" Mar'ia Dmitrievna said.

"Here then," said Kamenev, hauling out a man's head and holding it up to the light of the moon. "Recognize it?"

The head was shaved on top; the eyes were sunk beneath protrusions of the bony forehead; the mouth was surrounded by a small, close-cropped dark beard and trimmed mustache; one eye was wide-open, the other half-closed; the shaven cranium was hacked open but not cut all the way through; the nose was covered with dark, dried, caked blood. The neck was wound about with a blood-soaked towel. Despite all the wounds to the head, a child-like kindness expressed itself on the blue lips.

Mar'ia Dmitrievna looked at the skull, and, saying nothing, averted her body and strode rapidly into the house.

Butler couldn't tear his eyes away from the terrifying head. It was the head of that very same Hadji Murat with whom he had so recently spent several evenings in friendly conversation.

"How'd it happen? Who killed him? Where?" he asked.

"He tried to run off, we caught him," Kamenev said, passing the head to the Cossack, then going inside the house with Butler.

"He died like a real man," Kamenev said.

"But, how did this all happen?"

"Just wait a bit. When Ivan Matveevich comes back, I'll give you all the details. Anyway, that's why I'm here. I ride around to all the forts and *auls*, and show it."

They sent for Ivan Matveevich, and, when he finally returned home—drunk and accompanied by two other, extremely drunk officers—he roused himself to embrace Kamenev.

"I brought you Hadji Murat's head," Kamenev said.

"You're lying! They killed him?"

"Yes. He tried to run away."

"I said, he'd scam us. So where is it? The head? Show me."

They yelled for the Cossack, and he brought the sack with the head in it. They took out the head, and Ivan Matveevich, with drunken eyes, looked at it for a long time.

"Well, all the same he was a fine fellow," he said. "Give him here, I'll give him a kiss."

"Yes, it's true, a devilish, dashing head," said one of the officers.

When everyone had looked over the head, they gave it back to the Cossack. The Cossack put it in the sack, trying to set it on the floor so that it bumped as lightly as possible.

"So, Kamenev, you make a speech when you're showing it?" asked one officer.

"No, let me kiss him, he gave me his saber," Ivan Matveevich shouted.

Butler went out on the porch. Mar'ia Dmitrievna was sitting on the second step. She glanced at Butler and angrily turned away.

"What's with you, Mar'ia Dmitrievna?" asked Butler.

"You're all butchers. I can't stand it. Butchers, that's what," she said, pulling herself erect.

"The same thing could happen to any of us," Butler said, not knowing what to say. "That's war."

"War?" screamed Mar'ia Dmitrievna. "Some war! Butchers! That's all you are. A dead body should be given back to the earth, instead you scoff at it. Butchers, really!" she repeated, then and she stepped down off the porch and walked away from him toward the house's back door.

Butler returned to the living room and asked Kamenev to relate in detail how the whole affair had happened.

And Kamenev did as requested.

Here is what happened.

XXV

Hadji Murat was allowed to go out riding, but close to town and always with a Cossack escort. The Cossacks in Nukha numbered only half a company, of whom around ten were assigned to the staff officers; the others were supposed to do guard detail every other day in groups of ten. At first, therefore, ten Cossacks were sent on detail with Hadji Murat; later it was decided to send out a detail of five on condition that Hadji Murat not take with him a full complement of bodyguards, but on April 25 Hadji Murat went riding with all five of his men. As Hadji Murat mounted his horse, the watch commander had noticed that all five bodyguards apparently intended to go riding with him, so the commander had said to him that he was not allowed to take all of them with him, but Hadji

Murat, as if he hadn't heard, had touched his horse to go, and the watch commander had not insisted. With the Cossacks rode a non-commissioned officer, a man sporting the Cross of St. George for bravery, his hair fringe-cut, the young, strapping, tanned, and robust Nazarov. He was the oldest son of a poor family of Old Believers, who grew up without a father and fed his elderly mother, his three sisters, and two brothers.

"Look, Nazarov, don't let him ride far!" shouted the watch commander.

"Aye, Aye, Your Excellency," answered Nazarov and, his rifle strapped across his back, he rose in his stirrups, then eased his fine, strong, angular-muzzled chestnut gelding into a trot. Four Cossacks rode with him: Ferapontov, tall and thin, a real thief and looter, the very one who had sold gunpowder to Gamzalo; Ignatov, a soldier finishing up his hitch, a no-longer young, strapping peasant, who bragged about his strength; Mishkin, a weak-limbed adolescent at whom everyone laughed; and Petrakov, young, fair-haired, his mother's only son, always gentle and cheerful.

Since dawn it had been foggy, but by breakfast the weather had cleared, and now the sun was shining on the newly-sprouted foliage, on the young, virgin grass, on the tender sprouts of grain, and on the rippling waters in the fast-flowing stream visible to the left of the road. Hadji Murat's horse moved slowly forward; the Cossacks and his bodyguards, not lagging behind, followed after him. The horses ambled along the road beyond the fort. They encountered women with baskets on their heads, soldiers on wagons, and creaking ox-drawn carts. Having gone out a mile or so, Hadji Murat spurred his white Kabardian horse; he set a pace that required his bodyguards to go at a brisk trot. The Cossacks rode at the same speed.

"Ah, he's got a fine horse under him," said Ferapontov. "Let him turn against us, and I'll sit on that horse myself."

"You bet, brother. They'd give three hundred rubles for that horse in Tbilisi."

"But I could pass him on mine," Nazarov said.

"No way you'd pass him," said Ferapontov.

Hadji Murat kept increasing his pace.

"Hey, *kunak*, that's not allowed. Slow down," shouted Nazarov, pushing to overtake Hadji Murat.

Hadji Murat looked around and, saying nothing, continued to ride at the same speed, not slackening his pace.

"Look, they're up to something, the devils," said Ignatov. "See, whipping their horses."

In this way they rode half a mile toward the mountains.

"Halt, I say!" Nazarov shouted again.

Hadji Murat neither answered nor looked back, but only increased his pace again, going from a trot to a gallop.

"Bastard! You won't escape!" shouted Nazarov, cut to the quick.

He struck his massive, chestnut gelding with his whip, then, standing in his stirrups and bending forward, rode at full speed after Hadji Murat

The sky was so clear, the air so fresh, the strength of life so joyfully played in Nazarov's soul as he blended into a single being with his good, strong horse and flew down the level road after Hadji Murat, that the possibility did not enter his head that something unfortunate, distressing or terrible might happen to him. He was rejoicing that with every stride he was gaining on Hadji Murat and drawing closer to him. Hadji Murat sensed by the approaching hoof clatter from Nazarov's massive horse that the Cossack would overtake him shortly, and, drawing his pistol with his right hand, with his left he began to gently rein in the Kabardian, which was excited by the chase and which also heard the hoof clatter from behind.

"Halt, I say!" shouted Nazarov, almost pulling even with Hadji Murat and extending his hand to grab the Karbardian's bridle. But he had not succeeded in grabbing the bridle when a shot rang out.

"What are you doing?" shouted Nazarov, clutching his chest. "Blast 'em, boys," he cried, reeling forward then falling across the bow of his saddle.

But the mountaineers pulled their weapons first, and they shot the Cossacks with their pistols and slashed them with their sabers. Nazarov hung across the neck of his frightened horse, which carried him in a circle around his comrades. A horse fell on Ignatov, pinning his leg underneath. Two mountaineers grabbed their swords and, without dismounting, slashed him about the head and arms. Petrakov was about to rush to his comrades' assistance, when two bullets, one in his back and one in his side, burned into him, so he tumbled like a sack of potatoes from his horse.

Mishkin turned his horse around and galloped toward the fort. Khanefi and Khan-Mahoma hurtled after him, but he was already far ahead, and the mountaineers could not catch him.

Having ascertained that they couldn't catch the Cossack, Khanefi and Khan-Mahoma returned to the group. Gamzalo finished off Ignatov with his dagger, stabbed Nazarov too, and threw him down off his horse. Khan-Mahoma took the cartridge bags off the dead. Khanefi wanted to take Nazarov's horse, but Hadji Murat shouted at him to leave it and dashed forward down the road. His *murids* galloped after him, chasing away Petrakov's horse which was following them. They were already two miles or so from Nukha among some rice fields, when a shot rang out from a tower in the fort, sounding the alarm.

All the while, Petrakov was lying on his back, his stomach split open and his young face turned to the heavens; gasping like a fish out of water, he was slowly expiring.

"Oh, by the souls of our forefathers, what have they done!" cried the commander of the fort, taking his head in his hands, when he learned of Hadji Murat's escape. "They've cost me my head. They've let him get away, the scoundrels!" he shouted, when he heard Mishkin's report.

A general alarm was sounded: not only were all Cossacks in the vicinity sent in pursuit of the fugitives, so too was every available militiaman from pacified *awuls*. A reward of one thousand rubles was promised to whomever brought in Hadji Murat, dead or alive. So two hours after Hadji Murat and his retinue had escaped from the Cossacks, more than two hundred men on horseback had galloped off behind the chief of police to locate and apprehend the fugitives.

After travelling a few miles down the main road, Hadji Murat reined in his heavy-breathing white horse, which was now gray with sweat. To the right of the road were visible the *saklyas* and minaret of Belardzhik *awul*, to the left there were fields at the end of which a river could be seen. Although the way to the mountains was to the right, Hadji Murat turned in the opposite direction, to the left, reasoning that his pursuers would head toward the mountains. Meanwhile, abandoning the road, he would ford the Alazan, come out onto the main highway where no one would expect him, then follow the river as far as the forest, and, crossing the river again, make his way to the mountains. Having decided this, he turned to the left. But it proved impossible to reach the river. The rice field through which they had to ride had just been flooded as always happened in the spring, and it had turned into a quagmire into which the horses' hooves sunk to the pasterns. Hadji Murat and his bodyguards zigzagged first to the right, then to the left in search of a drier spot, but the field into which they had ventured had been flooded evenly and was completely saturated by water. The horses, their feet sounding like popping bottle corks, kept trying to pull their sunken hooves out of the sticky mud, and, breathing heavily after having gone a few feet, kept stopping.

The men struggled on this way until dusk, but still they had not reached the river. To the left was a small elevated island covered by small-leafed bushes, so Hadji Murat decided to ride into these bushes and, giving a rest to his worn-out horses, to spend the night.

Having made it into the underbrush, Hadji Murat and his bodyguards dismounted their horses and, hobbling them, allowed them to feed, while they themselves ate bread and cheese they had prepared. The young moon that at first had lit the sky had now set behind the mountains, so the night was dark. In Nukha there had been a great many nightingales. Even in these bushes there were two of them. While Hadji Murat and his men were making noise as they made their way through the underbrush, the nightingales had stayed quiet. But as soon as the men had quieted down, the birds began to chatter and call to each other again. Hadji Murat, taking in the sounds of the night, involuntarily listened to them.

And their whistling reminded him of that song about Hamza that he had heard early that same morning when going out for water. Any minute now, he might find himself in Hamza's very situation. As soon as he realized that things would turn out precisely that way, he suddenly became very serious. He unfolded his *burka* and performed his prayers. Scarcely had he finished them when he heard sounds approaching the bushes. The sounds came from a large number of horses' hooves smacking through the quagmire. Sharp-eyed Khan-Mahoma, running to one end of the underbrush, made out through the darkness the black shadows of horses and riders. Khanefi saw the same group from the other side. It was Karganov, the district military commander and his militia.

"Well, then, we'll fight as Hamza did," thought Hadji Murat.

After the alarm had been given, Karganov had plunged into the hunt for Hadji Murat with a company of militiamen and Cossacks but had found no sign of him anywhere. Having lost hope, Karganov had already turned for home when, just before nightfall, he had run across an old Tatar man. Karganov had asked the old man if he had seen six men on horseback. The old man answered that he had. He had seen six riders wander through a rice field and go into the thicket, where he usually gathered firewood. Taking the old man with him, Karganov had turned around to find the thicket, where the sight of hobbled horses assured him that Hadji Murat was there; Karganov had then surrounded the thicket under cover of the night and had waited for morning to take Hadji Murat, dead or alive.

Realizing that he was surrounded, Hadji Murat noticed an old ditch in the middle of the thicket; he decided to dig in there and defend himself as long as his ammunition and strength would permit. He informed his men of this plan, and ordered them to raise an earthen rampart in front of the ditch. And the bodyguards immediately got busy cutting branches, digging up the earth with their daggers and building the rampart. Hadji Murat worked with them.

As soon as it started to get light, the commander of the company militia rode up close to the thicket and yelled:

"Hey, Hadji Murat, surrender! We are many, and you are few."

In answer from the ditch came a puff of smoke, then a rifle cracked, its bullet struck the militiaman's horse, which reared up under him and began to fall. Soon thereafter, shots rang out from the rifles of the militiamen standing on the perimeter of the thicket, and their bullets, whistling and buzzing, began clipping off leaves and branches and landing in the earth rampart, yet they didn't strike the men squatting behind the mound. Only Gamzalo's straggling horse was hit by gunfire. The animal was wounded in the head. It didn't fall, but, breaking its hobble, crashed through the underbrush, rushed up to the other horses, and having pressed itself against them, spilled its blood on the young grass. Hadji Murat and his men only fired when one of the militiamen moved forward, and they rarely missed their mark. Three militiamen were wounded and the rest, far from resolving to attack Hadji Murat and his men, moved further away from them and fired only from a distance and randomly.

The battle continued this way for more than an hour. The sun had risen half-way through the trees, and Hadji Murat had already begun to think about jumping on the horses and trying to break through to the river when shouts from a large, newly-arrived party were heard. This was the Mekhtulian, Hadji-Aga, and his men. There were two hundred of them. Hadji-Aga had once been Hadji Murat's *kunak* and had lived with him in the mountains, but later had defected to the Russians. With them was Akhmet-Khan, the son of Hadji Murat's enemy. Hadji-Aga began just as Karganov had done, shouting to Hadji Murat to surrender, but, just as on the first occasion, Hadji Murat answered with a rifle shot.

"Sabers, boys!" shouted Hadji-Aga, grabbing his weapon, and there issued forth the sound of a hundred men's voices as they rushed loudly into the thicket.

The militiamen ran into the thicket, but from behind the earth rampart several shots cracked out in succession. Three men fell and the attack faltered, then from the edge of the thicket the militia returned fire. As they fired, they gradually approached the rampart, running from bush to bush. Several succeeded in taking cover; several others fell to bullets from Hadji Murat and his men. Hadji Murat fired without missing; Gamzalo also rarely wasted a shot and yelped with joy each time he saw his bullet find its mark. Kurban sat at the edge of the mound singing, "*La ilaha illa Allah!*" he did not rush his shots, but they seldom hit their target. Eldar's whole body was shaking with impatience to charge the enemy with his dagger, so he fired often and erratically, constantly looking over at Hadji Murat and peering over the rampart. The hirsute Khanefi, sleeves rolled up, did the work of a servant even here. He loaded the guns that Hadji Murat and Kurban handed him, carefully driving home with an iron ramrod the bullets wrapped in an oily piece of rag and pouring dry powder from the powder horn into the firing pan. Khan-Mahoma did not squat down in the ditch like the others, but ran from the ditch to the horses, driving them to a safer spot, and shrieking incessantly he fired without using a gun rest for his rifle barrel. He was the first to be wounded. A bullet struck him in the neck, and he sat back, spitting blood and cursing. The next to be wounded was Hadji Murat. A bullet passed through his shoulder. Hadji Murat tore some cotton matting from his *beshmet*, stopped up the wound, and went on firing.

"Let's charge them with our swords," Eldar said for the third time.

He peered out from behind the earth mound, ready to hurl himself at the enemy, but at that very moment a bullet hit him, he staggered and fell backwards onto Hadji Murat's leg. Hadji Murat looked down at him. His wonderful, ram's eyes gazed fixedly and seriously at Hadji Murat. His mouth, its upper lip protruding like a child's, twitched without opening. Hadji Murat pulled his leg out from under Eldar and continued firing. Khanefi bent over Eldar's dead body and began to take the unused cartridges out of his *cherkesska*. Kurban all the while kept singing, slowly loading and taking aim.

The enemy, running from bush to bush with whoops and shrieks, was advancing ever closer. Another bullet struck Hadji Murat in his left side. He lay in the ditch and again, taking a piece of matting from his *beshmet*, stopped up the wound. The wound in his side was mortal, and he felt that he was dying. With unusual speed memories and images succeeded one another in his imagination. First he saw before him the mighty Abununtsal-Khan holding up his sliced, hanging cheek and charging his enemies, dagger in his hand; then he saw feeble, bloodless old Vorontsov with the white, crafty face, and even heard his soft voice; then he saw his son Yusuf, then his wife Sofiat, then the red-bearded, squint-eyed, pale face of his adversary Shamil.

And all of these memories ran through his imagination without summoning up any feelings in him: neither pity, nor anger nor any kind of desire. All this seemed insignificant in comparison to what was about to begin or rather had already begun in him. Meanwhile, his powerful body continued the thing it had begun. He gathered his last strength, raised himself out of the ditch, fired his pistol and hit one of the men running up to him. The man fell. Then he pulled himself completely out of the ditch and with his dagger in his hand went forward, limping heavily, to meet the enemy. Several shots rang out; he staggered and fell. Several militiamen sprang at the fallen body with triumphant shouts. But what had seemed like a dead body to them suddenly began to stir. First the bloody, shaved, turbanless head rose, then the torso stood erect, and, gripping the tree, the man had raised himself up to full height. He seemed so terrifying that those running at him stopped in their tracks. But suddenly he shuddered, staggered away from the tree, then from his full posture, like a scythed thistle, he fell forward on his face and did not move again.

He didn't move, but he could still feel. When Hadji-Aga, the first of those running up to reach him, struck his head with a large dagger, it seemed to him that they were beating his head with a hammer, and he couldn't understand who was doing this and why. That was his last consciousness of any connection with his body. He felt nothing further, so that when his enemies stomped on him and stabbed him, this had nothing to do with him. Hadji-Aga placed his foot on the back of the body and cut the head off with two blows, then carefully, so as not to stain his shoes with blood, used his foot to roll the head away from the body. Bright red blood gushed out of the severed neck, dark red blood poured from the head onto the grass.

Karganov, Hadji-Aga, Akhmet-Khan, and all the militiamen, like hunters over a dead animal, gathered up the bodies of Hadji Murat and his men (Khanefi, Kurban, and Gamzalo had been bound together), then, standing among the bushes amid the gun smoke and talking joyfully, they had celebrated their victory.

The nightingales, silent while the firing lasted, started trilling again, the one close at hand being first to sing, the one on the far side following suit.

It was this death of which the crushed thistle in the midst of the ploughed field reminded me.

Notes

1   Susan Layton, *Russian Literature and Empire: Conquest of the Caucasus from Pushkin to Tolstoi* (Cambridge, UK: Cambridge University Press, 1994), p. 336, n. 3.
2   "*Hadji Murat* has been unjustly neglected by foreign readers, no doubt because of the infelicitous rendering of the colloquial speech of soldiers and tribesmen which mars the standard translations, and the lack of polish which a final revision would have ensured." R. F. Christian, "The Later Stories," in Edward Wasiolek, ed., *Critical Essays on Tolstoi* (Boston: G. K. Hall & Co., 1986), p. 190.
3   Ibid.
4   Harold Bloom, "Introduction," in Harold Bloom, ed., *Leo Tolstoy* (New York: Chelsea House Publishers, 1986), pp. 1–2.
5   Ibid., p. 5.

Part III

WAR OF WORLDS

A COMMENTARY ON THE TWO TEXTS IN THEIR HISTORICAL CONTEXT

Gary Hamburg

The earliest reported encounters of the Eastern Slavs with the Islamic world occurred in the eighth and ninth centuries, when traders from Kievan Rus' journeyed southwest toward the Danubian basin and southeast toward the Caucasus and Central Asia. On the basis of these episodic commercial connections, the writer Ibn Khurdadhbih included the people of Rus' in his classic geography of the Islamic world.[1] By the tenth century more systematic contact between the Rus and their distant Muslim neighbors had led to the first religious disputes between emissaries of the Kievan principality and Islamic peoples to the south. A legendary reflection of these disputes was recorded in the first Kievan historical chronicle, *Povest' vremennykh let* [*Tale of Bygone Years*], under the year 986, when Prince Vladimir demanded that Muslims, probably Danubian Bulgars, explain their faith.[2] After hearing their explication, Vladimir commented that Russians could never accept Islam because "Russians love [alcoholic] drink, and we cannot be without it."

By the mid-fifteenth century the Orthodox Russians could no longer dismiss Islam as casually as Prince Vladimir once had done. With the capture of Constantinople by Muslim power in 1453, Russians faced a powerful challenge to their faith and to their political identity that the long centuries of Byzantine ascendancy had enabled them to avoid. Attempting to turn the disquieting events in Constantinople to advantage, the Muscovite Grand Duke Ivan III (1462–1505) strove to depict himself as the morally legitimate successor to the fallen Byzantine royal house—a move that also entailed a declaration of hostility toward the sultans in Istanbul. In 1510 the monk Filofei confidently predicted to Ivan's successor, Vasilii III that, after the fall of the first two Romes, Moscow would stand eternally as the "Third Rome." Given Ottoman might in southern and east-central Europe, however, the famous doctrine of the Third Rome was more bluster and wishful thinking than real assertion of Russia's eternal primacy, for no Muscovite realistically hoped to match the Ottomans militarily.

By the middle of the sixteenth century the Muscovite political elite was caught between religious hostility toward its Islamic rivals and grudging admiration for the Ottomans' military successes. An odd mixture of hatred for and awe of the Ottomans characterized the writings of Ivan Semenovich Peresvetov, a military officer and minor courtier to Grand Duke Ivan IV. Peresvetov's best-known work, *Skazanie o Magmete-saltane* [*Legend of Sultan Mahmet*], admitted that the Islamic "infidel" had done God's will by overthrowing the Byzantine state, thereby punishing corrupt Greek nobles for their cupidity and lack of faith. Yet Peresvetov praised the sultan as a strong and wise ruler and forwarded to Ivan a program of proposed reforms intended to reshape the Russian state apparatus and army on the model of the sultanate. If Peresvetov had had his way, Muscovy would have flattered a deadly foreign rival by emulating it.[3]

Muscovy's expansion to the south, punctuated by the capture of Kazan' and Astrakhan in the 1550s, quickly transformed Russia's Islamic problem from an external threat into a domestic issue, for many of the peoples living in so-called Tatary were Muslims. Over the next two centuries Muscovite Grand Dukes and their successors, the Romanov tsars, struggled to overcome this internal difficulty. A recent history of the empire in this period has described the relationship between Russians and non-Russians in the south as "one of mutual non-comprehension at best and savage exploitation at worst."[4] On the one hand, the Russians made no attempt to destroy the Islamic faith within the enlarged empire: they permitted Muslims to worship in their mosques, to select their religious leaders, and to educate their children in the Quran. The general policy exchanged limited religious toleration for payment of taxes and performance of public duties under the law. The result was the emergence within the empire of a Muslim population that was to some degree separate from, even insulated from, its Russian masters.[5] On the other hand, the Russians were never entirely satisfied with this arrangement, so that they periodically sought to revise its terms. In the eighteenth century, for example, the Tatars were subjected to intense pressures to convert to Russian Orthodoxy. Under Empress Catherine II Tatar nobles were forbidden to own Christian serfs, but, by converting to Orthodoxy, these same nobles could gain the right to own Christian serfs and to receive a three-year exemption from taxation. Meanwhile, after 1700 thousands of Bashkirs, mostly Sunni Muslims, were forced into Russian military service, a duty they detested since it meant serving under the command of "infidels." The Bashkirs repaid their Russian masters by raising rebellion four times in the century. Finally, whenever the Russian army invaded Circassia on its way to the Black Sea coast, an act repeated under several tsars, officers invariably captured Circassian women and later sold them into slavery at auction.[6] Thus, imperial policies toward subject Muslims were contradictory, at the one moment accommodationist, at another moment assimilationist or punitive.

Assessing the relative success of Russian policies toward the Muslims before 1800 is no easy matter. In general, as the empire pressed hard to the south, the Russian army gradually overcame military resistance to its presence, established fortifications, and assisted ethnic Russians to establish communities near the frontiers. As we have noted, internal resistance to the expanding empire was episodic and was put down with great brutality when it occurred, but perhaps the great surprise is that in some areas of Muslim demographic dominance there was less organized armed resistance to the Russians than one might have expected. Probably by the mid-eighteenth century the Russians' advantages in steppe warfare were insuperable to indigenous Muslim peoples. However, even with their many advantages, the Russians were not immune from attack across the permeable frontier line: well into the reign of Catherine II the Crimean Tatars posed a threat to the empire's territorial integrity and domestic tranquility. Moreover, the further south the Russian military went, the less secure it became: lines of communication were stretched; the favorable steppe terrain yielded to the mountains of the Caucasus where it was more difficult to find and destroy raiders or opposing armies; and, as one crossed the ridges of the Caucasus, Russian troops approached ever more closely territories long controlled by the Ottoman and Persian empires.

I

In the late eighteenth century the Iranian, Ottoman, and Russian governments entered the decisive phase in their protracted competition for mastery of the strategically vital Caucasus region—the ethnically diverse, religiously mixed territory on either side of the Caucasus mountain range between the Black and Caspian seas. Although the Iranian and Ottoman empires had been contracting for some time due to Russian pressure and mounting internal difficulties, their expulsion from the Caucasus was by no means inevitable.

As the historian Nikolas K. Gvosdev has convincingly demonstrated, Russian policy toward the south lacked consistency. After the Russo-Turkish war of 1768–1774, a powerful faction in the Russian government led by Catherine II's favorite Grigorii Aleksandrovich Potemkin advocated expansion in the south—the annexation of the Crimea followed by the creation of Russian protectorates in the North Caucasus and Georgia, culminating in the military removal of the Ottomans from the eastern Black Sea Coast and the eventual Russian colonization of the Transcaucasus. This grandiose vision soon became the template for Russian policy, but it was briefly abandoned after Catherine's death when her son Paul decided to withdraw Russian troops from Georgia. After Alexander I's succession to the throne in 1801 Russian policy in the south again fell into question when the tsar's closest advisors—members of the reformist-minded Unofficial Committee—called on the sovereign to content himself with proper governance of Russia's existing territories. Not until September 12, 1801, when Alexander issued his "Manifesto to the Georgian People," did the Russian government finally set its will on annexation of Georgia and hegemonic control of the rest of Caucasus.[7]

The Russian drive southward brought in its wake murderous diplomatic intrigues and periodic wars with the Ottomans and Persians. From 1787 to 1791 the Turks sought to destroy Russian fortifications in the North Caucasus, thereby to weaken Russia's hold over the Crimea. In 1795 the Iranian Shah Agha Muhammad Khan invaded Georgia where he sacked and burned Tbilisi in an attempt to recover Persia's former tributary. In late 1806 the Ottomans again declared war on Russia, partly to push Russia out of the Danubian basin but also to recover the Caucasus; simultaneously, the Persians made an alliance with Napoleon in hopes of securing his support for Russian withdrawal from the southern Caucasus. Unfortunately for the two Muslim empires, their military efforts proved uncoordinated and too desultory to effect the desired objectives. At Bucharest in May 1812 the Ottomans reluctantly made peace with Russians, granting them control of the Black Sea ports at Sukhumi and Redout-Kale and recognizing the Russian protectorates in Western Georgia. The next year at Gulistan the shah of Iran renounced his pretensions to govern Georgia, Northern Azerbaijan, and Daghestan in the North Caucasus. The treaties of Bucharest and Gulistan provided no more than an intermission in the imperial struggle to control the Caucasus. By 1824, the shah's diplomats had made clear their dissatisfaction with the territorial arrangements made at Gulistan. On the ground the Russian military commander Aleksandr Petrovich Ermolov soon concluded that the shah intended war.[8] In July 1826 the Iranian regular army crossed the river Araks with the evident goal of pushing the Russians out of Georgia and the Caucasus generally. The plan collapsed almost at once: within eighteen months the Russian infantry under general Ermolov and Ivan F. Paskiewicz had seized the Iranian provinces of Yerevan and Nakhichevan, and had compelled the shah to renounce all territory above the Araks River. Meanwhile, war was expected between the Ottomans and Russians over Greek independence and control of the eastern Black Sea coast. In the Caucasus theater the Russians quickly seized the Turkish fortress at Kars, and routed most of the Ottoman forces along the eastern Black Sea coast. By July 1829 the Russian army had seized the city of Erzurum, the major Ottoman garrison in Western Armenia. In September the Ottomans and Russians signed a peace treaty at Adrianople. Under its provisions the victorious Russians returned Kars and Erzurum to Ottoman control; in exchange, they won the sultan's agreement to withdraw Turkish troops from most of the southern Black Sea coast and to recognize Russian possession of Georgia, parts of Armenia and other occupied areas of the Southern Caucasus.

By the standard of nineteenth-century diplomacy, the treaties of Turkmanchai and Adrianople constituted an unmitigated triumph for Russia. Following decades of struggle, the army had expelled the Muslim empires from the entire Caucasus region. To generals Ermolov and Paskiewicz the victory was a point of professional pride and a justified marker of social prestige. Admirers compared Ermolov to a Roman general; friends called his successor "Paskiewicz Erivanskii" in honor of the Armenian conquest.

Yet the Russian penetration of the Caucasus cannot be regarded as an unalloyed achievement, if only because it encouraged in the governing elites an overweening arrogance toward the indigenous peoples of the region. General

Ermolov described the inhabitants of the Caucasus as "Asiatics." In order to rule them, he resorted to prophylactic cruelty: "I held by necessity to many Asiatic customs and I grasped that the proconsul of the Caucasus [i.e., Ermolov himself] could not tame the cruelty of local manners by softheartedness." He boasted of acting "with bestial face" and shouting "at the top of my lungs" to cow his opponents.[9] When facing opposition from subjects in Russian-occupied zones, he acted brutally. In Guria, he declared: "rebellious villages were destroyed and burned, orchards and vineyards were cut to the root, and for many years the traitors will not return to their original position. Extreme poverty shall be their punishment."[10] He stated that "I desire that the terror of my name should guard our frontiers more potently than chains or fortresses, that my word should be for the natives a law more inevitable than death."[11]

Condescension toward the indigenous peoples of the Caucasus was not confined to Ermolov. Semen Bronevskii, an official with experience on Georgia and author of the best early nineteenth-century ethnography of the Caucasus, wrote that "the *mores* of [these] peoples may be termed 'savage', for anyone whose life is spent among the cliffs and among mountains must necessarily be uncultured [*gruby*]."[12] Even those public figures who regretted Russia's reliance on the sword to pacify the Caucasus still considered the local peoples unenlightened and undeveloped. The diplomat and playwright Aleksandr Griboedov thought annexation by Russia in the interest of the mountain peoples. He proposed a preposterous scheme whereby Russian peasants and merchants would be transplanted into the Caucasus so as to teach the locals how to exploit the natural wealth of the region.[13] The writer and dissident A. S. Pushkin, whose poetry lauded the free spirit of the mountain peoples, nevertheless considered them savage Asiatics. As Susan Layton has noted, the final stanzas of Pushkin's 1822 "Prisoner of the Caucasus" celebrated Russia's "heroism" for "Leaving a trail of black contagion to deal a death blow to the tribes."[14] Pushkin's travel memoir of his journey to the Russian front lines in 1829 described the road from Novocherkassk to Tbilisi as a "transition from Europe to Asia." His Tbilisi was full of "Asiatic structures and the bazaar," his Erzurum was a backward city of "Asiatic poverty, Asiatic vice." In the travel memoir Pushkin called Paskiewicz a "blazing Hero."[15]

Of course, Russians' arrogance toward the "savage," "uncultured" "Asiatic" inhabitants of the Caucasus was sometimes tempered by the hope that the conquest of the Caucasus be effected by non-military means. Griboedov famously observed that "one can get one's way for only a time by employing fear and freely dispensing gifts: the only way to reconcile conquered peoples with the victors' banners is to introduce a properly functioning court system."[16] The Decembrist Nikolai I. Lorer, who took part in punitive expeditions against the "insubordinate" mountain peoples, wrote flatly: "Fire and the sword will bring no benefit, and who gave us the right to bring education by force to peoples who are content with their liberty and property?"[17] These reservations about the means used to effect Russia's goals in the Caucasus were nevertheless perfectly consistent with the elite's belief that Russia must bring "civilization" to the benighted area. And, in any case, the scruples of educated Russians had little impact on the tsar. Shortly after the taking of Erzurum, Nicholas I ordered General Paskiewicz to set his sights on a glorious and most vital enterprise of direct utility [to Russia]—the permanent pacification of the mountain peoples or the annihilation of those who do not submit."[18]

To be sure, in carrying out the emperor's cold-blooded policy toward the indigenous peoples, the Russians enjoyed a few successes. In portions of Georgia and Armenia the Christian population was favorably inclined toward their Russian "protectors." The mostly Christian elites in Georgia cautiously accepted their new masters wherever doing so would leave their former privileges intact or might offer new opportunities to benefit.[19] Elsewhere, however, the reception of the Russian administration was skeptical or openly hostile.

In the North Caucasus along the Black Sea coast, the mostly Muslim Circassians had long resisted Russian rule. Between 1785 and 1791 they had joined Shaykh Mansur's *ghazwa* against Russia; fifty years later memories of this holy war were perpetuated in their popular songs. Between 1820 and 1864 the Circassians fought against the Russians sporadically, but with increasing determination. On his way to Erzurum in 1829 Pushkin concluded simply: "The Circassians hate us. We have driven them from their pastures; whole *awuls* belonging to them have been sacked; entire clans destroyed."[20] After their final defeat in 1864, between half a million and a million Circassians emigrated from the Russian-occupied Caucasus to Ottoman lands.[21]

At the eastern end of the North Caucasus the Russians confronted even greater challenges. Here there was nothing like a modern state structure. In mountainous Avaria in Daghestan, for example, there were forty "free communities" consisting of at least fifteen different nationalities, each zealously guarding its own small villages or *awuls* and its own precious meadows for grazing sheep or horses.[22] Within these communities there was only a modest degree of social differentiation. By custom, property holding was communal, but sometimes hereditary clan leaders controlled meadowlands and hence could demand payment of access fees; in some cases clan leaders owned dozens or hundreds of livestock. Still, this economic differentiation was never as sharp as that existing in Russia, because juridical serfdom had not developed in the region and because the economic privileges of clan leaders were sharply curtailed by customary constraints. Furthermore, members of the mountain communities regarded themselves as free: they traveled without constraint within their small domains and, with the spread of Islam throughout the region, an increasing number of males made the pilgrimage to Mecca. In this environment, where authority was horizontally dispersed and a certain *ésprit de la liberté* animated community members, Russian officials found it exceptionally difficult to establish a firm foothold.

The time-honored imperial strategy of co-opting local leaders into service had only transitory success. The Russians offered their "protection" to secular leaders who promised "loyalty to the Russian throne," but the mountain authorities treated these oaths more as empty formalities than sacred obligations. For example, between 1802 and 1806 the Russians arranged six protectorates in Chechnia and neighboring Daghestan: under one of these arrangements the Avar Sultan Ahmad Khan received the Russian military rank of major-general; under another the *qadi* of Tabarsaran got the rank of colonel. Nevertheless, these kindnesses did nothing to guarantee loyalty to Russia in the subsequent wars with Iran and the Ottoman Empire.[23] The best that the Russians could do under the circumstances was to assert their presence in the North Caucasus by building forts. Several of these forts, among them the outpost at Vladikavkaz (1783), predated the nineteenth century, but most were constructed after 1800 as Russia sought ways to project its power in the region. Under Ermolov the Russians built Groznaia (1819), Vnezapnaia (1820), and Burnaia (1821) in the heart of Chechnia; then the Russians extended their fortifications to the south and east into Daghestan all the way to Derbend on the Caspian coast. By 1830 roughly thirty thousand soldiers occupied the region.

While the construction of fortifications announced the Russians' determination to govern the northeastern Caucasus, it did little to endear the empire to the native peoples of the region. Building defensible strongholds and the roads to link them entailed clearing forested areas and sometimes displacing villages. The serf soldiers, who did this backbreaking labor and who lived in the forts, had to provision themselves from local resources. Russian units generally requisitioned land and livestock from the surrounding territory, thus disrupting the precarious local economy and earning the indigenous peoples' irritation.

Russia's many wars against the Muslim empires, its steady incursion into the Northern Caucasus, its consequent disruption of the regional environment and economy, its threat to the autonomy of proud, self-determining local communities —all these factors provoked among the religiously-minded peoples of the Northeastern Caucasus a series of mobilizations in defense of Islam.

The movement initiated by the self-proclaimed imam, Shaykh Mansur, constituted the first of these mobilizations. After its origins in 1785, Mansur's movement within a few months spread through his native Chechnia and into neighboring Daghestan. It also won adherents among the Circassians in western North Caucasus, as we noted above. Although the mechanisms by which the movement propagated itself remain obscure, circumstantial evidence suggests that Mansur's ideas may have been circulated by the Sufi confraternity active in the region, the Naqshbandiyya. At any rate, as the historian Alexandre Bennigsen has noted, the Naqshbandis' preaching coincided with Mansur's: both sought an Islamic lifestyle in accordance with the sacred law, or *sharia*; and both preached a holy war against Russian "infidels" and against anyone defending customary law over *sharia*.[24] While the Russians defeated Mansur by 1791, they neither suppressed his religious ideas nor destroyed the Sufi confraternity that shared these notions.

Moshe Gammer has traced the "chain" of Naqshbandi preachers in the Caucasus in the late eighteenth/early nineteenth century. The most dynamic teacher associated with the order at the turn of the century was Shaykh Khalid, who established himself in the formerly Persian-held province of Shirvan, in Azeri territory. His follower Shaykh Ismail trained Shayk Khas Muhammad, who taught the Daghestani masters Shaykh Muhammad al-Yaraghi and Shaykh Jamal al-Din. All these holy men pleaded with Muslims to imitate the Prophet Muhammad, to conform to the *sharia*, to repent their sins. It is not clear whether, before 1830, Muhammad al-Yaraghi and Jamal al-Din called on their followers to fight a *ghazwa* [holy war, plural *ghazawat*] against the Russian "infidels": what is clear is that these two increasingly influential religious teachers demanded Muslims purify themselves *in preparation for* a holy war.[25] Only after the Russian victories over the Persians and the Ottomans in 1828 and 1829 did the Naqshbandi holy men decide to make an unequivocal effort to raise Muslims against the Russian hegemon.[26] The Muslim mobilization in 1830—the second defensive movement by the indigenous peoples in the North Caucasus against Russia—generated the social context of the events discussed in the present book.

II

The Naqshbandi order of Sufis originated in fourteenth-century Bukhara under the inspiration of the learned Baha al-Din Naqshband (1317–1389). His teaching borrowed heavily from Persian sources, particularly 'Abd al-Khaliq al-Ghujduwani, who insisted that Muslims inwardly remember God with every breath they take and that they outwardly emulate the Prophet Muhammad. To perfect the practices recommended by al-Ghujduwani, Baha al-Din insisted that his followers employ the silent method of "recollecting God" [*dhikr*], a form of prayer in which the adept calls to mind the Islamic creed or one of the Ninety-Nine Names of God and meditates on its significance. The object of the silent *dhikr* was to concentrate the believer's heart on God's presence so completely that deviation from the *sharia* would be virtually unthinkable. Like other Sufi masters, Baha al-Din thought it very important that there be a close relationship between the master and his students, such that through their disciplined conversations there be a meeting of minds, an experience of spiritual unity. Unlike many of his predecessors, however, Baha al-Din de-emphasized the emotional, ecstatic dimensions of Sufi mysticism, opting instead for an orientation of greater sobriety. To be sure, he considered spiritual intoxication a great achievement, even a sign of "sainthood" [*auliya*]; however, he regarded perfection in the discharge of religious duties as the true goal of Sufism, for as one approached that perfection, one came ever closer to emulation of the Prophet.[27]

From Bukhara the Naqshbandiyya spread west toward Istanbul, where it established itself by the end of the fifteenth century, and east onto the Indian subcontinent, where it found receptive soil among the Mughal emperors and ruling elites. The most important Indian Naqshbandi holy man was Shaykh Ahmad Sirhindi al-Faruqi (1564–1624), whose contribution to Naqshbandi doctrine was to demand that infidel practices permitted by law in Muslim countries be purged from the civil codes, so that civil law would correspond to the *sharia*. While asking believers rigorously to obey *sharia*, Sirhindi acknowledged that ordinary people might have difficulty interpreting the hidden essence [*haqiqa*] of divine law. Therefore, he asked these ordinary believers to listen carefully to spiritual guides, whose knowledge of God was more profound and whose understanding of *sharia* was consequently deeper. By so doing, Sirhindi expanded the writ of Sufism, transforming it from an esoteric discipline pursued by a small number of especially dedicated, prayerful men into a path to be followed by society as a whole. It would surely be an exaggeration to claim that Sirhindi "politicized" Sufism, since from the beginning Sufi leaders had interested themselves, most often indirectly, in political matters; nevertheless, by underlining the duty to provide moral instruction to the masses and ruling elites alike, Sirhindi made explicit Sufism's political dimension.[28] His desire religiously to purify the civil laws, his high estimation of Sufi masters as guides to public policy, and his focus of the importance of politics were transmitted to the entire line of future Naqshbandi teachers.[29]

Although the North Caucasus was near the geographical epicenter of Naqshbandi activity, the Naqshbandiyya's hold over peoples of the region remained superficial until the late eighteenth/early nineteenth century. We noted above that Shaykh Mansur's preaching coincided in some respects with Naqshbandi ideas, but the evidence for Naqshbandi involvement in his movement remains circumstantial at best. Only with the preaching of Shaykh Diya al-Din Khalid al-Shahrazuri al-Kurdamiri (1779–1820) and of his followers did the Naqshbandiyya win a sizeable constituency in the Caucasus. A significant factor in the Khalidis' popularity there was their ability to take advantage of the growing indigenous opposition to Russian penetration of the North Caucasus. Their success in mobilizing anti-Russian sentiment cannot be ascribed to primitive nationalism, however, since it sprang directly from Shaykh Khalid's distinctively Sufi teaching.

Like his Naqshbandi predecessors, Khalid taught that, if Muslims would be saved, they must obey God's law. For Khalid as for his predecessors, the *sharia* laid upon individual believers the duty to pray five times a day, to fast at prescribed times, to refrain from consuming spiritually "unhealthy" substances (alcohol and tobacco), and to make pilgrimage to Mecca. Khalid added, however, that individual observance of *sharia* was not possible under non-Islamic rule. Individual obedience to God's law could only take place in a context of a believing community governed by a "pure-hearted' Muslim. In other words, Khalid argued that salvation for believers was only possible in an Islamic state. Given the imminent danger that Russian infidels might impose Christian rule upon the Caucasus, Khalid's advocacy of Islamic rule had special poignancy.

Like other Naqshbandi teachers before him, Khalid insisted that ordinary believers listen attentively to trained spiritual guides. Now, however, he strove to bring to the master–disciple relationship a religious sophistication and dynamism it had previously lacked. Khalid believed that God passes to the master spiritual aids which the master can then convey almost effortlessly to his disciples, thereby sharpening the disciples' spiritual awareness. To perform this service, the master himself must approach spiritual "perfection" by undeviatingly obeying *sharia* and by manifesting humility before God and the believing community. Meanwhile, the disciple must accept wholeheartedly the master's spiritual authority: only by properly "keeping company" with the master can the disciple find direction toward God. Lack of commitment to the master, Khalid felt, would inhibit the disciple's progress toward God. To facilitate spiritual obedience to the master, Khalid recommended that disciples contemplate the master's "spiritual image," that is, to picture him standing immediately before and "between two eyebrows," then to draw the master's image downward into the heart. This intense contemplation of the master constituted the appropriate preparation for the silent *dhikr*. Among Khalid's followers, the recollection of God generally took the form of reciting the Islamic creed "There is no god but God," although in rare instances it involved repetition of the word "Allah," the so-called "Name of Splendor."[30]

Khalid's teaching attracted attention throughout the Islamic world—in Kurdistan, Iraq, Syria, and Anatolia—but also in Daghestan, where Muhammad al-Yaraghi and Shaykh Jamal al-Din al-Ghazi-Ghumuqi propagated his ideas. Before falling under Khalid's spiritual influence, Muhammad al-Yaraghi already held a reputation as the most learned scholar in Daghestan. His "conversion" into the Naqshbandiyya-Khalidiyya had two consequences. First, he publicly repented his past offenses against the Muslim community, particularly his diversion of religious contributions to his own pocketbook. He now renounced his property, distributed his wealth to the community, and devoted himself to charitable acts. This dramatic volte-face impressed the public and made it curious about the spiritual key to his transformation. Muhammad al-Yaraghi used this curiosity as the opening to call upon fellow believers to repent their sins, to reject infidel practices, and to return to *sharia*. Second, persuaded by Khalid's teaching that salvation can only be achieved in the context of a self-governing Islamic community, Muhammad al-Yaraghi began openly to attack Daghestan's Russian masters. "As long as we remain under the infidels' supremacy, we are covered with shame," he said. "The prayers of slaves are not heard in Heaven ... All your ablutions, your repentance and sacrifices, all your holy deeds are without value so long as the Muscovites supervise your lives. Even your marriages and children are illegitimate as long as the Muscovites rule over you. So how can you serve God if you are serving the Russians?"[31]

This uncompromising message led in 1824 to a confrontation between Muhammad al-Yaraghi and the local secular potentate, Aslan Khan, a client of the Russian General Ermolov. When Aslan Khan, following Ermolov's directive, ordered Muhammad al-Yaraghi to stop his provocative preaching, Muhammad al-Yaraghi refused: "You are wrong, O Khan. How can you possibly follow the path of the faithful and at the same time be the infidel's slave?"[32]

For his part Shaykh Jamal al-Din pursued a less public but equally fruitful course of action. According to the historian of the Daghestani Sufis, Anna Zelkina, Jamal al-Din "was the first North Caucasian Naqshbandi sheikh to compose a treatise on Naqshbandi doctrine and practices."[33] In his book *al-Adab al-Murdhiyya fi al-Tariqa al-Naqshbandiyya*, Jamal al-Din elaborated the broad outlines of Khalid's teaching.[34] He associated repentance and return to *sharia* with entrance into the Sufi order. Jamal al-Din attached special significance to the presence and wisdom of the spiritual master (*murshid*) for the guidance of the novice (*murid* or *salik*). "If someone who performs *dhikr* invokes the name of God by the entire range of *dhikhrs* but without the instruction of a master, he will not reach perfection. That which a *salik* finds in *suhba* [keeping company] with a perfect master in one second he will not find by reading one thousand books or in a thousand-year exercise ..."[35]

Thus, the centrality of the master–disciple relationship for the Khalidiyya was a point of devotional practice that had far-reaching political significance in the North Caucasus. There the leading Khalidi masters came to think that certain obstacles stood in the way of the people's path to God. Among these obstacles were local customs that tolerated the consumption of alcohol and tobacco, that permitted deviation from prescribed prayer and fasting, that underestimated the importance of religious pilgrimage, and—perhaps most significantly of all—that discouraged believers' self-surrender to God. To overcome these obstacles the Khalidi masters demanded that their disciples help enforce proper behavior in the community, to assist in spiritual "purification" of the errant, to effect return to the divinely-prescribed path. In practical terms, this meant vigilant prohibition of unhealthy substances, adherence to prayer, and dietary rules, insistence on the *hajj*, and calling on Muslims to surrender their lives to God. Although the Khalidi masters and their disciples regarded themselves as members of the community of believers, their campaign to impose spiritual discipline had the inevitable effect of setting themselves against the ungodly and lukewarm, and above the community itself. Hence, even among Muslim believers in the North Caucasus region, there were those who selfishly opposed the Khalidi or who felt that Khalidi rigorism went too far in trampling down local custom. When the Khalidi encountered such opposition, they appealed to the authority of the Quran, to the Prophet's instructions; they reminded the doubters of the local master's place in the "chain" of Islamic teachers; they employed all the tools of charismatic authority—techniques of preaching, manifesting spiritual confidence, and the like. Failing by such means, they did not scruple to use force against their opponents. Thus, the campaign for godly ways gradually transformed the North Caucasus into an arena where Khalidi masters imposed their spiritual understanding on entire communities. The Khalidi worldview cultivated religious habits of mind convenient to the construction of a theocratic state in which a charismatic master could wield absolute authority through his faithful disciples.

Perhaps understandably, Russian observers of the North Caucasus misread the Khalidi campaign for godliness as an attempt to seize political power in the region. The Russians saw the relationship between spiritual guide (*murshid*) and his would-be disciple (*murid*) as a means of exercising authority over the *murid* and hence of imposing the *murshid*'s will on society. When Russian troops confronted the empire's armed opponents in the North Caucasus, the most dangerous fighters were the devoted *murid* horsemen. Hence Russians began to refer to their adversaries as *murids* [*miuridy*], and to the long war in the North Caucasus as the "Murid War" [*miuridskaia voina*]. They tended, again understandably, to distinguish "traditional Islam" from *miuridizm*, a fanatical revolutionary movement having, as they saw it, little or nothing in common with Islam.[36] This misunderstanding of the Khalidi-Naqshbandi campaign for godliness, coupled with the Russians' dismissive attitude toward the "Asiatic" tribes of the region, reinforced the brutal instincts of Russian field commanders.

III

The war between the mountain peoples of the North Caucasus and Russia was the result of two conflicting, irreconcilable visions—the Khalidi vision of a godly society dedicated to Quranic justice and the Russian imperial design for a "pacified" Caucasus subordinated to the will of the Orthodox emperor. The clash between these radically incompatible projects was, at first, implicit in the assumptions of the two principals but only sporadically actualized in organized violence. However, as Russians inserted more troops unto the region, the local population became increasingly irritated and the Muslim religious leadership more strident in its effort to mobilize the people in defense of Islamic ways. As this occurred, there were more outbreaks of violence and a growth in the scale of fighting from isolated *awuls* to entire zones. Symbolically, the Russians could date the war's origin to 1829, when Nicholas I framed the policy of "pacification or annihilation." The mountain peoples, for their part, could locate the war's beginning in Imam Ghazi Muhammad's 1830 proclamation of *ghazwa* against the Russian "infidels." In reality, the war emerged ineluctably out of the ever-more intense cultural collision between Islamic peoples and the Orthodox empire.

In the military sense, the mountain conflict mixed conventional fighting with quick hit-and-run raids characteristic of an unconventional "dirty" war. The Russian army enjoyed an overwhelming numerical superiority vis-à-vis the mountaineers. Gammer has estimated that the Russian government had committed roughly 30,000 men to the Caucasus circa 1830; of these, nearly 85 percent were regular infantry. The Russian generals liked to campaign with sizable units: thus, already in May 1830 Major-General Rozen led 6,000 troops against the mountaineers' stronghold at Gimrah; two years later in August 1832 he commanded a force of 15,000–20,000 men in Lesser Chechnia. By the 1850s, the Russian commitment had increased to nearly 200,000 troops.[37] For most of the war, Russian troops possessed an advantage in armaments, being supplied with field artillery whereas the mountaineers had very few artillery guns. The recurrent hope of the Russian generals was to draw their enemy into the open field where withering rifle and artillery fire might destroy mounted horsemen, or to trap the rebels in one of their headquarters where a siege might decimate them. Meanwhile, the Russian generals extended the network of fortifications and military roads begun by Ermolov. Around the forts and along the roads they free-cut trees, so as to deny the adversary forest camouflage. The idea was to penetrate everywhere in the region, then surround and strangle the outnumbered mountaineers.

Sometimes the Russian strategy worked well. For example, in late October 1832 the imperial army laid siege to the town of Gimrah, where Ghazi Muhammad and his forces were trapped. Eventually, they killed all but two of the resisters, including Ghazi Muhammad himself. In 1838 the Russians penned up the mountaineers at Akhulgoh in northern Daghestan. There, Russian forces pounded the village with artillery, then took it in hand-to-hand combat. They wounded the charismatic Imam Shamil who barely escaped with his life.

The Russians' periodic successes, however, did not enable them to drive the mountaineers to early defeat. The Russian army was not always able to take advantage of its numerical superiority, for its soldiers regularly fell prey to poor diet, inadequate clothing and the virtual absence of sanitation. Gammer asserts that "battle casualties accounted for only one in eleven deaths" on the Russian side.[38] Furthermore, the Russian army's virtual monopoly on field artillery in the first years of the war seldom translated into an actual advantage in firepower: field guns proved difficult to maneuver in the high mountains, so the enemy could escape before the heavy weapons were fired. After 1843, the rebels had accumulated enough captured artillery pieces to break the Russians' monopoly, and soon they managed to forge their own guns. The mountaineers also learned to turn Russian siege tactics against imperial fortifications, and were not above luring Russian troops onto unfavorable ground where they could be quickly decimated. Near Darghiyya in 1845, Shamil's forces trapped hundreds of ill-provisioned Russian troops and cut them to pieces when they tried to break out of the encirclement: nearly 1,000 Russians were killed and another 2,700 were wounded in this battle, nicknamed the "biscuit expedition."[39] Thus, in spite of the Russians' nominal advantages, the indigenous insurgents sometimes held their own in conventional fighting.

That said, the bulk of the fighting must still be classified as unconventional warfare. When Russian troops advanced along roads in their ponderous columns, the mountaineers hit them with sniper fire from camouflaged locations or fell on stragglers in lightning sorties, only then to disappear into the surrounding terrain. When Russians undertook major initiatives, as in Viceroy Mikhail Semenovich Vorontsov's campaign of 1845, the mountaineers yielded ground, but not before razing all villages in the area and carrying away villagers and supplies, leaving to the Russians devastated wilderness. The mountaineers learned the guerrilla art of merging into the indigenous population whence they had come, only to re-emerge when the Russians least expected. This tactic frustrated the Russian high command, though it also reinforced the intuition that almost all locals sympathized with the resisters if they were not themselves insurgents. Thus, the Russians confronted an adversary that was almost simultaneously unseen and yet ubiquitous—a typical earmark of unconventional warfare.

The mountaineers gradually developed sophisticated techniques of psychological warfare. On the one hand, they sought to intimidate the Russian civilian population and to terrorize locals who sided with the Russians. Thus, in 1831 at the undefended settlement of Qidhlar, the insurgents killed 126 civilians and captured another 168, most of them women. Later, in 1854 in the Alazan valley, the mountaineers carried off hundreds of civilian captives, including two Georgian princesses and their French governess.[40] When the mountaineers could arrange ransom payments or prisoner exchanges, they did so. But some Russian captives, particularly males, were simply put to work, usually at tasks of direct military significance. When local elites collaborated with the Russians, the insurgents could be implacable: in 1834 the entire Avar ruling house in the village of Khunzakh was wiped out by the rebel leaders; in 1839, when a delegation of locals asked Shamil to submit to the Russians, he warned that, in future, anyone undertaking such a mission "would be hanged."[41] In 1845, three locals who had entered the Russian camp at Andi without authorization from the insurgent commanders were arrested then beheaded as a warning to other potential collaborators.[42]

This policy of intimidation was balanced by shrewd, if self-interested, generosity. The insurgents tried, within limits, to treat captives humanely. They did so in part to encourage desertion by Russian troops. To Russian defectors the mountaineers offered release from serfdom; if defectors converted to Islam, they were given the possibility of marriage to a local woman. By Shamil's orders, both captives and defectors who remained loyal to the Orthodox faith were allowed to worship freely. Partly as a consequence of these open-handed policies and partly as a result of the difficult conditions prevailing in the Russian army, the number of Russian deserters reached "several hundred at least" by Gammer's calculation.[43]

Meanwhile, the Russians employed their own unconventional tactics. They seized livestock in insurgent-controlled territory or prevented hostile villagers from grazing animals on lowland pastures—a crude form of economic coercion. Russian commanders sometimes burnt every village in the army's path, as general Veliaminov did in winter 1830–1831 in Daghestan. In cases where they encountered prolonged resistance, as at Saltah in 1847, the Russians polluted water supplies with their excrement to deny drink to the enemy. When Saltah fell, the Russians systematically destroyed the town.[44] Alongside these efforts to demoralize the insurgents and terrorize the indigenous population, the Russians tried to organize the assassination of enemy leaders. In 1830 they sought to have Ghazi Muhammad killed; after 1834 they tried repeatedly to locate and kill Shamil.

Like the insurgents, the Russians employed certain techniques of psychological warfare. Sporadically they issued statements to the local population promising respect for Islamic practices.[45] In 1845, after his appointment as viceroy over the Caucasus region, Prince Vorontsov ordered the printing of a calendar showing the dates of religious festivals for Sunni and Shi'i Muslims, as well as for Orthodox Christians.[46] The point of this calendar was to advertise Vorontsov's (and Russia's) tolerance toward "peaceful" Muslims. Later in 1847, Vorontsov asked a defector from Shamil's forces, Sulayman Efendi, to denounce Shamil as a non-Muslim; the resulting document was then distributed widely in the North Caucasus. Vorontsov's intention was to give indigenous peoples a religious justification for opposing Shamil's brand of Sufi Islam. Vorontsov also made it a practice to treat well prominent defectors from the insurgent armies. Finally, Vorontsov tried to encourage local people to seek Russian protection: in 1846–1847 about 3,000 Chechen families were relocated near the outskirts of newly-built Russian forts.[47]

Such inducements to collaborate with the Russians were accompanied by practices designed to humiliate insurgents. In 1840, the Russians arrested the Avar noble Hadji Murat on suspicion of secret collaboration with Imam Shamil. While under detention, Hadji Murat was beaten, and a Russian officer spat on him. When he escaped detention, the Russians burned his house and confiscated his livestock.[48] Such actions aimed to demonstrate to him and other collaborators their helplessness before imperial power, to strip them of their dignity and manhood. The Russian attempt in 1840 to disarm the Chechens was another deliberate ritual humiliation: it had little to do with imperial security in the direct sense, and everything to do with signifying utter submission to the new Russian masters. Unfortunately for the Russians, shaming the indigenous peoples generally provoked resisters to engage in new acts of defiance. No less an authority than D. A. Miliutin, the future minister of war, warned that disarmament of the mountaineers in violation of local custom was counterproductive to Russian interests.[49]

To these unconventional methods of waging war the Russians added another tactic: Gammer has called it "demographic warfare." At first, the Russians focused their attention narrowly on creating new settlements to defend strategic roads and fortified points. Under provisions of the 1837 statute on military settlements, the Russians gave common serf soldiers who had served at least fifteen years in the army the opportunity to settle their families in new military colonies. The treasury supplied the colonists with building materials for their houses, land for tilling, and draught animals. In exchange, the colonists were obliged to help defend the local territory against insurgents.[50] More ominously, the Russians began to think about larger-scale relocations of the local populations. In the late 1830s the Russian military command started to shift various tribes (Nazranovs, Karabulaks, Ingush) to new venues in the Caucasus. At the same time, leading military strategists proposed massive resettlements of the Terek Cossacks southward to the base of the Caucasus mountains so as to neutralize the non-Russian peoples of the region.[51]

By 1855 the Russian high command had decided that demographic warfare might play a key role in the empire's new strategy to subdue the North Caucasus. The link between forced population resettlements and security considerations was clearly articulated in the memorandum written by General Nikolai

Nikolaevich Murav'ev on assuming Vorontsov's old office of imperial viceroy to the Caucasus in December 1855. In the memorandum Murav'ev argued that Russia could not compel insurgents to submit to it, even if it introduced more troops to the mountain region and allotted them land under the 1837 military resettlement plan. Russia's military colonists, Murav'ev noted, "were burdened by the need to act as local sentries to defend their homes and thus lacked the means to congregate in large numbers to carry out offensive thrusts against the adversary." On the Russians' left flank in Chechnia, the security difficulties were especially acute because numerous Chechens fleeing from Shamil's control had crowded into the areas surrounding Russian fortresses. These dirt-poor refugees were "farming lands belonging to Cossacks" and, in addition, were "receiving significant welfare assistance from our treasury in the form of food subsidies." Murav'ev foresaw that these refugees would not become economically self-supporting any time soon, and that therefore they would constitute a continual danger to Russian soldiers. "To avoid this unfortunate situation," Murav'ev wrote, "we have no other means but to expel these people [vykalit' sikh liudei] to our rear lines or some place even further away. Here arises a new question to which we must attend: where to?"

After considering the options, Murav'ev suggested resettling the inhabitants "in the sandy, arid expanses" currently occupied by the nomadic Nogai peoples. Absent such a resettlement scheme, he claimed that "the victories we are now achieving will remain without positive consequence."[52] Incidentally, in the Northwestern Caucasus Murav'ev proposed the same approach be taken toward rebellious Circassians: "When the campaign has concluded, then once and for all the peoples we call Circassians, along with any Caucasian tribes that now support Shamil, must be detached [otdeleny]" from their homes. Again, Murav'ev left open the location of the resettlement zone.

In his presentation of the Murav'ev memorandum, Gammer has quoted a letter from a Russian field officer stationed in Groznaia. The officer characterized the Murav'ev proposal as "fantasy": "It was decided that for the [complete] pacification of the Caucasus [to occur], it would be necessary to transfer the conquered population to Vologda province or whatever other empty land [that may be available], and it was also decided, in a council in Stavropol', to send all the Chechens to Manych ..." The officer maintained that Murav'ev's plan was dropped only when the Chechens made it clear to Russian commanders that "they would rather perish to the man than accept the loss of their homeland."[53] Gammer has asserted that Murav'ev's "act of folly" in writing the memorandum "contributed to [his] replacement" by Aleksandr Ivanovich Bariatinskii.[54]

Gammer correctly observed that the Murav'ev plan was not carried out in 1856 because the first stages of its implementation seemed to stiffen Chechen resistance to the Russians and therefore threatened to prolong the war. However, as we shall note below, the Russian military authorities did not give up on the concept of population resettlement as a means of solidifying their control over the Caucasus. Bariatinskii himself strongly advocated population resettlements as part of the Russian "peace plan" in Chechnia and Daghestan. Moreover, in the Western Caucasus, the 1864 Russian victory over the Circassians led to massive Circassian flight into Ottoman lands, a flight the Russian authorities did little or nothing to arrest. At the very least, the evidence supports a claim that Murav'ev's 1855/1856 advocacy of population resettlement represented a common pattern of high-level Russian strategic thinking about dealing with the Caucasian insurgents toward the end of the mountain war.

As additional archival evidence becomes available, we may discover that the Murav'ev memorandum was part of a self-conscious military campaign to launch systematic ethnic cleansing of the Caucasus. How else shall we account for Murav'ev's stated desire "to expel" entire peoples from their homelands, to "detach" them or "separate" them from the Caucasus region? Moreover, is it not obvious from Murav'ev's interest in the sandy-soiled, arid terrain on which roamed the Nogai tribes that Russian policy contemplated physical punishment of the mountaineers as well as their displacement to new homes? Did Murav'ev not suspect that hundreds of refugees would perish in the difficult new environment? A distinguished historian has recently argued that ethnic cleansing was a quintessentially twentieth-century phenomenon.[55] Evidence from the mountain war, however, may suggest otherwise.

During the mountain war the indigenous peoples of the Northeast Caucasus experienced "on their own skins" the consequences of Russian military expansion into their native land. The destruction of forests everywhere along military roads, the building of unwanted fortresses housing Russian troops to whom local peoples were expected to submit themselves, the intrusion of Russian civilians and strange or unwelcome institutions into mountain life, the resettlement or killing of those who resisted Russian power—all these were direct or indirect results of Russian policy between 1830 and 1859. To be sure, some indigenous villagers profited from the Russian presence through commerce or simply through the relative peace that the Russian army imposed in certain areas of Chechnia and Daghestan; moreover, it is surely true that some members of elite mountain clans cut favorable deals with the Russians in return for collaboration with the army. Nevertheless, the general record of these years strongly suggests that the consolidation of empire in the Northeast Caucasus was a devastating process for many of Russia's newest subjects.

In light of Russia's bloody conquest of the Caucasus region, we should think twice before agreeing with those historians who claim that the Russian empire "was not a colonial power in the European sense of the term," and that its rule "was positive not only for the Russian ruling elite, but for the entire Russian state and the peoples within it."[56] We should also perhaps be wary of those scholars who invite us to shift our attention from the conquest of peoples to the "constructive" aspects of Russian colonization, for such an invitation may imply that understanding the dynamics of "frontier exchanges" and the creation of "new social identities" on the "mixed ground of ethnic frontiers" should take precedence in our minds over the military and cultural destruction that constituted the central acts in the Caucasus in the middle of the nineteenth century.[57]

IV

From 1829 to 1859 the insurgents did battle with the Russian army, in the process tying down between 30,000 and 200,000 troops. This struggle required brave determination, to be sure, but also unusual organizational skills. Not the least of the insurgents' achievements was the construction in Daghestan and Chechnia of a rudimentary Islamic state. At the center of the nascent state stood three successive spiritual leaders or imams: Ghazi Muhammad (1829–1832), Hamza Bek (1832–1834), and Shamil (1834–1859).

About the emergence of Ghazi Muhammad and Hamza Bek we know relatively little, but the path of Shamil to the imamate has been carefully studied. From childhood Shamil pursued the "right path" of Islam: he learned the Quran by heart, as bright young boys were expected to do; in early adolescence, in the company of a spiritual guide, he secreted himself in a cave to pray, stopping up his ears with wax to block out distractions; at age fifteen he left home to travel across Daghestan in search of teachers who could instruct him in theology and Islamic law. By the time he reached manhood, Shamil had earned a reputation among the best Daghestani scholars as a promising student, conversant with the most important Arabic texts of Islamic jurisprudence.[58]

Yet Shamil did not commit himself to religious scholarship, in spite of his affection for his teachers and his life-long love of books.[59] His greater interest was to discover how he might embody Islamic teachings in the mountain society that surrounded him. There is a legend, indicative but almost surely apocryphal, that as an adolescent he demanded that his father stop cultivating grapes for the wine trade on the grounds that alcohol consumption is forbidden by the Quran.[60] In the late 1820s Shamil joined the campaign of his childhood friend Muhammad to preach the destruction of customary law throughout Daghestan and to impose in its place the *sharia*. As this preaching campaign picked up momentum, Muhammad and Shamil faced opposition, sometimes violent, from the local secular elite, whose privileges were rooted in customary regulations. They also confronted their former teacher, Jamal al-Din al-Ghazi-Ghumuqi, who insisted they confine their efforts on behalf of the *sharia* to peaceful agitation—a plea that Shamil at first heeded, then resisted.[61] At any rate, by the late 1820s Shamil's mastering passion was the ordering of mountain life under Islamic law—a passion that was widely, if not universally, shared by other religious leaders of his generation.

The small Islamic state that began to emerge under the three imams in the early 1830s committed itself to returning mountain society to godly ways—a goal that required the elimination of Russian influences on Islamic life but also the eradication of corruption within the Muslim community itself. To achieve this outsized objective the imams wielded power springing from their moral authority and personal charisma—power that, if not unlimited, was at least undivided. In our terms, the imams pretended to absolute secular as well as religious authority: they were theocrats.

The imams transmitted their authority through their faithful disciples or *murids*. In Shamil's state, the most trusted *murids* acted as his personal retinue. Others were appointed *naibs* (deputies), to take charge of religious, political, and military administration in particular areas of the Caucasus. At its zenith in the 1830s, Shamil's imamate exercised at least nominal control over a territory some 900 kilometers in circumference in Chechnia and Daghestan. Roughly two dozen *naibs* divided responsibility for administration across this region, each *naib* having oversight of a greater or lesser district within the region. The *naibs* carried out a series of tasks, each crucial for the insurgency's survival. Following the *sharia* they established procedures for the recruitment of military men in their districts: in the 1840s every ten households had to supply an armed horseman, giving each *naib* no less than 300 cavalry men to disport against the Russians. The *naibs* also had the duty to oversee tax collections. Under Shamil there was an in-kind levy of one-tenth of the grain harvest, and a fee was assessed on herders of livestock. The *naibs* were obliged to turn over to the imam's treasury one-fifth of any booty seized during military action. Finally, the *naibs* carried out decisions of the religious authorities concerning Islamic law, although the *naibs* themselves had no power to render judgment on the *sharia*.[62]

In specifically religious matters, the *naibs* relied on the judgment of those learned in the Quran. In every district there was a *mufti* appointed by the *naib* but having autonomous status to act as arbiter in religious disputes. The *mufti* could reprove the *naib* if the latter violated the *sharia*. Under the *mufti* there were some dozens of *qadis*: generally each *qadi* prayed in the village mosque, collected money to support it, and enforced the rules of godly behavior in his own *awul*. The *qadis*, however, operated under the *muftis'* watchful eyes. It should also be noted that, since taxation was meant to follow the prescriptions of Islamic law, the *mufti* acted as the primary tax collector in each district, making sure that the various levies were equitable and transmitting the gathered funds to the *naib*.

Although Shamil made some effort to differentiate the duties of *naibs* and *muftis*, their jurisdictions overlapped—just as one might expect in a theocratic government where every official was God's instrument. Surely, however, a result of this functional overlapping was to enhance the imam's control over the movement: in every district he had two parallel lines of control, two autonomous sources of information, two operatives that, in case of need, could be played off one against the other. Shamil's expert manipulation of these levers of power contributed to his longevity in office.

Although the imams led the Naqshbandi resistance against Russia, they did not stand alone at the government's center. Important issues were discussed by a council of elders, consisting of thirty-two members. This council (*diwan*) met every day except Friday. It advised the imam on religious and administrative matters, and issued decisions in his absence at the front. Under Shamil after 1842 there was a second, smaller council—scholars call it a "secret council" or "privy council"—to deal with the imamate's most pressing problems. Its resolutions were subject to review by the *diwan* and by a group of Muslim scholars, the *ulama.* Periodically Shamil summoned conferences of *naibs* and *ulama* to discuss strategic decisions too large to be disposed in the traditional venues.[63]

One of the hallmarks of the imamate was the use of elaborately polite, formal Arabic in internal political correspondence. Despite the devastation of the mountain war, over a hundred of Shamil's letters survive.[64] When writing to a large audience of the faithful, as he did in 1850, Shamil began with the salutation: "In the name of God, the Merciful, the Compassionate. Praise be to God, to Him alone; prayer and peace be to Him, after whom no one is Prophet. And multitudinous greetings from the just imam Shamil to each *naib*, *qadi*, *murid*, and to all other Muslims."[65] When writing to an individual Muslim, Shamil used other formulas, often referring to his addressee as "brother." For example, a letter of 1855 to one of his *naibs* commenced: "From the emir of the faithful Shamil to his brother, *naib* Khazy. Peace to you." Even when there was tension between the imam and his correspondent, as in the unpleasant rivalry with Hadji Murat, Shamil preserved the formal courtesies. In 1850 he wrote a letter beginning: "Peace to you. To my beloved brother, Hadji Murat."[66] Shamil's epistolary courtesy was rooted in local custom, to be sure, but it must also have been rooted in the Quranic order to regard every Muslim as an equal under God's eyes, for, by contrast, Shamil's correspondence with Russian generals lacked the "obligatory" references to brotherhood and to peace.[67] If the Quran commanded that Muslim believers respect the dignity of all other believers, it instructed them to be wary of non-believers.

At various junctures, the imams had to contend against internal opposition. In 1830, for example, when Jamal al-Din opposed Imam Ghazi Muhammad's call for *ghazwa* against the Russians, the imam sent *murids* to Jamal al-Din's village where they leveled his house.[68] In 1834 Imam Hamza Bek encountered resistance from the Avar khan's household: he responded by taking two of the khan's sons hostages; later the hostages, their brothers, and mother were killed by *murids*, perhaps on the imam's order.[69] The rumor of the imam's responsibility for this killing prompted distant relatives to assassinate Hamza Bek at the Khunzakh mosque before Friday noon prayers.

Shamil's most serious opposition came from the Avar Hadji Murat. An ally and foster brother of the slain Avar khans, Hadji Murat briefly ruled Avaristan in the 1830s. During this period he collaborated with the Russian authorities, fought against the insurgents, and made no secret of his wish to take revenge on Shamil, whom he held personally responsible for murdering the khans. However, in 1840, the Russian general Frants Karlovich Klüge von Klugenau ordered Hadji Murat's arrest on the charge of initiating clandestine contact with Shamil—a charge that Hadji Murat indignantly protested. After the arrest, a Russian officer beat Hadji Murat and spat on him—a humiliation of the sort mentioned earlier. Feeling the injustice and ingratitude of this treatment, Hadji Murat escaped from Russian captivity and joined the Islamic resistance. Apparently, the invitation to join Shamil came from the imam himself. Shamil offered Hadji Murat the position of *naib* in Avaristan. The two men pledged to co-operate against the common enemy, the Russians; they promised to forget their blood feud as well, but it is inconceivable that either did so. The result was a political-religious *mariage de convenance* that lasted over a decade.

Hadji Murat brought to the resistance a high order of military skills. He quickly became a thorn in the Russians' side, and by late 1842 he had helped virtually clear Avaristan of Russian troops. When the Russians counterattacked in 1843 taking Hadji Murat's native *awul* Khunzakh, he led a successful attempt to retake the territory; during this sortie he followed Shamil's order to set fire to *awuls* surrounding Khunzakh. Thereafter he played a leading role in the expansion of the Islamic state into Daghestan, earning a justified reputation as the resistance's finest field commander after Shamil. In view of Hadji Murat's contributions to the insurgency, Shamil promoted him to the rank of *mudir* ["director" or "leader"]. This office entailed supervision of other *naibs* in Daghestan: it was the highest military rank in the Islamic state below the imam.

By 1850, Shamil and Hadji Murat were the principal figures in the mountaineers' resistance to Russia, their leadership acknowledged throughout the Caucasus and beyond. Yet their relationship, never easy because of the repressed blood feud, remained tense. As imam, Shamil stood at the epicenter of the Khalidi-Naqshbandi brotherhood, but Hadji Murat was something of a latecomer to the defense of Islam. As a young man, he had not followed the godly path, putting worldly advancement above religion. After embracing Islam, he had become a devoted practitioner of meditative prayer and a *murshid* in his own right, but he never subordinated himself to Shamil through the Naqshbandi initiation rite. Shamil's *murids*, therefore, viewed Hadji Murat warily, as an outsider. Muhammad Tahir al-Qarakhi, Shamil's secretary and the chronicler of the resistance movement, referred to the imam's rival as one of the Khunzakh "hypocrites"—repeating the Quranic description of the Prophet's opponents in Mecca.

Between Shamil and Hadji Murat there was also a nasty disagreement over the leadership of the movement in the event of the imam's death. Evidently, in 1842 Shamil and his privy council had decided that, should the imam die, the mantle of leadership would pass to his minor son Ghazi Muhammad. This secret resolution was announced by Shamil six years later, in March 1848, when Ghazi Muhammad was eighteen years old. Hadji Murat, irritated by Shamil's dynastic plan and wounded by the imam's lack of confidence in him, publicly opposed the announced succession. Hadji Murat told associates that he himself should be Shamil's successor. Moshe Gammer believes that this disagreement over the succession led Shamil to "engineer a confrontation with his lieutenant in order to secure his son's succession."[70]

According to the mountain chronicler Muhammad al-Qarakhi, in the summer of 1268/1851 Shamil sent three *naibs* to Qaytaq-Tabarsaran, there to impose the *sharia* and to raise the inhabitants to arms against the Russians. This mission, involving nearly 3,000 troops, failed abysmally, leading Shamil to dismiss from office the unsuccessful *naibs*. In the wake of this setback, Hadji

Murat volunteered to try his hand at accomplishing the same goals. He asked Shamil for a force of 500 cavalry to invade the region.

Al-Qarakhi claimed that between Shamil's instructions and Hadji Murat's battle plan there was a sharp divergence. According to al-Qarakhi, Shamil expected Hadji Murat and his troops "to set up a fortified camp" near Qaytaq, to construct there a "fortress inaccessible [to the enemy] and to establish their administration among the residents." Hadji Murat, however, "had no intention of doing so." According to al-Qarakhi, Hadji Murat took hostages from the family of the local secular leader, the *shamkal* of Targhu. Al-Qarakhi offered no explanation of the hostage-taking, but the military context makes it clear that Hadji Murat intended to use the hostages as leverage to compel the *shamkal* to side with the resistance. Once the *shamkal* had joined the insurgency, Hadji Murat expected the common people to follow their leader.

In Qaytaq-Tabarsaran Hadji Murat's horsemen fell on the village Buynakh, sacked the residence of the *shamkal's* uncle, Abumuslim-Shakhvalikhan, killed the uncle, and carried off his wife and children. The cavalrymen also seized "all the weapons there, women's valuables, and so on." When the horsemen entered Khaidak, the inhabitants petitioned for the captives' release, in return for which the villagers promised to ask the *shamkal* to join the insurgency. According to al-Qarakhi, Hadji Murat "paid no attention" to this entreaty. Instead, Hadji Murat "went on his customary way, plundering and abducting [inhabitants of the area], here and there. His cavalrymen dragged their hostages wherever they went, like a mother cat drags her kittens." Unfortunately for Hadji Murat, the strategy of seizing hostages and plundering backfired: "the people of those *vilayats* [provinces] made no agreement with him and did not coalesce around him." The campaign ended in a disorganized retreat. On returning to headquarters, Hadji Murat was dismissed from office by Shamil.[71]

Al-Qarakhi described Hadji Murat as "saddened and utterly depressed" after being dismissed from office. In response to this unwelcome development, Hadji Murat "and those who went along with him" started bitterly criticizing the imam. They succeeded in winning support from "the majority" of Khunzakh's residents, who proceeded to "disobey the imam" and "to carry out Hadji Murat's orders." In other words, Hadji Murat persuaded residents of his home district to break with Shamil.

To quell the mutiny before it spread beyond Khunzakh, Shamil sent troops to confront the rebels and to arrest Hadji Murat. In this armed showdown, al-Qarakhi asserted, the "entire people completely dissociated themselves from Hadji Murat, who then fell under the imam's judgment." Holding Hadji Murat's life in his hands, Shamil nevertheless "pardoned" all the transgressions of the rebellious former *naib*. In spite of this pardon, however, Hadji Murat was a marked man. According to al-Qarakhi, "henceforth Hadji Murat found no refuge under any roof, no rest in any home." The chronicler said that the desperate Hadji Murat "feared slander," and so prepared to escape the imam's control. He "liquidated most of his personal property," taking care to hide whatever valuables he could not transport. Then he fled to the Russians, taking with him all the money he could lay hands upon. Having saved himself, Hadji Murat abandoned his family and children, but, on arriving behind Russian lines, he sent an appeal to Shamil asking for his family's release. The imam ignored the appeal. When Hadji Murat repeated it, Shamil responded: "O fool! You have committed apostasy from Islam. I am no fool, so I shall not release your family into apostasy."[72]

Al-Qarakhi attributed to Hadji Murat every vice a *murid* should avoid—pride, disobedience to religious authority, greed, theft, faithlessness to family, cowardice, and apostasy. He laid responsibility for Hadji Murat's removal from office squarely on the *naib*, not on the imam. Meanwhile, al-Qarakhi described Shamil as politically consistent (he removed from office all the unsuccessful *naibs*, Hadji Murat as well as the three predecessors) and merciful (he forgave Hadji Murat's transgressions). In al-Qarakhi's chronicle, there was no hint that Shamil "engineered" the 1851 confrontation with Hadji Murat. Instead, the chronicle showed Shamil responding to a disagreeable state of affairs fostered by a flawed subordinate.

Is it possible to reconcile Gammer's analysis of the Hadji Murat affair with al-Qarakhi's presentation of it, or at least to combine elements of the two accounts into a single, coherent interpretation?

Gammer's reading of the events behind Hadji Murat's defection is plausible. We know that by the early 1830s Shamil was already a central figure in the Naqshbandiyya-Khalidiyya, whereas Hadji Murat initially opposed the Sufi call for holy war against the Russians. After the assassination of the Avar khans in 1834, there had been bad blood between Shamil and Hadji Murat. We can assume that even after Hadji Murat joined the insurrection against the Russians in 1840, the imam eyed him with considerable suspicion. Certainly the suspicion would have intensified if, after the succession announcement of 1848, Hadji Murat had publicly opposed the imam's choice of a minor son as successor. It is conceivable that, after this moment of public opposition on Hadji Murat's part, Shamil awaited a pretext to act against the *naib*, and it is possible that he found such a pretext in 1851 when Hadji Murat's campaign in Qaytaq-Tabarsaran collapsed. Still, there is a difference between awaiting a convenient moment to settle a political score and actively "engineering" a confrontation with a rival. Moreover, if Shamil had wanted to force Hadji Murat out of military command, he could certainly have done so in 1848 without awaiting further events, or he might have chosen another occasion more proximate to 1848. Why, in other words, did Shamil wait three years to remove Hadji Murat as *naib*? If Gammer's hypothesis that the imam sought confrontation with Hadji Murat is not inconsistent with the evidence, neither is it compelling.

Al-Qarakhi's presentation of the 1851 confrontation helps us to understand the sequence of events immediately preceding Hadji Murat's defection from the Russians: the cavalry's retreat from hostile territory, Shamil's decision to remove Hadji Murat as *naib*, Hadji Murat's opposition to that decision, his arrest and trial by the imam, the dramatic pardon, the disgraced *naib*'s isolation in the imamate, his liquidation of personal property and final decision to flee to the Russians. Yet, if al-Qarakhi's chronicle of events is crisp and internally consistent, it is also one-sided.

The first mission to Qaytaq-Tabarsaran had failed despite the imam's commitment of nearly 3,000 troops. Hadji Murat's decision to undertake the campaign with only 500 cavalrymen was perhaps an act of hubris, but it was also a courageous step that must have impressed even the hardened Shamil. It is unlikely that Shamil would have sacrificed 500 men on a doomed mission, so the imam must have thought there was some chance of Hadji Murat succeeding where others had not. It is unlikely that Shamil gave orders to cavalrymen to establish a fortified camp and to build a fortress "inaccessible" to the Russians. After all, 3,000 foot soldiers had failed to hold a position in Qaytaq-Tabarsaran. Why would Shamil have thought that a lesser number of cavalry could stake out a defensible position? Moreover, experience had taught Shamil that the Russians could attack virtually any fortification, for the imperial army had laid siege to countless rebel strongholds in mountainous Daghestan. Much more sensible in military terms was Hadji Murat's plan of removing the political obstacle to the insurgency's spread in Qaytaq-Tabarsaran—namely, the *shamkal* and family. A force of 500 horsemen would have been well suited precisely to the taking of elite hostages, and Hadji Murat would have been the best possible negotiator for the imam's cause. Therefore, al-Qarakhi's suggestion is not credible that in Qaytaq-Tabarsaran Hadji Murat acted against the imam's instructions. We are on safer ground to assume that in Qaytaq-Tabarsaran Hadji Murat followed rather than defied the imam's explicit instructions.

Hadji Murat's seizure of the *shamkal*'s sister-in-law and her family was neither an act of sexual depravity nor an indicator of the *naib*'s indiscipline. It was a military step, almost certainly sanctioned by Shamil. The seizure of the *shamkal*'s property—weapons and women's valuables—was standard procedure in a war where booty was one of the chief sources of the imamate's revenue. Hadji Murat's refusal to surrender the *shamkal*'s family to the people of Qaytaq also had a military motivation: the hostages were his only leverage over the *shamkal*. Unfortunately, the *shamkal* was not moved to make concessions by the capture of his relatives, nor was the populace more inclined after the hostage taking to support the insurgents. Hadji Murat therefore found himself moving aimlessly "here and there" around the countryside, taking with him the hostages, as a "mother cat drags her kittens." His situation was ridiculous, as al-Qarakhi later took pleasure in pointing out. Hadji Murat soon gave up the mission as a dead end. He retreated from the field in humiliation.

Shamil removed Hadji Murat from office for two reasons. First, he had fired the three *naibs* who had failed in the first mission; to be consistent, he now had to remove Hadji Murat as well. Second, Hadji Murat's failure was Shamil's failure, because Shamil had almost certainly approved Hadji Murat's plan of hostage taking. Under the circumstances, the *naib* would have to take the fall for the imam, for, in the imamate, the only indispensable person was the imam.

Hadji Murat's crime was to oppose Shamil's decree removing him from office. This opposition gained a sympathetic hearing from Hadji Murat's townsmen in Khunzakh before the imam sent troops to arrest the mutinous former *naib*. The trial of Hadji Murat had as its justification the imamate's very survival: Shamil, fearing a widening of internal opposition to his rule, had no choice but to put Hadji Murat in the dock.

Al-Qarakhi's chronicle was deliberately silent about the formal charges against Hadji Murat. To acknowledge that the mountaineers' second most famous general had been tried for treason would not have been prudent. Nor did the chronicler mention the court's verdict: death to the "traitor." Yet to every attentive reader of al-Qarakhi's chronicle, the nature of the charges against Hadji Murat and the attendant penalty would have been obvious enough. Instead of emphasizing the imam's implacable justice, al-Qarakhi focused on Shamil's mercy. In spite of Hadji Murat's grave offenses, the imam at least publicly forgave them. When Hadji Murat, ungrateful to the imam and to God, refused to accept this mercy and defected to the infidels, he committed apostasy. To Shamil and to al-Qarakhi it was politically and religiously vital to label Hadji Murat an apostate from Islam.

By indirection, however, al-Qarakhi's chronicle subverted the very message its author attempted to propagate. Al-Qarakhi informed his readers that the disgraced Hadji Murat "found no refuge under any roof, no rest in any home." It added that Hadji Murat had fled to the Russians, "fear[ing] slander." What could be the meaning of these words? If Shamil's pardon were genuine, if Hadji Murat's transgressions had really been forgiven, why could he not find refuge anywhere in his country? Did Hadji Murat's countrymen shun him? At whose direction? And if most doors were closed to him, why could he not take shelter among friends in Khunzakh? Al-Qarakhi's words actually tell us that Hadji Murat had not really received a pardon after all. The former *naib*, "saddened and utterly depressed," was hunted by Shamil's agents who, knives drawn, lurked in the mountain shadows.

Was Hadji Murat a coward? Did he defect to the infidels to escape death at the imam's hands? Although al-Qarakhi implied such, the implication cannot stand scrutiny. As a fighter for Islam, Hadji Murat had faced death many times without flinching. He did not fear death as such, but he found it abhorrent to die in dishonor, hunted by "men of God" who would give him no opportunity to clear his name from the charge of treason. It was in this sense alone that Hadji Murat "feared slander." The accusation of apostasy was the most powerful arrow in the imam's quiver, but it cannot be taken seriously either: we know from many sources that in Russian custody Hadji Murat never foreswore Islam, and al-Qarakhi himself knew that Hadji Murat had died in 1852 trying to escape from the Russians.

Once in Russian custody, Hadji Murat called on Shamil to release his family from captivity. He surely did not expect the imam to do so, but the request put the moral responsibility for the family's fate squarely on the imam. Hadji Murat also tried to effect his family's release through the Russians: in return for their assistance in rescuing his family, Hadji Murat held out the prospect of military collaboration against Shamil. Under the right circumstances, his intervention against Shamil might have been decisive, provided he could have presented himself to the mountaineers as a true Islamic alternative to Shamil. Hadji Murat probably realized that the Russians had no intention of supporting a viable Islamic alternative to Shamil: the point of the imperial presence in the North Caucasus was to destroy the autonomy of the indigenous people and to render Islam helpless before Russian authority. Hadji Murat's high-stakes gamble on the Russians was a desperate play for time; by December 1851, he had no good alternatives. In the event, the Russians chose to hold Hadji Murat as a captive trophy, much as a lion tamer holds a captured beast, feeding him, parading him this way and that, but offering the "animal" no chance to demonstrate his feral strength. Hadji Murat's death on May 7, 1852 was an overdetermined outcome of the Russians' policy.

The killing of Hadji Murat removed Shamil's greatest rival from the political arena, thus ending the most serious internal threat to the Islamic state. The insurgency would now succeed or fail by virtue of the military contest with Russia.

V

In 1852 the insurgents' military prospects against Russia were not rosy. Although Shamil's forces bloodied the imperial army in numerous intense engagements, the Russian campaign systematically drove the insurgents out of Greater Chechnia. The insurgents nervously cast about for ways to expand their struggle geographically. The plan of winning new recruits in southern Daghestan had collapsed the previous year, and the war in Chechnia had gone badly. Therefore, the insurgents had to look west toward the Circassians and the Ottoman Empire for help. In late 1852/early 1853, as the chances of a new war between Russia and the Ottoman Empire increased, Shamil's "western" strategy began to look potentially more fruitful. A vigorous Turkish offensive against the Russians might open the door to a simultaneous attack in the North Caucasus from Circassians in the west and Shamil's forces in the east. In March 1853, a letter from Shamil to the Ottoman emperor practically begged for such co-operation.[73]

While awaiting Turkish intervention in the Caucasus, Shamil took his own measures to stir up a wide anti-Russian movement throughout the region. In August 1853 he led 10,000 men into Kakheti in eastern Georgia where he hoped to arouse the Muslim minority to join the insurgency. In spring 1854 Shamil sent his *naib* Muhammad Amin into Circassia. Muhammad Amin tried to persuade various clans to join Shamil in a major offensive against the Russians, but he discovered only mixed support for the imam's plan.[74]

Although neither of these initiatives yielded the desired results, the imam did not despair because, in January 1854, France and Britain entered the Crimean war in alliance with the Ottomans. Thereafter, Shamil anticipated a devastating Allied blow against Russian forces all along the Black Sea coast. Nor was he the only military leader awaiting that event. The Russian General N. A. Read advised Tsar Nicholas I that Russia should evacuate Georgia and the eastern Caucasus, for Read did not believe Russian troops would be able to hold their ground against an Allied assault.[75] Incidentally, the expectation of an Allied advance into the Caucasus was widely shared in Europe among intellectuals. Karl Marx wrote in 1854 that a Turkish invasion might bring about a junction of forces with the mountaineers and "may at once cut off the communication, at least by land, of the Russian army south of the Caucasus with Russia—a result that may lead to the total destruction of that army."[76]

In fact, however, the Allied offensive concentrated not on the Caucasus but on destroying the Russians' Black Sea fleet and on taking the naval base at Sevastopol in Crimea. Not until the late autumn of 1855 did the Turks mount an offensive in Transcaucasia, but this incursion lacked co-ordination with the Circassians and the eastern Caucasus insurgency. Whatever chance had existed for a general Islamic uprising against the Russians had slipped away.[77]

With the signing of the Peace of Paris in 1856, Russia lost its naval bases in the Black Sea and with them the possibility for a decisive advance against the Ottoman Empire through Anatolia. What it gained was the opportunity to concentrate its already mobilized forces against Shamil's insurgents. The architect of Russian military policy toward the insurgents after 1856 was Prince Alexsandr Ivanovich Bariatinskii. He called for a large-scale offensive against the rebels in Chechnia and Daghestan and won Tsar Alexander II's approval for the plan. Within three years Bariatinskii's army had beaten all organized resistance in the eastern Caucasus and secured the capture of Shamil.[78]

Bariatinskii's military victory opened the way to a Russian plan for the absorption of the now conquered Caucasus. Bariatinskii demanded the restoration of customary law and the gradual introduction of Russian civil law in the region. Both these steps meant to destroy the hold of the *sharia* in the eastern Caucasus, thus removing the influence of the Sufi brotherhood over civil society. Simultaneously, Bariatinskii called on the St. Petersburg government to revive dormant Orthodox influences in the Caucasus and to work for the general spread of Christianity in the region.[79] Bariatinskii's plan suggested that the Russian administration ended the fight against the Islamic insurgents as it had begun the struggle: the confrontation was a war of two civilizations, two religious messianisms, two worlds.

VI

When Shamil surrendered to Field Marshal Bariatinskii in August 1859, he became a pawn in the field marshal's scheme to promote ever more rapid Russian penetration of the Caucasus. Bariatinskii arranged for Shamil to travel to St. Petersburg, where the imam would meet assorted members of high society as well as high military and civilian officials. On the way to the capital Alexander II himself granted the imam an audience and promised that, in future, the belligerents of the Caucasus war would live together in amity. Government escorts showed Shamil the marvels of Russian industry and culture, then took him to an estate in Kaluga province where the imam spent most of the next decade. In 1870, in fulfillment of a pledge made by Bariatinskii, Russian authorities allowed Shamil to make pilgrimage to Mecca.[80]

Bariatinskii's ostentatiously courteous treatment of Shamil had nothing to do with altruism. The field marshal expected Russian kindnesses to the imam to be repaid in the coin of submission by the North Caucasus to Russia's imperial embrace. In the first instance, he hoped Muslim leaders in Daghestan and Chechnia would never again directly challenge Russian authority, for they would see from Russia's equable treatment of Shamil that the path of peace would bring large rewards. Second, Bariatinskii expected the "peaceful resolution" in the eastern Caucasus to drive the Circassian resisters to make peace as well. Alexander II and Bariatinskii persuaded Shamil to write the Circassian leader Muhammad Amin a letter calling on him to capitulate to be Russians.[81] Third, Bariatinskii looked to Shamil to endorse massive population shifts in the North Caucasus: either voluntary immigration from the Caucasus to unpopulated sections of the Russian empire or emigration to Ottoman lands.[82] Fourth, Bariatinskii wanted to use Shamil as a living advertisement of Russia's civilizing mission in "Asia." On the one hand, Shamil would be presented to the public as a brave, intelligent, resourceful individual—that is, as a worthy adversary to Russian power now become a valuable ally. On the other hand, by acknowledging Russia's military, technological, and political superiority, Shamil would prove the limits of Islam as civilizational force. Only by contact with vigorous Russia could the *élan vital* of the North Caucasus's many peoples be restored. In Bariatinskii's view, Russia's duty to itself and to the benighted North Caucasus was to spread enlightenment there.

Until 1870 Bariatinskii and other imperial planners did their best to take advantage of Shamil's surrender, and surely their public relations campaign had its successes. After 1859, Shamil did nothing to stir up resistance in the eastern Caucasus: the insurrection had been beaten—a fact he recognized as God's will. The imam also did what he was asked to promote peace between Russians and Circassians, although we have no evidence that anyone in the western Caucasus now heeded his advice. Shamil listened to Bariatinskii's proposals promoting "voluntary" emigration from the North Caucasus, but did nothing to further those schemes. Except in Circassia where tens of thousands fled to Anatolia in 1864, Bariatinskii's extravagant plan for russifying the Caucasus collapsed of its own weight. Shamil's most important gesture of "partnership" with the Russians was his decision in 1866 to swear an oath of allegiance to Tsar Alexander II.

Lest we conclude that Shamil's defeat caused him to rethink his religious allegiance or that it deprived him altogether of political agency, we must note well his curious correspondence with the Algerian independence fighter 'Abd al-Qadir. In a letter dated the year 1277 (July 8/20, 1861), Shamil praised 'Abd al-Qadir for "having criticized the misdeeds of those who have transgressed God's laws." In response 'Abd al-Qadir wrote: "We have come from God and we shall return to Him. Alas! The pious are few, rare are those who defend and uphold the right. Even those learned in sacred knowledge imagine that the foundation of Islam is violence, the absence of pity, bestial cruelty, and tyranny. It is good to endure such things patiently, but we ask God's help against them." Between the lines of this correspondence it is possible to read Shamil's enduring commitment to Islam and its defense against the unrighteous.[83]

'Abd al-Qadir had learned of Shamil's desire to make pilgrimage to Mecca. He prayed that God would grant the imam's wish. In 1865 Shamil wrote 'Abd al-Qadir: "I have no goal more pressing or more important than this [visiting Mecca and Medina] and then to die in the faith, in the holy precincts, the locus of revelation and forgiveness."[84] Perhaps Shamil's voluntary oath of allegiance to the tsar the next year was the imam's well-considered first step toward Mecca. In February 1869, after many delays, the Russian government gave the imam formal permission to visit the longed for holy lands. He departed for Mecca in 1870 and died at Medina in 1871. Unlike so many other subjects of the Russian government, Shamil died having achieved his deepest personal ambition.

VII

The mountain war in the North Caucasus generated thousands of documents, most from Russian officials but also a large number from the mountain peoples.[85] Among mountain sources, however, only two chronicles dealt comprehensively with the military campaigns and their religious context. The first was kept by Qurban 'Ali al-'Ashilti and edited by Imam Shamil himself. Unfortunately, after Shamil's surrender this irreplaceable source was burned by the author out of fear that the chronicle would be used by the Russians as the basis for mass arrests.[86] The second was Muhammad Tahir al-Qarakhi's *The Shining of Daghestani Swords in Certain Campaigns of Shamil*. This document, treasured by the mountaineers and widely circulated—sometimes in shortened, altered or otherwise corrupted redactions—was not published in a reliable scholarly edition until 1941. Yet, today, specialists recognize it as perhaps the single most revealing indigenous account of the mountain war.

The compiler of *The Shining of Daghestani Swords*, in spite of his prominence in the Sufi brotherhood, remains to us an obscure figure. We know virtually nothing of his early life except that he studied under the *alim* Hajj Dibir of Khunuk. There al-Qarakhi mastered Quranic Arabic, familiarized himself with principles of Islamic law, read the *Life of the Prophet* and Arabic poetry. Al-Qarakhi's knowledge of Arabic was not unusual in early nineteenth-century Daghestan. The Soviet Arabist I. Iu. Krachkovskii has shown that, across the eastern portion of the North Caucasus among the peoples of Daghestan, Chechnia, and Ingushetia, there was a serious interest in classical Arabic dating to the late eighteenth century.[87] Marius Canard has added that Arabic instruction was routinely provided to young boys in Daghestan mountain communities. Shamil himself began reading Arabic at age six.[88] For most of the nineteenth century, Arabic constituted the written *lingua franca* of the North Caucasus, a link connecting the diverse peoples of the region with each other and to the wider Islamic world.[89]

Al-Qarakhi's intense religiosity and his consequent devotion to the sacred language of Arabic led him to identify with the mountain insurgency from its outset and to celebrate its great deeds. When the "first imam" Ghazi Muhammad was killed at Gimrah in 1832, al-Qarakhi mourned the passing in an Arabic elegy. Al-Qarakhi's acquaintance with Shamil can be assumed at this time because Shamil arranged Ghazi Muhammad's burial rites.[90] In 1846 al-Qarakhi was attached to Shamil as an expert in Islamic matters. After the battle at Kutisha, al-Qarakhi composed an Arabic poem "for the imam's consolation and for the noble *naibs'* exhortation."[91] Two years later after the defeat at Akhdi, he wrote similar consolatory verses for the imam.[92] From the evidence it is not clear to what extent al-Qarakhi involved himself in actual fighting between 1832 and 1849, but an explanatory aside in his chronicle hinted that he had seen action before the Russians besieged the insurgents' fortress at Chokha in 1849. That siege, however, left him a "weakened and broken" man, unable to participate any longer in the *ghazwa* because of "weakness and pain in his joints."[93]

In the winter of 1850 al-Qarakhi settled in the *awul* Darghiyya. There he became one of Shamil's closest lieutenants, his confidant and virtual alter ego. The moment of al-Qarakhi's transformation apparently occurred when the imam consulted his inner circle concerning the wisdom of naming his second son Ghazi Muhammad the *naib* of Qarata. The so-called "consultation" amounted to an exercise in divination based on a Quranic verse. Al-Qarakhi "saw immediately that the sense of the Quranic line ... indicates that the office of *naib* has been ordained to him [Ghazi Muhummed]." Persuaded by al-Qarakhi's exegesis, the imam proceeded to name his second son to the position, even though Ghazi Muhammad had not yet reached his majority. After performing this service for Shamil, al-Qarakhi was invited to live "in the imam's quarters." "Season after season" al-Qarakhi stayed there until 1855, when Shamil's eldest son Jamal al-Din returned from Russian captivity.[94]

At some point after 1850 al-Qarakhi received from Shamil a directive to prepare a chronicle of the mountain war. This was a very sensitive assignment with profound political implications. In the event of victory over the Russians, the chronicle would identify Shamil, as the human architect of the mountaineers' triumph, with God's wisdom; in the event of defeat, the document would convey to future warriors the precious memory of a holy war gloriously waged in God's name. Al-Qarakhi dutifully gathered materials for the chronicle until the prisoner exchange of March 1855 freed Shamil's eldest son Jamal al-Din from Russian confinement.[95]

The return of Jamal al-Din evidently disrupted the fragile comity in the Naqshbandi leadership. After sixteen years among the Russians, Jamal al-Din had learned the Russian language and Russian customs. He had developed friendships with his captors, including General Leontii Pavlovich Nikolai, who helped negotiate the prisoner exchange.[96] Almost immediately after being reunited with his father, Jamal al-Din and his cousin Hamza "spoke with the imam about making peace with the Russian tsar and urged him towards it." These pleas for peace did not impress the imam, but they did excite irritation at Shamil's eldest son and nephew: "It was said," al-Qarakhi reported, "that [the Russians] freed these two only for this [peace initiative]."[97] The hint in the lines is palpable: Jamal al-Din and al-Qarakhi quarreled over peace policy. Although the imam took al-Qarakhi's position on the political matter, he could not be seen as choosing intimacy with a trusted advisor over his son. That is the likeliest explanation for the termination of Shamil's close relationship with al-Qarakhi.

During the subsequent fighting against the Russians, al-Qarakhi "became separated from Shamil."[98] The separation may have occurred because al-Qarakhi was physically unable to campaign, whereas the imam rushed from place to place in a vain effort to stave off defeat. Perhaps, however, the "separation" happened suddenly, in late July/early August 1859, when the remnants of Shamil's state collapsed swiftly under Russian pressure. Between August 21 and September 6, 1859 Shamil and his immediate entourage were trapped in the mountain *awul* Ghunib. By the time the final siege had commenced, al-Qarakhi had come to the attention of the Russian high command. Perhaps Bariatinskii learned of al-Qarakhi's status in the Naqshbandi brotherhood from General L. P. Nikolai who had cultivated close relations with the insurgents and had been involved in the 1855 peace feelers. At any rate, in late August al-Qarakhi was sent by the Russians into Ghunib to negotiate Shamil's surrender.

In *The Shining of Daghestani Swords* al-Qarakhi offered us a brief glimpse of this enterprise:

> Then the commander of the Russians, the baron, summoned the blind Muhammad Efendi al-Huyami, who had lived in Qarakh as Shamil's companion, Muhammad Tahir al-Qarakhi, and his student Hajiyaw al-Qarakhi, and he sent them to the imam for negotiations about peace.
>
> When they had reached the fortress Ghunib, the imam decided that no one might enter the fortress except those who would stay with him. The Efendi and Muhammad Tahir then returned [to the Russians], but Hajiyaw entered the fortress and remained with Shamil. Because of this, Hajiyaw subsequently fell into great misfortune: for a certain time he was imprisoned, where he worked like a slave, but only later was he liberated.[99]

This laconic passage offers fertile ground for speculation. Why did al-Qarakhi describe the "Russian commander" as "baron?" Bariatinskii, the actual commander and viceroy of the Caucasus, held the title of "prince." The "baron" on the scene was General Nikolai, mentioned above as peace negotiator in 1855. Did al-Qarakhi confuse Bariatinskii's rank? Or did he take Baron Nikolai as commander? The apparent confusion probably indicates that al-Qarakhi was called suddenly into the presence of someone with whom he was not familiar. What was the criterion of selection for the team of three intermediaries? The two senior intermediaries had long histories with Shamil: Muhammad Efendi had served as *naib* at the height of the insurgency before losing his sight; Muhammad Tahir had been a leading spiritual consultant to Shamil, part of the *ulama*. Perhaps the younger Hajiyaw was selected as scribe. Why did the two senior intermediaries turn away at the fortress gate? They probably understood Shamil's condition for entering as a demand for loyalty: "He who is not with me is against me." At this point they would not join Shamil in a suicidal defense of a mountain fortress. Their ultimate loyalty was to God, whose will had been made clear enough. Probably the young Hajiyaw felt the urge to suffer for the sake of Islam.

We have only fragmentary information on al-Qarakhi's fate after Shamil's surrender on September 6, 1859. The chronicle noted that Shamil, his two sons and their families were taken under Russian escort to the camp at Qakhal, then to the fortress at Temir-Khan-Shura, and thence to meet Tsar Alexander II. Others were "released ... each to his own native place."[100] After his service to Shamil, al-Qarakhi apparently eventually made his way to Temir-Khan-Shura, where he spent the rest of his life as a religious judge. During this period he wrote several lengthy treatises on Islamic law. He died in 1882.

While at Temir-Khan-Shura, al-Qarakhi maintained contact with veterans of the insurgency. For example, he returned to Shamil's son Ghazi Muhammad valuable books that had been looted from the imam's "treasury" by someone in the *awul* Qurush.[101] In addition, al-Qarakhi gathered from his wide contacts information bearing on the fate of the most prominent insurgents—Sultan Daniyal, Shaykh Muhammad Efendi, and, of course, Imam Shamil. From what we can discern, this information came in the form of oral reports but also letters and written memoirs that al-Qarakhi obtained. On at least one occasion, al-Qarakhi reacted publicly to a written account that disparaged Shamil. Someone passed to al-Qarakhi a verse by Hajj Yusuf al-Yaksavi, who declared: "Shamil's victories are dust, although they made him imam." As trustee of the movement's history, al-Qarakhi composed a verse challenging that insult: "Shamil's victories were great deeds, and that is why they made him imam."[102]

At Temir-Khan-Shura, al-Qarakhi kept a small archive consisting of the original version of his chronicle covering the years 1830 to 1855, and of materials that he had collected subsequently. Before his death in 1882, he made factual corrections to the original chronicle and added accounts of the insurgency's defeat, of Shamil's visit to St. Petersburg, and of the imam's pilgrimage to Mecca.

Al-Qarakhi also introduced his son Habibullah to the history of the mountain war. After his father's death Habibullah acted as guardian of *The Shining of*

Daghestani Swords. He sought out additional written materials about Shamil and made additional changes to the chronicle. In 1904, Habibullah tried unsuccessfully to gain permission from the imperial censor to publish *The Shining of Daghestani Swords* in Arabic language at Temir-Khan-Shura. Neither father nor son managed to see a printed version of the manuscript in which their very lives were invested.

VIII

Two passages in *The Shining of Daghestani Swords* explain how Muhammad Tahir al-Qarakhi composed the chronicle. The first passage by al-Qarakhi himself was inserted at the end of the entry on Jamal al-Din's return from Russian captivity:

> Here is the conclusion of the material gathered by Muhammad Tahir during his residence with the imam and based on conversations of the imam and his lieutenants who participate in the campaigns. Later he [Muhammad Tahir] supplemented what he gathered earlier with testimony about events that occurred subsequently, after the original material had been collected.[103]

The second passage was written by Habibullah after his father's death but on the basis of oral testimony from al-Qarakhi:

> The reason for the compilation of this book is that Imam Shamil (May God have mercy on him!) said time after time to Muhammad Tahir: "I would like to gather stories about the events that have occurred in my time; however, I cannot find the leisure for it because of preoccupation with all sorts of matters and with military campaigns." Then in the winter of one year he [Shamil] kept company with [Muhammad Tahir] in Darghiyya. They sat at dusk together and Shamil dictated and narrated what had occurred in non-Arabic language, then Muhammad Tahir translated the account into Arabic and by daylight recorded what Shamil had said. For events at which Shamil was not present, he [Shamil] summoned an eyewitness to tell what had occurred, and Muhammad Tahir wrote it down. This was how he compiled the book to the end of the chapter on Jamal al-Din's return from the infidels' camp. From that point to the end he gathered material in accordance with what people had learned or heard, except for what I [Habibullah] added from the imam's letters ... or changed in the interest of the cause."[104]

These passages pointed to Shamil as the main force behind *The Shining of Daghestani Swords.* The imam set the book's subject ("events that have occurred in my time"); he determined the time and place where the book's material was gathered ("one winter" "at dusk" in Darghiyya); he laid down ground rules for providing material (he recollected events in his native "non-Arabic" tongue, and selected eyewitnesses to supplement his deficient memory). Al-Qarakhi wanted readers to understand the first two-thirds of *The Shining of Daghestani Swords* as an authoritative text, "dictated and narrated" by the imam himself. Al-Qarakhi's own role was that of faithful emanuensis: translator into Arabic, transcriber, and compiler of the materials provided by the imam. At several points, al-Qarakhi described himself as an "intermediary" between Shamil and the future reader.

To be sure, *The Shining of Daghestani Swords* allows us to hear the imam's voice and to share his assessment of events. But we should not forget al-Qarakhi's intermediacy, for he took the raw material supplied by Shamil and shaped it into a blend of two genres familiar to his Muslim public.

The first genre is biography of the Muslim hero and holy man. The main model for such biography is the *Sira*, the life of the prophet Muhammad himself. The most widely read version of the prophet's life, written in the ninth century by Ibn Ishaq, gave colorful accounts of Muhammad's confrontations with unbelievers; thus, it set the pattern for future narratives of holy war waged by Muhammad's successors. In the Sufi world, the *Sira* template was linked to the celebration and commemoration of "friends of the faithful" or "friends of God"—that is, to narratives of those close to God who assumed special responsibility for enforcing obedience to divine law and who enjoyed God's special protection. The lives of these "friends of God" [*awliya*] have sometimes been compared to the lives of Christian saints in as much as the "friends of God" can intervene with God on behalf of the believer and sometimes call on supernatural gifts to perform worthy deeds. Two crucial differences between the concept of Christian sainthood and the Islamic notion of *awliya* are that, in Islam, there is no formal canonization of individuals close to God and that, in Islam, it was therefore possible to attribute full sanctity to living persons. Thus, the capacious rubric of Muslim hagiography could easily accommodate a narrative attributing supernatural gifts to a Sufi master like Shamil.[105]

In *The Shining of Daghestani Swords* al-Qarakhi ascribed to Shamil the gift of foreseeing the future. For example, while under siege at Akhulgoh in 1839, Shamil saw in a dream the deaths at Shubut of his wife Jawhara and infant son Sa'id.[106] After leaving Akhulgoh, he made his way to Shubut where he verified the passing of his dear ones. In 1843, during a desperate moment at Ansal, Shamil dreamt the legend of Sultan Mahmud who cleansed the dirty well of Ghazna. Shamil's companion Amir Khan interpreted the legend as an augury of victory—a victory secured quickly thereafter.[107] Sometimes al-Qarakhi connected the gift of foreseeing the future with Shamil's cat-like skill in avoiding danger. Thus, at Gimrah in 1832 Shamil dreamt that he would find himself trapped in a house, that Russians would break through the roof and fire upon him, and that he would escape by running out of the door. The next day during the actual fighting Shamil narrowly extricated himself from precisely such a predicament. Although badly wounded, he made his way to a nearby cave; that night he avoided death from exposure to cold by heating the cave with the warm air issuing from his stomach wound.[108]

In *The Shining of Daghestani Swords* al-Qarakhi provided readers with numerous accounts of Shamil's escapes from danger. In 1830, while trying to impose the *sharia* in Khunzakh, Shamil was disarmed, then nearly beaten to death by his religious opponents. He was saved by Darvish Nur Muhammad on the first night of Ramadan.[109] In 1837, a loyal lieutenant saved him from death at 'Ish, near Khunzakh.[110] Twice before the siege at Akhulgoh the imam escaped death: near Tarad-Inkhal "bullets showered him from every direction, and ... God the All-Powerful saved him from injury"; at Irghin he and a lieutenant escaped Russian pursuers unwounded, despite "five bullet holes in his *burka*."[111] After the Akhulgoh siege in September 1839, Shamil was attacked in his quarters by "an evil, strong and vicious man named Gubash." Lacking his weapons and unable to summon immediate assistance, Shamil sustained "twelve knife wounds to his body and seven cuts to his lower abdomen," plus "broken ribs" and "bite wounds to the arm and head" before the terrifying assailant was overcome.[112] In 1847, when Vorontsov attacked the fortress at Saltah, "the soldiers' bullets did not strike their targets, not even one in a hundred did so," while the bullets of Shamil's forces "were unerring, not a single bullet fell to the ground."[113]

To these incidents when Shamil escaped injury or death we must add those moments when God saved his property. "Three times the *awul* Gimrah burned, but Shamil's house never caught fire," al-Qarakhi informed us. "Shamil's house at 'Ashilta did not burn when the rest of the *awul* did, nor did his residence in Akhulgoh burn when the Russians mobilized themselves for that siege. That is how God the most high assisted Shamil and us in our faith."[114] During the imam's escape from Akhulgoh, he "left behind his books and supplies. He struck the book *Insan al-'Uyun*, copied by the famous scholar Sa'id al-Harakani, and exclaimed: 'What enemy will attain you?' But God the most high by his great power returned the book to Shamil."[115] In 1859 in the *awul* Qurush Shamil's treasurer Hajiyaw al-'Uruti and the *qadis* of the *awul* "took for themselves those books [of Shamil] they considered best." Later the *qadis* repented the theft and handed over the books to al-Qarakhi for return to Shamil. The books included a manuscript of the *Meccan Bestowal* written by al-Quduqi.[116]

As "friends of God" the imams could reasonably hope for God's protection through nature. Thus, in 1831 during the campaign outside the fortress at Qidhlar "a host of black ravens obscured the sun," thereby depriving Russian soldiers of information about Ghazi Muhammad's troop dispositions. "Swirling above the Russians' fortress, the ravens' cries distracted them and threw them into confusion."[117] Fourteen years later during Vorontsov's attempt to take Darghiyya in early summer the Russians were caught by an unexpected snowstorm. Trapped for "more than a week" in "heavy snow and strong winds," they lost horses and ran through their food supply.[118] That such events were part of God's rage against the Russian infidels was made clear by al-Qarakhi who quoted an anonymous letter to Vorontsov:

Ah, you dog, Vorontsov. May God break your legs, cut off your arms, blind your eyes and make dumb your tongue! You have summoned misfortune upon us. Because of your evil deeds five misfortunes have befallen us. You drove the majority of our men into a place of perdition where they perished. Cholera has assailed us. Locusts have flown upon us in clouds and forced us into hunger. A powerful earthquake has destroyed our homes and villages. And all because of your evil deeds![119]

On rare occasions, Imam Shamil seemed to exercise control over time, natural objects, and human events. After the siege at Akhulgoh Shamil's seven-year-old son Ghazi Muhammad neither ate nor drank for two days. On the third day Shamil promised that, at the summit of a nearby mountain, food and water would be found for the weakened boy. There, in that unlikely venue, a stray ally provided bread, cheese, and drink to Ghazi Muhammad.[120] In summer 1843 at the siege of Ansal, Russian troops retreated so long as Shamil was watching them through a spyglass. "As soon as the troops were obscured from his sight, however, the imam's troops began to retreat. But when the mist dispersed, he saw the soldiers in the same place they had been before the Russians' advance and his troops' retreat."[121]

By highlighting the instances when Shamil and the other imams enjoyed God's special favor, al-Qarakhi prepared his readers to classify the Naqshbandi leaders as true descendants of the prophet Muhammad. The Muslim scholar Hajiyaw al-'Uruti reported that "if [Imam] Ghazi Muhammad and I had lived before the coming of our prophet [Muhammad] ... then would I have said that Ghazi Muhammad is the prophet."[122] This same "prophetic" Ghazi Muhammad prophesied that: "Shamil will live long ... I have been told [in a dream] that Shamil's contribution will last to eternity."[123] On leaving 'Ashilta in 1834, Shamil compared himself to Muhammad:

I part with you [people of 'Ashilta] because I cannot establish faith in your heart. The best creature of God the Most High, Muhammad (May God's blessing and peace be upon him!), abandoned the finest place in creation, Mecca, when he could not spread the true faith there.[124]

At the successful siege of Irghin in 1839, Shamil told his soldiers that their momentary pusillanimity was like that of Muhammad's soldiers during the battle of 'Uhud. He predicted they would be victorious just as the prophet's troops had been—another implied comparison of himself to Muhammad.[125] Even in moments of military difficulty, however, the parallels between Muhammad's time and the mountain rebellion were carefully observed. After the rout of Shamil's forces at Kutisha in 1846, al-Qarakhi intoned:

Thus it was, but the Most High God said in the glowing book of revelations to his great emissary and noble servant, our master and prophet

Muhammad (May God's blessing and peace be upon him!): "Even in these days we insist on taking our place among the people."[126]

The decline of rebel power in the late 1840s and the defeat of the Naqshbandi insurgency in 1859 forced al-Qarakhi and his readers to consider whether the insurgency had enjoyed God's blessing at all, and it raised the corollary question of whether the imams were really "friends of God." To the first question al-Qarakhi gave inconsistent answers. On the one hand, he asserted that God's will is always done. After the débâcle at Akhdi in 1848 when Shamil's troops failed to take the small Russian fortress, al-Qarakhi wrote consolatory verses. He asked: "Should one be sad when all is foreordained?" His answer expressed the central axiom of Islamic theodicy: "We strive, in fact, to attain only what has been foreordained."[127] On the other hand, al-Qarakhi quoted Shamil's assertions that, behind the insurgency's defeats, stood violation of the *sharia*. In 1849, after the defeat at Choka, the imam scolded his *naibs*: "You do not hold to the religion of God the most high, who is your ruler and creator, except by your thumb and little finger."[128] After Shamil's failed offensive in the Alazan valley in 1854, God sent the imam's troops "nothing but humiliation and defeat, isolation and retreat." The reasons for the endless disasters that followed were "the arrogance and pride of [his] lieutenants, their dereliction of duty and lack of support; in the imam's family, disobedience and obstruction of his will; in the people, dissatisfaction with their rulers and disapproval of [the leaders'] obstructionism."[129] In other words, the Muslims' general failure to do God's bidding explained the movement's failure to achieve the "foreordained" success.

In approaching the question whether Shamil was a genuine "friend of God," al-Qarakhi confronted not only the catastrophic defeat of the movement Shamil had led but the imam's embarrassing surrender to infidels. Why did the famous warrior for Islam choose not to die a martyr's death? To answer this disconcerting question, al-Qarakhi depicted Shamil in 1859 as the last true believer surrounded by traitors to the insurrection. Everywhere, even in his own family council, Shamil demanded rigorous adherence to the *sharia*, but everywhere his words fell on deaf ears. Inside Ghunib, the imam "pleaded, cajoled and admonished those gathered in the mosque, everyone together and each individual, calling each by name, summoning them to battle, to fall for the faith and to seek out death in the fray, but not a single person expressed such a desire, even his two sons ..." Totally isolated among his closest followers, Shamil finally accepted surrender "only thanks to [the] ... urgings [of his son Ghazi Muhammad]."[130] Even after consenting to surrender, Shamil made the condition that "if the Russians should separate him from his lieutenants or if they should disarm these lieutenants, that [he and his lieutenants] should give battle and should dare attack the Russians, seeking death in battle ... Nevertheless, the Russians interposed themselves between Shamil and his lieutenants and took away Shamil's weapons ..."[131] Thus, al-Qarakhi's narrative showed the imam as faithful to the end, despite his followers' fear and deception.

Yet al-Qarakhi himself appeared unpersuaded by this very account. If Shamil were really a holy warrior in the Islamic tradition, he would have died alone for the cause, unpersuaded by the easy counsel to surrender. After all, the imam had once sworn to his *naibs* "on the Quran that he would never make peace with the Russians save on the conditions prescribed by the Quran."[132] Therefore, al-Qarakhi sought another way of demonstrating that Shamil was truly a "friend of God." The narrative's "external proofs" of the imam's holiness included the Turkish sultan's kissing of Shamil's hand in 1870, when the imam visited Mecca on the *hajj*; the Russian tsar's decision to grant Shamil a twenty-thousand-ruble annual subsidy for life; the ruler of Egypt's invitation to the imam to sit alongside him; and the Sharif of Mecca's elevation of Shamil to the pulpit of the Mecca mosque. According to al-Qarakhi, the most convincing evidence of the imam's spiritual greatness was his "passage, like that of gold through fire, through all events and difficulties until the very moment when God the most high took his soul, the soul of one elected, into the fragrant presence of the prophet (May God's blessing and peace be upon him!)."[133]

The second genre to which *The Shining of Daghestani Swords* belongs is the historical chronicle. In the European West, the chronicle was a venerable form of historical writing associated with antiquity, the Middle Ages, and, to a lesser degree with the Italian Renaissance: even Leonardo Bruni's "modern" history of Florence *Historiarum Florentini populi libri* (1415–1429) belonged in formal terms to the rubric of chronicle. Yet by the eighteenth century leading European historians considered chronicling an outmoded, even disreputable method of writing history. This scholarly dismissal of the chronicle owed something to a turn against ecclesiastical and political history: Giambattista Vico's *Principi di scienza nuova* (1725), Voltaire's *Essai sur les moeurs* (1756), and Johann Gottfried Herder's *Ideen zur Philosophie der Geschichte der Menschheit* (1784–1791) all abandoned chronological narrative in favor of thematically organized cultural history. In the eighteenth century's most famous historical work, Edward Gibbon scoffed at chronicles, which, he said, "repeat a tedious and uniform tale of weakness and misery." He claimed his "philosophical" narrative would compensate the reader by the "Superior merits of interest and perspicuity."[134] In Russia the chronicle had a longer run. It was the dominant mode of historical writing from the twelfth-century *Povest' vremennykh let* [*Tale of Bygone Years*] through to the early seventeenth- century *Time of Troubles*.[135] Yet even N. M. Karamzin's *Istoriia gosudarstva Rossiiskago* (1816–1829) bore earmarks of the chronicle form. Let us recall Pushkin's penetrating witticism: "Karamzin is our first historian and last chronicler."[136]

In most of the Islamic world after the tenth century, the favored method of presenting historical information was the annalistic chronicle. The historian's goal was to gather documentary or personal testimony, test its reliability, then arrange it in the appropriate sequence on the Islamic calendar (generally thought to begin at the hegira (July 15, 622 A.D. according to the Gregorian calendar). Perhaps the first great example of this mode of writing was the *Tarikh al-Rusul wa al-Muluk*, a universal history of humanity from the Creation to the time of the chronicler Abu Jafar al-Tabari (d. 923). Between the tenth and sixteenth centuries the focus of historiography tended to narrow. Now the subject was a political leader, a dynasty or a particular locale, but the relevant materials were ordered by year, as before.[137] Throughout this stretch of centuries, there were no professional historians in the Islamic world, nor was there any recognition of history as a recognized discipline. In parts of the Ottoman empire—Egypt, for example—both the quality and quantity of historical writing may have diminished between the sixteenth century and the beginning of the nineteenth century. One scholar has assessed this work with brutal frankness: "Ottoman-Egyptian historiography represents the nadir of a long and often glorious historical tradition. The structure of the chronicle declined in Ottoman times even further from its already threadbare Mamluk format, and the sheer quantity of historical writing tapered off dramatically. Historical style became a mixture of bone-dry chronology and empty *saj'* [decorative literary] convention."[138] Only with 'Abd al-Rahman al-Jabarti's analytical chronicle *Aja'ib al-Athar fi al-Tarajim wa al-Akhbar* [*Wondrous Seeds of Men and Their Deeds*] (written c. 1798, published 1879–1880), Rifaah al-Tahtawi's thematically organized public history *Manakib al-Albab al-Misriyyah fi Mabahij al-Adab al-Asriyyah* [*Paths of Egyptian Hearts in the Joys of Contemporary Arts*] (1869), and his historical translation project did the shift away from "bone-dry" chronicle to analytical history occur.[139]

In Central Asia, as Adeeb Khalid has demonstrated, the courts at Kokand, Bukhara, and Khiva "were active centers for the writing of history" between the early sixteenth and the mid-nineteenth centuries. However, historiographical production generally limited itself to the manuscript form, and the impetus for writing usually came from the local ruler or court elites who sought literary justification of their governance. Moreover, as in the Ottoman empire, historians almost aways preferred the chronicle genre. The most substantial work of Central Asian historiography before the late nineteenth century, Shir Muhammad Munis' *Firdaws al-Iqbal* (written 1805–1828), consisted largely of annalistic chronicle.[140]

Al-Qarakhi's *The Shining of Daghestani Swords* therefore exemplified a mode of historical writing only recently abandoned in Western Europe and Russia, and still dominant in much of the Islamic world. Like most early Islamic and Ottoman historians, al-Qarakhi was an amateur rather than a professional. Like his contemporaries in Central Asia and many of his predecessors in the Ottoman domains, he produced a manuscript form of his chronicle without the expectation that the work would be printed. Again like the Central Asians but also like his Russian coeval Karamzin, al-Qarakhi wrote at the behest of the local ruler and would-be dynast.

Like other Muslim historians, al-Qarakhi assiduously gathered first-hand testimony from Shamil and other veterans of the mountain insurrection. He then arranged this testimony according to the dates of the Islamic calendar. For that portion of the chronicle dealing with the post-1855 period, al-Qarakhi gathered documentary and oral testimony. Everywhere he indicated his source of information, so that readers would be able to judge its reliability. In cases where he himself witnessed an event or participated in a conversation, al-Qarakhi alerted his readers. Yet his intention was apparently not to insist on his own priv-ileged access to events, but to underline the trustworthiness of evidence from an eyewitness. Like fellow historians, al-Qarakhi was deliberately self-effacing: he described himself as a simple "conveyor" of testimony, a "reliable rapporteur."

Still, al-Qarakhi was not a slavish adherent to the chronicle format. When nothing noteworthy occurred in a given year, he passed over the interval without commentary. Since his information on the post-1855 period was fragmentary, his account of Shamil's surrender, glorified captivity by the Russians, and pilgrimage to Mecca was also episodic. Lacking the year-by-year exposition typical of the chronicle's first portion, the second portion of *The Shining of Daghestani Swords* had a looser structure and freer tone sometimes reminiscent of a memoiristic essay. It is almost as if *The Shining of Daghestani Swords* consisted of two discrete historical forms artificially linked together. Or—to cast the stylistic divergences in other terms—it is as if *The Shining of Daghestani Swords*, composed and corrected over a period of decades, embodied in its fractured text the transi-tion in historical writing then occurring throughout the Islamic world.

The "after-life" of *The Shining of Daghestani Swords* is itself curious. The Soviet translator of al-Qarakhi's text, A. M. Barabanov, has established that Russian authorities became aware of the chronicle's existence "immediately after Shamil's capture, if not earlier."[141] Pavel Giliarovich Przewalski, a police officer who guarded Shamil in Kaluga from 1860 to 1862, attempted to translate the first portion of the chronicle into Russian. Przewalski showed the translation to Shamil and asked the imam to approve its authenticity. According to I. N. Zakhar'in-Iakunin, Shamil "who had not inspected the original [in Przewalski's custody] and who did not read Russian at all, categorically refused to sign the translation."[142] The Przewalski translation, dated November 1, 1860, was given by Przewalski himself to Nikolai Fedorovich Dubrovin, who inspected it during the writing of his history of the mountain war.[143]

At approximately the same time, the Russian general Lazarev obtained a copy of the Arabic manuscript, which he passed to Adol'f Petrovich Berzhe (Berguet). A student of the Chechens and of the mountain peoples generally, Berzhe also translated *The Shining of Daghestani Swords* but gave up after three chapters.[144] Unfortunately, accordingly to Barabanov, Berzhe gave the Arabic manuscript "to someone else," then did not receive the manuscript back, so "it disappeared."[145] For whatever reason, Berzhe did not publish *The Shining of Daghestani Swords* in his twelve-volume edition of archeographic materials on the Caucasus and the mountain war.[146]

In spite of the early Russian interest in *The Shining of Daghestani Swords* and the existence of two translations (one complete but inadequate, the other partial), the chronicle remained virtually unknown outside of al-Qarakhi's circle. Barabanov has speculated that neither Dubrovin nor Berzhe dared publish it because the work, "full of hatred and contempt toward Daghestan's enslavers and replete with descriptions of the mountaineers' heroism," did not coincide with the Russian interest in presenting the war as a "victorious" campaign by its generals and army. "Daghestan had been subjugated once and for all, Shamil had been captured and sent to Kaluga. The generals, the 'heroes and victors,' were receiving their promotions and medals; they were writing memoirs; historians preparing the multi-volume descriptions of the Caucasus war successfully got along without local sources; they made do with the narratives and reports provided by the generals and viceroys. For the real facts of the recent long and bloody fighting nobody had any use."[147]

Indeed, the Russian authorities soon listed *The Shining of Daghestani Swords* as a "subversive Islamic book," whose publication at "Muslim presses" within the empire was forbidden. In 1902 al-Qarakhi's son Habibullah explored the possibility of printing an abridged Arabic language version of *The Shining of Daghestani Swords* at Makhachkala. Al-Qarakhi's prospective editor, Muhammad Mirza Mavraev advised Habibullah to change the title to something innocuous like *The Hardened Hearts of Daghestan* (!) and to eliminate expressions "slandering the Russian government." In March 1904, Habibullah sent the softened text to Mavraev, but the editor did not succeed in persuading the imperial censor to license publication. *The Shining of Daghestani Swords*, even 45 years after Shamil's surrender, remained too incendiary to print anywhere in Russia.[148]

IX

Lev Tolstoi first encountered the Caucasus in the literature of Pushkin, A. A. Bestvzhev-Marlinskii, and M. Iu. Lermontov. One of his popular biographers, Henri Troyat, gave Tolstoi credit for knowing by heart the Caucasian poems of Pushkin and Lermontov.[149] Tolstoi himself, writing in an unpublished 1852 essay, disclosed that he had read Marlinskii "with delight" along with "all of Lermontov's Caucasian works." With little exaggeration, Tolstoi confessed that such imaginative literature was his "only source of knowledge about the Caucasus" before arriving there in May 1851.[150]

Of course, it is no simple matter to define precisely the contours of Tolstoi's literary "knowledge." Susan Layton's *Russian Literature and Empire* outlined the principal tendencies of pre-Tostoian Russian writing about the Caucasus. These included: the depiction of the indigenous peoples as savage, Asiatic "others"; the attribution to the mountaineers of certain vices (cruelty in warfare, sexual predation) and virtues (fearlessness, anarchic love of liberty) lacking in their "civilized" Russian counterparts; the depiction of the Caucasus itself as the mirror opposite of Russia—that is, as an exotic clime where neither agriculture nor serfdom, neither autocracy nor Christianity had taken root. On these points of reference, Russian writers constructed an intoxicatingly rich literary discourse whose hallmark was profound ambivalence toward the Caucasus. On the one hand, writers rejected the native peoples as immoral savages threatening everything for which Russians properly stood; on the other hand, these very same writers admired Caucasian fierceness, envied warriors' imputed sexual prowess, and sought to emulate the mountaineers' anarchic ways. In other words, hatred toward and love of the mountaineers cohabited in the classic Russian writers before Tolstoi.[151]

On the evidence of the essay fragment "Notes on the Caucasus. A Journey to Mamakai-Yurt," Tolstoi himself was drawn to the Caucasus as a site where extraordinary natural vistas and the natives' exotic customs would provide raw materials to his own unfettered imagination. He confessed:

> I have long ago forgotten Marlinskii's and Lermontov's poems, but from the images contained in them I have manufactured different poems, a thousand times more seductive than the originals ... Have you ever read verse in a half-familiar language, verse that you know to be first rate? Without deciphering the meaning of each phrase, you continue to read, and from certain words that you do comprehend, you construct in your mind an utterly different meaning—one that may be unclear, vague and unrelated to the original syntax, yet more beautiful and poetic. For the longest time the Caucasus for me was that poem in an unfamiliar language.[152]

The "poem in an unfamiliar language" constructed in Tolstoi's mind out of pieces of Russian literature slowly receded as the young writer confronted the prosaic realities of the imperial presence in the Caucasus. In June 1851 he lived as his brother Nikolai's guest in the Russian fortress at Staryi Yurt. He found nature disappointing: "up to this point—nothing diverting."[153] The officers and soldiers at the fortress were of low caliber, such that it became impossible for the two Tolstoi brothers "not to admit our mutual superiority over the others."[154] Lev Nikolaevich soon found himself tempted to gamble at cards to impress these very same "obviously inferior" officers: by early July he had lost 850 rubles. On top of that indignity, he had "gotten completely drunk" and "had slept with a woman" whom he did not love and who repudiated his subsequent advances. Trapped in the banal, vice-ridden routine of the Russian occupying army without actually being part of the armed forces, Tolstoi admitted that his behavior had been "very stupid"—"an abomination!"[155]

Depressed by the vileness of his surrounding milieu and by his own moral flaws, Tolstoi nevertheless retained his characteristic curiosity, that astonishingly energetic greediness to know himself and the world's secrets that would mark virtually every page of his writing. In late June 1851, General Bariatinskii invited Tolsoi—at this point still a civilian—to accompany an army squadron on a raid against two Chechen villages. During the raid on June 27 and 28, the Russians met significant resistance. According to the military historian M. A. Ianzhul, the Russians lost 13 men, killed or wounded; the imperial artillery expended over 300 rounds. In the end, Ianzhul noted, the Russians destroyed most of the fields under cultivation around the two *awuls*.[156]

Although official accounts left no trace of Tolstoi's role in this particular raid, his diary and subsequent fiction provide us ample materials for speculation. The diary entry for July 3, 1851, the first entry after his return from action, noted a bad conscience:

> I was on a raid. [There] also I behaved badly: involuntarily I allowed myself to be intimidated by [General] Bariatinskii. Yet I am so weak, so vile, I have done so little worthwhile, that I am bound to succumb to the influence of every B[ariatinskii] who comes along.[157]

In the 1852 short story "*Nabeg*" ["The Raid"] Tolstoi's narrator, a volunteer observer, watched in comfortable indifference the razing of an unnamed Chechen *awul*:

> There a roof is pulled down, an axe strikes a sturdy tree, soldiers break through a plank door; here a haystack, a fence, a *saklya* bursts into flames, and a thick column of smoke rises into the clear air. A Cossack drags a heavy sack of flour on a carpet; a happy-looking soldier carries from a *saklya* a tin basin and some rags; another gives chase to two chickens, which he kills near the fence while cackling with laughter; a third has found an enormous *kumgan* [pouch] of milk, he drinks from it, then with a loud belly laugh throws it down onto the ground.[158]

Amid the chaos, the narrator overheard the humiliation of a helpless old Chechen man. Then he witnessed what he (mistakenly) assumed to be the beating or murder of a Chechen child. A crying sound resembling a child's rang through the village, followed by the voice of a Don Cossack: "Hey, don't use your fist, they'll see you. Have a knife, Evstigneich? Gimme the knife."[159]

Early drafts of the short story also alluded to disturbing incidents. Variant five of the first rough draft provided a similar account of the *awul*'s destruction, and mentioned "a frightened old Chechen man who had not managed to escape." This variant did not describe the beating of a Chechen child, rather the beating of a Chechen woman carrying a young child. "A quick-moving soldier caught her from behind, grabbed her sack, but she would not let it go. The soldier then took his rifle in both hands and struck the woman full-force in the back. She fell, her shirt covered with blood, her child burst into tears."[160]

Horrified by the violence, the narrator in the variant accused the soldier of a terrible crime against the sixth commandment. The narrator promised that the perpetrator would answer on his deathbed for this crime:

> in your imagination you will see a terrible picture: lifeless eyes, a thin stream of red blood and a deep wound on the back beneath a blue shirt, the cloudy eyes will penetrate yours with an inexpressible sadness, the bare-headed child will look at you with horror, and the voice of conscience will quietly but distinctly render its terrible verdict on you.[161]

213

Tolstoi's commentaries on the Chechen raid suggest that on June 27 and 28, 1851 he witnessed the looting and torching of a Chechen *awul*, the public humiliation of a withered old Chechen man too slow to escape the village, and the beating of a young Chechen—a young mother or a child. Tolstoi's conscience rebelled against these acts, yet he did not dare expose them. "Involuntarily/against [his] conscience" he "allowed [himself] to be intimidated by [General] Bariatinskii."

To this speculation about Tolstoi's moral pliability in the Caucasus, we must add another point: in 1851 he was an unusual 23-year-old in search of war's hidden essence. Writing in variant seven of the third draft of "Raid," Tolstoi's autobiographical narrator confessed:

> War has always fascinated me. But war not in the sense of great generals' strategies—my mind refuses to keep track of these grandiose actions: I don't understand them at all—rather what has always interested me is the main fact of war—killing. I want most of all to know in what manner and under the influence of which emotion one soldier has killed another, rather than the disposition of forces at Austerlitz or Borodino ... One question has preoccupied me: under the influence of which emotion does one person decide without apparent self-interest to submit himself to peril and, even more surprisingly, to kill another individual like himself? I have always wanted to know whether this happens under the influence of hatred; but one cannot really suppose that every warrior hates [his adversaries] continuously. I should also weigh the factors of self-defense and duty, although I have rarely observed [them]. I rule out the instinct of self-preservation proper, because, in my book, it ought to prompt every soldier to hide or to run away [from battle], not to fight.[162]

Where better to tease out an answer to the mystery of organized violence than on the mountain slopes of the northeastern Caucasus?

Shortly after the Chechen raid of late July 1851, Tolstoi decided to join the Russian army. Apparently, his curiosity about killing outweighed his revulsion to it. Besides, Tolstoi badly desired to succeed in high society: a glorious army career and a medal for bravery could serve as his passports into society's favor. In August he discussed an officer's commission with General Bariatinskii. In late October he went to Tbilisi to secure the necessary papers—a process that stretched over three months. The government finally gave him permission to enter the army in February 1852, but it delayed his officer's commission until just before his transfer from the Caucasus to the Crimea in 1854. In all, Tolstoi spent two years and seven months in the Caucasus, roughly two years of it on active military duty.

Tolstoi's first duty assignment was assistant artillerist [*unosnyi feierverker*] in the fourth battery of the twentieth artillery brigade. In early February 1852 his unit saw action in Chechnia, where its mission was to clear the forest roads from the fortress at Kurinskoe southwest across the Michik River. During this mission his unit fought a large force of approximately 6,000 mountaineers commanded by Shamil himself. On February 18 Tolstoi's battery fell under artillery bombardment. A shell destroyed the gun wagon a few yards in front of him; shrapnel hit the wheel of the wagon next to him. Another shell struck and killed his horse. Tolstoi estimated that if the enemy artillery had shifted its aim "by one one-thousandth of a degree to either side I would have been killed."[163] A year later Tolstoi's unit cleared forest in virtually the same area. Between February 17 and March 9 the twentieth artillery brigade helped destroy two *awuls*, Gurdali and Mazlagash, just southwest of the Michik River in Greater Chechnia. Official military histories of the battle along the Michik on February 17 claimed that Russian forces sustained only 11 wounded whereas Shamil's forces lost 500 men.[164] For his participation in this apparently lopsided victory Tolstoi was considered for a St. George Cross, a decoration for bravery in battle. His brigade commander, Colonel L. F. Levin, nominated him for immediate promotion to officer rank.

Although we have no reason to question Tolstoi's efficiency in maneuvering and firing artillery pieces, at least one unofficial memorist of the Michik River skirmish has offered a starkly different account of the battle. According to the Cossack officer V. A. Poltoratskii, the Chechen insurgents had prepared to defend the river's embankments against cavalry attack by erecting firing screens of tree branches and rock. They fled under artillery bombardment, sustaining casualties in the process. The Russian "victory" therefore consisted of retaking the same ground occupied the year before by driving insurgents from an indefensible position. Moreover, according to Poltoratskii, the Russian command had arranged the entire encounter in such a way that the cavalry commander, Baron Nikolai, could sweep down on the insurgents and secure a medal for "storming" the enemy. Unfortunately, when the cavalry attacked "only one thing was lacking—the enemy."[165] Tolstoi himself, in the story *"Rubka lesa"* ["Clearing Forest"] based on the battle, summarized the encounter briefly: "The fight went successfully: we heard that the Cossacks made a glorious sweep and took three Tatar bodies; our infantry did its job and lost only six wounded; [our] artillery lost one man and two horses."[166] Judging by Poltaratskii and Tolstoi, the battle for the Michik River was a small, sordid victory in a long dirty war.

The aftermath of the battle proved disappointing for Tolstoi. He did not receive his medal for bravery, nor did he get his longed-for promotion to officer rank. Indeed, on the very eve of the award's ceremony in his brigade, he was arrested for failing to appear for guard duty. He had gotten involved in a game of chess and forgotten his assignment.[167] Incarcerated for the first (and only) time in his life, he decided to submit papers of resignation from the military service. A draft letter to General Bariatinskii expressed his frustrated ambition:

All this would mean nothing to me ... if it were not necessary to explain to my relatives and acquaintances how it is that, after two years service in the Caucasus while enjoying the favor of Prince Bariatinskii, I have not received a single decoration and am not even an officer.[168]

In August 1853, Tolstoi wrote his aunt that he wanted to resign from the military: "It would take too long and would be too tedious to explain to you all the unpleasant obstacles I have encountered since my arrival; I will say simply that I am fed up and I want to leave the service as soon as possible."[169] Tolstoi's unhappy tenure in the Caucasus ended in January 1854—not with his retirement, but with his transfer to the Turkish front in the Crimean War. To his brother Sergei he wrote: "Since I am forced to fight somewhere, I think it more pleasant to fight in Turkey than here."

Thus, Tolstoi's decision to enter military service did not yield the medals, rank, and glory he had sought. Perhaps, however, it taught him something significant about the mystery of organized killing. Army life, he discovered, involves corruption of the human spirit away from the battlefield. Soldiers and officers engage in gambling, drinking, fornication, and other "diversions." On the battlefield, they do little that is glorious: they fire heavy weapons at enemy positions, killing from a distance; they attack and burn small villages, victimizing women and children in the process. After the slaughter has ended, officers exaggerate the number of enemy casualties, and would-be officers scheme for promotion. Death, when it comes to a comrade, is a mere statistic.

X

In the Caucasus Tolstoi focused his attention on himself and his comrades in arms. His short stories of the period explored the mentality of Russian common soldiers and lower-grade officers, but he wrote almost nothing about the indigenous peoples in whose land he lived.[170] Nor did he study in any serious manner the religion and culture they died for in isolated villages and river hollows. Yet, in a few noteworthy particulars, the Caucasus left its mark on his consciousness.

Four months after arriving in the Caucasus, Tolstoi solicited lessons singing Kalmyk songs from a young Cossack named Mark.[171] By late August he had begun to study the local Turkic language that the Russians called "Tatar."[172] On August 26 he wrote laconically: "since morning ... studying Tatar with young women."[173] A year later Tolstoi was collecting Chechen songs from two acquaintances, Balta (Bulta) Isaev and Sado Miserbiev.[174] These songs he recorded phonetically in his diary, along with rough translations. Tolstoi's interest in mountain languages and songs enabled him to incorporate dozens of mountain terms and examples of verse in the text of *Hadji Murat*.

Tolstoi's friendship with Sado Miserbiev was itself an important indicator of the degree of Tolstoi's interest in the local culture. While stationed at Staryi Yurt, Tolstoi participated in the officers' evening gambling. Occasionally, Chechens from a nearby *awul* were admitted to these sessions, probably because they were easy marks for the card sharps. Sado, who could neither read nor keep accurate tallies, was a consistent loser in these crooked games. Tolstoi hated dishonest card playing, so he befriended Sado: "I never played against him, I persuaded him not to play, I explained that the others were cheating him and proposed to play in his place. He was terribly grateful to me, so he gave me a sack of money. In accordance with the local custom of exchanging gifts, I gave him a cheap rifle for which I had paid eight rubles." Touched by this kindness, Sado invited Tolstoi to dine at his *saklya* and to become his *kunak*.

Tolstoi soon learned that becoming a *kunak* entailed another, more elaborate exchange of gifts. Sado offered Tolstoi his horse, his weapon or anything else he might desire: eventually, he persuaded Tolstoi to accept a saber worth one hundred rubles. In return, Tolstoi offered Sado a silver watch given to him by his brother Nikolai. This second exchange of gifts bound the two men in friendship til death: "*on devient amis à la vie et à la mort.*" In Tolstoi's frank explanation of the term, being a *kunak* meant "that if I ask for all his money, or his woman, or his weapons, or anything else of value, then he must give it me and I, in turn, may not refuse him anything."[175]

Twice Sado demonstrated to Tolstoi the value of this friendship. In January 1852 Sado won from Prince F. G. Knorring enough money to redeem Tolstoi's 500-ruble gambling debt to the prince.[176] Then, in June 1853, Sado saved Tolstoi's life when their column was attacked by twenty mountaineers. In his diary account of the incident, Tolstoi wrote only that: "I almost fell into captivity … I was pale after the Chechens chased me."[177] However, years later he admitted to his brother-in-law Stepan Andreevich Bers that he owed his life to Sado's horse and to the Chechen's quick thinking under fire.[178]

Tolstoi used his memories of Sado at various points in *Hadji Murat*. The friendship between the junior officer Butler and Hadji Murat was likely drawn on the lines of Tolstoi's relationship with Sado. The exchange of dagger for silver watch between Hadji Murat and Semën Vorontsov probably followed the pattern of the second gift exchange between Sado and Tolstoi. The significance of the relationship between *kunaks* colored several passages in *Hadji Murat*, and it served as the main proof of the indigenous peoples' sense of honor. Finally, as many commentators have noticed, Tolstoi assigned the name "Sado" to Hadji Murat's host in the Chechen *awul* from which the latter escaped under duress. Sado's loyalty and nobility of spirit in *Hadji Murat* were Tolstoi's belated tributes to his loyal Chechen friend *à la vie et à la mort*.

Most important for our purposes was Tolstoi's exposure to news about his future hero, Hadji Murat. In late November 1851 Hadji Murat surrendered himself to Russian custody. Tolstoi learned about this event in Tbilisi, where he had arrived on November 1 in hope of arranging the paperwork for entrance into the army.[179] In a letter to his brother Sergei dated December 23, 1851, he reported the event, adding a short assessment:

> If you're dying to flaunt the latest from the Caucasus, you can relate
> that the second in command after Shamil, a certain Hadji Murat, has

just recently [*na dniakh*] handed himself over to the Russian government. This was the most daring *dzhigit* and bravest fellow in all Chechnia, yet he has now disgraced himself [*sdelal podlost'*—literally, "done a base deed"].[180]

The reference to the timing of Hadji Murat's defection suggests that Tolstoi read about the event in the local newspaper or heard about it by word of mouth, but not from anyone immediately involved in the surrender. The characterization of Hadji Murat's status as the "second in command after Shamil" repeated the claims of Russian authorities about the significance of their achievement in securing the defection: Tolstoi was, in this sense, part of the Russians' "spin" operation. The last phrase of the passage—"yet he has now disgraced himself"—departed from the patriotic tone of the preceding sentences. Now Tolstoi judged Hadji Murat not from the perspective of a Russian imperialist, but from the perspective of a Russian noble wed to the European code of honor. A nobleman was to take up arms in outraged honor; to surrender before satisfying the demand of the code was to disgrace oneself.

Three months later, in March 1852, Tolstoi learned more about Hadji Murat from a Chechen named Durda: "He [Durda] told me about the squabble [*stychka*] between Hadji Murat and Arslan-Khan at the mosque." The reference here was perhaps a confused account of pivotal events of 1834: the killing of the Avar royal household at Khunzakh by Hamza Bek, a killing said by some to be inspired by Aslan-Khan; the subsequent revenge killing of Hamza Bek on September 19, 1834 as he entered the Khunzakh mosque for Friday prayers; and Hadji Murat's part in both events—observer of the royal murders and participant in the revenge "hit" on the second imam. The account relayed by Durda, if it narrated the 1834 events, wrongly placed Aslan-Khan at the mosque. The other possible referent for the story was a rumor that in January 1852, just before his escape from the Russians, Hadji Murat had attended the mosque at Tash-Kichu, where he was said to have had an altercation with several Ghumuq princes, including a blood enemy named Arslan-Khan. Whatever the shape of the tale, Tolstoi seemed to be impressed: "It would have been interesting to see them," he wrote.[181] One of these accounts, much altered in Tolstoi's artistic retelling, would later become the basis of Chapter XX of *Hadji Murat*.

We have no other firm information about Tolstoi and Hadji Murat from the writer's service years in the Caucasus. The hints in Tolstoi's diary, however, are worth pondering. On October 23, 1853 he recorded absentmindedly: "Kazi Mullah [Ghazi Muhammad] appeared on the scene in 1832 during the Polish campaign; Hamzat Bek succeeded him."[182] Apparently, Tolstoi was trying to sort out the origins of the insurgency in the North Caucasus based on his reading of a short book by Iakov Ivanovich Kostenetskii.[183] He was also thinking about connections between the past and present. His next diary entry began: "The past conditions the future."[184] We also know that in November 1853 Tolstoi served briefly under Colonel Iosif Ivanovich Karganov who, in early 1852, had been involved in the chase leading to Hadji Murat's death. Tolstoi may have heard first-hand from Karganov about Hadji Murat's last days. We know that Tolstoi remembered Kurganov's name for a half century: in 1902, in connection with the writing of *Hadji Murat* he wrote Karganov's son for information.[185]

Thus, during his Caucasus service term, Tolstoi acquainted himself with at least some of the main points in Hadji Murat's life.

XI

Tolstoi left the Caucasus in January 1854. He carried with him a profound appreciation of the psychology of the Russian forces in the Caucasus, a first-hand knowledge of army life, and insight into the violence of the mountain war. In his short fiction of the 1850s—"The Raid" and "Clearing Forest"—he shared his developing understanding with readers. Later, in his extended tale *Cossacks* (1863), he offered a masterful sketch of the frontier people who served as the foundation of imperial Russian power in the Caucasus. Yet, in spite of his friend-ship with individual Chechens and his familiarity with the life of the Avar defector Hadji Murat, Tolstoi did not succeed in depicting the Caucasus from a native perspective. His only attempt to do so—an early draft of *Cossacks* called "The Runaway"—fell flat because he lacked a detailed knowledge of mountain ways.

Susan Layton was certainly correct when she noted: "despite these contacts with tribesmen in their native realm, Tolstoi experienced a loss of confidence and artistic inspiration in writing about the subject ... [He] failed at this point to find his own way of depicting the Muslim *dzhigit* on home ground."[186] Not until 1896, when he began to write *Hadji Murat*, did Tolstoi attempt to bridge the vast cultural chasm separating Russians from the alien Islamic world of the northern Caucausus.

How can we explain Tolstoi's strange decision four decades after leaving the Causasus to return to the still sensitive theme of the Russian conquest, but this time from what he took to be a native perspective?

In one sense, the answer to this question is straightforward. Tolstoi never forgot the story of Hadji Murat's defection. In 1862, for example, he narrated the outlines of Hadji Murat's tale to peasant students at Iasnaia Poliana: "We talked about mountain brigands. [The peasants] remembered the Caucasian history that I had related long ago, and I began to talk again about runaways, Cossacks and about Hadji Murat."[187] Over time, Tolstoi's curiosity about Hadji Murat deepened and his knowledge expanded. Between 1875 and 1896 Tolstoi read various historical accounts of the mountain war that mentioned Hadji Murat. Especially influential on Tolstoi were the memoirs of V. A. Poltoratskii, which he read twice—once on original publication in 1883 and again on repub-lication in 1895. Coupled with this interest in Hadji Murat was Tolstoi's growing conviction that the mountain war was a crucial event in Russian history, one no less significant for its time than the Napoleonic invasion was for Alexandrine

Russia. Furthermore, the mountain war posed for Tolstoi a series of artistic challenges: to take Russia's literature on the Caucasus in a new, more realistic and
truthful direction; to employ in analysis of the mountain war some of the same
techniques perfected in *War and Peace*; to come to terms with the lives of common
people living in the Russian empire but not of ethnic Russian stock. In other
words, if we accept this reasoning, Tolstoi's decision to write *Hadji Murat* was the
belated, but virtually inevitable consequence of the great writer's personal experience, historical interests, and artistic ambition.

This overdetermined explanation, however, ignores what may be the most
interesting factor in Tolstoi's thinking about the mountain war—namely, the link
between his spiritual "conversion" in the 1870s and his attempt to reinterpret the
place of Islam in the lives of common people in the Caucasus and elsewhere in
the Muslim world.

Tolstoi's intellectual crisis in the 1870s has almost always been analyzed in the
terms proposed by Tolstoi himself in the spiritual autobiography *Ispoved'*
[*Confession*] (1882). According to this text, sometime in 1877 Tolstoi lost his sense
of purpose: "Life became hateful to me. An irresistible force drew me to rid
myself of it by whatever means."[188] Depressed and suicidal, the famous author
fruitlessly sought among secular philosophers for life's meaning. Finding no
answer there, he concluded that, in principle, reason alone cannot uncover life's
significance. He therefore sought meaning in Orthodox religion, in the everyday
conviction of Russian peasants who lived "not for their own needs, but for God."
He discovered in their unreflective faith a spiritual confidence that he himself
lacked and a clear ethical commitment to the common good he felt was almost
completely absent among Russia's wealthy elites. From this appreciation of the
Russian peasantry's spiritual self-assurance Tolstoi moved toward a Christianity
grounded in the ethical precepts enunciated by Jesus during the Sermon on the
Mount: "Thou shalt not be angry, thou shalt not commit adultery, thou shalt not
swear oaths or judge thy neighbors, thou shalt not resist evil by evil, and thou
shalt have no enemies." Wholeheartedly embracing these precepts as the essence
of Christianity, Tolstoi rejected other beliefs as incidental or even inimical to its
social message. Thus, he saw no reason to believe in Jesus as the son of God, the
second person of the trinity: for Tolstoi, Jesus was not God, but a prophet and
holy man, the most profound spiritual teacher ever to have lived. Because Tolstoi
denied Jesus' divinity, he naturally rejected the miracles attributed to him in the
gospels. Nor could Tolstoi accept Jesus' resurrection from the dead or Jesus'
promise of an afterlife. By the time Tolstoi had finished stripping Christianity of
these dogmatic "incidentals," he had completely redefined it from a revealed
supernatural faith to a this-worldly code of ethics. In Tolstoi's *Confession*, the
writer's "conversion" experience traced a circle: from childhood faith, to worldly
debauchery and disillusionment, back to childlike faith. Substituting other words,
we might describe the circular journey as hermetic to Christian civilization:
Tolstoi moved from naïve Christian belief to disbelief, back to naïve Christian
belief.

Yet Tolstoi's spiritual path was far more erratic and much less solipsistically Christian than *Confession* suggested. His thinking about religious matters was linked to Russia's confrontation with the Islamic world, to doubts about Christianity's universal validity, to unresolved personal guilt about his role in the mountain war many years earlier.

In various places, Tolstoi dated the most severe moment of his religious crisis to 1877, the year after hundreds of Russian nobles had begun raising money to support the Orthodox Serbs against the Turks and had joined the campaign as volunteer fighters. The public support for a religious crusade against the Turkish infidels, particularly the sending of volunteer fighters, could not help but remind Tolstoi of his own past in the Caucasus and raise for him the repressed question of the validity of other faiths, especially Islam, as paths to salvation. In the eighth part of *Anna Karenina* (1877) Tolstoi's fictional alter ego rediscovers his spiritual kinship with Russia's Orthodox peasants, then asks: "'Well, what about Jews, Muslims, Confucians, Buddhists—What about them? Are these hundreds of millions of people deprived of this sublime blessing [the reassurance of faith] without which life has no meaning?'" After some hesitation, Levin dodges the question. He declares that "'the question about other belief systems and their attitudes toward God I have neither the right nor the possibility to answer.'"[189]

This evasion, uncharacteristic for Levin who everywhere else in the novel presses uncomfortable questions to a logical answer, was necessary if Tolstoi wished to avoid problems with the ecclesiastical censors. Yet, as Tolstoi surely knew, most readers would answer the question for Levin on the basis of the novel's larger design. Part eight commences by describing the public forces behind the volunteer crusade against the Turks and by airing the self-serving patriotic rhetoric of the volunteers. By allowing the morally compromised Vronskii and his supercilious, manipulative well-wisher, the Countess Lidiia, to embody the volunteer cause, Tolstoi signaled clear disapproval of the religious patriots. Meanwhile, in his diaries, where he could afford to be forthcoming, Tolstoi went beyond the evasion of his fictional hero. There Tolstoi asserted that all human beings seek meaning in life; all cultures find that meaning through religion in the promise of salvation; and the key to salvation in all the major religions is self-renunciation—living selflessly.[190] Tolstoi was already approaching the intuition he would later make the subject of passionate investigation—namely, the sense that all religions, stripped of dogmatic incidentals, are identical.

In that same year 1877, Russia declared war on Turkey. This new stage in the confrontation between Orthodox Russia and the Muslim Turks was even more wrenching for Tolstoi. During the war's two-year span he fought his own inner struggle over faith and violence.

On the one hand, Tolstoi sought to find common ground with the Turks. In August 1877 he took his family to visit Turkish prisoners of war interned in Tula province. According to his wife Sofiia Andreevna, "Levochka asked [the prisoners] whether they had a Quran and who was mullah; when they gathered around us, it turned out that each of them had a Quran in a small pouch."[191] By

January 1878 Tolstoi had concluded that he could not accept the Russian Orthodox classification of the Muslim Turks as enemies: "when tradition tells me, 'Let us pray that more Turks be slain,' then, listening not to my reason but to the vague but insistent voice of my heart, I say: 'this tradition is false.'"[192] Behind this "vague but insistent voice" of Tolstoi's heart lay submerged guilt over his own conduct in the Caucasus. In May 1878 Tolstoi plunged into "horror and the pain of repentance" over "all the lamentable deeds [*merzosti*]" of his youth. He was thinking of the "lamentable deeds" done in the Caucasus while with his brother Sergei. "For everything I did in the military I can fabricate an explanation. But [after] many years and the conquest of the enemy this [explanation] is blasphemy. A Christian ought to pray for enemies, not against them."[193] It was self-reproach and repentance over his terrible behavior in the Causus that underlay the famous, otherwise inexplicable, passage in *Confession* in which Tolstoi cried:

> I cannot recall those years [of youth] without horror, loathing and heartache. I killed people in war, summoned others to duels in order to kill them, gambled at cards; I devoured the fruit of the peasants' labor and punished them; I fornicated and practiced deceit. Lying, thieving, promiscuity of all kinds, drunkeness, violence, murder ... there was not a crime I did not commit, and yet I was praised for it all and my contemporaries considered, and still consider me, a relatively moral man.

Revulsion at his own past and disgust over the contemporary slaughter of his fellow human beings in the name of Christianity drove Tolsoi toward a break with Orthodoxy. In chapter 15 of *Confession* he wrote:

> When I turned my attention to what is done in the name of religion I was horrified and very nearly withdrew from the Orthodox church entirely ...
> During this time [1877–1878] Russia was at war. And in the name of Christian love Russians were killing their brothers. There was no way to avoid hearing about this. There was no way to ignore the fact that murder is evil and contrary to the most fundamental tenets of any faith.[194]

Tolstoi's repugnance at the Turkish war, however, cohabited with an instinctive distrust of the Turks and a patriotic spirit strangely at odds with his incipient pacifism. During the above-mentioned August 1877 visit to Turkish prisoners of war, Sofiia Andreevna confided:

> "When [the prisoners] gathered round us and crowded in upon us, there was one moment when we became terrified, so we quickly walked

away. At first sight they are almost all fine young men, still, as with all people, there are some who are terrifying and unpleasant, but the rest have glorious faces."[195]

It was as if the Tolstois, enjoying their common humanity with the Turks, were suddenly reminded that these prisoners of war might consider privileged Russians infidels worthy to be dispatched. As to the war itself, Tolstoi followed newspaper reports with trepidation. One biographer has hinted that what upset Tolstoi most was not the fratricidal killing at the front, but the spectacle of Russia's weakness. "How could it be that Russia, which had in 1854 fought so stoutly against three great powers (Turkey, France and Britain), now had problems coping with Turkey alone?"[196] As the tide of battle turned in Russia's favor in fall 1877, Tolstoi expressed his satisfaction. On October19 he wrote N. N. Strakhov: "The news you sent me on the war is very interesting and pleasant." Tolstoi celebrated the appointment of his old comrade at arms, Lieutenant-General Nikolai Nikolaevich Obruchev, to leadership status.[197] Three weeks later he wrote the poet patriot Afanasii Afanas'evich Fet a salutation on Russia's capture of the Turkish fortress at Kars: "Thank God, we have taken Kars. I have stopped worrying."[198] Apparently, the kvas patriot in Tolstoi was still in fighting fettle.

Tolstoi was well aware of the horrendous contradictions in his views toward war, the Islamic "enemy," and religion. Between 1878 and 1896 he worked to resolve those contradictions by pursuing two very different projects. The first of these was to plan a novel on the early years of Nicholas I's reign. Tolstoi's idea was apparently to follow the Decembrist revolutionaries from their failed palace coup in late 1825 to their places of exile in Siberia and the Caucasus. In the mountains roughly 2,800 of the conspirators who had participated directly or indirectly in the political dissidence of 1825 were assigned to work either in the civil service or the army. Many of the latter were compelled to fight in the Russo-Turkish war of 1828–1829, or to engage in suppression of resistance to Russian rule from the indigenous peoples of the region.

Tolstoi gathered material for this novel from literary sources in the fall of 1877. Indeed, on the same day he wrote Fet to rejoice in the victory at Kars, he wrote Strakhov to solicit books on the 1828–1829 Russo-Turkish war.[199] Tolstoi's intuition was that, in the Decembrists' response to Islam, to the Turkish "menace," and to indigenous insurgency in the Caucasus he might find a solution to his own dilemmas. That Tolstoi was interested precisely in the Decembrists' religious sensibilities is confirmed by two pieces of evidence. On March 14, 1878 he sent an inquiry to the Decembrist Aleksandr Petrovich Beliaev to ask if Beliaev "might have the religious work or memoris of [Pavel Sergeevich] Bobrishchev-Pushkin, which he wrote in Chita, and [Alexsandr Petrovich] Bariatinskii's response."[200] The second piece of evidence confirming Tolstoi's fascination with the Decembrists' religious sensibilities was a variant of the novel focused on the Decembrist Aleksandr Ivanovich Odoevskii. That variant was set to begin at the Easter morning service in a country church "during the communion service, after the reading of the Gospel, by candle light."[201] It is worth noting that Odoevskii was a remarkable figure—a cousin of Griboedov, the author of the Decembrists' "*Nash otvet*" ["Our Response"] to Pushkin, the hero of Lermontov's poem "*Pamiati A. I. O-go*" ("To the Memory of A. I. O[doevskii]"). He was also a deeply committed Christian, described by contemporaries as "a Christian without the sanctimoniousness, a lover of suffering." Originally sent to hard labor in Siberia, Odoevskii pleaded to be sent to the Caucasus. Griboedov asked General Paskiewicz to arrange the transfer in December 1828. The government refused to consider the transfer until ten years later when Nicholas I personally decided to post Odoevskii to the Caucasus as an infantryman.[202] Thus, in selecting Odoevskii as a possible hero of his planned novel on the Decembrists, Tolstoi picked the emblematic figure whose life brought together Russia, political dissent, the Caucasus, and "Christianity without sanctimoniousness."

The second project through which Tolstoi sought to resolve the tensions in his views of Islam was an investigation of Islamic religious teaching. The object of the investigation was to discover whether Islam, properly understood, was a militant religion inconsistent with Christianity or whether its teachings, fully consistent with Tolstoi's ethical Christianity, had been deliberately distorted by Muslim clerics seeking to exercise state power. Tolstoi launched this research project only after he had worked out his interpretation of Christianity and Judaism—that is, only in the mid-1890s. The focus of Tolstoi's interest was the nineteenth-century Persian religious teacher Sayyid Ali-Muhammad Shirazi (1235/1819–1266/1850).

Born into a Shi'ite merchant family, Sayyid Ali-Muhammad fell under the influence of the Shaykhis, a religious group awaiting the appearance of a new prophet, or *mahdi*, who would reinvigorate the faithful by perfecting the teachings of Muhammad. In 1260/1844, the Shaykhis recognized Sayyid Ali-Muhammad as *Bab*, the "gateway to truth," the initiator of a new prophetic cycle. Followers of the Bab, nicknamed Babis, proclaimed him "the mirror of the breath of God."

Sayyid Ali-Muhammad taught that, at the end of each prophetic cycle, God destroys the old material world and rebuilds it in closer conformity to the spiritual truth. Accordingly, each prophetic cycle must commence with a new set of rules matching the newly-expressed will of God. This meant that the Quran and *sharia*, which had constituted the prophetic book and spiritual law during Muhammad's prophetic cycle, were now superseded by a new prophetic book, the *Bayan*, and by a new moral code. Sayyid 'Ali Muhammad did not see this teaching as a religious revolution, because it treated Islam as a noble stage in the elaboration of God's will, just as Muhammad had regarded Judaism and Christianity as noble, but superseded prophetic cycles. From the perspective of the Persian crown and Shi'ite religious authorities, however, the Babis were dangerous revolutionaries set on the abolition of *shari'a* and the destruction of Islam.

Soon after Sayyid Ali-Muhammad's execution in 1850, the Babis split into two groups. The majority, the Baha'is, developed Babism in a new direction. They taught that prophetic truths could be found in a variety of religious confessions. For them Adam, Abraham, Jesus, Zoroaster, Muhammad, and the *Bab* were all "mirrors of God's breath," while Confucius and the Buddha were recognized as "spiritual masters" falling just short of prophetic status. They taught that heaven and hell do not actually exist, being instead symbols of believers' destination at the end of the path to knowing God. They rejected killing of infidels, for they thought it pointless to murder the spiritually unenlightened. These doctrines translated into a conviction that the human race is one, that all religions are essentially identical, and that no prejudice of any sort should be permitted, given the essential unity of humanity and the identity of all religions. The Baha'is called for the abolition of wealth and poverty in all nations so that all believers might approach God on equal terms.[203]

Tolstoi became interested in the Baha'is teaching on the unity and equality of human beings sometime in summer 1894. The trigger for this interest was a series of letters from Ol'ga Sergeevna Lebedeva, Tolstoi's translator into Turkish language. On August 1 Lebedeva described the Ottoman authorities as despots who "smother every idea in infancy," while the Turkish people were "gentle, magnanimous, faithful believers who look tolerantly on Christians." Lebedeva promised to send Tolstoi her book "finding the point in common between Christianity and Islam in the hope of somehow uniting these two religions, something that would be most helpful for Russia which has so many millions of Muslim subjects. I intend to extract lines from the Quran and gospel that resemble one another, to comment on them, and compile the book."[204] In a follow-up letter on August 18, Lebedeva told Tolstoi: "I have even found a Muslim sect very close to Christianity, by means of which it might be possible to effect the unification of Muslims with Orthodoxy. This is the sect of Babids or Babis. Perhaps you have heard of it?"[205] Two weeks later, in a letter dated September 3, 1894, Lebedeva summarized the Babis' theology, listed their sacred books, and described their current situation in the Ottoman empire.

Tolstoi welcomed Lebedeva's attempt to find common ground between Islam and Christianity. In a letter on September 4 1894 he warned that a mechanical juxtaposition of similar passages from the Quran and the gospels would do little to further the unity of religions: He contended it would be better to gather the passages expressing the "fundamental vital experiential-moral religious truths, which are ... identical in all religions, and second [to show] that Christianity and Islam have the same sources and they differ only in their deviations from these sources, and that it will only require Christians from their perspective and Muslims from theirs to abandon these deviations and both religious will then inevitably coincide."[206] On September 22 Tolstoi invited Lebedeva to send him "extracts" from the writings of Sayyid Ali-Muhammad Shirazi illuminating the basic "moral and social" teachings of the Babis. However, he found the Babis' theology impenetrable: "I think that in the *Bab*'s own books this teaching is lost in Oriental effusiveness and in strained efforts to show [Babism's] proximity to the Quran."[207]

Four years later, in September 1898, Tolstoi received from the German poet Rainer-Marie Rilke a book by the Orientalist F. C. Andreas on the Persian Babis.[208] Prompted by this gift, he renewed his research on the Babis. In 1903 he told the Russia poet Isabella Arkad'evna Grinevskaia that the Baha'is "have a great future."

> I know about the Babis and have been studying their teaching for a long time. It seems to me that this is a doctrine, like all the other rationalist social, religious doctrines that have recently appeared from those maimed by the priestly devotees of the original religions: Brahminism, Buddhism, Judaism, Christianity and Islam. [These doctrines] have a great future because they all, having rejected the monstrous accretions common to the original religions, will coalesce into a single religion of humanity. Therefore the teachings of the Babis, to the degree it has cast out the old Muslim superstitions (unfortunately, something like these superstitions can be found in the teachings of the *Bab* himself), and to the degree that it holds to the basic ideas of brotherhood, equality and love—also has a great future.[209]

By 1904, however, Tolstoi had decided he could no longer find in the Baha'is an analog to his own ethical Christianity. In a letter to the French attorney Hippolyte Dreyfus in April 1904, Tolstoi excoriated the Baha'ullah's *Book of Certitude*: "I regret to inform you that reading this book has completely disenchanted me with the Baha'ullah's teaching. The book contains nothing but insignificant and pretentious phrases that simply confirm old superstitious and are completely empty of genuine moral or religious content."[210]

Neither Tolstoi's historical research into the Decembrist movement and Russo-Turkish war of 1828–1829 nor his investigation of the Baha'i movement led to a resolution of his own contradictory views toward Islam. He never finished the novel on the Decembrists and the Caucasus, perhaps because their own understanding of Islam was as flawed as his own. For a time, both before and during the writing of *Hadji Murat*, he had tried to imagine Baha'ism as a gentler, more authentic form of Islam. But the teachings of the Baha'i masters, however attractive they seemed in the social and moral sense, were shot through with "superstitions." And, in any case, the Baha'is were a sect persecuted by Muslim authorities in the Ottoman empire and Persia. They had no influence in the Caucasus of the 1850s when Tolstoi served as soldier, and no impact on the Russo-Turkish war of 1877–1878. If Tolstoi wanted to resolve his own love–hate relationship with Islam, if he wanted to lay the ghosts of the mountain war, he would have to trust his own crooked eye.

XII

On July 18, 1896 Tolstoi visited his brother Sergei Nikolaevich at the Pirogovo estate 35 kilometers from Iasnaia Poliana. While walking on the estate's periphery, Tolstoi saw a raspberry thistle or Tatar bush, with three stalks: "one broken, its dirt-covered white flower hanging to the side; another broken and trampled into the mud, its stem run over and blackened by dirt; the third stalk protruding to the side, also covered with dust, but alive and in its middle portion still flowering." The trampled but resilient thistle reminded Tolstoi immediately of Hadji Murat, perhaps because he had come to associate an invincible life force with the Caucasus mountaineers.

Returning to Iasnaia Poliana, Tolstoi spent three weeks re-reading books on the Caucasus war. On August 10 he visited his sister Mariia Nikolaevna at Shamordino, the women's monastery next to Optina Pustyn'—site of the monastery made famous by F. M. Dostoevskii and V. S. Solov'ev as a locus of Orthodox wisdom. There, in the quiet of this rural sanctuary, Tolstoi wrote the first draft of *Hadji Murat*—a story which at this stage confined itself to the narrow biographical theme of Hadji Murat's defection to the Russians and eventual death. On concluding the tale with the dying Hadji Murat's exclamation, "Allah," Tolstoi recorded the date of composition in his notebook: August 14, 1896.[211]

Two months later, when the moment of white-hot inspiration had passed, Tolstoi re-read his story. Now he decided, the tale was "no good [ne to]." To improve it, he would have to extend its scope to include the entire period of the mountain rebellion and its principal figure, Shamil. This fateful artistic decision to widen the story-line launched Tolstoi on an obsessive search for printed and manuscript materials on the Caucasus and forced him, as he collected those materials, to revise his narrative strategy. He did not complete *Hadji Murat* until December 1904, more than eight years after he first put pen to paper. Thus, the gestation period of Tolstoi's last masterpiece exceeded that of his monumental early fiction—*War and Peace* and *Anna Karenina*.

From Tolstoi's letters and diary we can reconstruct the main stages in the composition of *Hadji Murat*. From late 1896 to May 1898 Tolstoi requisitioned and read books on the Caucasus. On December 27, 1896 he asked his friend Vladimir Vasil'evich Stasov to send him information on "history, geography, the ethnography of the Avar khanate."[212] Using his own library resources and Stasov's list of books, Tolstoi consulted nearly five thousand pages of reference material. He read carefully the memoirs of Arnold L'vovich Zisserman and Vladimir Alekseevich Poltoratskii, both veterans of the Caucasus war.[213] Although Poltoratskii's memoirs had been excerpted in the journal *Istoricheskii Vestnik*, Tolstoi visited Poltoratskii himself and read 27 volumes of manuscript memoirs and diaries.[214] He read relevant portions of the multi-volume *Sbornik materialov dlia opisaniia mestnostei i plemen Kavkaza* (*Collected Materials for the Description of Places and Tribes of the Caucasus*);[215] he also looked at the *Sbornik svedenii o kavkazskikh gortsakh*, making over 300 notes. Tolstoi studied Adol'f Petrovich Berzhe's 12-volume edition of archeological papers on the Caucasus.[216] Out of this vast corpus of information Tolstoi added to his story several scenes involving the Russian military and officialdom: the description of soldiers on ambush, the encounter between Hadji Murat and the Vorontsovs, the letter from Viceroy Vorontsov to war minister Aleksandr Ivanovich Chernyshev, the conversation between Hadji Murat and Vorontsov's adjutant Mikhail Tarielovich Loris-Melikov about the mountaineer's past. However, throughout this period of intensive research Tolstoi struggled with his main character. On December 21, 1897 he confided to his diary: "I have been thinking through Hadji Murat, but it's a struggle and I lack confidence." Three months later he added: "There is a toy called English 'peepshow': you look under a glass cover and you see one thing, then another. That is how to show Hadji Murat: brave fighter, religious fanatic, etc."[217] Tolstoi's idea was to reveal his hero kaleidoscopically, by presenting various facets and hoping they all would add up. But the technique didn't help, because the terms in which Tolstoi perceived his subject prevented him from drawing Hadji Murat as a sympathetic human being. At this point the working title of Tolstoi's story was "*Ghazawat*" and the hero was, among other things, a "religious fanatic." Frustrated by his lack of progress, Tolstoi dropped the story in May 1898. He did not resume work on it until March 1901.

The second stage in writing *Hadji Murat* lasted from March 1901 to late September 1902. During this period Tolstoi continued to consult books on the Caucasus, but now his use of the historical and ethnographic record became more focused and highly selective. For example, he re-read E. A. Verderevskii's edition of the captivity memoirs produced by Princess Orbeliani. Now, however, Tolstoi used the material to good effect in constructing a portrait of Shamil and Shamil's retinue—a major addition to the text. Tolstoi also re-read his notes on mountain folklore from *Sbornik svedenii o kavkazskikh gortsakh*. He incorporated into chapter 1 of *Hadji Murat* various aphorisms and proverbs drawn from that source; he also incorporated mountain songs from that source into chapter 24.[218]

The major thematic addition of this period was an exploration of imperial decision-making on the Caucasus. Earlier drafts of *Hadji Murat* had mentioned the Vorontsovs and the letter from Viceroy Vorontsov to war minister Chernyshev. Now Tolstoi did further research on these characters. He read parts of the multi-volume Vorontsov papers in search of information on the disastrous "biscuit expedition" of 1845 and to find the original French text of the Vorontsov–Chernyshev letter.[219] On June 20, 1902 Tolstoi visited the Vorontsov palace at Alupka, where he studied portraits of Mikhail Semenovich Vorontsov and family. Tolstoi's companion on this trip Pavel Aleksandrovich Bulanzhe (Boulanger) wrote later that Tolstoi's "sharp eye seemed to record every trait and subtlety of the faces that peered from within the picture frames."[220] Meanwhile Tolstoi's search for the Vorontsov–Chernyshev letter failed to turn up the original text, despite an inquiry to grand Duke Nikolai Mikhailovich, the Romanov family historian.[221]

As Tolstoi pressed his investigation of Russia's war in the Caucasus, he naturally began to consider the pivotal role played by Tsar Nicholas I in that conflict.

In August 1902 Tolstoi sent his friend Stasov a request for anything on the history of Nicholas I and for the court journal [kamer-fur'ierskii zhurnal] containing the record of the tsar's daily appointments.[222] That same month he wrote Grand Duke Nikolai Mikhailovich asking for the tsar's correspondence with the Vorontsovs "and for Nicholas I's inscription on memoranda and reports concerning the Caucasus in those years."[223] For the most part, Tolstoi's research on Nicholas I proved fruitless: he learned that the sought-after court journal had not been published, and he had no luck finding a printed version of the tsar's correspondence with Vorontsov. Still, the insights he garnered from printed sources comprised a solid foundation for the first drafts of the famous capsule biography of Nicholas I that would appear in chapter 15 of *Hadji Murat*.

At this point in the genesis of *Hadji Murat*, Tolstoi had begun to sound critical notes toward Russian policy in the Caucasus. The strongest evidence of his disagreement with the government's view was his sketch of a raid on an unnamed Chechen village, a sketch that became the basis for chapters 16 and 17 in the final version of the tale. In the sketch, probably based on personal experience in the raid of June 27 and 28, 1851, Tolstoi's *alter ego*, the easy-going, dissolute Captain Butler, watched soldiers set an entire village to the torch. During this deliberate orgy of destruction, Butler felt only the "joy of life," the anticipation of a medal, and "respect for his comrades and Russian friends." He did not notice the other side of war: "Death, the wounds of soldiers and officers and mountaineers did not present themselves to his imagination. He even unconsciously [*bezsoznatel'no*], in order to preserve his poetic image of war, never looked at the dead and wounded."[224]

In the wake of the *awul*'s destruction, however, Chechen survivors dealt not with war's "poetry" but with its mean prose. Aside from burnt houses with fouled interiors, torched haystacks, and beehives, a well polluted by excrement, they faced human losses that the war-intoxicated Butler "unconsciously" did not register. The currant-eyed, 15-year-old son of the villager Sado lay dead, bayonetted in the back. His mother, raped by soldiers, stood wailing over his body. Two other dead bodies were brought to the *awul*'s center, there to be mourned by relatives. To this infernal scene Tolstoi added two paragraphs that sprang from forty years of bad conscience, four decades of trying to understand his own complicity in murder, two score years of attempting to fathom the perspective of the mountaineers:

> About hating the Russians no one said a single word. The feeling gripping every Chechen from the youngest to the oldest was stronger than hatred. The feeling was not hatred but a refusal to recognize these Russian dogs as human beings, a feeling of such revulsion, disgust and incomprehension in the face of these creatures' senseless cruelty that the desire to exterminate them, like the desire to exterminate rats, poisonous spiders, and wolves, was just as natural a feeling as self-preservation.

The inhabitants had a choice: to stay there and restore by dint of terrible effort all that had been built up by great labor and that had been so easily and senselessly destroyed, meanwhile expecting at any minute a repetition of the same destruction, or, contrary to the laws of their religion and to their sense of revulsion toward and suspicion of the Russians, to submit to their adversaries. After praying, the elders unanimously agreed to send Shamil a messenger asking for his help, then they immediately began to rebuild the destroyed village.[225]

As Tolstoi mightily strove to see from the mountaineers' perspective what could not be seen from the Russian side, he ascribed ever-greater dignity to his hero, Hadji Murat. In the August/September 1902 draft, the hero acquired a military bearing, spiritual awareness, and economy of expression that suggested a rare nobility of character. Whereas in the early phase of the empire's penetration into the Caucasus, Russian generals had styled themselves Roman heroes, now Russia's greatest writer attributed classical dignity to the empire's arch enemy: a complete transvaluation of values.

The third stage of writing *Hadji Murat* lasted from October 1902 to December 1904. In this period Tolstoi gathered hundreds of small details pertaining to his characters' physical characteristics, behaviors, and outlooks. As we shall see, this research immensely enriched *Hadji Murat* but also shifted its literary center of gravity in a critical way.

During this two-year period Tolstoi doggedly hunted down material about his protagonist. In December 1902 he wrote Ivan Iosifovich Korganov, the son of Colonel Iosif Ivanovich Korganov, asking for information about Hadji Murat. The questions Tolstoi put were quite specific:

1. Did Hadji Murat live in a separate house or with your father [during Hadji Murat's stay in Nukha]? How was the house arranged?

2. Was his clothing some how distinct compared to that of ordinary mountaineers?

3. On the day he fled [toward the mountains], did he and his retinue ride out with rifles on their shoulders or unarmed? [226]

Korganov informed Tolstoi that his memory could not be trusted because "at that time I was only ten years old, and my range of interests [krugozor] was narrow." Nevertheless, Korganov invited Tolstoi to inquire with his 82-year old mother, who was "very healthy and with excellent memory." On receipt of Korganov's invitation, Tolstoi immediately sent a second letter of inquiry to the aged Korganova:

My questions follow:

1. Did he [Hadji Murat] speak even a little Russian?

2. Whose were the horses on which he tried to escape? His own or others'? Were these good horses and of what color were they?

3. Did he limp noticeably?

4. The house, in which you lived on the top floor and he below, did it have a garden?

5. Was he strict in observing the Muslim religious practices—the five daily prayers and so on?[227]

With his usual thoroughness, Tolstoi paid an emanuensus to deliver this letter and to record Korganova's answers.

Simultaneously with this investigation of Hadji Murat, Tolstoi plunged into a separate program of research on Tsar Nicholas I. Irritated by his inability to obtain published versions of Nicholas's court journals and correspondence, Tolstoi tried to circumvent these obstacles by calling on his connections in the literary world and high society. He trusted his ideological ally, the Georgian writer Il'ia Petrovich Nakashidze, with the commission to obtain from Tbilisi archives "the most characteristic resolutions of Nikolai Pavlovich concerning the broadest possible range of issue pertaining especially to the years [18]51 to [18]55, and, the main thing, to late [18]51 and early [18]52."[228] With this request Tolstoi enclosed a note to Lieutenant-General Vasilii Aleksandrovich Potto, the director of the Tbilisi Military-Historical Archive, asking full co-operation with his emanuensis. The strategy was to secure from Tbilisi what might not be obtained in St. Petersburg. Simultaneously, Tolstoi wrote Stasov, asking him whether an emanuensis could be sent to the archives in St. Petersburg to examine the manuscript court journals "for five or six days of late 1851 and early 1852." Almost as an afterthought, Tolstoi asked for "books containing Nicholas' resolutions. Even if books can't be sent, maybe copies could be made of the most characteristic resolutions" for the years 1848–1851.[229] Still, in spite of the clear widening of his interests in Nicholas' reign, Tolstoi told his aunt Aleksandra Andreevna that "I am writing not a biography of Nicholas I, but several scenes from his life essential to my story *Hadji Murat*.[230]

By April 1903, however, Tolstoi had begun to reconsider Nicholas' character from an even wider perspective. To Grand Duke Nikolai Mikhailovich he wrote: "I would have composed a rather negative picture of your grandfather's character and personality, but … I changed my verdict and have been trying to penetrate more deeply into his soul and what made him who he was."[231] In mid-May 1903 Tolstoi wrote his brother Sergei Nikolaevich: "I am writing about

Nikolai Pavlovich, and it is very interesting to me."[232] Early the next month he told his daughter Mariia Lvov'na Obolenskaia: "I am busy with Nik[olai] Pav[lovich] and seem to be clarifying what I need ... This, you see, is proof that I am writing about power."[233] On June 4 he confessed to Pavel Ivanovich Biriukov that the chapter on Nicholas I in *Hadji Murat* was now "disproportionally long" [*neproportsional'na*], but he claimed the length was "necessary to illustrate my understanding of power [*vlasti*]."[234] For the moment, however, he decided "not to touch" *Hadji Murat*, even as he continued to read material on Nicholas I.[235] "If it became necessary," however, Tolstoi reserved the prerogative "to write separately" on Nicholas.[236] Tolstoi's resolve to leave in *Hadji Murat* the long chapter on Nicholas I did not become final until February 1904.[237]

Tolstoi's determination to place a definitive portrait of Nicholas I within the confines of *Hadji Murat* shifted the thematic focal point of the tale from the mountain insurgency as such to the "Tolstoian" theme of depotism. That Tolstoi was aware of the shift was already clear from his letters to Obolenskaia and Biriukov, but Tolstoi made his intention even more explicit in a conversation recorded by the historian Sergei Nikolaevich Shul'gin in mid-June 1903. Tolstoi told Shul'gin:

> I have taken up not just Hadji Murat and his tragic fate but also the extremely curious parallelism of the two main antagonists of that epoch—Shamil and Nicholas, who together seem to constitute the two poles of governmental absolutism—the Asiatic and the European. In particular, one trait in Nicholas is striking—he often contradicts himself without noticing it and he thinks himself always absolutely correct. That is evidently how people of his milieu raised him to think, the spirit around him overflowing with servile flattery.[238]

XIII

In final form *Hadji Murat* was a tale about power, about despotism in its European and Asiatic forms. Structurally, the tale assumed pyramidal shape: the action began in the Caucasus, ascended the bureaucratic pyramid to its apex in St. Petersburg, then descended again to the Caucasus. The central chapters of *Hadji Murat* focused on the center of the empire, the emperor in the Winter Palace in the capital. Tolstoi knew the absurdity of claiming that St. Petersburg sat at Russia's geographic center, for Peter the Great's "window on the West" was just as peripheral spatially as was the North Caucasus. Yet in an empire the "center" is the locus of political authority, the galvanic point to which all compasses necessarily are drawn and from which ordering force invisibly flows. As if to underscore the significance of the tale's fascination with European despotism, the famous chapter 15 devoted to Nicholas I was the longest and densest in the piece. It occupied 12 of *Hadji Murat's* 117 printed pages; none of the other 24 chapters even approached that length. And, as we noted above, the chapter contained two years' research and reflection on Nicholas's character, style of government, and policies. Although Tolstoi devoted chapter 19 to Shamil and his privy council at Vedeno, that chapter was less than six pages long, and it lacked the psychological acuity, not to mention the referential density, of the chapter on Nicholas. For Tolstoi, Asiatic despotism was a mere counterpoint to European bureaucratic absolutism—the latter being the primary object of investigation and the former being secondary. Put another way, Tolstoi might have intended a story about corrupting power in Europe and the "Asiatic" Caucasus. What he wrote was a tale that, in spite of the many pages on the mountain war, recentered St. Petersburg and the imperial project instead of decentering them.

In *Hadji Murat* Russian power was depicted as a social, psychological, and cultural phenomenon. From the social pespective, power functioned through social hierarchy; indeed, in Tolstoi's opinion, power and social stratification were inextricably, perhaps causally, linked. The imperial government passed information from the killing fields of the Caucasus up to St. Petersburg's elite officials and thence to the tsar; the tsar's orders were transmitted down the service ladder to the Caucasus where those orders were murderously implemented. Although the effect of a particular decree was not always what the tsar intended, his command had tangible, bloody results: witness the description in chapters 16 and 17 of the Chechen *awul*'s destruction. Gone from *Hadji Murat* was the conceit of *War and Peace* that those highest in government have virtually no power over events. This transformation in Tolstoi's notion of power carried vast consequences for his humble characters, who now became the monarch's rough instruments in the mountain war. True, we cannot say that serf soldiers were His Majesty's willing executioners: Avdeev was swept into the infantry by the serf recruitment system and family coercion, as chapter 2 instructed us. Yet these serf infantrymen and Cossack cavalrymen wreaked such devastation on Chechen *awuls* that they might as well have been willing executioners. Russia's common soldiers, then, were power's victims and tools. Whether victims or victimizers, however, they lacked the agency Tolstoi had accorded to Platon Karataev in *War and Peace*.

The psychological earmarks of power in *Hadji Murat* were mendacity and narcissism. Among common soldiers the natural impulse of attachment to fellow human beings—witness Avdeev's enthusiastic report of conversation with the Chechen intermediaries in chapter 2—was submerged by the military "imperative" to remember that the other would "slit your guts." In the officer corps falsehood was more deeply rooted: battles were arranged so as to advance careers, enemy casualty figures were inflated, superior officers were routinely deceived. Among policy-makers the art of lying was finely honed: Vorontsov senior's verbal commications with Hadji Murat consisted of a courtier's non-commital circumlocutions in which there was no word of truth; war minister Chernyshev arranged the presentation of "facts" to suit his own ends. The tsar was himself a master of the bright shining lie; indeed, Nicholas breathed deception. Linked to lying was self-preservation and self-promotion. Among soldiers the lie of hatred toward the "shaveheads" was helpful in mobilizing the vigilance needed for survival but also in earning the respect of comrades; for officers the dangers of battle served to inflate self-esteem and to win decorations; for policy-makers lying was the sole means of political survival and therefore the skill requisite for advancement; to Nicholas mendacity operated as a means of governing but also as the psychological underpinning of His Majesty's boundless self-love. In chapter 15 Nicholas' biggest lies were the assertions of his unique probity ("there is only one honest person in Russia") and unmatched greatness. Unlike Peter the Great who presented himself as Russia's most humble servant, Nicholas bestrode the political stage as God's chosen narcissist.

In cultural terms Russian power exerted itself through the written word. Whereas the oral exchanges among common soldiers generally represented a window on their spontaneous, natural, and "true" emotions, printed reports generally constituted calculated lies—the "unnatural" medium of "artificial" hierarchy. Susan Layton is right to note that *Hadji Murat* devalued the written word as "false mediation."[239] One might add that the more European the literary word, the more false: hence, the courtiers' use of French over Russian was a cultural marker of falsehood.

In *Hadji Murat* religion in its two guises informed the cultural order. Among common soldiers the "true" religion of self-renunication and simple piety had space to operate: Avdeev gave up his own happiness for his brother's sake; in chapter 7 the fatally-wounded Avdeev manfully faced death, asking for a candle in a last pious moment of self-surrender. Tolstoi showed the false guise of religion—religion as power—in chapter 15. After seducing a virginal teenager at a court dance, Nicholas prayed formulaic prayers to which he ascribed no meaning. At a religious service he compared the body of his amorous conquest to the ample charms of his "official" mistress Nelidova. Worst of all, he based his political decisions not on self-sacrificial love but on self-aggrandizing hatred for others—for unhappy Poles and rebellious mountaineers.

Meanwhile, *Hadji Murat* treated Shamil's "Asiatic" despotism as a comparable but lesser-scale instance of power. Within the mountain societies, power created a hierarchy of three sorts: the authority of the khanates as described by Hadji Murat in chapter 11; the religious power of the *murshids* over their *murids*; and the hierarchy of rank in the mountaineers' army. Surmounting all three social pyramids was Shamil, who destroyed the rival khanates, and enforced his personal authority in the religious community and in the insurgent army. As in the Russian case, the operation of power among the mountaineers depended upon deception and was linked to the leader's inflated self-image. In chapter 19 we see Shamil returning to his headquarters at Vedeno knowing that the insurgents' war was going badly yet doing all he could to sustain his followers' universal conviction that the Russians had been defeated. The essence of his deception was theatrical projection of a brave, uncompromising image to his followers. Like Nicholas, Shamil stifled in himself feelings of natural compassion and self-renunciation. The imam's treatment of Hadji Murat's captive son Yusif in chapter 19 (he pledges not to kill, but to blind Yusif) was a perfect analogue to Nicholas's "mercy" toward the Polish student (no capital punishment, but 12,000 strokes of the rod). In the end, Shamil's cruelty in the name of God was a self-deception that perpetuated the insurgent leader's "greatness."

The most interesting feature of Asiatic despotism in *Hadji Murat* was the treatment of religion as a cultural system. On the one hand, the tale highlighted the piety of the mountaineers. The first sounds Hadji Murat heard on riding into the *awul* Makhket were "the strained singing of muezzin, calling villagers to prayer. The hero punctiliously observed the Muslim rituals praying five times a day, washing himself in the rite of purification and so on. Hadji Murat and his *murids* offered to women a reverential respect that stood in stark contrast to the Russian habits of familiarity and sexual fliration. The *murids'* obedience to their master was regarded as a religious duty. Even the exhausted Shamil, hoping for a liaison with his favorite wife, surrendered himself to midday prayer, which was for him "as essential as his daily bread." And—the acid test for Tolstoi—just before his final skirmish with the Russians, Hadji Murat performed his prayers. For the mountaineers the "true" religion of piety, respect for others, and self-sacrifice constituted virtually the entire cultural landscape. Nevertheless, as in the Russian case, the natural religion competed with a false, worldly religiosity. We encounter religion as power in Shamil, who ordered violators of the *sharia* punished and treated others with hatred. We see a perversion of "true" religion in the *murid* system of obedience. We even discover in Hadji Murat himself a willingness to take money from the corrupt Russians—a *pactus diabolis* that he did not survive.

If we compare European with Asiatic despotism, then, we discover substantial similarities "under the skin" along with the not inconsiderable difference that European absolutism, being more "advanced," was more hierarchical, more mendacious and narcissistic, and more hostile to "true" religion. In Tolstoi's criterion of judgment, political power was inherently evil, so that being a "great power" entailed concentrated evil. A great state, like Russia, was, axiomatically, more evil than an aspiring state, like Shamil's imamate.

We can scarcely be surprised about Tolstoi's revulsion against political authority. Hostility to the state sprang directly from his pacifist reading of the *Sermon on the Mount*, and it informed his novel *Resurrection* (1899) as well as his 1902 letter to Tsar Nicholas II.[240] What is surprising, however, is the hidden element of calculation that probably accounted for Tolstoi's elaboration of the Hadji Murat incident. Hadji Murat was the perfect liminal figure: he fought on both sides of the mountain war, first against Shamil, then alongside him; he had held political authority on both sides, first in Avaria and later in the imamate; in 1851–1852 he sought personal advantage by crossing back to the Russian side; his tragedy was that, like the falcon in the Tavlinian story recounted in chapter 22, he finally belonged to no flock. As a border figure, Hadji Murat afforded Tolstoi the "neutral" perspective on the mountain war he needed in order to condemn power politics on both sides.

Yet if Tolstoi succeeded in viewing through the marvelous lens afforded by Hadji Murat the structures of power in the Russian empire and the North Caucasus, he failed in the enterprise of cultural crossing and religious mediation. How could he, possessed by formidable erudition and gifted with relentless intelligence, have fallen short of the mark in a task he was seemingly born to carry out?

From the outset Tolstoi's interest in the mountain war was idiosyncratically confessional. Having gone to the Caucasus to discover war's terrible secret—why men kill one another—he had guiltily watched a Chechen *awul* laid waste, then had himself taken part in the killing game. Tormented by bad conscience for decades, Tolstoi had seized on *Hadji Murat* as the vehicle of settling accounts. The apology sounded in the tale's first page when the narrator, seeking to add a Tatar thistle to his bouquet, wrested the flower violently from its stalk, in the process wounding his own hand on the plant's protruding thorns. "I regretted needlessly destroying a flower that had looked beautiful in its proper place, and I threw it away." We know from the subsequent paragraphs and from Tolstoi's diaries that the Tatar thistle was the emblem of the mountaineers' life force. Susan Layton has argued that the narrator's despoilment of the symbolic thistle inculpated Tolstoi "in his nation's failure to connect properly and find a *modus vivendi* with the Muslim tribes." The verdict is exactly right, but Layton did not stress the specificity of Tolstoi's confession. He did not write *Hadji Murat* for an "ideal audience" of his upper-class Russian peers whom he wished to admonish for their forebears' crimes in the Caucasus. Indeed, the evidence of his correspondence with Chertkov indicated a firm resolve not to publish the story in his lifetime.[241] Tolstoi wrote mainly for himself: to express his sorrow, to "explain" himself to himself.

The confession, signalled by the tale's first page, reached its climax in chapters 16 and 17, recounting the destruction of the *awul* Makhket. As we have seen, the events of the raid in *Hadji Murat* follow the script of Tolstoi's early diaries and fiction. Where guilt presses on the soul, the urge to confess repeatedly overwhelms the sinner, leading to a repetition of the guilt narrative—a point made by Dostoevskii in *Crime and Punishment*. In *Hadji Murat* Tolstoi repeated the details of his criminal deeds. He relived the awful raid of 1852 vicariously, first through the superficial, heedless officer Butler, then through the injured and offended Chechen villagers.

The confession was surely sincere, but we must not miss the paradoxical element of exculpation. Butler, the commanding officer during the destruction of Makhket, acted unconciously, or rather, conscious only of life's joy and of the positive side of war. He did not "see" the evil he had done, for he was caught in the machine of imperial power. In fact, every character in *Hadji Murat* was implicated, to a greater or lesser degree, in one or the other of the two power structures, and, to that degree, was unfree. Even Tsar Nicholas I, the embodiment of malice and deceptiveness, was the product of a milieu that determined his character and dictated his (dys)functional behavior.

By confessing his guilt, then displacing it onto the mechanism of imperial Russian power, Tolstoi directed readers' attention away from the complexities of mountain culture. His self-laceration and inculpation of imperial power created in *Hadji Murat* a narrative asymmetry. What purported to be a story of the Caucasus became, by virtue of Tolstoi's moral-ideological obsession with himself and with his imperial masters, another tale about the Russian conquest of the region.

It may be objected that the Russocentrism of *Hadji Murat* was balanced by Tolstoi's deep research into mountain ethnography and politics and by his profound sympathy for Russia's victims. In this respect, whatever the unevenness of the tale, *Hadji Murat* represented mountain life in a more compellingly realistic fashion than did its fictional precursors. The objection is well taken, and yet ...

And yet Tolstoi did not identify the mainspring of mountain cultural life, the driving force behind the mountaineers' resistance to Russia: the distinctive religious credo of the Sufi brotherhood. As we have seen, Tolstoi rejected the supernatural element of religious belief. For him, "true" religion was altruism, self-sacrifice, and charity. This "true" religion was at the heart of every confessional credo, so that "true" Christians and "true" Muslims must be alike. The author's compassion in *Hadji Murat* extended equally to common Russian soldiers and their mountain adversaries, because both instinctively felt sympathy for others even as both were by power forced to do unnatural evil deeds. The unstated hypothesis was that, absent power, the two peoples would be identical in their religious outlooks.

As we saw in our analysis of al-Qarakhi's chronicle, however, the Islamic insurgents lived by the will of Allah. They understood Shamil to be a figure raised by God for the purpose of saving believers from the infidel Russians. The warrants for their faith included Shamil's many escapes from enemies and from death itself—escapes inexplicable to infidels but transparently explicable to believers. The ties that bound together the mountain armies were not the interstices common to all states—bureaucracies, armies, written laws—but the unseen bonds of common belief. For Tolstoi, Shamil was an Asiatic despot, an analog to Nicholas I. For al-Qarakhi, Shamil was imam—a spiritual master far advanced on the path to God whose behavior should be emulated and whose will should be obeyed because it proceeded from knowledge of God.

Perhaps Tolstoi was unlucky in having no access to al-Qarakhi's *The Shining of Daghestani Swords*. Tolstoi did not know Przewalski's translation of the chronicle. Although Dubrovin had consulted it during the writing of his history of the mountain war, Tolstoi did not refer to Dubrovin's work.[242] Nor did Berzhe include *The Shining of Daghestani Swords* in his monumental edition of documents on Russia's mountain war,[243] a set of documents that Tolstoi read carefully and annotated. Nor did Tolstoi seek out in the far-away Caucasus native eyewitnesses of the mountain wars. He remained unaware of his contemporary Habibullah, al-Qarakhi's faithful son, who at the very moment Tolstoi completed *Hadji Murat* was trying to publish *The Shining of Daghestani Swords*.

Tolstoi may have been unlucky, but it is difficult to suppose that al-Qarakhi's chronicle would have changed in any essential the narrative direction of *Hadji Murat*. As he had dispensed with the supernatural in Russian Orthodoxy, Tolstoi would certainly have discarded the "superstitious" components of *The Shining of Daghestani Swords*. Like his fictional *alter ego* Butler, Tolstoi could see only what his consciousness allowed him to see.

Tolstoi stood in the line of religious enlighteners who sought to save religions from themselves by reducing them to their ethical imperatives. Like his predecessor Voltaire who warred against church and absolutist state, Tolstoi saw human beings as essentially good and noble until corrupted by power. Like Rousseau, he saw a nearly unsullied spirit of generosity and wisdom reposed in the common man. He knew too much about the world not to mark the differences between cultures, but he thought the differences superficial: underneath the peasant kaftan and mountaineer's *burka* there beat the same heart. But what he discarded of religion, its supernatural component, its maddeningly, idiosyncratically alien conceptions about God, that discarded thing was what made religion attractive to its adherents, that thing made each religion distinctive and irreducible.

If Russians would understand the Other in the North Caucasus, they would have to apprehend the Other's God. Put another way, for Russians to cross completely the cultural chasm between the Orthodox world and the Islamic world, they would have to revere, if not worship with the Sufis, *al-Muqtadir*, God the Decreer of Destiny.

That the Russians would not do. Empires have their imperatives, the first of which is security. So long as the Ottoman Turks imperilled Russia's southern borders, so long as their co-religionists in the Caucasus anxiously awaited for that threat to materialize in order that they might rise up and throw off the hated Russian yoke, so long as the Russian empire's Islamic peoples refused to disappear quietly into the good night of historical oblivion, the Russian elites' task was plain: intimidate, subdue, oppress, displace or annihilate their internal Muslim opponents.

Nor, in the final analysis, could Lev Nikolaevich Tolstoi bring himself to embrace the warring mountaineers and their militant religion. Hadji Murat twice crossed over to the Russians, and twice he returned to the mountains, on both occasions sowing death among the Russians. He died fighting for his "freedom," for his God, for the *ghazwa*. In the Caucasus, as outside it, Tolstoi, try as he might, could find no kinder, gentler Islam. Tolstoi's nightmare vision—Hadji Murat's severed head lifted as a trophy of Russia's vaunted power—was the bloody surreality he ultimately acknowledged. Eerily, in December 1897 Tolstoi's friend Gavriil Andreevich Rusanov had shown the great writer a drawing of Hadji Murat's leonine face, whose curving brow and shapely skull were so expertly limned that the shaken writer wrote in his diary: "Rusanov has Hadji Murat's head."[244] From that moment to his death in 1910 Tolstoi was haunted, as Russia is today haunted, by the disembodied Other from the Caucasus.

A COMMENTARY ON THE TWO TEXTS

Notes

1 Ibn Khurdadhbih (825–911) wrote a geographical treatise, *Kitab al-Masalik wa'l-mamalik* [Book of Itineraries and Kingdoms], that became one of the standard geography texts in the Arabic language. For a short biographical note and bibliography, s.v. *Encyclopedia of Islam* (2nd edition), article "Ibn Khurdadhbih."

2 See *Povest' vremennykh let. Chast' pervaia. Tekst i perevod.* (Izdatel'stvo ANSSSR: Moscow–Leningrad, 1950), pp. 59–60; *Povest' vremennykh let. Chast' vtoraia. Prilozheniia* (Izdatel'stvo ANSSSR: Moscow–Leningrad, 1950), pp. 328–329. For Arabic versions of Vladimir's religious "test," see "Sbornik anekdotov," *Zapiski Vostochnogo otdeleniia Russkogo arkheologicheskogo obshchestva, Tom IX* (St. Petersburg, 1896), pp. 262–267.

3 On Peresvetov and like-minded reformers see the magisterial book by Aleksandr Aleksandrovich Zimin, *I. S. Peresvetov i ego sovremenniki. Ocherki po istorii russkoi obshchestvenno-politicheskoi mysli serediny XVI veka* (Izdatel'stvo ANSSSR: Moscow, 1958).

4 See Janet M. Hartley, *A Social History of the Russian Empire 1650–1825* (Longman: London and New York, 1999), p. 74.

5 The Russian–Tatar interaction is as yet little understood, but the recent scholarly work of Allen J. Frank, *Muslim Religious Institutions in Imperial Russia. The Islamic World of Novuzensk District and the Kazakh Inner Horde, 1780–1910* (Brill: Leiden, Boston, Köln, 2001) suggests the degree to which Tatar Muslims managed to construct a semi-autonomous social world.

6 Hartley, *A Social History of the Russian Empire*, pp. 74–75.

7 See Nikolas K. Gvozdev, *Imperial Policies and Perspectives toward Georgia, 1760–1819* (London: Macmillan Press Ltd., 2000).

8 "Vsepoddanneishee pis'mo Ermolova ot 12 iiulia 1825 g.," *Cheteniia v Obshchestve Istorii i Drevnostei Rossii*, 1867, kn. 3, p. 177, quoted in Anatolii Vsevolodovich Fadeev, *Rossiia i Kavkaz pervoi treti XIX veka* (Moscow: ANSSSR, 1960), p. 192.

9 Mikhail Petrovich Pogodin, ed., *Aleksei Petrovich Ermolov. Materialy dlia ego biografii* (Moscow: 1863), pp. 23, 288–289.

10 *Zapiski Alekseia Petrovicha Ermolov s prilozheniiami v dvukh chastiiakh* (Moscow: 1865–1868), II, p. 112. Quoted in Natan Lakovlevich Eidel'man, *Byt' mozhet za khrebtom Kavkaza* (Moscow: Nauka, 1990), p. 39.

11 Quoted in Moshe Gammer, *Muslim Resistance to the Tsar: Shamil and the Conquest of Chechnia and Daghestan* (London: Frank Cass, 1994), p. 34.

12 Semen Bronevskii, *Noveishie geografischeskie istoricheskie izvestiia o Kavkaze v dvuzh tomakh* (Moscow, 1823), I, p. 32, quoted in Fadeev, *Rossiia i Kavkaz*, p. 347.

13 Griboedov's project entailed the establishment of a Russian "East India" company. The company would hold title to 120,000 desiatins of land on which it would grow "tropical products" for export. Apparently, Griboedov saw himself as the head of this monopolistic enterprise: he expected the right to use the Russian army against any enemies in the region, to build fortifications to control the Caucasus and so on. For a draft of the scheme see *Polnoe sobranie sochinenii Griboedova* (Moscow: 1889), I, pp. 135–153. Natan Eidel'man has analyzed the project in *Byt' mozhet za khrebtom Kavkaza*, pp. 107–118.

14 See Susan Layton, "Nineteenth-Century Russian Mythologies of Caucasian Savagery," in Daniel R. Brower and Edward J. Lazzerini, eds., *Russia's Orient. Imperial Borderlands and Peoples, 1700–1917.* (Bloomington and Indianapolis: Indiana University Press, 1997), pp. 80–100, here p. 87.

15 A. S. Pushkin, *Polnoe sobranie sochinenii* (Moscow: ANSSSR, 1948), 8/I, pp. 441–490, here pp. 446, 456, 477, 482.

16 A. S. Griboedov, *Sochineniia*, 1953, pp. 574–575, quoted in Fadeev, *Rossiia i Kavkaz*, p. 353.

17 Nikolai Ivanovich Lorer, *Zapiski dekabrista* (Moscow: 1931), p. 214.

18 M. M. Bliev, "K voprosu o vremeni prisoedineniia narodov Severnogo Kavkaza k Rossii," *Voprosy istorii*, 1970, no. 7, pp. 43–56, here p. 54.

19 Even so, Georgia was far from quiescent. In 1819, under the leadership of two bishops and their supporters within the landed nobility, the Imeritian elites resisted the reorganization of the Georgian church proposed by the Russian Exarch of Georgia. In 1828 there was a peasant uprising in Guriia. In 1832, Georgian officials plotted to assassinate Russian imperial officials at a ball in Tbilisi.

20 A. S. Pushkin, "Puteshestvie v Arzrum," p. 449.

21 On the prolonged Circassian struggle, see Paul B. Henze's fine article, "Circassian Resistance to Russia," in Maria Broxup, ed., *The North Caucasus Barrier. The Russian Advance toward the Muslim World* (New York: St. Martin's Press, 1992), pp. 62–111. For an analysis of Sheikh Mansur's rebellion, see Alexandre Bennigsen, "Un mouvement populaire au Caucase au XVIIIe siècle," *Cahiers du monde russe et sovietique* V/2 (1964), pp. 159–197, and Tarik Cemal Kutlu, *Kuzey Kafkasya' nin ilk Milli Mücahidi ve Önderi, Imam Mansur* (Istanbul: Bayrak Yayincilik, 1987). On the mass migration see Justin McCarthy, *Death and Exile: The Ethnic Cleansing of Ottoman Muslims 1821–1922* (Princeton, NJ: Darwin Press, 1995).

22 Fadeev, *Rossiia i Kavkaz*, p. 283; Rasul Madonedoran Magomedov, *Obshchestvenno – ekonomicheskii i politicheskii stroi Dagestana v XVIII – nachala XIX v.* (Makhachkala: Dagestanskii gos. univ., 1957), p. 83.

23 Fadeev, *Rossiia i Kavkaz*, p. 281.

24 Alexandre Bennigsen, "Au mouvement populaire au Caucase au XVIIIe siècle," pp. 176–179. For an overview of Sufi brotherhoods with occasional illuminating remarks on the Naqshbandi, see Carl W. Ernst, *The Shambala Guide to Sufism* (Boston and London: Shambala, 1997), pp. 120–146, and the more specialized J. Spencer Trimingham, *The Sufi Orders in Islam* (Oxford: Oxford University Press, 1971).

25 See Gammer, *Muslim Resistance to the Tsar*, pp. 39–44.

26 According to one Soviet source, the commitment to holy war came in 1824, when Muhammad al-Yaraghi and other Daghestani *ulama* associated the fulfillment of *sharia* with *ghazwa*. In this account, the first battles of the holy war were fought under Beibulat Taimazov against Russian forces at Amir-Adji-iurt and the *awul* Gerzel'. Fadeev, *Rossiia i Kavkaz*, p. 327. Other Soviet scholars hold that "holy war" was not prosecuted until 1830. The earlier confrontations between indigenous and Russian troops they interpreted as part of an "anti-colonial war" by the Chechens and Daghestanis. Their transparent calculation was to privilege the indigenous national movement over the "reactionary" Islamic religious movement. See, for example, ANSSR. Dagestanskii filial. *Istoriia Dagestana. Tom II* (Moscow: Nauka, 1968), pp. 79–88.

27 For brief but illuminating remarks on the Naqshbandiyya, see the classical book by Annemarie Schimmel, *Mystical Dimensions of Islam* (University of North Carolina Press: Chapel Hill, 1975), pp. 363–367.

28 On Sirhindi's teachings, see Schimmel, *Mystical Dimensions of Islam*, pp. 367–369.

29 On the origins and spread of Naqshbandi ideas see the splendid book of Anna Zelkina, *In Quest for God and Freedom. The Sufi Response to the Russian Advance in the North Caucasus* (New York: New York University Press, 2000), pp. 75–89, especially pp. 80, 86–87. For the Ninety-Nine Names of God and their place in Sufi prayer, see Ernst, *The Shambala Guide to Sufism*, pp. 81–119.

30 On the devotional practices of the Naqshbandiyya-Khalidiyya, see Hamid Algar, "Devotional Practices of the Khalidi Naqshbandis of Ottoman Turkey," in Raymond Lifchez, ed., *The Dervish Lodge. Architecture, Art and Sufism in Ottoman Turkey* (Berkeley, Los Angeles, Oxford: University of California Press, 1992), pp. 209–227.

31 See Friedrich von Bodenstedt, *Die Völker des Kaukasus und ihre Freiheitskämpfe gegen die Russen: Ein Beitrag zur neuersten Geschichte des Orients* (Frankfort: Kessler, 1848), pp. 161–162, quoted in Zelkina, *In Quest for God and Freedom*, pp. 106–107.

32 Bodenstedt, *Die Völker des Kaukasus*, p. 168, quoted in Zelkina, *In Quest for God and Freedom*, p. 117.

33 Zelkina, *In Quest for God and Freedom*, p. 109.

34 The Arabic text was published three-quarters of a century after its writing. See Jamal al-Din al-Ghazi-Ghumuqi, *al-Adab al-Murdiyya fi al-Tariqa al-Naqshbandiyya* (Petrovsk: 1905). Zelkina has made "a full translation" of this work, which she promises to publish in the near future with annotations. Zelkina, *In Quest for God and Freedom*, p. 108, fn. 1.

35 Jamal al-Din al-Ghazi-Ghumuqi, *al-Adab al-Murdhiyya fi al-Tariqa al-Naqshbandiyya*, pp. 32–33, quoted in Zelkina, *In Quest for God and Freedom*, pp. 114–115, my translation.

36 In a recent book Alexander Knysh has argued that "the Russian officers and colonial administrators, who produced most of the accounts of the Caucasus and its inhabitants, were captives to the European and Christian stereotypes and anxieties about Islam and the Muslims which were as rife in their age as they are today." Knysh noted that colonial administrators generally took a "conspiratorial view" of Sufism, regarding it as the core of the Muslim anti-colonial resistance; meanwhile, these officials looked on the "scriptural" Islam of the urban elites as more "civilized" and therefore more "manageable." In the Maghrib region, French officials called the Sufi orders "a new sort of religion born of Islam"; analogously, in the Caucasus, "their Russian colleagues railed against 'the blind zealotry' of *myuridizm*, *zikrizm*, and *dervish-estvo*, all of which were seen as a uniquely Caucasian (and innately militant) version of Islam. See Alexander Knysh, *Islamic Mysticism. A Short History* (Brill: Leiden, Boston, Köln, 2000), pp. 296–297.

37 Gammer, *Muslim Resistance to the Tsar*, pp. 24, 52, 58.

38 Ibid., p. 307, fn. 12.

39 Ibid., pp. 149–161.

40 Ibid., pp. 56, 271–273. The captives, generally well treated, were ransomed for silver at Qidhlar; they were exchanged for Russian-held prisoners and for silver at Alazan. The incident at Alazan provoked an international outcry against the "fanatic and barbarian" Shamil. It also led to publication of two important captivity narratives. E. A. Verderevskii, *Plen u Shamila* (St. Petersburg: 1856) and Edouard Merlieux, *Les Princesses Russes Prisonnières au Caucase. Souvenirs d'une Française Captive de Chamyl* (Paris: 1857), republished as Anna Drancey, *Princesses russes, prisonnièrres au Caucase* (Paris: A. Michel, 1980).

41 Gammer, *Muslim Resistance to the Tsar*, p. 99.

42 Ibid., p. 160.

43 Ibid., pp. 252–254.

44 Ibid., pp. 187–188.

45 For example, in 1843 Tsar Nicholas I personally directed Minister of War Chernyshev and General Neidgart to send proclamations to the mountaineers that Russia had no designs against their religion or property. See John F. Baddeley, *The Russian Conquest of the Caucasus* (London, 1908), pp. 379–380.

46 See Anthony L. H. Rhinelander, *Prince Michael Vorontsov. Viceroy to the Tsar* (Montreal Kingston: McGill-Queen's University Press, 1990), p. 175. See also RGIA fond 1268 (Kavkazkii komitet) op. 1, delo 799, ll. 1–3, letter from M. S. Vorontsov to Minister of War A. Chernyshev, June 19, 1845.

47 Gammer, *Muslim Resistance to the Tsar*, pp. 177–179.

48 Ibid., pp. 122–123.

49 See Miliutin's memorandum, "O polozhenii na Kavkaze," in RORGB fond 169 (Miliutina), k. 18, ed. khr. 13, l. 4; quoted in Ia. T. Sarapuu, "Kavkazskii vopros vo vzgliadakh i deiatel'nosti D.A. Miliutina, *Vestnik Moskovskogo universiteta. Seriia 8, Istoriia*, 1998, no. 3, pp. 71–89, here 81–82.

50 See K. M. Iachmenikhin, "Voennye poseleniia na Kavkaze v 30–50–e gody XIXv.," *Vestnik Moskovskogo universiteta. Seriia 8. Istoriia*, 1991, no. 4, pp. 18–28.

51 D. A. Miliutin complained in his 1840 memorandum "O polozhenii na Kavkaze" about the counterproductive policy of shifting local tribes to new settlements. Yet in his 1844 memo "Mysl' o razlichnykh obrazakh deistviia na Kavkaze," he decided that the only way to counteract the tribes' habit of staging bandit raids was to move ethnically Russian Cossacks to the border of the north Caucasus. The Cossacks, who shared the custom of raiding, would neutralize the non-Russian tribes. See Ia. T. Sarapuu, "Kavkazskii vopros vo vzgliadakh i deiatel'nosti D.A. Milutina," pp. 83–84.

52 See "Obshchii vzgliad gen. Murav'eva na voinu s gortsami na Kavkaze," *Akty sobrannye Kavkazskoiu arkheograficheskoiu kommissieiu, Tom 11*, pp. 65– 67.

53 See the letter from Rostislav Andreevich Fadeev to his father, July 2/14, 1856; quoted in Gammer, *Muslim Resistance to the Tsar*, pp. 277–278. For the original, see "Pis"ma Rostislava Andreevicha Fadeeva k rodnym," *Russkii vestnik*, October 1897, p. 64.

54 Gammer, *Muslim Resistance to the Tsar*, p. 278.

55 For the argument that ethnic cleansing was a twentieth-century phenomenon see Norman M. Naimark, *The Fires of Hatred: Ethnic Cleansing in Twentieth-Century Europe* (Cambridge, MA: Harvard University Press, 2001).

56 This is the curious argument of B. N. Mironov, *Sotsial'naia istoriia Rossii perioda imperii XVIII – nachalo XX v.: Genezis lichnosti, demokraticheskoi sem'i, granzhdanskogo obshchestva i pravovogo gosudarstva*. Tom 1 (Dmitrii Bulanin: St. Petersburg, 1999), pp. 64–65. Mironov's entire discursus on "the advantages of Russia's vast spaces," together with his ode to imperial rule, was dropped from the English-language translation of his "classic" book, probably because it would have offended American academic sensibilities. See Boris Mironov with Ben Eklof, *A Social History of Imperial Russia, 1700–1917* (Westview Press: Boulder, CO, 1999). To be fair to Mironov, we must note his awareness of the mountain war's cost, at least from the Russian perspective. He calculates that "Russia paid 200,000 lives to subjugate the Caucasus." He also cites the estimate of Russian diplomats that "after the subjugation of the Caucasus, roughly 400,000 people emigrated to Turkey." Mironov, *Sotsial'naia istoriia Rossii*. Tom 1, pp. 35–36. Astonishingly for a historian famed for his mathematical precision, Mironov does not distinguish between the Circassians in the northwest Caucasus, who emigrated en masse to Turkey in the 1860s, and the indigenous peoples of the northeast Caucasus, who after their defeat in 1859 largely remained in Chechnia and Daghestan.

57 See Thomas M. Barrett, "Lines of Uncertainty. The Frontiers of the Northern Caucasus," in Jane Burbank and David L. Ransel, eds., *Imperial Russia. New Histories for the Empire* (Indiana University Press: Bloomington and Indianapolis, 1998), pp. 148–73. To be sure, understanding social processes on the Caucasus frontier is a worthy goal, to be pursued for its instructiveness about the lived history of the empire. But it is ungenerous or mistaken to imply that previous scholarship on the Caucasus was somehow flawed because it has concentrated on the conquest and its deleterious results.

58 On Shamil's childhood see the excellent popular biography by Shapi Kaziev, *Imam Shamil'* (Moscow: Molodaia gvardiia, 2001), pp. 13–21. His spiritual guide in the mountain caves was a childhood friend, Muhammad, two years his elder, In 1830 this friend became the first imam of Daghestan, Ghazi Muhammad.

59 He became a book collector, proud of the small library of efficacious spiritual works he managed to amass. During the mountain war he carried his most precious volumes across the battlefields of Daghestan and Chechnia, bitterly lamenting the moments of peril when he had to abandon his books and rejoicing at their recovery. At several points in *The Shining of Daghestani Swords* al-Qarakhi mentioned Shamil's attachment to these books, which the imam appeared to regard as animate beings, worthy of direct address.

60 The legend has Shamil swearing on the *Quran* to kill himself if his father did not stop tending grapes – a virtual impossibility since the *Quran* forbids suicide.
61 See Kaziev, *Imam Shamil'*, p. 46.
62 *Istoriia Dagestana.* Tom II (Moscow, 1968), pp. 99–107.
63 These conferences convened in 1841 at Darghiyya and 1848 at Andi. The conferences resembled war councils since their principal aim was to co-ordinate military action. However, the Andi conference also dealt with treatment of Russian deserters, requisitioning of gunpowder, and rectifying certain abuses by the *naibs*. See *Istoriia Dagestana. Tom II*, p. 101.
64 For published versions of the letters, see Kh. A. Omarova, ed, *100 pisem Shamilia* (Makhachkala: Izdatel'stvo DNTS RAN, 1997) and R. Sh. Sharafutdinova, ed., *Araboiazychnye dokumenty epokhi Shamilia* (Moscow: Vostochnaia literatura RAN, 2001).
65 "Pis'mo Shamilia ko vsem naibam, kadiiam, miuridam i prochim musul'manam (v period s 6 noiabria 1850 g po 26 sentiabria 1851 g.), in *Araboiazychnye dokumenty epokhi Shamilia*, pp. 84–85.
66 "Pis'mo Shamilia Khadzhimuradu (ne pozdnee avgusta 1850 g.)," in *Araboiazychnye dokumenty epokhi Shamilia*, p. 160.
67 The imam's letter of 1836 to Major-General Klüge von Klugenau began: "From Shamil, a needy writer who entrusts all his affairs to the mighty protection of Allah" See "Pis'mo Shamilia general-maioru Kliuki [von Klugenau] (23 iiulia [1836 g.])," in *Araboiazychnye dokumenty epokhi Shamilia*, pp. 109–113. A shorter, but also less honorific saluation can be found in the letter of 1836 to Major-General Reut: "From Shamil, a poor slave of Allah, to General Reut." See "Pis'mo Shamilia general-maioru Reutu (22 noiabria 1836 g.; datiruetsia po date polucheniia dokumenta)," in *araboizychnye dokumenty epokhi Shamilia*, pp. 114–115.
68 Gammer, *Muslim Resistance to the Tsar*, p. 50.
69 This version of events was repeated in the novella *Hadji Murat.*
70 Gammer, *Muslim Resistance to the Tsar*, pp. 226, 243, 396, fn. 8, 402. Gammer calculated Ghazi Muhammad's age in 1842 as "seven or eight." Idem., p. 402, fn. 52. This would have made Ghazi Muhammad thirteen or fourteen years old in 1848. However, al-Qarakhi listed Ghazi Muhammad's age in 1850 as eighteen, which would have made the boy ten or eleven years old in 1842.
71 Al-Qarakhi, pp. 226–227/177–178.
72 Ibid., pp. 227/179.
73 Gammer, *Muslim Resistance to the Tsar*, p. 267.
74 W. E. D. Allen and Paul Muratoff, *Caucasian Battlefields. A History of the Wars on the Turco-Caucasian Border, 1828–1921* (Cambridge: Cambridge University Press, 1953), pp. 60, 66.
75 Allen and Muratoff, *Caucasian Battlefields*, p. 68.
76 Karl Marx, *The Eastern Question: Letters Written in 1853–1856 Dealing with the Events of the Crimean War* (London: 1897), p. 167.
77 Allen and Muratoff, *Caucasian Battlefields*, pp. 95–100.
78 On Bariatinskii see A. L. Zisserman, *Fel'dmarshal' Kniaz' Aleksandr Ivanovich Bariatinskii, 1815–1879*, 3 vols. (Moscow: 1890) and Alfred J. Rieber, *The Politics of Autocracy. Letters of Alexander II to Prince A. I. Bariatinskii 1857–1864* (Paris, the Haague: Mouton, 1966).
79 Rieber, *The Politics of Autocracy*, p. 69.
80 For details on Shamil's reception see Thomas M. Barrett, "The Remaking of the Lion of Daghestan: Shamil in Capitivity," *Russian Review*, 53: 3 (July 1994), pp. 353–366.
81 Barrett, "The Remaking of the Lion of Daghestan," p. 356; Shamil's letter may be found in *Akty sobrannye Kavkazskoiu arkheograficheskoiu komissieiu* (Tiflis, 1866–1904,) 12, p. 827.

82 Barrett, "The Remaking of the Lion of Daghestan," p. 357.
83 It is ironic that Abd al-Qadir, after fourteen years of struggle against the French in Algeria in support of Islam (1832–1846), surrendered to them in 1846 somewhat like Shamil did to the Russians in 1859.
84 See Marius Canard, "Chamil et Abdelkader," *Annales de l'Institute d'Etudes Orientales de la Faculté des Lettres d'Alger*, XIV (1956), pp. 231–256; reprinted in *idem. Miscellanea Orientalia* (London: Variorum Reprints, 1973). I wish to thank my colleague Paul M. Cobb for this reference.
85 Among these, especially valuable is the anthology Institut istorii, iazyka i literatury im. G. Tsadasy, *Dvizhenie gortsev severo-vostochnogo Kavkaza v 20–50 gg. XIX veka. Sbornik dokumentov* (Makhachkala: Dagestanskoe knizhnoe Izd-vo, 1959), which contains many proclamations and letters of Shamil. A more exhaustive primary source, mixing Russian and non-Russian documents, is *Akty, sobrannye Kavkazskoiu arkheograficheskoiu komissieiu* (Tiflis, 1866–1904), 12 vols.
86 See. G. Mallachikhan, "Predislovie," *Tri imama*, Society for Central Asian Studies, Reprint Series no. 16 (London: 1989), p. 7.
87 I. Kratchkovsky, "Daghestan et Yémen," in *Mélanges E. F. Gautier* (Paris, 1937), pp. 288–296.
88 Canard, "Chamil et Abedlkader," pp. 236–237.
89 A. M. Barabanov, "Vvedenie," in ANSSSR, Institut Vostokovedeniia, *Khronika Mukhammeda Takhira Al-Karakhi o Dagestanskikh voinakh v period Shamila* (Moscow: ANSSSR, 1941), p. 11.
90 Al-Qarakhi, *Khronika*, p. 57/27.
91 Ibid., p. 201/155.
92 Ibid., p. 213/165.
93 Ibid., p. 222/174..
94 Ibid., pp. 223–224/175–176.
95 Al-Qarakhi was very clear about the link between Jamal al-Din's return from captivity and the end of his work on the chronicle. Toward the end of the chapter "On the Return to the Imam of His Son Jamal al-Din," al-Qarakhi wrote: "This is the end of what Muhammad Tahir gathered during his time with the imam ...", *Khronika*, p. 239/189.
96 Gammer, *Muslim Resistance to the Tsar*, p. 275.
97 Al-Qarakhi, pp. 239–240/189.
98 Ibid., p. 248/197.
99 Ibid., p. 248/196–197.
100 Ibid., p. 250/198.
101 The looting occurred in August 1859 just before the Russians' final seige at Ghunib. Ibid., p. 249/198.
102 Ibid., pp. 251–254/199–203.
103 Ibid., p. 239/189.
104 Ibid., p. 315/256.
105 On Islamic notions of sainthood see Ernst, *The Shambala Guide to Sufism*, pp. 58–69.
106 Al-Qarakhi, pp. 108–110/71–73.
107 Ibid., pp. 155–156/115.
108 Ibid., pp. 53–56/24–28.
109 Ibid., p. 43/15.
110 Ibid., p. 86/52.
111 Ibid., pp. 94/59, 96/61.
112 Ibid., pp. 126–128/87–89. Note that the Prophet Muhammad also escaped death despite damage to his mantle.
113 Ibid., p. 206/158–159.
114 Ibid., p. 75/43. See also p. 89/54.

115 Ibid., pp. 108–109/72.
116 Ibid., pp. 246–247/195.
117 Ibid., p. 47/19–20.
118 Ibid., p. 181/137.
119 Ibid., pp. 194–195/149.
120 Ibid., pp. 114–115/76–77.
121 Ibid., p. 157/116.
122 Ibid., p. 51/23.
123 Ibid., pp. 49–50/21–22.
124 Ibid., p. 76/43–44.
125 Ibid., p. 96/61.
126 Ibid., p. 201/154; citation from *Quran*, 3:134.
127 Ibid., p. 213/165.
128 Ibid., p. 218/171
129 Ibid., p. 241/190.
130 Ibid., p. 249/197.
131 Ibid., p. 249–250/197–198.
132 Ibid., p. 185/140.
133 Ibid., pp. 254–255/203–204.
134 See his introductory remarks at the beginning of chapter 48, *The History of the Decline and Fall of the Roman Empire.*
135 See A. L. Shapiro, *Russkaia istoriografiia s drevneishikh vremen do 1917 g.: uchebnoe posobie* (Moscow: Assotsiatsiia "Rossiia": Izd-vo "Kul'tura," 1993).
136 For a lively analysis of Karamzin as historian, see Natan Iakovlevich Eidel'man, *Poslednii letopisets* (Moscow: Kniga, 1983).
137 For a splendid overview of Muslim historiography, s.v. *Encyclopedia of Islam* (2nd edition), article "Ta'rikh." See also the classic F. Rosenthal, *History of Muslim Historiography* (Leiden, 1952); and T. Khalidi, *Arabic Historical Thought in the Classical Period* (Cambridge, 1994).
138 See Jack A. Crabbs, Jr., *The Writing of History in Nineteenth-Century Egypt. A Study in National Transformation* (Cairo: The American University Press in Cairo, and Detroit: The Wayne State University Press, 1984), p. 39.
139 Although al-Jabarti remained a chronicler, Anouar Abdel-Malek has asserted that he was a "chronicler with a scholarly method striking in its rigor and richness of detail, and he was an observer–that is, an analyst of the European impact [on Egypt]. Anouar Abdel-Malek, *Idéologie et renaissance nationale. L'Egypt moderne* (Paris: Editions anthropos, 1969), p. 200. See also. Crabbs, *The Writing of History in Nineteenth-Century Egypt*, pp. 43–86. Al-Tahtawi himself probably translated twenty books from French into Arabic; see Albert Hourani, *Arabic Thought in the Liberal Age, 1798–1939* (London, New York, Toronto: Oxford University Press, 1962), p. 71. According to Crabbs, al-Tahtawi and his pupils in the Cairo School of Languages "translated in all over 1,000 books into Turkish and Arabic." Crabbs, *The Writing of History in Nineteenth-Century Egypt*, p. 72.
140 See Adeeb Khalid, "The Emergence of a Modern Central Asian Historical Consciousness," in Thomas Sanders, ed., *Historiography of Imperial Russia. The Profession and Writing of History in a Multi-National State* (Armonk, New York and London, England: M.E. Sharpe, 1999), pp. 433–452, here 434–438.
141 A. M. Barabanov, "Vvedenie," *Khronika Mukhammeda Takhira al-Karakhi*, pp. 9–10.
142 Ivan Nikolaevich Zakhar'in, *Vstrechi i vospominaniia; iz literaturnago i voennago mira* (St. Petersburg: Izd-vo M. V. Pirozhkova, 1903), p. 50; cited in Barabanov, "Vvedenie," p. 10.
143 See Nikolai Fedorovich Dubrovin, *Istoriia voiny i vladychestva russkikh na Kavkaze* (St. Petersburg: V. Tip. Departamenta udelov, 1871).

144 For his earlier work, see A. P. Berzhe, *Kratkii obzor gorskikh plemen na Kavkaze* (Tiflis, 1858), reprinted (Nal'chik: Kabardino-Balkarskoe otd-nie Vseros. Fonda Kul'tury, 1992), and idem., *Chechnia i chechentsy*, reprinted (Groznyi: Kniga, 1991).
145 Barabanov, "Vvedenie," p. 10.
146 *Akty, sobrannye Kavkazskoiu arkheograficheskoiu kommisssieiu* (Tiflis: Tip. Glavnago upravleniia namestnika Kavkazskogo, 1866–1904).
147 Barabanov, "Vvedenie," p. 11.
148 Ibid., pp. 25–27.
149 Henri Troyat, *Tolstoi*, trans. Nancy Amphoux (New York: Harmony Books, 1967), p. 77.
150 L. N. Tolstoi, "Zapiski o Kavkaze. Poezdka v Mamakai-Iurt," *Polnoe sobranie sochinenii v 90-i tomakh* (Moscow, Leningrad, 1928–1958), 3, p. 215.
151 See Susan Layton, *Russian Literature and Empire. Conquest of the Caucasus from Pushkin to Tolstoi* (Cambridge: Cambridge University Press, 1994), esp. pp. 89–155.
152 "Zapiski o Kavkaze," *Polnoe sobranie sochinenii*, 3, pp. 215–216.
153 L. N. Tolstoi, "Dnevnik" in *Polnoe sobranie sochinenii*, 46, p. 61, entry of June 11, 1851.
154 Ibid., p. 63, entry of June 11/12, 1851.
155 Ibid., pp. 64–65, entry of July 3, 1851.
156 See M. A. Ianzhul, *80 let boevoi i mirnoi zhizni 20-i art. brigady* (Tiflis: 1886–1887), 2 vols.; quoted in Sergei Sergeevich Doroshenko, *L.N. Tolstoi. Voin i patriot* (Moscow: Sovetskii pisatel', 1966), p. 61.
157 "Dnevnik," *Polnoe sobranie sochinenii*, 46, p. 65.
158 "Nabeg. Rasskaz volontera (1852)," *Polnoe sobranie sochinenii*, 3, pp. 15–39, here 34.
159 Ibid., p. 35.
160 Ibid., pp. 221–223.
161 Ibid., pp. 222–223.
162 "Varianty iz rukopisnykh redaktsii 'Nabega'," *Polnoe sobranie sochinenii*, 3, p. 228.
163 Doroshenko, *Lev Tolstoi. Voin i patriot*, pp. 78–79.
164 See Ianzhul, *80 let boevoi i mirnoi zhizn*, 2, pp. 127–129; A. M. Zaionchkovskii, *Vostochnaia voina 1853–1856 gg. v sviazi s sovremennoi ee politicheskoi obstanovki*, 2 vols. (St. Petersburg, 1913), 2.1, pp. 225–226.
165 V. A. Poltoratskii, "Vospominaniia," *Istoricheskii vestnik*, 1893, no. 6, 667–672, quoted in Doroshenko, *L. N. Tolstoi. Voin i patriot*, pp. 93–95.
166 L. N. Tolstoi, *Polnoe sobranie sochinenii*, 3, p. 60.
167 Doroshenko, *L. N. Tolstoi. Voin i patriot*, p. 97.
168 L. N. Tolstoi, "Pis'mo kniaziu A. I. Bariatinskomu," July 15, 1853, *Polnoe sobranie sochinenii*, 59, pp. 237–238.
169 L. N. Tolstoi, "Pis'mo T. A. Egol'skoi," late August 1853, *Polnoe sobranie sochinenii*, 59, p. 244.
170 The "exception" was his novella, "Kazaki" ["Cossacks"] (1863), which treated the Terek Cossacks as indigenous heroes. But this exception proved the rule: in reality, the Terek Cossacks were instruments of Russian conquest–frontier settlers, not truly indigenous to the Caucasus region.
171 "Dnevnik," *Polnoe sobranie sochinenii*, 46, pp. 82–86. Entry of August 10, 1851.
172 Ibid., p. 86, entry of August 22, 1851.
173 Ibid., p. 87, entry of August 22, 1851.
174 Ibid., pp. 89–90, entry of February 1, 1852.
175 L. N. Tolstoi, "Pis'mo T. A. Egol'skoi," January 6, 1852, *Polnoe sobranie sochinenii*, 59, pp. 145–149, here p. 147.
176 *Ibid.*, p. 148.
177 "Dnevnik," *Polnoe sobranie sochinenii*, 46, p. 162, entry of June 23, 1853.

178 Stepan Andreevich Bers, *Vospominaniia o grafe L. N. Tolstom*, (Smolensk, 1893), pp. 9–10. See also V. A. Poltoratskii, "Vospominaniia," *Istoricheski i vestnik*, 1893, no. 6, pp. 672–678.

179 Tolstoi and his brother left the north Caucasus on October 25. After arriving in Tbilisi on November 1, Tolstoi remained in the city until January 7, 1852. See Doroshenko, *L. N. Tolstoi. Voin i patriot*, pp. 64–67.

180 Tolstoi, "Pis'mo grafu Sergeiu Nikolaevichu Tolstomu i Mari'e Mikhailovne Shishkinoi," December 23, 1851, *Polnoe sobranie sochinenii*, 59, pp. 132–133.

181 See "Dnevnik," *Polnoe sobranie sochinenii*, 46, p. 96, entry of March 20, 1852.

182 "Dnevnik" *Polnoe sobranie sochinenii*, 46, p. 183, entry of October 23, 1853.

183 Ia. I. Kostenetskii, *Zapiski ob Avarskoi ekspeditsii na Kavkaze v 1837 godu*, 3 chasti (St. Petersburg, 1851).

184 "Dnevnik," *Polnoe sobranie sochinenii*, 46, p. 184, entry of October 24, 1853.

185 See "Primechaniia k dnevniku," *Polnoe sobranie sochinenii*, 46, p. 444, n. 1085.

186 Layton, *Russian Literature and Empire*, pp. 246–247.

187 L. N. Tolstoi, "Iasnopolianskaia shkola za noiabr' i dekabr' mesiatsy," *Polnoe sobranie sochinenii*, 8, p. 44.

188 L. N. Tolstoi, *Ispoved'*, *Polnoe sobranie sochinenii*, 23, p. 12.

189 L. N. Tolstoi, *Anna Karenina. Polnoe sobranie sochinenii*, 19, pp. 398–399.

190 "Dnevnik," *Polnoe sobranie sochinenii*, 48, pp. 187–189, entry of June 2, 1878.

191 N. N. Gusev, *Lev Nikolaevich Tolstoi. Materialy k biografii s 1870 po 1881 god.* (Moscow: Izdatel'stvo AN SSSR, 1963), p. 436.

192 "Pis'mo Nikolaiu Nikolaevichu Strakhovu," January 27, 1878, *Polnoe sobranie sochinenii*, 62, p. 381.

193 "Dnevnik," *Polnoe sobranie sochinenii*, 48, pp. 69–70, entry of May 22, 1878.

194 L. N. Tolstoi, *Ispoved'*, *Polnoe sobranie sochinenii*, 23, pp. 5, 55–56.

195 N. N. Gusev, *Lev Nikolaevich Tolstoi. Materialy k biografii s 1870 po 1881 god*, p. 436.

196 "Pis'mo N. N. Strakhovu," October 19, 1877, *Polnoe sobranie sochinenii*, 62, pp. 345–346.

197 Ibid.

198 "Pis'mo A. A. Fetu, November 11/12, 1877, *Polnoe sobranie sochinenii*, 62. p. 349.

199 See the letter to Strakhov of November 11/12, 1877: "Please, be so kind as to think about and render advice on the first part of Nikolai Pavlovich's reign and particularly on the war of 1828–1829." Strakhov sent N. Luk'ianovich's *Opisanie turetskoi voiny 1828 i 1829 godov*, 4 vols. (St. Petersburg: 1843–1847) and Paul Lacroix, *Histoire de la vie et du règne de Nicolas I, empereur de Russie*. See "Pis'mo N. N. Strakhovu," *Polnoe sobranie sochinenii*, 62, p. 349.

200 "Pis'mo Petru Nikolaevichu Svistunovu," March 14, 1878," *Polnoe sobranie sochinenii*, 62, p. 394. Svistunov, himself a Decembrist, was supposed to pass the inquiry to Beliaev, a Decembrist who did twelve years at hard labor in Siberia before being sent to the Caucasus in 1839. P. S. Bobrishchev-Pushkin and A. P. Bariatinskii were also Decembrists. The former had translated Pascal's *Pensées*; in May 1878 Tolstoi considered finding a publisher for this translation but dropped the plan. Gusev, *Lev Nikolaevich Tolstoi. Materialy po biografii s 1870 po 1881 god*, p. 495.

201 Gusev, Lev Nikolaevich Tolstoi. Materialy po biografii s 1870 po 1881 god, p. 493.

202 On Odoevskii see N. Ia. Eidel'man, *Byt' mozhet za khrebtom Kavkaza*, pp. 217–278.

203 S.v. *Encyclopedia of Islam* (2nd edition), articles "Bab," "Babis," "Baha'is."

204 "Pis'mo O.S. Lebedevy Levu Nikolaevichu Tolstomu," August 1, 1894, in Aleksandr Iosifovich Shifman, *Lev Tolstoi i Vostok* (Moscow: Izdatel'stvo Vostochnoi Literatury, 1960), pp. 405–409.

205 "Pis'mo O. S. Lebedevy Levu Nikolaevichu Tolstomu," August 18, 1894, in Shifman, *Lev Tostoi i Vostok*, p. 410.

206 "Pis'mo Ol'ge Sergeevne Lebedevoi," September 4, 1894, *Polnoe sobranie sochinenii*, 67, p. 215.

207 "Pis'mo Ol'ge Serveevne Lebedevoi," September 22, 1894, *Polnoe sobranie sochinenii*, 67, pp. 223–224.

208 Friedrich Carl Andreas, *Die Babi's in Persien. Ihre Geschichte und Lehre quellen mässig und nach eigener dargestellt* (Leipzig, 1896).

209 "Pis'mo Isabelle Arkad'evne Grinevskoi," October 22, 1903, *Polnoe sobranie sochinenii*, 74, 207–208.

210 "Pis'mo Ippolitu Dreifusu," April 18, 1904, *Polnoe sobranie sochinenii*, 75, pp. 77–78.

211 See "Varianty k 'Khadzi Muratu," *Polnoe sobranie sochinenii*, 35, pp. 284–307.

212 "Pis'mo Valdimiru Vasil'evich Stasovu," letter of December 27, 1896, *Polnoe sobranie sochinenii*, 69, p. 226.

213 See A. L. Zisserman, *Dvadtsat' piat' let na Kavkaze (1842–1867)*, 3 vols. (St. Petersburg, 1879–1884). V. A. Poltoratskii, "Vospominaniia," serialized in *Istoricheskii vestnik*, 1893.

214 "Pis'mo Vladimiru Vasil'evich Stasovu," January 4, 1897, *Polnoe sobranie sochinenii*, 70, p. 11.

215 *Sbornik materialov dlia opisaniia mestnostei i plemen Kavkaza*, 20 vols. (Tiflis: Tip. Kantseliarii glavnonachal'stvuiushchago grazhdanskoi chasti na Kavkaze, 1893–1895).

216 *Akty, sobrannye Kavkazskoiu arkheograficheskoiu kommissieiu* (Tiflis: 1866–1904), 12 vols.

217 "Khadzhi-Murat. "Istoriia pisaniia," *Polnoe sobranie sochinenii*, 35, pp. 593–594.

218 Ibid., pp. 601, 608.

219 *Arkhiv kniazia Vorontsova*, 40 vols. (Moscow: Tip. A. I. Mamontova, 1870–1895).

220 P. A. Bulanzhe, "Kak L. N. Tolstoi pisal 'Khadzhi-Murata," *Russkaia mysl'*, 1913, no. 6, pp. 79–80.

221 See "Pis'mo Velikomu Kniaziu Nikolaiu Mikhailovichu," letter of August 20, 1902, *Polnoe sobranie sochinenii*, 73, pp. 281–282.

222 "Pis'mo V. V. Stasovu," August 10, 1902, *Polnoe sobranie sochinenii*, 73, p. 276.

223 "Pis'mo Velikomu Kniaziu Nikolaiu Mikhailovichu," *Polnoe sobranie sochinenii*, 73, p. 282.

224 *Khadzhi-Murat, Polnoe sobranie sochinenii*, 35, p. 79.

225 Ibid., p. 81.

226 "Pis'mo Ivanu Iosiforichu Korganovu," letter of December 25, 1903, *Polnoe sobranie sochinenii*, 73, p. 353.

227 "Pis'mo Anne Avesalomonovne Korganoi," letter of January 8, 1903, *Polnoe sobranie sochinenii*, 74, p. 10.

228 Pis'mo Il'iu Petrovichu Nakashidze, letter of December 20, 1902, *Polnoe sobranie sochinenii*, 73, pp. 346–347.

229 "Pis'mo Vladimiru Vasil'evichu Stasova," letter of December 20, 1902, *Polnoe sobranie sochinenii*, 73, p. 348.

230 "Pis'mo Aleksandre Andreevne Tolstoi," letter of January 26, 1903, *Polnoe sobranie sochinenii*, 74, p. 24.

231 "Pis'mo Velikomu Kniaziu Nikolaiu Mikhailovichu," letter of April 1, 1903, *Polnoe sobranie sochinenii*, 74, p. 94.

232 "Pis'mo Sergeiu Nikolaevichu Tolstomu," May 18, 1903, *Polnoe sobranie sochinenii*, 74, p. 128.

233 "Pis'mo Marii Lvov'ne Obolenskoi," letter of June 3, 1903, *Polnoe sobranie sochinenii*, 74, p. 137.

234 "Pis'mo Pavlu Ivanovichu Biriukovu," letter of June 3, 1903, *Polnoe sobranie sochinenii*, 74, p. 140. He made the same point in a letter to Vladimir Grigor'evich Chertkov: "I'm writing something in *H[adji] M[urat]* about Nik[olai] Pavl[ovich], a separate chapter that, even if it will be disproportionately long compared with the whole,

fascinates me [chrezvychaino privlekaet menia]." "Pis'mo Vladimiru Grigor'evichu Chertkovu," June 11, 1903, *Polnoe sobranie sochinenii*, 88, p. 298.

235 "... I am reading about Nik[olai] Pavl[ovich], who interests me very much, and I am correcting *H[adji] M[urat]* so as not to touch it again ...," "Pis'mo Vladimiru Grigor'evichu Chertkovu," letter of June 30, 1903, *Polnoe sobranie sochinenii*, 88, pp. 300–301.

236 "Dnevnik," *Polnoe sobranie sochinenii*, 54, p. 178, entry of June 18, 1903.

237 See "Khadzhi-Murat. Istoriia pisaniia," *Polnoe sobranie sochinenii*, 35, p. 627.

238 S. N. Shul'gin, "Iz vospominanii o gr. L. N. Tolstom," in *L. N. Tolstoi v vospominaniiakh sovremennikov v dvukh tomakh* (Moscow: Gos. Izdatel'stvo khudozhestvennoi literatury, 1955), II, pp. 162–163.

239 Layton, *Russian Literature and Empire*, pp. 274–277.

240 For the latter see "Pis'mo Nikolaiu II," letter of January 16, 1902, *Polnoe sobranie sochinenii*, 73, pp. 184–191.

241 See "Pis'mo Vladimiru Grigor'evichu Chertkovu," letter of October 11, 1902, *Polnoe sobranie sochinenii*, 88, pp. 277–278.

242 Dubrovin's *Istoriia voiny i vladichestva russkikh na Kavkaze*, 6 vols. (St. Petersburg 1871–1888) did not extend beyond 1827; thus, Dubrovin did not incorporate al-Qarakhi in his narrative. In January 1896, Tolstoi received from V. V. Stasov a list of books on the Caucasus containing Dubrovin's history. Tolstoi struck Dubrovin from the list as irrelevant to his Caucasian tale. See "Khadzhi-Murat. Istoriia pisaniia," *Polnoe sobranie sochinenii*, 35, p. 588.

243 *Akty, sobrannye Kavkazskoiu arkheograficheskoi kommissieiu*, 12 vols. (Tiflis: 1866–1904).

244 See Nikolai Nikolaevich Gusev, *Letopis' zhizni i tvorchestva L'va Nikolaevicha Tolstogo. 1891–1910* (Moscow, 1958–1960), 2. p. 261. There is another, less probable version of this encounter with Hadji Murat's head. According to A. P. Sergeenko, the author of the *Hadji Murat* commentary in Tolstoi's *Complete Works*, Rusanov showed Tolstoi an oval mask whose curving brow and shape recalled the Avar hero. See "Khadzhi-Murat. Istoriia pisaniia," *Polnoe sobranie sochinenii*, 35, p. 592. More recent scholarship has sided with Gusev. See Lidiia Dmitrievna Opul'skaia, *Lev Nikolaevich Tolstoi. Materialy k biografii s 1892 po 1899 god* (Moscow: Nasledie, 1998), p. 269.

GLOSSARY

[Variants given in brackets are different versions of the same name and the Arabic adjectival forms of place names. For example, "al-Qarakhi" means "from Qarakh." Names in this book except for "Hadji Murat" are spelled as in Moshe Gammer, *Muslim Resistance to the Tsar* (London: Frank Cass, 1994). In the Tolstoi translation, versions of Muslim names are kept as close to the Russian originals as possible.]

Aghach Qala [Chumeskent]: Fort in thickly wooded mountains west of the Hindal area that was used at various times by Muslim leaders as a refuge from the Russians. Ghazi Muhammad, for example, used it a base from which to defend the Hindal area from Russian attacks in the spring of 1831.

Aghdash Awukh [Aktash Aukh]: Village on the Aktash River about 25 km south of Khasav Yurt.

Ahmad Khan [Akhmet-khan]: Hereditary ruler of Mekhtuli, a region just south of the territory of the *shamkhal*'s domain. The Russians installed Ahmad as the temporary ruler of the Avar area in 1836, which sparked a feud between him and Hadji Murat. Ahmad finally denounced Hadji Murat to the Russians as Shamil's collaborator, causing Hadji Murat to turn against the Russians until 1851. Ahmad died in the early 1840s.

Akhdi [Akhty]: Russian fort on the Samur River in southern Daghestan. Shamil besieged a Russian force there in the fall of 1848 to spark a general uprising in this area but did not succeed.

Akhulgoh: Mountain village in central Daghestan on the Andi Koysu River near 'Ashilta where Shamil made an unsuccessful stand against the Russians in 1839.

Alazan River: River south of Daghestan. The Alazan river valley was at the center of the "Lezghian Line"—a defensive line established by the Russians in the 1830s to protect Georgia from incursions.

'Andal: Area in the eastern part of the Avar region of Daghestan near the 'Andi Koysu River.

'Andi Koysu: River that runs through the heart of the Avar region of Daghestan.

Ansal [Untsukul/al-Ansali, al-Untsukuli]: Village in the Hindal region of central Daghestan.

Argun: River that runs from the northern Caucasus through central Chechnia.

'Ashilta [al-'Ashilti]: Shamil's home village in central Daghestan on the 'Andi Roysu River.

Atli Buyun: Village between Petrovsk and Temir-Khan-Shura where Ghazi Muhammad defeated a Russian force in 1831.

awul: Daghestani mountain village.

Avar [al-Avari]: One of the many Daghestani ethnic groups primarily living in central Daghestan in the areas between and near the 'Andi Koysu and Avar Koysu Rivers and in the area called Hindal or Koysubu.

Avar Koysu: River south of the 'Andi Koysu River and just south of the village of Khunzakh.

bairam: Islamic holiday.

Balagin [Balakan]: Village in the Alazan river valley south of Daghestan and northwest of the Russian fort at Zakartalah.

baraka: Blessing from God.

Bayan: Village in Chechnia.

beshmet: Quilted jacket popular in the Caucasus.

Bizu': Valley near Ghunib.

burka: Felt cloak worn over the *beshmet* by mountaineers in the Caucasus.

Burnaia: Russian fortress built in 1821 near the *shamkhal*'s capital, Targhu. "Burnaia" means "stormy" in Russian.

Buynakh: Village south of the Russian fortress of Temir-Khan-Shura.

Char [al-Chari]: Village south of Daghestan in the Chartalah region, near the Russian fort at Zakartalah.

Chartalah: Region south of Daghestan in the Alazan river valley.

cherkesska: Circassian hat commonly worn in the Caucasus.

Chernyshev, Prince Aleksandr Ivanovich: Russian minister of war in the 1840s.

chikhir: A type of brandy popular in the Caucasus.

Chirkah [Chirkei/al-Chirkawi]: Village on the Sulak River in northern Daghestan.

Chokha: Village on the Ghazi-Ghumuq Koysu River south of Saltah.

Daghestan: Mountainous region of the northern Caucasus just southeast of Chechnia. It now belongs to the republic of Azerbaijan and has been the site of significant fighting since the late 1990s between Chechens, other Muslims, and the Russian Army. It remains an unsettled area populated by groups speaking at least 29 distinctive languages.

Darghiyya [Dargo/al-Darghiyyi]: Village in the Salatawh region of northern Daghestan.

Derbend: City on the Caspian coast with a major Russian fort. It is approximately 125 km south of Petrovsk [Makhachkala].

Dolgorukii [Dolgorukov]: Prince Vasilli Andreevich: Russian minister of war after Chernyshev.

dzhigit [yigit]: Turkish (as used in the Caucasus) for "brave young man."

Enderi [Andreevskii Awul/Indiri/al-Indiri]: Village just north of the Caucasus and east of Chechnia near the Russian fort *Vnezapnaia.*

Ghazanish: Village near to and south of Temir-Khan-Shura.

ghazwa (plural *"ghazawat"*): Campaign or battle in an Islamic holy war.

Ghazi Muhammad [Kazi-Mulla]: Daghestani imam (leader) who created a religio-political movement against the Russians that he led from 1826 to 1832, when he was killed in combat near Gimrah, which was his birthplace. Shamil's eldest surviving son was named for him and later became an Ottoman general.

Ghazi-Ghumuq Koysu: River beginning in the mountains west of Qaytaq that flows north into the Sulak River.

Ghumuq plain: Area east of Chechnia in north Daghestan through which the Terek River flows.

Ghunib: Mountain plateau in central Daghestan near the Kara Koysu River where Shamil made his final stand against the Russians in 1859.

Gimrah [Gimry/al-Gimrawi]: The home village of Shamil and Ghazi Muhammad in the Hindal region.

Girgil [Gergebil]: Village south of Hindal near the Ghazi-Ghumuq Koysu where Shamil withstood a major Russian attack in 1847.

Grabbe, Lieutenant-General Pavel: Russian general who defeated Shamil at Akhulgoh in 1839.

Groznaia [Groznyi]: Site of an important Russian defensive fort in Chechnia built on the Sunja River in 1819. "Groznaia" means "menacing" in Russian.

Hadji Murat al-Khunzakhi: An Avar nobleman who had originally been loyal to the Russians. In November 1840, Ahmad Khan convinced the Russian commander in Khunzakh to arrest Hadji Murat on suspicion of secret ties to Shamil. Angry, Hadji Murat shifted allegiance to Shamil, under whose leadership he fought until 1851, when he rejoined the Russians, apparently due to some friction with the imam.

Hamza Bek [Hamza Bek]: Daghestani imam (1832–1834) who followed Ghazi Muhammad and preceded Shamil as leader of Muslim resistance to the Russians in Daghestan. He was killed in a battle in which many members of the traditional Avar ruling family were killed.

Harakan [Arakany/al-Harakani]: Village on the Ghazi-Ghumuq Koysu River in the Hindal region.

Hindal [Koysubu]: Area in central Daghestan near the Ghazi-Ghumuq Koysu River.

Hutsal [Gotsatl']: An important village in the Avar region that was the birthplace of the second imam, Hamza Bek.

Ihali [al-Ihali]: Village in the Avar area just south of the 'Andi Koysu River.

imam: In Islam originally "imam" meant "Muslim prayer leader." Later its meaning grew to sometimes include "community leader" and "ruler" more generally. In the context of the Eastern Caucasus in the nineteenth century, this term was applied successively to Ghazi Muhammad, Hamza Bek, and Shamil—the three *imams* of the Muslim resistance to the Russians in the Eastern Caucasus who led this movement from 1826 to 1859.

Indiri [al-Indiri]: Village in Chechnia just across the Aktash River from the *Vnezapnaia* fort.

Irpili [Erpeli]: Village just west of Temir-Khan-Shura.

'Irib: Village in central Daghestan near the Kara Koysu River.

izba: Russian word for a hut or peasant house.

Jamal al-Din: Shamil's son, named for the Naqshbandi leader Jamal al-Din al-Ghazi-Ghumuqi [Jamal Edin]. Jamal al-Din al-Ghazi-Ghumuqi became the principal *murshid* in Daghestan after the death of Muhammad al-Yaraghi and approved of the choice of Shamil as the third imam in 1834.

jihad: Often glossed as "holy war," it generally means striving to promote and defend Islam.

Kafr Ghumuq: Village just northeast of Temir-Khan-Shura.

Karata [al-Karati]: Village in the Avar region just south of the 'Andi Koysu River.

Khasav Yurt: Town in the Ghumuq plain in Chechnia.

Khunzakh [al-Khunzakhi]: Hadji Murat's home town just north of the Avar Koysu River, often depicted in al-Qarakhi's work as a somewhat fickle place. It was a center of the Avar people, often at odds with Shamil.

Klugenau, General Frants Klüge-von-: Russian general who fought Shamil during the 1840s.

kosh kol'dy: Turkish (as used in the Caucasus) phrase for "welcome."

koysu: Daghestani word for "river."

kunak: Turkish (as used in the Caucasus) word for "guest", who, according to Muslim tradition, should be fed and sheltered for three days. Having been someone's guest also would imply a continuing relationship with that person.

Kuydurmas [Gudermes]: Town east of Groznaia in Chechnia on the Sunja river.

Mekhelta [al-Mililti]: Village in the northern part of the Avar region just south of the Salatawh area.

Mekhtuli: Area east of the Avar region ruled by Ahmad Khan, whose capital was at Jengutay.

Michik River: River in Chechnia.

muezzin: Muslim prayer caller.

Muhammad al-Yaraghi: Naqshbandi master from Daghestan who had been Shamil's *shaykh* but died in the 1830s.

mullah: Word used by Tolstoi to mean "Islamic holy man."

murid: Generally, the term *murid* refers to any follower and disciple of a Sufi guide and mentor (a *murshid*). Although Shamil did not consider himself an actual Sufi *murshid*, al-Qarakhi often called Shamil's followers *murids*.

murshid: Sufi guide and mentor. Shamil considered his *murshid* to be Shaykh Muhammad al-Yaraghi, followed by Jamal al-Din al-Ghazi-Ghumuqi on al-Yaraghi's death. Al-Qarakhi did not refer to Shamil as a *murshid*.

Muzlik [Mozdok]: Town on the Terek River northeast of Groznaia.

naib: Arabic for "deputy." In the context of the nineteenth-century Caucasus, it meant military governor of a particular area in Daghestan or Chechnia appointed by Shamil to administer justice and lead troops there.

Naqshbandi order: Important Sufi order named for Muhammad Baha al-Din Naqshband, a fourteenth-century Central Asian Sufi master. The followers of this order are well known among Muslims for strongly emphasizing the reconciliation of mystical knowledge of God with strict Islamic orthodoxy. They are still quite numerous in diverse parts of the Islamic world including modern Turkey, Afghanistan, and Pakistan. The particular branch of the Naqshbandi order with which Shamil was affiliated, the Khalidiyya, spread to Daghestan through Shaykh Muhammad al-Yaraghi, who had been ordained as a *murshid* (spiritual leader) by Ismail al-Shirwani, a Naqshbandi leader from Azerbaijan who had been an early follower of Shaykh Khalid, founder of the Khalidiyya branch of the Naqshbandi order. Shamil was never referred to as a *murshid* in al-Qarakhi's work, although he was sometimes called "imam". He was always represented in al-Qarakhi's text as a *murid* (follower) of Shaykh Muhammad al-Yaraghi.

Orota [al-'Uruti]: Village in the Avar region of Daghestan just south of the 'Andi Koysu river.

Petrovsk [Makhachkala]: Russian fort town founded in 1843 on the Caspian coast near the *shamkhal*'s capital at Targhu that was near an early Russian fort site.

Qarakh [al-Qarakhi]: Region in the south central part of the Avar region of Daghestan east of the Avar Koysu River. Qarakh was the home region of the author of *The Shining of Daghestani Swords*, Muhammad Tahir al-Qarakhi.

Qaranay: Village on the road between Temir-Khan-Shura and Gimrah.

Qaytaq [Kaitakh, Kaitag, Khaydaq/al-Khaydaqi]: Region between the Avar area of Daghestan and Derbend. Qaytaq is northwest of the area of Tabarsaran.

Qidhlar [Kizlyar]: Important Russian fort on the Ghumuq plain about 120 kilometers north of central Daghestan.

Qubah [Kuba]: Town south of Daghestan fairly near the Caspian coast that experienced an anti-Russian uprising in 1837.

Rughcha [Rugdzha/al-Rughchawi]: Avar village on the Kara Koysu River west of Ghunib.

saklya: Simple dwelling in a mountain village in the Caucasus.

Salatawh [Salatau]: Mountainous region in southern Chechnia just north of Daghestan.

Saltah [Salty]: Village near the Kara Koysu River in central Daghestan.

sardar: A Persian word meaning "military commander." In *The Shining of Daghestani Swords* it is written "*sardal.*"

saubul: Turkish response phrase (as used in the Caucasus) to "welcome": "Be well."

Shamil: Third imam who ruled in Daghestan and struggled against the Russians from 1834 to 1859. Born in 1796, he died in 1871 on a pilgrimage to Mecca and Medina.

shamkhal: The hereditary ruler of a group of the Turkic Ghumuq people in the eastern Caucasus near the Caspian Sea. The *shamkhal's* capital was Targhu, near the Russian forts of Petrovsk and *Burnaia*. Beginning in the late eighteenth century, the *shamkhal* and his followers often allied with the Russians.

sharia: Islamic holy law primarily based on two sources: (1) The *Quran*, God's revelation to Muhammad through the angel Gabriel; and (2) the *Sunnah*, Muhammad's practices and sayings. All Muslims must believe in one God and obey his holy law as set forth in these two sources.

Tabarsaran [Tabassaran]: Region in southern Daghestan southeast of Qaytaq and just west of Derbend.

Targhu [Tarki]: A village next to the Russian fort *Burnaia* in Daghestan near the Caspian Sea. Capital of the *Shamkhal* a traditional ruler of the area along the Caspian coast.

Tatar: A Turkic people whose homeland is the region north of the Black Sea and the northern Caucasus.

Tiflis [Tbilisi]: The capital of Georgia.

Temir-Khan-Shura [Shura]: Important Russian fort in the northeastern Caucasus between the Caspian Sea and the Avar region of Daghestan.

Tiliq [al-Tiliqi]: Mountain village south of the Avar Koysu River.

Vedan [Vedeno, New Darghiyya]: One of Shamil's capitals in the northern Caucasus on the Khulkhulau river.

Vladikavkaz: Russian city on the Terek river north of the Caucasus founded in 1784.

Vnezapnaia: Russian fortress built in 1820 on the west bank of the Aktash River near Enderi. "Vnezapnaia" means "sudden" in Russian.

Vozdvizhenskoe [Vozdvizhensk]: Russian fortress built in 1844 on the west bank of the Argun River in Chechnia near Enderi. "Vozdvizhenskoe" means "elevated" in Russian.

Zakartalah [Zakataly]: Russian fort just south of the village of Char in the Alazan river valley south of Daghestan.

Zunuh: Village on the Arghun river in Chechnia.

Compiled by Ernest Tucker

INDEX

'Abd al-Karim al-Chirkawi (Shamil's secretary) 65
'Abd al-Khaliq al-Ghujduwani 178
'Abd al-Qadir (Algerian leader) 198–9
'Abd al-Rahman al-Jabarti, *Aja'ib al-Athar fi al-Tarajim wa al-Akhbar* 209
'Abd al-Rahman al-Qarakhi 35
'Abdullah al-'Ashilti 18
Abraham (prophet) 225
Abu Ja'far al-Tabari, *Tarikh al-Rusul wa al-Muluk*, 208
Abu Muslim 20, 58
Abumuslim-Shakhvalikhan 192
Adam (prophet) 225
adat (customary law) 11, 34, 39
Adrianople (Edirne) 174
Agakhal 34
Agha Muhammad Khan (Shah of Iran) 174
Aghach Qala (Chumeskent) 17, 19
Aghdash Awukh (Aktash Aukh) 18
Ahmad Khan al-Sahali (Akhmet-khan) 17, 31–5, 46, 177
Ahmad Sirhindi al-Faruqi, Shaykh 178
Akalich 34
Akhbirdil Muhammad al-Khunzakhi 37, 45, 47
Akhdi 53–5, 65, 200, 207
Akhulgoh x, 29, 36, 38, 42–8, 183, 204–6
al-'Abbas 69
Alazan (river valley) 164, 184, 207
Alexander I (Aleksandr I; Russian Tsar, 1801–25) 173
Alexander II (Aleksandr II; Russian Tsar, 1855–81) 65, 197–8, 202
Alexandria, Egypt 69
'Ali Mamad 55
'Alibek al-Khunzakhi 47

'Alibek ibn Khiriyasulaw 36
'Aligul Husayn 32
'Ali al-Gulzawi 31–2
'Ali Sultan 17
Allah (God) 180, 227, 237
Almakhal 48
al-Quduqi 63
al-Thughuri 33
Alupka 228
Amir Khan 204
Amirasol Muhammad al-Kudali 64
Anapa 67
Anatolia 180, 197–8
'Andal 15, 33–4, 49, 62
Andreas, F. C. 226
Ansal 15, 23–33, 73, 204, 206
Araks River 174
Argun 19, 81
Argutinskii 52–6, 152–3
Armenia 174–6
Arslan-Khan 218
Artlukh 48
'Ashilta 21, 28, 35, 205
Aslan al-Tsadaqari 65
Aslan Khan 180, 218
Astrakhan 172
Atli Buyun 17
Austerlitz 214
Avar (tribe) 25, 33, 39, 72, 177, 184–5, 190, 193, 218–9, 227, 238; (village) 34
Avaria 176, 235
Avdeev 76, 233–4
Azerbaijan 174
Azizay 50

Bab (Sayyid Ali-Muhammad) 224–5
Babis, Babism 224–6
Baha al-Din Naqshband 178

Baha'is, Baha'ism 225–6
Baha'ism 226
Baha'ullah, *Book of Certitude* 226
Bala li-Muhammad al-Birguni 47
Balagin 23
Balkh 12, 47, 71
Baqiyya 69
Baqulal 15–16, 31, 34, 36, 49, 62
Barabanov, A.M. viii, 8, 210
Bariatinskii Aleksandr Ivanovich, Prince 186, 197–8, 201–2, 212–16, 223
Barti Khan (Shamil's paternal uncle) 27–8, 32, 37–44, 47
Basaw 'Illaw 32
Bashkirs 172
Batir al-Militi 58
Bayan (village) 19, 49
Bayt al-Haram (Mecca) 65
Beliaev, Aleksandr Petrovich 223
Bennigsen, Alexandre 177
Bers, Stepan Andreevich 217
Berzhe (Berguet), Adol'f Petrovich 210, 227, 237
Bestvzhev-Marlinskii, A. A. 211
Biladi 49
Biri 33
Biriukov, Pavel Ivanovich 232
Bizu' 62–3
Black Sea 67, 172–4, 176, 197
Bloom, Harold 76
Bobrishchev-Pushkin, Pavel Sergeevich 223
Boguslavskii, Colonel 66
Borodino 214
Brahminism 226
Britain 196, 223
Bronevskii, Semen 175
Bruni, Leonardo, *Historiarum Florentini populi libri* 208
Bucharest (treaty) 174
Buddha, Buddhists 221, 225–6
Bukhara 12, 47, 71, 178, 209
Bukhdah 58
Bulanzhe (Boulanger), Pavel Aleksandrovich 228
Bulgars 171
Buq Muhammad 62
Buraw 19, 72
Burnaia 177
Burtinah 57
Butay 60
Butler, Captain 217, 229, 236, 238

Butsun 33
Buynakh 58, 192

Canard, Marius 200
Caspian Sea 173, 177
Catherine II (Russian Tsarina, 1762–1796) 172–3
Caucasus vi, viii, x, 1–6, 8, 10–12, 38, 171, 198–202, 210, 221–4, 226–30, 232–3, 236–8; nineteenth-century conflict between Russia and Shamil in 182–97; Russian advance into 173–82; Tolstoi and 211–20
Central Asia 47, 171, 209
chalandar 38–42
Chamaw al-Qaytaqi 21
Char 16–17, 59
Chartalah 16–17, 63
Chavchavadze 60
Chechens vi, 2, 19, 34, 48, 51, 57, 72, 74–5, 185–6, 212–18, 229, 233, 236
Chechnia ix, x, 18–22, 32, 49–50, 71–2, 177, 182, 186–9, 196–9, 210, 214–15, 218
Chernyshev, Minister of War Aleksandr Ivanovich 228, 233
Chertkov, V. G. 3, 236
Chiriq 45
Chirkah (Chirkei) 14, 17–19, 50
Chirqata 32, 36–7, 39
Chita 223
Chokha 50, 55–6, 72, 200, 207
Christian, R. F. 76
Christianity 4, 197, 211; and Tolstoi, 220–6
Christians 2, 51–2, 54, 69, 172, 176, 179, 185, 204, 224, 237
Chumal 18
Circassia 198
Circassians 18, 172, 176–7, 186–7, 196–8
Confucians 221
Confucius 225
Countess Lidiia 221
Crimea 173–4, 214
Crimean War x, 61, 196–7, 216

Daghestan ix, x, 4, 7, 8, 11–13, 21, 30, 37, 50, 61, 68, 71, 112, 174, 176–7, 180, 183–4, 187–9, 191, 194, 196–200, 210–11
Daniyal Sultan 53, 55, 62–3, 65, 202

Danubian Basin 171, 174
Darada 52
Darghiyya (Dargo) 57, 183, 190, 200, 203–5
Darvish Nur Muhammad al-Inkhawi 16, 205
Decembrists 223–4, 226
Derbend 18, 177
dhikr ["recollecting God"] 178, 180–1
Dibir al-'Andi 62
Dibir Hajiyaw 32–3
Dibir ibn Inkachilaw al-Khunzakhi 64
diwan 189
Diya al-Din Khalid al-Shahrazuri al-Kurdamiri, Shaykh 179
Dostoevskii, F. M., 227; and *Crime and Punishment*, 236
Dreyfus, Hippolyte 226
Dubrovin, Nikolai Fedorovich 210, 237
Durchali 52, 58
Durda 218

Eastern Caucasus 177, 197–8, 213–14
Eastern Slavs 171
Egypt 68, 208–9
Ermolov, Aleksandr Petrovich 174–5, 177, 180, 183
Erzurum 174–6

Fatima (Shamil's wife) 29, 45, 51
Fet, Afanasii Afanas'evich 223
Filofei 171
Foote, Paul 2
France 196, 223

Galalal 57
Gammer, Moshe 177, 182–6, 191, 193
Georgia, 173–6, 196–7
Georgians 1, 59–60, 173, 184, 231
Ghalbaz al-Karati 64
Gharashkiti 49
ghaza/ghazwa (military campaign) 7–8, 19, 21, 23, 35, 45, 47, 56, 182, 190, 200, 238
Ghazanish 17
Ghazi Muhammad (first imam) x, 7, 9, 11–25, 71–2, 74, 190
Ghazi Muhammad (Shamil's son) 29, 42–7, 56–65, 67–70
Ghaziyaw al-'Andali 44, 64
Ghaziyaw al-'Andi, 33–5, 39

Ghazna 204
Ghuluda 16
Ghumuq 110, 120, 148, 218
Ghunib x, 61–2, 64, 68, 201–2, 207
Ghursh al-Sughuri 64
Gibbon, Edward 208
Gimrah x, 9, 15–17, 19–29, 31–2, 37, 39, 45–6, 182–3, 200, 204–5
Girgil 50–1
Gorky, Maxim vi
Gospels 220, 225
Grabbe, Pavel 38
Griboedov, Aleksandr 175, 224
Grinevskaia, Isabella Arkad'evna 226
Groznyi (Groznaya) 59, 98, 177, 186
Gubash 205
Gulistan (treaty) 174
Gurdali 215
Guria 175
Gurzal Awul 51
Guwal 35, 62
Gvosdev, Nikolas K. 173

Habibullah 4, 8, 202–3, 211, 237
Hadith al-Mililti 16
Hadji Murat (novella), v, vi, ix, x, 2, 4–6, 8, 25, 46, 56, 58–9, 73–6, 175, 185, 190–6, 216–20, 226–38
Hadji Murat al-Khunzakhi v–vi, ix–x, 2, 4, 6, 8, 25, 46, 74–76, 185, 190–6, 216–20, 226–38; confrontation with Shamil 58–9
Hajiyaw al-'Uruti 20, 62–3, 205–6
Hajiyaw al-Qarakhi 63–4, 201
Hajiyaw ibn al-Tsitawi al-Huchuti 55
Hajiyaw ibn Ghaziyaw al-Karati 65
Hajiyaw ibn Hajj Dibir al-Qarakhi 63
hajj x, 67, 69, 72, 181, 208
Hajj Dibir 199
Hajj Ibrahim al-Chirkisi 64
Hajj Musa 55
Hajj Nasrullah al-Qabiri al-Kurali 64
Hajj Tashaw al-Indiri 32, 35
Hajj Yahya al-Chirkawi 53
Hajj Yusuf al-Yaksavi 202
halal 42
Hamza Bek (second imam) x, 7, 11–12, 15–17, 19, 25–7, 34, 71–2, 188, 190, 201, 218
Haqlal 35
Harakan 15
Hasan Husayn 20

Hasanalmuhammad al-Harikuli 24
Hashimi 14
Hazra 54–5
Herder, Johann Gottfried, *Ideen zur Philosophie der Geschichte der Menschheit* 208
Himmat al-Hutsaliyun 49
Hindal 16, 30
Hitin al-Danukhi 48
Husayn al-Girgili 58
Husayn ibn Ibrahim al-Gimrawi 26
Hutsal 33
Hutub 55

Ianzhul, M. A. 212
Iasnaia Poliana 219, 227
Ibn Khurdadhbih 171
Ibrahim al-Gimrawi 23, 58, 64
Ibrahim al-Husayn 39
'Id 24, 72
Idris 51
Ifuta 51
Ihali 19, 32
Ilisu 59
Ilya 50
Imanqalaw al-Jirfati 48
Indiri 18–19, 32, 35, 72
Ingush 185
Inkhub 62
Insan al-'Uyun 43, 205
Iran 12, 174, 177
Irghin River 36, 62, 205–6
'Iri 55
'Irib 53, 55, 62–3
Irpili 15, 18
'Isa Hajiyaw al-Chirkawi 47
Isaev, Balta (Bulta) 216
Isbahi al-Chirkawi 62
'Ish 30–2, 34, 205
Ishchali 63
Islam 2, 5–6, 9, 11–15, 37, 51, 54, 59, 61, 67–69, 71–4, 171, 176–9, 182, 184–5, 188, 191, 193, 195–6, 198–9, 202, 204, 207, 209, 220–1, 223–6, 238
Ismail Pasha 68–9, 74
Ismail, Shaykh 178
Istanbul (Islambol) 31, 73, 171, 176, 178; Shamil's stay in 66–70
Istoricheskii Vestnik, 227
Istoriia gosudarstva Rossiiskago, 208
Iusif *see* Yusuf
Ivan III (Russian Tsar, 1462–1505) 171

Jamal al-Chirkawi 21
Jamal al-Din (Shamil's son) 18, 29; returned to Shamil 57–61, 200–3; sent as a hostage to the Russians 38–40
Jamal al-Din al-Ghazi-Ghumuqi (religious leader) 12, 14, 69, 71, 188, 190, 200–3; led resistance to the Russians 178–81; and *al-Adab al-Murdhiyya fi al-Tariqa al-Naqshbandiyya* 181
Jamaw Khan al-Khaydaqi 58
Jarbilil 33
Javad Khan 49
Jawad Khan al-Darghiyyi 47, 49
Jawhara 43–5, 204
Jesus 220, 225
Jews 221
jihad 11–12, 72
Judaism 5, 224, 226

Ka'ba 13
Kafr Ghumuq 17–8
Kahal mountain 64
Kakheti 196
Kalal 62
Kalmyk 216
Kaluga x, 198, 210–1
Kamal al-Ghuludi 64
Karabulaks 185
Karalal 49
Karamzin, N. M. 208–9
Karata 57, 62
Karataev, Platon 233
Karganov, Colonel Iosif Ivanovich 218–19
Kars 174, 223
kashf 20
Kawthar 13, 71
Kazan' 172
Khaidak 192
Khalid, Adeeb 209
Khalid, Shaykh 178
Khalidiyya 180–1, 193
Khan Mukhul 22
Khas Muhammad, Shaykh 178
Khirik 33
Khiva 209
Khiz al-Chirqawi 47
Khudanatil Muhammad 49
Khunuk 199
Khunzakh 16, 21, 25–6, 31, 33–4, 51, 59, 72, 184, 190–2, 195, 205, 218
Kievan Rus' 171

Klugenau, Frants Klüge-von- 27–9, 33–4, 37, 190
Kokand 209
Korganov, Colonel Iosif Ivanovich 230
Korganova 230–1
Kostenetskii, Iakov Ivanovich 218
Krachkovskii, I. Iu. 8, 199
Krasnoe 106
kunak 217
Kurdistan 180
Kurinskoe 215
Kutisha 200, 206
Kuydurmas (Gudermes) 19

Layton, Susan, *Russian Literature and Empire*, 175, 211–12, 219, 234
Lazarev, General 210
Lebedeva, Ol'ga Sergeevna 225
Lermontov, M. Iu. viii, 211–12; and "Pamiati A. I. O-go" ["To the Memory of A. I. O[doevskii]"], 224
Lesser Chechnia 182
Levin, Colonel L. F. 215, 221
Life of the Prophet, see Muhammad ibn Ishaq
Lorer, Nikolai I. 175
Loris-Melikov, M. T. 228

Ma'arukh 49
Mahdi (son of the shamkhal) 27, 28
Mahmud (sultan of Ghazna) 204
Mahmud II (Ottoman Sultan) 67
Makhachkala 176, 190, 199, 211
Makhket 78, 235–6
manakib 7
Mansur, Shaykh 176–7, 179
Manych, 186
Marx, Karl 197
Maude, Aylmer vi, 2, 75
Mazlagash 215
Mecca 7, 12, 29, 47, 65, 67, 69–73, 176, 179, 191, 198–9, 202, 206, 208, 210
Meccan Bestowal see al-Quduqi
Medina x, 7–8, 12, 20, 47, 69–71, 73, 199
Mekhelta 15–16
Michik River 60, 215
Michit 80
Miliutin, D. A. 185
Milrik Murtaza 'Ali al-Chirkawi al-Mugharrib 64
Mirdai al-Tiliqi 35

Mirza Ali 55
Miserbiev, Sado 216
Misigulaw al-'Andi 54
Moscow 12, 66, 70, 171–2, 174–5, 178, 188–90, 197, 200, 208, 211–12, 221, 225, 228, 232, 238
Moses 38, 73–4
mudir 191
muezzin (Muslim prayer caller) 22, 48, 78, 235
mufti 55, 69, 189
Mughal India 178
Muhammad (prophet) 2, 7, 11–14, 20, 178, 204, 206–7, 224
Muhammad Amin, 196, 198
Muhammad Efendi al-Humi 55
Muhammad Efendi al-Yaraghi 14, 18–20, 25, 72
Muhammad ibn 'Abd al-Latif al-Ilisuwi, 55
Muhammad ibn Ishaq,*Sira (Life of Muhammad)* 7, 199, 204
Muhammad ibn Ma'ruf al-Nuqushi, 55
Muhammad Kamil (Shamil's son) 69
Muhammad al-Mahdi (Muslim messiah) 47, 57, 74, 224
Muhammad Mirza Khan al-Ghumuqi 35
Muhammed Mirza Mavraev 211
Muhammad Naqshbandi, Shaykh 47
Muhammad Shafi 49
Muhammad Sultan 22
Muhammad Tahir al-Qarakhi v–ix, 1–9, 11, 21, 35, 56–8, 63–4, 66–7, 70, 74, 76, 188, 191–5, 237; and *The Shining of Daghestani Swords* 198–211
Muhammad Tilaw 57
Muhammad al-'Uradi al-Hidali 58
Muhras Shu'ayb 60
Mulla Ramazan al-Chari 35
Murav'ev, General Nikolai Nikolaevich 186–7
murid (follower/disciple) 27, 38, 49, 78–81, 118–19, 149, 156, 181–2, 190, 193, 235
"Murid War" 182
murshid (Sufi Muslim spiritual guide) 181–2, 191, 234
Murtaza 'Ali al-'Uruti 56
Murtaza 'Ali al-Chirqawi 47
Murtaza 'Ali al-Dhuldi al-Qarakhi 21
Murtaza 'Ali al-Haradarikhiyan 49
Murtaza al-'Urkachi al-Mugharrib 64
Murtaza Lasol Muhammad 33, 50

murtaziq 33, 73
Musa al-Balagini 44
Musa al-Balatkini 49
Muslims 4, 7, 11, 13, 33, 42, 61, 65, 171–2,
    178–9, 181, 184–5, 190, 207, 221, 225,
    237
Mustafa Khan al-Shirvani 50

naib 21, 33, 48, 51, 54–9, 62–4, 76,
    189–90, 192–6, 200, 202
Nakashidze, Il'ia Petrovich 231
Nakhbakal 43
Nakhichevan 174
Napoleon 174
Naqshbandi Sufi order (Naqshbandiyya) 7,
    8, 12, 14, 47, 71–2, 177–9, 181–2, 189,
    191, 201, 206–7
Nasrullah 64
Nazranovs 185
Nelidova 234
New Darghiyyah *see* Vedeno
Nichik 53, 55
Nicholas I (Russian Tsar, 1825–1855) 4, 61,
    184, 197, 228, 231, 235–6
Nicolai (Nikolai), General Leontii
    Pavlovich 37, 175, 185, 201–2, 210,
    223, 238
Nogai 186–7
North Caucasus 1, 173–4, 176–9, 181–2,
    185, 196, 198–200, 217–18, 232, 236,
    238
Nukha 230
Nukhuh 59
Nur Ali 49
Nur Muhammad al-Qarakhi 58

Obolenskaia, Mariia Lvov'na 232
Obruchev, Lieutenant-General Nikolai
    Nikolaevich 223
Orota 32–3
Odoevskii, Aleksandr Ivanovich, *"Nash otvet"*
    ["Our Response"] 223–4
Optina Pustyn' 227
Orbeliani, Princess 228
Orthodox/Orthodoxy 4, 171–2, 182,
    184–5, 197, 220–2, 225, 227, 238
Ottomans/Ottoman Empire 7–8, 66–9,
    171–4, 176–8, 187, 196–8, 209, 225–6,
    238

padishah 66–8

Pakhu Bike 16, 72
Paskiewicz, Ivan F. 174–6, 224
Paul I (Russian Tsar, 1796–1801) 173
Peace of Paris 197
Peresvetov, Ivan Semenovich 172
Persia *see* Iran
Peter the Great (Russian Tsar, 1682–1725)
    232, 234
pharaoh 69
Piri Awul 17
Pirogovo 227
Poltoratskii, V. A. 215, 219, 227
Potemkin, Grigorii Aleksandrovich 173
Potto, Lieutenant-General Vasilii
    Aleksandrovich 231
Povest' vremennykh let [*Tale of Bygone Years*],
    171
Prince Vladimir 171
Przewalski, Pavel Giliarovich 210, 237
Pullo 38–9, 47
Pushkin, A. S. 175–6, 208, 211, 224

Qachar 21
qadi (Muslim judge) 177, 189–90, 205
Qadi al-Ishichali 54, 58, 62
Qakhal 202
Qarakh ix, 7, 63–4, 201
al-Qarakhi *see* Muhammad Tahir
    al-Qarakhi
Qaral 33
Qaralal 34
Qaralala 63
Qaranay 15
Qarata 200
Qaytaq 58, 74, 191–4
Qibid Muhammad 28, 51, 63
Qidhlar 18–19, 27, 47, 52, 184, 205
Qinsir 63
Qubah 54
al-Quduqi, *Meccan Bestowal* 63, 205
Quran 11–13, 30, 70–4, 172, 181, 188–90,
    207–8, 221, 224–6
Qurban 'Ali al-'Ashilti 199
Qurbanli Muhammad al-Batsadi 62
Quruda 51
Qurush 63, 202, 205

Rajabil Muhammad al-Chirkawi 26
Raqahchi 59
Read, General N. A. 197
Redout-Kale 174

Renaissance 208
Resurrection 235
Rifaah al-Tahtawi, *Manakib al-Albab al-Misriyyah fi Mabahij al-Adab al-'Asriyyah* 209
Rigil-Nukhu 26
Rihiq 34
Rilke, Rainer-Maria 226
Romanov, Grand Duke Nikolai Mikhailovich 228
Rome 171
Rousseau, J.-J. 238
Rozen, Major-General 182
Rughchah 26, 58, 62
Runovskii, Capt. 65
Rus' 171
Rusanov, Gavriil Andreevich 238
Russians 56–70, 76, 171–91, 193–231, 233–8
Russo-Turkish War (1768–1774) 173
Russo-Turkish War (1828–1829) 223, 226
Russo-Turkish War (1877–1878) 226

Sa'id (infant son of Shamil) 204
Sa'id al-Harakani 21, 23, 43, 205
Sa'id al-Ihali 19, 32
Sado 216, 217, 229
Salatawh 18
Salih 43, 49
Saltah 50, 52–3, 184, 205
Sbornik materialov dlia opisaniia mestnostei i plemen Kavkaza [*Collected Materials for the Description of Places and Tribes of the Caucasus*] 227
Sbornik svedenii o kavkazskikh gortsakh [*Collected Materials on the Caucasian Mountain Peoples*] 227
Serbs 221
Sermon on the Mount 220, 235
Sevastopol' x, 197
Shafi'i rite (Islamic legal school) 27
Shahgirinskii Gates 83, 93
Shahwal Khan 58
Shali 57, 59
Shamil, v–x, 1, 2, 4, 6–9, 11, 12, 183–6, 188, 190, 198–203, 210–11, 215, 217–18, 227–8, 230, 232–5, 237, 250–5; became third imam 25; death 69; defended Islamic values and practices 24–5, 27, 29–31, 33, 35, 37; depicted as a Muslim holy man 204–9; houses not burned 29, 36; last stand at Ghunib 64–65; meeting with Russians 37–9; mentioned in Tolstoi's Hadji Murat 78, 80, 82, 89, 91–2, 96–7, 107, 109–12, 115–24, 130, 135, 138, 141–5, 152–5, 158–9, 166; political and military leadership 188–97; relationship with Ghazi Muhammad 20; relationship with Hadji Murat 59; showed bravery and persistence 19, 22–3, 26, 28, 31, 35, 40, 42, 44; trip to Mecca and Medina 67–9; trip to St. Petersburg 65–7
shamkhal 14, 17, 20, 27–8, 58, 71
Shamkhal Birdi 50
Shan Kiray 58–9
Sharakh 35
sharia (Islamic holy law) 11–15, 23–5, 27, 30, 33, 35, 46, 58, 68, 70–1, 73–4, 177–81, 188–9, 191, 197, 205, 207, 224, 235
Sharif of Mecca 208
Shawana the Christian 69
Sha'ban al-Buhnudi, Shaykh 17
Shaykhis 224
Shi'a 224
The Shining of Daghestani Swords v–vi, 1–8, 12–13, 48, 56, 67, 74, 76, 188, 199, 201–5, 208–11, 237–8; *see also* Muhammad Tahir al-Qarakhi
Shir Muhammad Munis, *Firdaws al-Iqbal* 209
Shirakhal, 54
Shirazi, Sayyid Ali-Muhammed, *Bayan* 224–5
Shirvan 178
Shuayb al-Tsamuturi 49
Shubut 49, 204
Shul'gin, Sergei Nikolaevich 232
Siberia 12, 47, 99, 223–4
Silikul Muhammad al-Tanusi, 47
Sira see Muhammad Ibn Ishaq
Skazanie o Magmete-saltane [*Legend of Sultan Mahmet*] 172
Solov'ev, V. S. 227
Solzhenitsyn, Aleksandr vi, x
St. Petersburg 8, 12, 65–6, 76, 171, 184, 197, 202, 210, 215, 218, 223, 227, 231–3, 237
Staryi Yurt, 212, 216
Stasov, Vladimir Vasil'evich 227, 229, 231
Stavropol 186
Strakhov, N. N. 223
Sufis x, 2, 7–8, 12, 14, 57, 71–2, 177–9, 181–2, 185, 193, 197, 199, 204, 237

Sufism 177–82, 204
Sughur 55
Sukhumi 174
Sulayman Efendi 185
Sultan Bek al-Dilimi 45, 74
Sultan Mahmud 74, 204
Sultanaw al-Rughchawi 26
Sunja 59
sunna 36, 73
Sunni Muslim 73, 172
Surkhai al-Kuluwi 33, 47
Syria 180

Tabarsaran (Tabassaran) 18, 58, 74, 177, 191–4
Tah Nosalal, 33
Tahir al-Ansali 26 41, 43
Tandub 62–3
Tarad-Inkhal 205
Targhu 17, 23, 72, 192
tariqat (Sufi order) 14
Tash-Kichu 148, 218
Tatar 76–8, 96, 113, 116, 124, 139, 148–9, 165, 172, 215–16, 227, 236
Tatary 172
Tattakh 49
Tbilisi Military-Historical Archive 231
Tbilisi (Tiflis) 17, 174–6, 198–9, 210, 212, 214, 217, 231, 227–8, 237
Temir-Khan-Shura 28, 108, 120, 202
Terek Cossacks 185, 216
The Hardened Hearts of Daghestan 211
"Third Rome" 171
Tiflis see Tbilisi
Tikhonov 89, 93
Tiklal 35
Tiliq 35–6, 51, 63
Time of Troubles, 208
Tolstaia, Aleksandra Andreevna 231
Tolstaia, Mariia Nikolaevna 227
Tolstaia, Sofiia Andreevna 221–2
Tolstoi, Lev, v–x, 2, 4, 6, 8, 46, 56, 75–6; and Anna Karenina, 221, 227; and Baha'i faith 225–6; and Hadji Murat 211–24, 227–38; and Ispoved' [Confession] 220–2; and "Notes on the Caucasus. A Journey to Mamakai-Yurt", 212; and "Nabeg" ["The Raid"] 213; and "Rubka lesa" ["Clearing Forest"] 215; and War and Peace 2, 220, 227, 233
Tolstoi, Nikolai 212, 217
Tolstoi, Sergei 216–7, 222, 227, 231

Transcaucasia 197
Troyat, Henri 211
Tsadaqar 53
Tsuntiya 60
Tsurib 63
Tumal 62
Turach al-Karati 56
Turkey 7, 216, 221, 223, 180, 187; see also Ottomans/Ottoman Empire
Turkmanchai (treaty) 174
Tush al-Karati 65

Uhlib 53
'Uhud 206
ulama 178, 190, 202
Ulub 26
Umar al-Akalichi 34
Unofficial Committee 173
Ur 44
Uritirk 17
'Urkach 33
'Uthmanu 21
Uysunghur 60

Vavilo, 88, 89
Vedan (Vedeno, New Darghiyya) 49, 80, 141, 143–4, 153, 155, 233–4
Veliaminov, General 184
Verderevskii, E. A. 228
Vico, Giambattista, Principi di scienza nuova 208
vilayat (province) 192
Vladikavkaz 72, 177
Vladimir, Prince 171
Vnezapnaia 72, 177
Voltaire 238; and Essai sur les moeurs 208
Vorontsov, M. S., 50–3, 183–6, 205–6, 217, 228–9, 233
Vorontsov, S. M. (son of M.S. Vorontsov) 228; establishment of a kunak relationship with Hadji Murat 217
Vronskii 221

Western Caucasus 187

Yerevan 174
Yunus 37–43, 45, 48–9, 60
Yusuf (Hadji Murat's son) 234–5

Zahida 69
Zakhar'in-Iakunin, I. N. 210

zakon (Russian law) 53, 56, 74
Zandiqi 48, 74
Zelkina, Anna 181

Zisserman, Arnold L'vovich 227
Zoroaster 225
Zunuh 34

CPSIA information can be obtained at www.ICGtesting.com
Printed in the USA
LVOW10s2131030214

372144LV00002B/34/P